NICHOLAS OF CUSA AND HIS AGE:
INTELLECT AND SPIRITUALITY

STUDIES IN THE HISTORY
OF
CHRISTIAN THOUGHT

FOUNDED BY HEIKO A. OBERMAN

EDITED BY

ROBERT J. BAST, Knoxville, Tennessee

IN COOPERATION WITH

HENRY CHADWICK, Cambridge
SCOTT H. HENDRIX, Princeton, New Jersey
BRIAN TIERNEY, Ithaca, New York
ARJO VANDERJAGT, Groningen
JOHN VAN ENGEN, Notre Dame, Indiana

VOLUME CV

THOMAS M. IZBICKI AND CHRISTOPHER M. BELLITTO (EDS.)

NICHOLAS OF CUSA AND HIS AGE:
INTELLECT AND SPIRITUALITY

NICHOLAS OF CUSA AND HIS AGE: INTELLECT AND SPIRITUALITY

Essays Dedicated to the Memory of F. Edward Cranz,
Thomas P. McTighe and Charles Trinkaus

EDITED BY

THOMAS M. IZBICKI

AND

CHRISTOPHER M. BELLITTO

BRILL
LEIDEN · BOSTON · KÖLN
2002

This book is printed on acid-free paper.

Library of Congress Cataloging-in-Publication Data

Nicholas of Cusa and his age : essays dedicated to the memory of F. Edward Cranz, Thomas P. McTighe, and Charles Trinkaus / edited by Thomas M. Izbicki and Christopher M. Bellitto.
    p.   cm. — (Studies in the history of Christian thought, v. 105)
    Includes bibliographical references and index.
    ISBN 9004125574
    1. Nicholas, of Cusa, Cardinal, 1401-1464. I. Izbicki, Thomas M.
II. Bellitto, Christopher M. III. Series.

B765.N54 N475   2002
230'.2'092—dc21

2002021550
CIP

Die Deutsche Bibliothek - CIP-Einheitsaufnahme

Nicholas of cusa and his age : intellect and spirituality ; essays dedicated to the memory of F. Edward Cranz, Thomas P. McTighe, and Charles Trinkaus / ed. by Thomas M. Izbicki and Christopher M. Bellitto. – Leiden ; Boston ; Köln : Brill, 2002
  (Studies in the history of Christian thought ; Vol. 105)
  ISBN 90–04–12557–4

ISSN 0081-8607
ISBN 90 04 12557 4

PRINTED IN THE NETHERLANDS

CONTENTS

ACKNOWLEDGEMENTS

Thomas M. Izbicki and Christopher M. Bellitto

The American Cusanus Society joins with scholarly organizations in Japan and throughout Europe, especially Germany, in marking the sixth centenary of Nicholas of Cusa's birth. Many of these articles began as papers at the biennial study group held at Gettysburg Lutheran Seminary, to whose president and staff we express our thanks for past hospitality and financial support, and at the International Congress on Medieval Studies held each May at Western Michigan University. We are grateful to the team of international scholars who shared their work at those sessions and who generously expanded their studies into the articles presented here. Robert Bast, the new editor of the Brill series *Studies in the History of Christian Thought,* graciously accepted this longstanding project. We are also grateful to Professor Andrew Gow, editor of the series *Studies in the History of Medieval and Reformation Thought,* for his editorial advice. We express special thanks and admiration to Kim Breighner who provided computer expertise of the first rank to make this volume a seamless whole; her task and achievements are particularly remarkable given the myriad of word processing programs and multiple of languages involved in the essays which follow.

As the American Cusanus Society celebrates this special anniversary of Nicholas of Cusa's life and work, we recall three distinguished leaders of the Society who recently passed away: F. Edward Cranz, Thomas P. McTighe, and Charles Trinkaus. We note, too, the passing of another great scholar and friend of the Society, Heiko Oberman, who supported this and previous volumes on Cusanus that were published by Brill and organized by the American Cusanus Society. We hope our efforts do justice to their scholarship and friendship.

IN MEMORIAM: F. EDWARD CRANZ,
THOMAS P. McTIGHE, AND CHARLES TRINKAUS

Morimichi Watanabe

It is a great honor to write a preface to this book which is published in memory and honor of three distinguished members of the American Cusanus Society who passed away in recent years. As President of the Society, I feel privileged to be able to write briefly in this preface about their scholarly achievements in general and their contributions to the growth of the Society in particular. I shall discuss them below in order of my coming in contact with them.

It was in Bressanone (Brixen), Italy in September 1964 that I first met Professor Thomas P. McTighe (1922-1997). We had come separately to Bressanone to attend an international congress commemorating the fifth centenary of the death of Nicholas of Cusa in 1464. A lanky scholar, whose publications on "The Meaning of the Couple *complicatio-explicatio* in the Philosophy of Nicholas of Cusa," "Nicholas of Cusa as a Forerunner of Modern Science," and others I knew about, he was cordial, warm and friendly to me from the beginning. He certainly gave me a greater degree of confidence in myself than I had before my arrival in Bressanone, as I faced the prospect of presenting a paper on Cusanus in the presence of famous Cusanus scholars. The session was under the chairmanship of Professor Raymond Klibansky, indisputably the dean of Cusanus scholars at that time and even now. Professor McTighe's own paper at Bressanone was on "Nicholas of Cusa's Theory of Science and its Metaphysical Background." I still remember well that, on the last day of the congress, we saw each other at the Bressanone railway station and exchanged warm greetings.

After the establishment of the American Cusanus Society in 1983, I asked Professor McTighe to serve as a member of the Executive Committee. In addition to appealing to scholars like myself, who were primarily interested in the political and legal ideas of Cusanus, the Society certainly needed scholars whose expertise was in his philosophical and theological ideas. I had no hesitation in turning to him for advice and help in this area. He, in turn, helped me a great deal and worked hard for the Society in many ways. In the beginning of its history especially, the Society's financial status was still weak, though not precarious. I remember with gratitude that he said to me many times: "Mori, let me know if you need. . . ." I know also that, during the time of his membership in the Executive Committee, he helped other members of the Society in their scholarly, editorial, and other endeavors. Professor McTighe was a kind, gentle, generous, and learned scholar whose guidance and encouragement warmed and strengthened the minds of members who turned to him for advice and guidance.

Bressanone was also the place where I first met Professor F. Edward Cranz (1914-1998). I had heard about him from Paul O. Kristeller and about his joint work with Professor Kristeller on a big project, the *Catalogus Translationum et Commentariorum*. It was a surprise and a pleasure to meet him at the Cusanus Congress, which was held in a beautiful Tyrolean town. As the day of delivering my paper on Cusanus and his concept of toleration neared, I was clearly nervous in general and worried in particular about an adjective which I used in the text of my paper. Without possessing a dictionary on my first trip to Europe, I turned

to him for help. Out of kindness, he explained the matter clearly to a post-
doctoral novice in Cusanus studies. His help made it possible for me to present
the paper without stumbling. The paper he himself presented at the congress,
entitled "The Transmutation of Platonism in the Development of Nicolaus
Cusanus and of Martin Luther," was a learned piece of work based on many years
of research, analysis, and reflection.

As in the case of Professor McTighe, I turned to Professor Cranz for help and
support after 1983. I can say definitely that, as a member of the Board of
Advisors of the Society from 1985 to 1998, he contributed a great deal to the
growth and development of the Society. Of course, his scholarly contributions
to Cusanus scholarship, both through his important later publications and at our
meetings and sessions, were to be expected; but it was also his personality and,
to put it differently, his being part of our activities that encouraged members of
the Society. He was a fatherlike figure to many. His simple, unassuming, and
gentle attitude to others and even his famous fondness for bicycling, hiking, and
climbing mountains, sometimes with a Cusanus text in its Heidelberg edition,
quickly endeared him to those members who came in contact with him. If I
understand the testimonies of his colleagues and friends correctly, throughout the
time of his association with the Society, he enjoyed participating in our
meetings and activities; and, as a result, his engagement with Cusanus and
Cusanian philosophy and ideas became increasingly intense. We are, naturally,
very pleased about and proud of the development.

Professor Cranz's emphasis in his publications on the importance of studying
not only Cusanus' earlier works, of which only the *De docta ignorantia* is often
emphasized by many, but also his later works, such as the *De visione Dei*, the
De beryllo, the *De aequalitate*, the *De principio*, the *De possest*, the *De non
aliud*, the *Compendium*, and the *De apice theoriae*, was a great contribution to
Cusanus scholarship. This approach has resulted in what might be called a
developmental theory of Cusanus' philosophy. We must remember, at the same
time, that, during his busy years, he worked on and completed two gigantic
projects, Vols. 2 and 7 of the *Catalogus Translationum et Commentariorum* as
its Associate Editor and Vols. 3-6 of the *Catalogus* as its Editor-in-Chief
(Washington, DC, 1960-1986), and *The Microfilm Corpus of Unpublished
Inventories of Latin Manuscripts Through 1600 A.D.* (New London, 1987).

In comparison with Professors McTighe and Cranz, Professor Charles
Trinkaus (1911-1999) established contact with the Society a little later. He was,
of course, very well known as a leading scholar in the study of Renaissance
humanism because of such famous works as *Adversity's Noblemen: The Italian
Humanists on Happiness* (New York, 1940); *In Our Image and Likeness:
Humanity and Divinity in Italian Humanist Thought*, 2 vols. (London, 1970);
The Pursuit of Holiness in Late Medieval and Renaissance Religion, edited with
Heiko A. Oberman (Leiden, 1974), *The Scope of Renaissance Humanism* (Ann
Arbor, 1985), and others. His great interest not only in many Italian humanists
but also in Erasmus of Rotterdam was clear in his publications. These publica-
tions indicated as a whole that the author was interested in and concerned about
the role of religion in Renaissance thought and humanism to a much greater
degree than some previous interpreters of the Renaissance, like Jacob Burckhardt,

had been. With this inclination and approach to late medieval and Renaissance times, it is easy to see how he found Cusanus studies interesting and agreeable.

Professor Trinkaus attended and delivered a plenary address at the Society's first biennial conference held at Gettysburg Lutheran Seminary on October 24-26, 1986. The general theme of the conference was Cusanus' *De pace fidei;* the title of the plenary lecture was "Renaissance Treatises on Non-Christian Religions." Thus began our close and happy association with him and his wife, Professor Pauline M. Watts, who had recently published her *Nicolaus Cusanus: A Fifteenth-Century Vision of Man* (Leiden, 1982). In fact, we were so happy that a party was given on his birthday, October 25, an event which was repeated whenever he participated in the following biennial conferences of the Society at Gettysburg. With a tremendous amount of knowledge about Renaissance intellectual and religious ideas, he was able to advise and enlighten members of the Society gently and persuasively. He was a wise, learned, and experienced advisor to many of us. We were very pleased that he accepted in 1990 our invitation to serve on the Board of Advisors of the Society. In his obituary, published in the *American Cusanus Society Newsletter,* 16, No. 2 (December 1999), Professor Louis Dupré wrote:

> This learned and good man, an honor to American scholarship and a true humanist, died as he had lived, quietly and serenely - his body gradually leaving a mind alert to the end. To me, and I think to many of us, he remains an inspiring model, but not one that we may hope to emulate. I remain deeply grateful to his presence among us.

How true the statement is.

I am sure that not only the contributors to this volume, but also other members of the Society, will join me in expressing our deep respect and gratitude to these three distinguished and learned scholars. I should add that our heartfelt thanks go to the editors of this volume for their hard editorial work to produce this book to be published under the auspices of the American Cusanus Society.

The basic text used is the edition of the Heidelberg Academy:

>*Nicolai de Cusa Opera omnia iussu et auctoritate Academiae Litterarum Heidelbergensis* (Hamburg, 1932-) = h.

Works are usually cited by book, chapter, and section number; h by volume and page. For example, *De coniecturis* I, 1, #5 (h III, 7-8) refers to *De coniecturis,* Book One, Chapter One, Section Five (in the Heidelberg edition, Volume Three, pages 7-8).

Where volumes in h have appeared in more than one edition, both are cited, and the later editions are indicated by suprascript numbers, e.g. V and V^2.

Several works have not yet appeared in h, but may be found in the following editions:

>*De visione dei.* Jasper Hopkins, *Nicholas of Cusa's Dialectical Mysticism: Text, Translation, and Interpretive Study of* De visione dei (Minneapolis, 1985).

>*De ludo globi.* Cited from Nicolaus Cusa, *Opera,* 3 vols. (Paris, 1514). I, 99-114 is reproduced photographically in *Nicholas de Cusa,* De ludo globi: *The Game of Spheres,* translation and introduction by Pauline Moffitt Watts (New York, 1986).

>*Sermones.* h contains many Sermons. Others may be found excerpted in the Paris 1514 edition under the title *Excitationum libri decem* (II, fol. 7^r-188^r [*sic,* for 190]).

The sources of the translations used are indicated in the notes to the individual articles.

Most of the works in h are also found, though not in a critical edition and with minimal annotation, in Nikolaus von Kues, *Philosophisch-theologische Schriften,* ed. Leo Gabriel, with a German translation by Dietlind and Wilhelm Dupré, 3 vols. (Vienna, 1967; reprinted Vienna, 1982).

The following is a summary of Cusanus' works preceded by volume number in h:

I. *De docta ignorantia,* ed. E. Hoffmann and R. Klibansky (1932).

II. *Apologia doctae ignorantiae,* ed. R. Klibansky (1932).

III. *De coniecturis,* ed. J. Koch and K. Bormann, with H.G. Senger (1972).

IV. *Opuscula* I, ed. P. Wilpert (1959):
>*De deo abscondito*
>*De quaerendo deum*
>*De filiatione dei*
>*De dato patris luminum*
>*Coniectura de ultimis diebus*
>*De genesi*

V. *Idiota de sapientia. Idiota de mente,* ed. L. Baur (1937); *Idiota de staticis experimentis,* ed. L. Baur (1937).

V^2. *Idiota de sapientia. Idiota de mente,* ed. R. Steiger (1983).
>*Idiota de staticis experimentis,* ed. L. Baur (1983).

VII. *De pace fidei cum epistula ad Ioannem de Segobia,* ed. R. Klibansky and H. Bascour (1959).

VII^2. *De pace fidei cum epistula ad Ioannem de Segobia,* ed. R. Klibansky and H. Bascour (1970).

VIII. *Cribratio Alkorani,* ed. L. Hagemann (1986).

X, 2. *Opuscula* II:

    Fasciculus 2. *De deo unitrino principio.*

    b. *Tu quis es (De principio),* ed. K. Bormann and A.D. Riemann (1988).

XI, 1. *De beryllo,* ed. L. Baur (1940).

XI, 1^2. *De beryllo,* ed. J. G. Senger and K. Bormann (1988).

XI, 2. *Trialogus de possest,* ed. R. Steiger (1973).

XI, 3. *Compendium,* ed. B. Decker and K. Bormann (1964).

XII. *De venatione sapientiae; De apice theoriae,* ed. R. Klibansky and J. G. Senger (1981).

XIII. *Directio speculantis seu de non aliud,* ed. L. Baur and P. Wilpert (1944).

XIV, 1, 2, 3, 4. *De concordantia catholica,* ed. G. Kallen (1959- 1968).

XVI, 1, 2, 3, 4. *Sermones* (1430-1441), Sermons I-XXVI, ed. R. Haubst, M. Bodewig, and W. Krämer (1970-1985).

XVII. 1. *Sermones* II (1443-1452), Sermons XXVII-XXXIX, ed. R. Haubst and H. Schnarr (1983).

XVII, 2. *Sermones* II (1443-1452), Sermons XL-XLVIII, ed. R. Haubst and H. Schnarr (1991).

XVIII, 1. *Sermones* III (1452-1455), Sermons CXXII-CXL, ed. R. Haubst and H. Pauli (1995).

PART ONE

CUSANUS IN CONTEXT

LINES OF CONVERGENCE: SOME REMARKS ON SPIRIT AND MIND IN THE WORK OF NICHOLAS OF CUSA

Wilhelm Dupré

Depending on the perspective we choose, we can approach Cusanus as a writer who resumes and develops themes of traditional spirituality or as an author who problematizes the meaning of the spiritual tradition in ways which make it necessary to speak of distinct features in his understanding of spirituality. In this paper I would like to concentrate on the second approach. What distinguishes this approach from the first one is the understanding of the human being as creator of its own world and of history as the place where this creativity begins to become visible in forms of different worlds. To the extent that this understanding succeeds, it permits us not merely to focus on the principles, the elements and the conditions of human world creation, but it also becomes a tremendous challenge to apply its insights to one's own world and to structure and restructure its meaning accordingly.

To outline some of the features of a spirituality which finds its expression in and through the dynamics of human world creation, I will proceed as follows. I begin with a sketch of the place where spirituality becomes an issue in the thought of Nicholas of Cusa. In the two steps that follow, I intend to discuss the meaning of spirit and mind respectively. I conclude with a few remarks on highlights in the assessment of the spirituality of Cusanus.

Place of Questioning

In a formal sense we could describe the spirituality of Cusanus as anticipation and enactment of an ongoing synthesis between the God-given meaning of unfolding the human potential and the intention to structure one's life accordingly: first as human being, then as Christian, and finally as the person one happens to be because of circumstances and by vocation.[1]

The central idea in this description is the complementarity between *complicatio* and *explicatio*, between enfolding and unfolding, as a comprehensive feature of all being and becoming. Whatever we know is marked by evolution and development. Every being is, in essence, becoming, with variable beginnings and results, and its specific form is a structured whole without which nothing exists. In fact, if we focus on ourselves and the whole of mankind, there can be no doubt that we are, as individuals who have been born and grown up, and as cultures which emerged in history, the result of multiple processes, and that the unfolding of mankind provides the milieu in which we find the form and features of our humanity.

However, what distinguishes humans from other beings we are aware of is both the need and the ability to relate to these processes, and to begin anew in this relation. In the necessities of becoming we encounter the freedom of making decisions and giving preferences. In the experience of actions we face multiple

---

[1] I refer to his sermon *Erunt novissimi primi et primi novissimi,* in *Excitationum libri decem,* in *Opera,* 3 vols. (Paris, 1514), 2.75v.

options and the task of shaping our lives within limits and in ways which confirm responsibility in conjunction with fairness and nobility.

The conditions of being human are such that spirituality becomes part of them: in one way or another we have to fill the gap that opens up between intention and reality.[2] There is, as we could say today, no culture and tradition which, by being culture and tradition, did not manifest its particular mentality in the form of lifestyles. But for the same reason that spirituality is cultural destiny, we might as well cultivate it and try to improve its meaning to the best of our abilities. The attempt to do so can be recognized in the profiles of spiritual traditions. In the light of this recognition the idea of spirituality becomes an expression of concerns for the essentials in life and gains meaning as a symbol for the acquisition of insights which serve as guides in coping with these concerns.

I mention these points because they indicate where we have to place Cusanus. As a humanist and pastor he is deeply interested in the spiritual aspects of his age and the improvement of his own spirituality, as well as that of his contemporaries. But if we ask how he pursues these interests, the two features which I have mentioned at the beginning of this paper are of particular importance. On the one hand, he follows tradition and shares in the practices of the spiritual life of his time. On the other hand, he tries to reach his goals through the understanding of spiritual processes and by integrating this understanding with the actual form of life. In the first instance he is inspired by traditional wisdom.[3] His questions and approaches resume themes and proceed along lines which reflect the implicit dynamics of the spiritual life of his age. In the second instance, it is this life and its history which are the subject of his inquiries. In their reality they precede the modes of perception and understanding. But because they are accessible in the form of signs, it becomes all important, as Cusanus tells us in the second chapter of his *Compendium,*[4] that we try to understand them, wherever and in whatsoever way they occur, as thoroughly as possible if we intend to respond to the unfathomable meaning of being and reality.

The direct involvement of Cusanus in spiritual issues is superseded by the attempt to combine this involvement with observations which focus on these issues in their entirety. Neither one of these two features is in itself sufficient to portray the meaning of Cusanus' spirituality. We can explore them separately,

---

[2] I use the word "spirituality" here as a vague indication of the mode and manners in which we relate to mind and mental matters. When Cusanus speaks of *spiritualitas,* he uses this word in contrast to *temporalitas,* and as a reference to the dimension of perpetuity.

[3] See, for instance, the inspiring "Essays in Honor of Morimichi Watanabe by the American Cusanus Society," which have been edited by Gerald Christianson and Thomas M. Izbicki in *Nicholas of Cusa in Search of God and Wisdom* (Leiden, 1991).

[4] *Philosophisch-Theologische   Schriften,* ed. Leo Gabriel, 3 vols. (Wien, 1964), 2.650.

and discuss the predominance of the one over the other. But, in the end, it is the attempted synthesis between them which comes first, if we intend to grasp the spiritual dimensions in the thought and life of Nicholas.

The Seminal Meaning of Spirit(s)

Cusanus speaks at various occasions about the spirit that manifests itself in the works and attitudes of human beings. He refers to the spirit of this world which manifests itself in avarice, lust and arrogance. In contrast to this spirit he points to the spirits of truthfulness, love and obedience as spirits of another world. When considering the idea that one and the same soul enlivens different bodies in succession, he rejects "migration" (reincarnation) with the argument that "a particular soul is proportionated to its body in such a way that it is impossible for that soul to animate another body," but he remarks that this idea does indeed apply to the spirit which "can be one in such a way that it raises up again in another person even if it appears to have died in somebody and left him." To prove his point he refers to Jesus who was believed by some to be John the Baptist, or Elias, or Jeremias, or another of the prophets (Mt 16:14)— "not that he was John the Baptist or Elias personally, but that the spirit was in Him which had been in John and Elias." Cusanus concludes his deliberation with the words: "that and how there is one spirit where there is one faith, can be understood if we attend to the fact that it is one faith which incites the spirit in many in order to be strengthened by the power of the one whom one trusts."[5]

I mention this last point because it clearly indicates that a particular configuration of attitudes and ways of thinking can be associated with the word "spirit" in the thought of Cusanus, and that it makes sense to inquire about his understanding of spiritual configurations. Of course, if we assume that some kind of spirituality can be found in all human beings, and that age and culture are marked by the spirit they disclose, then it is no more than sensible to ask, for instance, about the spirituality of Cusanus and the age in which he lived. But there is a considerable difference whether this question is brought to bear on others from the outside or meets itself in the course of this attempt.

Indeed, if we follow the suggestions which Cusanus made in chapter twenty-five of *De venatione sapientiae*,[6] a whole "philosophy of the spirit" comes into focus. These suggestions concern the "field of connection" as one of ten areas where the "hunt for wisdom" could (and should) be undertaken. The basic idea is the persistent and encompassing force of desire and love as the primary manifestation of the spirit in various forms of connection, and the realization that nothing exists without and outside its connecting force. More specifically, these suggestions center around the "spirit of wisdom" as it descends into and ignites the "spirit of the intellectual nature," with its love and desire, and the prospect of continuous happiness. Cusanus is convinced that only "few

---

[5]*Medius vestrum stetit*, in *Excitationes,* fol. 124r.

[6]h XII,25,73.

philosophers" have recognized the meaning of "intellectual love" and the "principle of connection" in which everything subsists, and adds that much can be found about this subject in his *sermones*.

The Latin *spiritus*, the Greek *pneuma*, the Hebrew *ruah* and *el* are terms which in the view of Cusanus refer primarily to the experience of blowing winds, breath, breathing, and force. "When breathing or respiring we let out breath or spirit.... When the wind blows, the air appears in living motion."[7] The wind is "a spirit which rises in the air and either opens the clouds to rain out or forces them to disperse."[8] Cusanus uses these images in his *sermones* as metaphors for the work and the ways of the Holy Spirit. But because of their association with motion and movements they have also a more direct bearing. As "motion that proceeds from a mover and a movable," the spirit belongs to all things.[9] In a way, there are as many spirits as there are different kinds of motion. The world is filled with spirits, or as he puts it (by quoting Cicero) in Sermon CCLXXXV: "everything is filled with Jupiter."[10] Each thing is marked by spirits: stones and minerals have their spirit, the wine is filled with spirit. In each organism we find the spirit and various (arterial and other) spirits that keep it alive. Soul and intellect are connected with their specific spirits. Whatever moves, is moved by the spirit that causes this motion.[11]

In view of all these spirits one might wonder whether it makes any sense to continue with the usage of the word "spirit," or whether it would not be more reasonable to treat these animistic notions with benign neglect. But Cusanus cannot be put aside that easily. Though it is true that the world dissolves in a multiplicity of spirits, what must not be neglected is the fact that reality returns in terms of various connections and formable as well as reformable unions and unities. In its multiple meanings, the notion of the spirit attests to the whole-ness of being and reality. The force of attraction which we observe in flowing waters, when walking on the ground, or between magnet and iron turns out to be an experience which applies analogously to all instances of experience and reality. And, if the spirit designates the principle of indeterminate motions (as it

---

[7]*Alleluia. Veni Sancte Spiritus* [Sermo CCLXXXV (1457), Vat. lat. 1245 [hereafter V2], fol. 275ra. Cusanus refers expressly to the Greek and Hebrew terms at several occasions.

[8]*In dominica Judica* [Sermo CLIII (1454)], V2, fol. 50ra. From a biographical point of view one could connect these references with Cusanus' experience at sea, his extensive travels in all kinds of weather, and the lightning flash of understanding in the mode of incomprehensibility which inspired him to write the books *On Learned Ignorance*. This connection has been suggested by (the late) Rem Jonges who wrote his Master's Thesis on *The Spirituality of Nicholas of Cusa,* University of Nijmegen, 1989.

[9]*De visione Dei,* h VI,19,84.

[10]*Iovis omnia sunt plena, Alleluia,* V2, fol. 275vb.

[11]See *De mente,* XIII (h V,13,147).

becomes obvious when we do not know from where the wind blows and where it is going), it does so inasmuch as these motions assume specific meanings in the course of their development.

To speak of the spirit implies that we think of the bond that connects the specific in the form of parts and distinctions. In a general sense it refers to being in motion and to movement as being. When taken in its fullness, the spirit stands for the motions which are typical for the species and what can be accomplished within the limits of a particular being. As in all other things, "to the extent that a human being is one, there can be no greater love [*dilectio*, from *diligere*, to value highly, to appreciate, to love] than the spirit's love to the body, even if the body rebels in poor health (*secundum carnem*)."[12] In its essence, however, the spirit is spirit because of its seminal meaning. In the metaphor of egg and semen it points to, and recalls, the beginnings out of which reality unfolds and to which it returns inasmuch as they coincide with the end from which all desires originated in the first place. Or to quote from *De coniecturis* (II, 7):

> I have spoken about seeds and trees. But you should try to take up these problems in their totality by making conjectures with regard to minerals, vegetal objects, animals and all perceptible things. And you should use them symbolically also with regard to rational and intellectual things. For, out of the seed of admiration grows a reasonable tree, with fruits that are similar to admiration and, elicited by admiration, this tree erects its own tree of reason. Then, from the seminal beginnings of demonstration, comes forth an intellectual tree which lets seminal principles grow out of itself, through which, in turn, ascends the tree of the intellect.

The picture which appears in the lines of spiritual relations is such that it makes sense to shift one's perspective and to associate the word spirit primarily with events in the mental dimensions of humanity. The nature that unfolds by responding freely to the calls of its spirits offers itself as a paramount example for redefining the meaning of spirit and the spiritual. In contrast to the experience of blowing winds we now have to think of movements and forces which are part of human interiority and carry us in realms beyond the world of material and temporal phenomena. It is only at this point that carnal and spiritual nature drift apart and should be distinguished because they belong to different dimensions.

The shift in meaning which comes to rest in the mental dimensions of humanity can be summed up in the statement that God is the "absolute spirit" and that the "free spirit" which, in human beings, designates the ability to receive and accept the seeds of the divine spirit, belongs to the world of "spiritual

---

12*Sedete quoadusque,* [Sermo LVIII (1446)], nr. 5 (h XVII/4 in press). Cusanus mentions this aspect in order to explain that God loves his world even though it rebels against God.

nature."[13] Within this frame of reference, Cusanus relates to the Spirit as the spark of God's fire, which becomes all-consuming if the soul is ready to let itself be ignited.[14] Or as he puts it in *De quaerendo Deum* (III):[15]

> Our intellectual spirit has the power of fire within itself. For no other reason has this spirit been sent by God to earth than to burn and to grow into a flame. When aroused in wonder and astonishment, it grows as if the wind blew into a fire and brought its potentiality in actuality.

But, since various spirits of this and the other world are already at work within the confines of the human species and each individual being, we might as well turn to them and listen to the message they convey in the forms and under the conditions of their occurrence. Cusanus speaks of a spiritual or divine instinct within us (which, I would like to add, probably knows of God long before we speak of Him, or reject name and notion). In following the traces of love and desire, he observes the spectacle of various and even contrasting encounters where we succeed and fail, become prudent, wise and happy, or fall into the pitfalls of arrogance, injustice and fear. In their seminal significance and within the order of all things, those spirits are the voice of God who speaks within us, if we listen to this voice in our conscience and do what the spirit tells us.

It is a wide field of fascinating and rich connections which opens up if we turn to our internal being and consider the various movements from outside as they come together within human interiority, but also and especially if we pay attention to the motions which originate in this interiority and point beyond this world to the firmament of divine beauty. But, as we rejoice in the idea that our spirit is free and noble and nobody's subject, meant to serve God out of love and not in fear, we discover also that the center of our being surpasses the confinements of body and soul.[16] To refer to the spirit implies that we become spiritual both in the sense that we let the seeds of the spirit grow and that we grow together with, and are born anew in, the spiritual virtues they anticipate. Cusanus expresses this view by pointing out that justice and wisdom, for instance, do not merely mean that we cultivate habits which are just and wise, but that they become the soul of our being. In a sermon of 1457 he stresses the difference between the changing qualities of perceptible things and the achievement of spiritual perfections because "they receive neither being, nor division, nor number from their subjects." Instead, it is:

---

[13]See, for instance, *Sedete quoadusque,* [Sermo LVIII], nr. 4 (h XVII/4 in press).

[14]See, for instance, *Loquimini ad petram coram eis, et dabit vobis aquas,* [Sermo CCLXXIV (1457)], V2, fol. 236va: "Spiritus enim est quasi scintilla ignis Dei, qui dicitur ignis consumens."

[15]h IV,3,43.

[16]See, for instance, *Loquimini ad petram coram eis, et dabit vobis aquas,* [Sermo CCLXXIV (1457)], V2, fol. 236va.

they which give to a subject its total being inasmuch as appears in this mode, as one can see when considering justice and the just person. They are prior to the subjects and the subjects are in them. To the extent that somebody is just he receives all his being from justice to the effect that justice is truly parent and father of the just person—like the soul which gives being to the body. Properly speaking it is the body which exists in the soul and not the soul which exists in the body. Therefore, the soul will not perish when the body has been destroyed. Likewise, one can say that justice is perpetual and immortal. For it is obvious that justice, wisdom, and other virtues of this kind do not die with a person who is just and wise, even if the opposite seems to be the case in the eyes of those who ignore [the true meaning of justice and wisdom]. It is thus one spirit that fills the heart of the faithful, giving them their being spiritual; that is, one spirit above all unity and number. And so you see that the relationship between justice and the just person is one thing; and the relationship between whiteness and what is white another thing, because whiteness receives its being from what is white... The habits of virtues are in those who are virtuous, but in such a way that they are confirmations and configurations with regard to justice and to God Himself from whom they come. I refer to configurations not as to a figure that has been shaped within them and which is attached to, and rooted in, the one who is virtuous, but as they are in continuous becoming, like the splendor in a medium and an image in a mirror....[17]

That the center of being human is neither body nor soul but lies halfway between the temporal and the spiritual is consequent upon the dynamics of connective relations. Whatever exists subsists by virtue of these relations and the order they initiate both in the world as a whole and in each thing separately. To see things in accordance with their substance (*substantialiter*) does not mean that we stare ourselves blind by looking at particular objects, but that we become aware of the movements in which they are constituted and kept in balance through multiple interactions and reciprocal dependencies. Moreover, if such is the world in which we live, it also means that it is up to the free spirit to create its own worlds by bringing things together in its own ways and, what is even more important, by joining the world of the divine as it appears in the light of God's Holy Spirit. Freedom and thought conjoin with nature and grace:

No other nature can become better by itself, but is what it is under the rule of necessity which keeps it like that. Only intellectual nature has the principles within it, through which it can become better, and therefore more like God and more susceptible to God. That is why the intellectual light is better than any other light, because it penetrates everything and is like the ray of eternal light or the light of the sun of justice... On its own grounds the intellectual nature is capable of lifting itself up to God, in order to see and to collect

---

17*Alleluia,* fol. 275va.

within itself the quiddity of things in which it becomes aware of the outpouring goodness of God who is the quiddity of all quiddities.[18]

By locating the center of being human within the horizon of time and eternity, Cusanus finds a position which makes it possible to appreciate spiritual transformations ontologically and to relate to the idea of the hidden Christ as goal and focus of the spiritual life. As a pastor, he does not only preach the gospel; but, with the biblical image of Jesus in mind, he also asks himself and his listeners to search for Jesus in each and all of us. For "we will not find Him, if we do not find Him in ourselves."[19] However, if we intend to be successful in our search for the meaning of spiritual transformations and the hidden Christ as their proper focus, we must know how to read the signs and signals of the spirit and distinguish them from misleading impressions. In the realization of this task, we depend on the life we lead and whether this life is consonant with the principles of order and peace; or, as the Bible says: "ye shall know [false prophets] by their fruits" (Mt 7:16). But it is also a task which challenges the mind with all its faculties and possibilities.

The Mind as Center of Mediation

When Cusanus speaks of the mind (*mens*), he refers to it as the invisible and untouchable place where human beings become conscious of themselves and where they are connected with all and everything. It is the medium where the senses and passions of the soul join with the will and the intellectual faculties, and where world and life contract to an instrument that permits us to measure things in accordance with this instrument's own principles. In its singularity the mind discovers features of universality and recognizes itself as the eye (*oculus mentis*) that perceives the rays of beauty and intelligence. By following the movements of contraction in reverse, and by thinking of its own limits, it becomes essential to the mind that it understands itself in relation and contrast to the absolute and eternal mind both as goal and as measure of all mental efforts, which it glimpses

---

[18]*Pax hominibus bonae voluntatis,* [Sermo CLXVIII (1455)], V2, fol. 60va.

[19]*Confide, filia,* [Sermo XLI (1444)], quoted in Wolfgang Lentzen-Deis, *Den Glauben Christi teilen: Theologie und Verkündigung bei Nikolaus von Kues* (Stuttgart, 1991), p. 182. Next to this sermon the author brings also the text of Sermones XXII, XLII, XLIII, XLIV, XLVI, and CCLXXX in Latin with a German translation. See also Sermon XLI, h XVII/2, nr. 7; and Alfred Kaiser, *Möglichkeiten und Grenzen einer Christologie "von unten": Der christologische Neuansatz "von unten" bei Piet Schoonenberg und dessen Weiterführung in der Sicht des Nikolaus von Kues* (Münster, 1992). Apart from the classical texts by Maurice de Gandillac (*La Philosophie de Nicolas de Cues* [Paris, 1941]) and Rudolf Haubst (*Die Christologie des Nikolaus von Kues* [Freiburg, 1956]), see also Peter J. Casarella, "His Name is Jesus: Negative Theology and Christology in Two Writings of Nicholas of Cusa from 1440" in *Nicholas of Cusa on Christ and the Church,* ed. Gerald Christianson and Thomas M. Izbicki (Leiden, 1996), pp. 281-307.

in lightning flashes and momentary breaches, but which it does not reach except in forms which are brought into being as it unfolds in the right direction.

Though the mind is identical with the soul in its functions, it differs from the soul as it connects in widening circles with the meanings of truth and divine simplicity. In the course of this connection the mind discovers itself as creator of the human world but also becomes aware of its own needs with regard to soul and body, and of mind and soul with regard to the spiritual food that keeps them alive in one and the same search for wisdom and immortality. The awareness of these needs is a strong incentive to be and to become ever more attentive to the various aspects of reality, the differences in perception, knowledge and understanding, and the possible insights which pertain to the life of desires and emotions, to the cultivation of virtues and communication, and to the ways of holiness and salvation. Because the mind is not identical with the spirit except in the sense that it is of a spiritual nature which is capable of receiving spirits and impulses, it is free to chime in with the freedom of will and intellect, to accompany them with its judgments, and to grow into its own realm while growing together with the unfolding of being human.

The theory of understanding which evolves under these conditions is marked by the notion that the created mind becomes acquainted with things by measuring them and that it creates by assimilation, but goodness, beauty and peace are by no means less important. In Sermon CLXVIII he remarks:

We are unable not to desire peace because nothing subsists without peace. Peace means the unifying connection between circumference and center. The center is the place of peace and rest. Peace can only be where extremes meet, and the place of peace is the middle. Substance cannot be found in the form which gives being, nor in the subject matter: it is found in the center of connective rest, peace or mediation. Stable and permanent truth does not exist outside peace. There is no science of the medium of peace, through which stable truth is seen, though everything is understood much better, if the mind makes use of this middle. Authors who wrote about truth with elegance tried hard to reduce the variety of opinions to the medium of peace. We see that all sciences come down to modes of expressing the vision of peace. In moral matters we see that virtue is mediation and peace. Peace is the heaven of the blessed. For, strictly speaking, blessed are those who keep the middle. A philosopher who encounters many oppositions investigates many things through which he likes to ascend to truth. As long as he turns around in opposites, he does not see peace. In fact, the place of truth is peace, which cannot be reached by ratiocination, but will be found only on the other side of opposites as it surpasses all sense and reason.... The place of substance is peace. The more a thing participates in the stability of peace, the nobler it becomes. And what you see with regard to peace, consider likewise with regard to the good and to life.[20]

---

[20]*Pax hominibus bonae voluntatis,* [Sermo CLXVIII (1455)], n. 17, V2, fol. 60ra, 60rb.

However, whether we think of the mind as it understands by measuring things and becoming creative through assimilation or focus on its relationship with order and peace and whatever they entail, in either case it is important to note that we remain within the circle of humanity. The moves and movements are ecstatic in character. In their beginnings they aim at the ultimate. But the ultimate recedes; and, as it does, we realize that its meaning escapes all proportion. Whatever we understand, we understand and judge in a human way.[21] Even if we speak of God and refer to the God of all creation, we can do it in no other way than by relating to God as our God and as God of our intentions. The name itself is a human conjecture in the horizon of infinity. And likewise, if we think of God as Holy Trinity or of Christ as one person in two natures, we still try to make sense of the limit of infinity in accordance with the best of our understanding.

In *De docta ignorantia* Cusanus does not yet discuss the meaning of mind. His main concern in this work is the exploration of all reality and the specification of limits as they appear in "infinitizing" reflection upon all and everything against the background of utter maximality.[22] His object of inquiry is world and universe as the space within which the pursuit of knowledge and understanding makes sense inasmuch as the whole of thought and being provides the parameters we need for an adequate (that is, humanly adequate) assessment of being and truth. Since the knowledge of this whole is essential to sound and free thinking, the obstinate tendency to ignore this almost completely needs to be reversed and enlightened as to itself. By following the indications of this reversal, and thus, by proceeding in the dawning light of learned ignorance, Cusanus comes to the assessment of ultimate limits as they might be discovered when the science of maximality will be developed, and as they are already and implicitly acknowledged when relating to God, the Universe and Christ. However, if we take into consideration that the approach toward the ultimate passes through different kinds of composite perception, reasoning, and understanding (*De docta ignorantia* II,1 [h I, pp. 61-65]), or that human nature is, as microcosm, the counterpart of macrocosm (*De docta ignorantia* III,3 [h I, pp. 125-129]), then we have to conclude that the limits imposed by the whole "prior" to contraction are limits of the whole in the contractions of human nature: whereas the whole concentrates in the mind, it is the mind which provides the ground

---

[21]*De visione Dei,* 6,19: "Homo non potest iudicare nisi humaniter."

[22]The idea of the geometrical limit which Cusanus develops in the first book of *De docta ignorantia* is one of the instances of this reflection. Cusanus uses this idea to facilitate the application of infinitesimal thinking to other instances of "serial" connections within a total context; that is, as a means to cross "metaphysical waters" [Sermo CCLXXIV (1457)]—see Sermo CCLXXIV (1457), V2, 236vb, and not, or in a very remote sense only, as a precursor of Leibniz and Newton. See also Donald F. Duclow, *The Learned Ignorance: Its Symbolism, Logic and Foundations in Dionysius the Areopagite, John Scotus Eriugena and Nicholas of Cusa,* Ph.D. Dissertation, Bryn Mawr College, 1974, especially the section on "The Anthropology of the Limit-Situation," pp. 229ff.

where divine spirit-seeds germinate and grow toward the ultimate horizon of all reality. What began as a kind of immediate exploration of ultimate limits, returns in contracted form—that is, if we turn to the mind as it unfolds toward infinity.

We do not know what Cusanus had precisely in mind when he announced his work *On Conjectures* in the second and third book of *On Learned Ignorance*. The contemporaneous discussion of signs and his reading of Proclus are worth being mentioned.[23] Nor would I be surprised if issues like history, freedom, consensus, "the principles of political and constitutional organization,"[24] and so forth, which he had treated in *The Catholic Concordance,* were still nagging at his mind. But whatever the answer may be, it is both consistent and a sign of his genius that he continued his work on the nature of maximality with a theory of conjectural art and self-understanding as its focus (in the last chapter of *De coniecturis*), and that he finished the project of learned ignorance with the thematization of the mind in dialogues with a layman (*Idiota de sapientia, de mente, de staticis experimentis*). As to their primary intention, these works do not differ from the books *On Learned Ignorance*. But, in concentrating on the mind as "spiracle of life in the image and likeness of God," he added new glamor and different perspectives to his project. As his inquiries culminated in the idea that the human being is a living image of God's wisdom which becomes what it is by growing together with wisdom, justice, beauty and all the other qualities of divine splendor, he succeeded not only in his attempt to come to a deeper understanding of reality, but also opened the way to relate to the "objectifications" of the mind and to study them on their own grounds.

Issues in Spirituality

Among the many issues which could be raised in connection with the spirituality of Cusanus, I would like to bring up three points. The first relates to the compositional character of being human; the second concerns the meaning of Christ; and the third is a reference to the connection and tension between insight and lifestyle.

1) I have already indicated that the emphasis on connective relations moves the center of humanity from its bodily enclosures to the realm of meanings and meaningful actions. This point is important because of the ontological status it attributes to deeds and attitudes, to structures and organizations, and to the interactions between human beings. The creations of human beings, the achievements of virtues, the deeds of compassion and piety are more than qualities of a malleable substance; they are realities in their own rights.

23See, for instance, Rudolf Haubst, *Streifzüge in die cusanische Theologie* (Münster, 1991), pp. 243ff, Chapter VIII. "Am Nichtteilnehmbaren teilhaben." Zu einem Leitsatz der cusanischen "Einheitsmetaphysik" und Geistphilosophie.

24Paul E. Sigmund, "Nicholas of Cusa on the Constitution of the Church" in *Nicholas of Cusa on Christ and the Church,* p. 129.

In his sermon *Debitores sumus,* Cusanus expresses his view as follows:

The civil life is good when it is set to do to others what we like to be done
to ourselves, as Christ teaches us in the seventh chapter of St. Matthew
when He says that laws and prophets which talk about this life are contained
in this commandment.[25] But contemplative life is the true life of the
intellectual spirit. This life is most joyous, and eternal, without any
conflicting opposites. The life of the flesh contrasts with the life of the
spirit, like lust with contemplation. Therefore, if we live in accordance with
the flesh, we die in terms of the spirit. Reason verges toward animality.
However, if we live in accordance with the spirit, carnal life will be
mortified. But, if we live in conformity with the composition of both, we
lead a human and civil life, where all things are done in their time. First we
do what is part of animal life, then what belongs to the divine life, and
finally what concerns human life.[26]

The central concern is, of course, the divine life. But basically it is the whole
spectrum of being human which has to be taken into consideration. Civil life
and spiritual life have to grow together with that of the body; and, when they do,
order, amiability and beauty will be, according to Cusanus, trustworthy guides
that tell us whether we are on the right track or not.

The oppositions to which Cusanus relates are not new. In his preference for
the spiritual life, he refers not only to the Bible but to Plato, Aristotle, Cicero,
and others. But, whereas modern thinking tends to dichotomize the world of the
senses and the world of reason and excludes the meaning of substance from
functionality and spiritual contents, he focuses on the composition and the net of
seminal relations when he thinks in terms of substantiality and perfection. It is a
perspective which, in view of modernity and the need for post-modern reorienta-
tion, points to possible alternatives in the pre-modern period which might have
been seeds of different developments and still could be of vital importance, if we
understand ourselves and the present world correctly.[27]

2) The second point is closely connected with the first one, even though it
belongs to a different order. The idea of Christ as "nodal point" of the universe
had already been developed by Cusanus in the third book of *De docta ignorantia*.

---

[25]See 7:12: "Therefore all things whatsoever ye would that men should do to
you, do ye even so to them: for this is the law and the prophets."

[26]*Debitores sumus* [Sermo CXCVII (1455)], V2, fol.111vb.

[27]See Kuhgai Yamamoto who sees the possibility of a *second renaissance* in
connection with the work of Cusanus: "*Dies sanctificatus* und der Ursprung der
Religionsphilosophie," MFCG 19 (1991): 221-230; Louis Dupré, *Passage to
Modernity: An Essay in the Hermeneutics of Nature and Culture* (New Haven, 1993),
esp. pp. 182ff; and Iñigo Bocken, "Kommunikation und Mutmassung," in *Karl
Jaspers - Philosophy on the Way To "World Philosophy." Philosophie auf dem Weg
zur "Weltphilosophie,"* ed. Leonard Ehrlich and Richard Wisser (Stuttgart, 1999),
pp. 141-146.

At least partly inspired by St. Paul and Meister Eckhart,[28] he speaks in his sermons of human beings as sons of God and refers, as I have already indicated, to the hidden Christ or Jesus in each of us.

This reference gains in importance if we connect it, as Cusanus does, with the belief that Christ is "the way, the truth, and the life" and that "no man cometh unto the Father, but by [Him]" (Jn 14:6). In line with the question about the thrust and purpose of spirituality, we could say that it is answered by the idea and reality of Christ as focus and vanishing point of the movements and motions within the limits of humanity. Therefore, it is Christ whom we have to seek and to find in the configurations of spiritual growth, both as ultimate goal in the relation between God and humanity and as the essential limit of all endeavors into the right direction.

This conclusion agrees with the parameters of ultimate reality as they have been outlined by Cusanus. But do these parameters also agree with the conclusion that "because humanity exists only in the contraction to this or that human being, it is not possible that more than one true human being could ascend to union with maximality?" Cusanus accepts at this point the general assumptions of his tradition, which is fair enough; but there remains the question of internal consistency. Moreover, since historical consciousness has passed through different stages of understanding, and because the religions of this world ask for global ecumenicity, there are strong reasons to return to this point and to inquire about the meaning of Christ, especially if Christ could be the central notion of all spirituality—not only because Christian faith is focused on Christ in its trust in Jesus of Nazareth, but because the spirit of justice, love, and believing carries us already into a christological dimension.

Though the "rule of learned ignorance" makes it necessary to distinguish between the extremes of "more" and of "less,"[29] the connection itself forbids total separation because it precedes this necessity. The assumption of an actual maximum or minimum is reasonable, and even necessary if it has an explaining function, but on our side of the infinite limit it is not absolute because the idea of approximation is retained in this maximum or minimum, and not merely as a qualification of understanding. Singularity does not oppose plurality. As a sign of absolute unity it confirms order within and among plural things and occurrences:

> Each creature finds its singular mode in assimilation to the absolute One. Because what is many through creation cannot be found apart from its

---

[28]See, for instance, Klaus Kremer, "Gott - in allem alles, in nichts nichts: Bedeutung und Herkunft dieser Lehre des Nikolaus von Kues," MCFG 17 (1986): 188-219; and Donald F. Duclow, "Nicholas of Cusa in the Margins of Meister Eckhart: Codex Cusanus 21," in *Nicholas of Cusa in Search of God and Wisdom,* pp. 57-69.

[29]I refer to the axiom "that we can never come to a pure and simple maximum or a pure and simple minimum with regard to things which assume more or less, even though it is best possible to arrive at an actual maximum and minimum;" see *De venatione sapientiae* (h XII,26,79) XXVI.

assimilation to the absolute One, things become concordant in the diversity of singularity. And this is the harmony of the world.[30]

If I read Cusanus correctly, I would rather say that the belief in Jesus as Christ means that we are able, and challenged, to seek and to find Christ in each of us in accordance with the example Jesus has given, and in relation with the communities and realities that have been inspired by His example. The example itself is such that the uniqueness of Jesus and His faith in God makes us think of the coincidence between human singularity and divine universality, and follow Him, if God, and only God, can be adored and glorified. In His human nature Jesus was not almighty, and as revelation of God He remains a mystery of grace. Love, as Cusanus understands it, requires reciprocity. We cannot love our neighbor if we do not acknowledge the same divine origin in human beings and in the various manifestations of being human, inasmuch as, and to the extent that, they are concrete signs of divine perfection. This view might be worrying if belief in God ends up with belief in Jesus as superman. But, if we think of inter-religious dialogue and true peace among religions, it opens up new vistas where nobody has to give up his faith because the singularity of Jesus implies the recognition of divine universality, even though this, like any other faith, including that of Christian believers, might have to change considerably because of the hidden Christ in the center of its own history.[31]

3) With the third and final point on the connection and tension between insights and lifestyle I touch upon one of the most troubling and, at the same time, most fascinating problems of human beings. The problem is most troubling because of the deep split in human nature which it indicates. As we know from personal and historical experiences, we tend to disregard our insights and act against better judgments. And often enough, we either do not know how to coordinate life and understanding or are afraid to do so. But the problem is also most fascinating because it underlines our ability to live by insights, to develop them and to transform ourselves and ways of life accordingly. Besides, if we face all sorts of dissonances in attitudes and intentions, we may discover that there has been more wisdom in the way we have actually behaved than we realized at the time, or that culture and tradition protect us against spurious insights and take care of us in ways which are not so bad after all. On the other hand, if we follow this last line, we have to add that culture, tradition, and personal lifestyle can also be far worse than we ever expected, while we thought they were good. Unfortunately, we are not aware of this, as long as we act in good faith and accept, as Cusanus points out in *De pace fidei*, our customs to be true for no

---

[30]*Maria optimam partem elegit* [Sermo LXXI (1446)] nr. 12 (forthcoming in h XVII/5). For a better understanding of these and related problems see also Alfred Kaiser, "Die Christologie des Nikolaus von Kues im Urteil von Isaak August Dorners (1809-1884)," MFCG 19 (1991): 196-220.

[31]See also Birgit H. Helander's thesis that "in reality, unity is already present," but that we do not see it in our blindness in *Nicolaus Cusanus als Wegbereiter auch der heutigen Ökumene* (Uppsala, 1993), pp. 225ff.

other reason than because they are our customs. But it is a conclusion we have to draw when we observe other cultures and people and approach them and ourselves in historical dimensions.

The various strands of experience and observation which are brought together in the problem of spiritual orientation are clearly present in the thought and life of Nicholas of Cusa. In his attempt to gain genuine insights he follows the road of knowledge and reflections. But, like the sages of India, he thinks and develops his thought also within and between the lines of holy Scripture and the documents of his tradition. And, if we focus on his life and career, we see that he attunes himself to the mood of his age and relates to his personal ideals more or less in terms of contemporary understanding. Whether and to what extent he succeeds in integrating his insights into the spiritual dimensions of humanity is difficult to say. By exploring the whole circle of being human, and by focusing on variable circles within it, he is able to reevaluate possible configurations; but the extent to which he makes use of this possibility needs very careful studies, not only of *De visione Dei*, for instance, where we could say that he thinks also of "strategies" in reaching the goals of spirituality,[32] but of his biography as well. But because and to the extent that his thoughts touch on most elementary issues, the import of his reflections to the study of spirituality can hardly be exaggerated. In his life and thought he is one of the great symbols which shed light on the human situation and help us to find our way, if we follow this light. It is at this point that I would like to speak of lines of convergence both in the sense that the seeds of the spirit are the beginning of all being and becoming, and that they unite with their beginning when they are growing into perfection.

---

[32]I refer here to the connection between spirituality and strategies as Robert J. Schreiter has introduced it in his seminal book on *The Ministry of Reconciliation: Spirituality and Strategies* (New York, 1998).

PROLEGOMENA TO NICHOLAS OF CUSA'S THEORY
OF RELIGIOUS SYMBOLS

Louis Dupré

Any sign refers to a reality that differs from its own. It may do so without having an intrinsic relation to that to which it refers, or it may in some way partake of the nature of the signified. In the former case we speak of a signal or conventional sign; in the latter of a symbol. The conventional sign's meaning is arbitrary and univocal, a shortcut agreed upon to replace a more complex signification. The symbol, on the contrary, is no merely instrumental product of thought; it *adds* a surplus of meaning and, rather than replacing it, it *represents* the signified.

How one reality can represent another presupposes an ontological principle, namely, that being is expressive, that it possesses itself in otherness. The more self-possession, the greater the capacity to express and to be expressed. This expressiveness forms the ontological ground of symbolic representation. Cognition itself depends on the mind's expressive power which enables it to project itself upon the other and to assume it into its own ideal nature. The mind's ontological excellence becomes manifest in its capacity to convert literally anything into a symbol of itself.

Modern interpretations made under nominalist influence tend to ignore this ontological significance. Instead of recognizing in the cognitive act a return of the mind upon itself, capable of converting any object into an image of itself, they have weakened symbolic activity to establishing an external similarity between one object and another. Such an extrinsic relatedness may suffice for a conventional sign. But a symbol in the strict sense does more than resemble the symbolized; it *partakes* of its own reality. Participation, contrary to similarity, reflects an intrinsic bond. The modern de-ontologization of the symbol caused a major problem for the justification of religious symbolism. Indeed, in religious symbolization similarity plays no part at all, since the mind possesses no basis for comparison; it ignores what God is "like." The so-called analogy of being by itself provides no adequate support for God talk. Analogy is merely a logical devise for *defining* a relation among terms; it contributes nothing toward discovering the nature of an unknown term in a relation. Hence it presents no basis for relating two entities of which one is unknown. Nor does the assumption that God is the efficient cause of all things support a symbolic representation of the transcendent. As long as the relation between Creator and creature is restricted to efficient causality it still remains *extrinsic*. Only a formal causality establishes the kind of *intrinsic* participative relation that justifies symbolic language about God.

The idea of divine participation itself received several meanings during its long life in western thought. Platonists conceived of it as the result of an emanation; Christians saw it in a context of creation. But on one basic principle they agreed: symbols of the divine were grounded in the divine expressiveness. In Eckhart's mystical theology, this ontological foundation of religious symbols implied that God, the hidden, absolute first Principle, inhabits its primary expression in the divine Word and, through that Word, the entire creation. Yet even though all things partake in the divine Being, that Being remains unknown in Itself. Eckhart denies that any similarity can exist between the manifest (the creation) and its unmanifest source. How could what surpasses all determinations be similar to the determined? The dissimilarity between the finite and the infinite appears absolute: the two share no common "property." Nevertheless the finite's immanence in God entails that each creature is more intimately related to God than to any other creature. Moreover, God, surpassing all distinctions, cannot be any more dissimilar than similar:

> What is as dissimilar as the infinite and the finite? And...what is as dis-similar as that which has no genus in common with another thing?... [Yet] what is as similar to something else as that which possesses and receives its total existence from the order and relation it has to something else, a thing whose total existence is drawn from this other and has this as an exemplar? But this is the way that the creature is related to God....

The creature possesses no qualities that distinguish it from the Creator. Hence God is as much like the creature as He is unlike. Eckhart concludes:

> Nothing is as dissimilar as the Creator and any creature. In the second place, nothing is as similar as the Creator and any creature. And in the third place, nothing is as equally dissimilar and similar to anything else as God and the creature are dissimilar and similar in the same degree.

Alois Dempf declared this statement the most beautiful classical text on the *analogia entis* of the entire Middle Ages.[1] This may be true provided one does not understand the *analogia* in the common, Thomistic sense, as Dempf does.

Eckhart conceives the analogy between God and the creature as starting in God, rather than in the creature. C.F. Kelley has called this a "reverse" analogy.[2] In its *essence* the creature coincides with God, and that forms the basis of his mysticism. In its contingent *existence*, however, the creature has nothing in common with its Creator. Thus God is at once totally immanent in the creature and totally transcends it. Eckhart does not deny the efficient causality of the creative act as source of its existence. But while efficient causality alone would detach the creature from God, the creature's uncreated *essence* remains permanently *within* God's Word. This ontological union of the creature with God constitutes its formal essence. Eckhart, the negative theologian, considered the dialectic of similarity and dissimilarity, of being and non-being, of immanence and transcendence, inherent in Christian doctrine and left the

---

[1] Eckhart's two texts appear in *Commentary on Exodus* #112-115, in *Die deutschen und lateinischen Werke* (Stuttgart and Berlin, 1936-), vol. 2, *The Latin Works,* ed. Joseph Koch, p. 50. See also *Meister Eckhart, Teacher and Preacher,* trans. Bernard McGinn (New York, 1986), pp. 81-82; Alois Dempf, *Meister Eckhart* (München, 1960), p. 98.

[2] C.F. Kelley, *Meister Eckhart on Divine Knowledge* (New Haven, 1977), pp. 165-172.

antinomies standing. He simply *assumed* the presence of God in the soul: he felt no need to prove what to him appeared obvious.

Cusanus lived in a different climate and wrote from a different perspective. His work constituted a philosophical ontology wherein each concept, including that of God, had to be justified and placed within a comprehensive order of reality.[3] For that reason Cusanus was forced to overcome the oppositions in his system, instead of leaving them unresolved, as Eckhart had done. According to *De coniecturis* and in *De visione Dei*, the manifold becomes intelligible only through the one. In his 1956 study of *De coniecturis* the German medievalist Josef Koch interpreted that work as the transition from a traditional metaphysics of Being (still present in *De docta ignorantia*) to a metaphysics of unity. While the former starts from "below" and then, via the *analogy of being*, ascends from the multiplicity of creation to an absolute principle, the metaphysics of unity, even as Eckhart's reverse analogy, moves from the first principle of unity to the multiplicity of derived beings. The One is *within* as much as *beyond* the many. Koch may have been mistaken in describing *De docta ignorantia* as a *metaphysics of being* in the traditional sense. If so, he was by no means the only one, as Haubst's commentaries on that work show. Nor am I sure that *De coniecturis* is altogether a Neoplatonic work, as Koch claims. Nonetheless, the shift that occurs from *De docta ignorantia* to *De coniecturis* runs in the direction shown by Eckhart: from *similarity* to *identity*. Identity through participation appears indeed to be the fundamental principle underlying the metaphysics of unity adopted in *De coniecturis*.

Does Cusanus also maintain a similarity between God and creation as Eckhart had done? Yes, but only with respect to the human mind. The mind alone may be called an image of God. It acts "like" God as it converts "traces" (Bonaventure's *vestigia*) or signs into *symbols* that participate in God. In the act of knowing, it brings a mere multiplicity to an ideal unity. In *De docta ignorantia* Cusanus had shown how the assumption of an absolute *maximum* conditions all cognitive acts. In *De coniecturis* and such later works as *De non-aliud* and *De visione Dei*, he increasingly stresses how only the *presence* of the One enables the mind to subsume all otherness under unity—the very essence of knowing.[4] Each cognitive act implicitly symbolizes God's presence, without ever knowing God Himself. The mind, then, is an "image" of an unknown original. Cusanus follows here the long-standing Neoplatonic reading of the verse of Genesis, "He created them into His own image," as applying to the *presence* of the divine Logos in the soul. In and through this presence the mind is capable of thinking, that is, measuring and combining things with one another.

---

[3]Cf. Hans Hof, *Scintilla animae* (Lund, 1952).

[4]Cf., Josef Stallmach, "Geist als Einheit und Andersheit: Die Noologie des Cusanus in *De coniecturis* and *De quaerendo Deum*," MFCG (1975): 86-124.

For Cusanus, knowing consists of comparing. In *Idiota de mente* he defines mind as "what measures" (*Mentem quidem a mensurando dici conicio*).[5] Yet, paradoxically, the mind never knows the measure of its knowledge—that to which it compares all objects—the *absolute maximum* and the *absolute unum*. Any form of knowledge, then, is a mixture of knowing and not-knowing. Full knowledge would require a coincidence of being and knowing. Human knowledge merely *refers* to the signified without ever coinciding with it. It remains "conjectural" because of the unbridgeable distance that separates it from its own measure. The conjecture, Cusanus explains in *De coniecturis*, opens up a limited perspective on reality. If taken together with all other perspectives, it constitutes the *maximum contractum*, that is, the universe as a whole which unites all contracted opposites.[6] Yet even that universe, though surpassing all finite perspectives, remains a *specific* totality that emanates and differs from the *maximum absolutum*. In that *maximum absolutum* all perspectives coincide. It remains present in the *maximum contractum* and, through it, constitutes all finite reality: "God is present in all things through the mediation of the universe."[7] Mathematics, the science that derives multiplicity from unity and reduces multiplicity to unity, enables the mind in some way to partake of the "measuring" unity. It mediates between the unknown but actively present divine exemplar and our concrete knowledge of the world.

> The essence of number is therefore the prime exemplar of the mind. For indeed, one finds impressed in it from the first the trinity, or the unitrinity, contracted in plurality. In that we conjecture symbolically from the rational numbers of our mind in respect to the real ineffable numbers of the divine Mind, we indeed say that number is the prime exemplar of things in the mind of the Composer, just as the number arising from our rationality is the exemplar of the imaginal world.[8]

In this passage taken from *De coniecturis*, Cusanus highlights the profound metaphysical significance of mathematical concepts. They exemplify the finite universe and symbolize its divine model.

In Sections 6 and 7 of *Idiota de mente*, Cusanus shows how in the number the unifying power of the mind symbolizes God's unity as source of all created diversity. Even as the mind out of its unity brings forth an infinity of numbers, so does God's unity express itself in an infinity of works. Whereas sensibility,

---

[5] *Idiota de mente*, ch. I, Strassburg edition (1488), reedited by Paul Wilpert in *Werke,* 2 vols. (Berlin, 1967), 1.238.

[6] *De docta ignorantia*, II, 4, # 113, *Werke,* 1.46.

[7] DDI, II, 5, # 117.

[8] *De coniecturis*, § 9, *Werke,* 1.123; *On Conjectures*, trans. William F. Wertz in *Toward a New Council of Florence* (Washington, DC, 1993), p. 61.

imagination, and reason merely assimilate external data, in its higher intuitive power the mind reduces all multiplicity to its own unity.

> In this fashion mind grasps everything intuitively in its own simplicity. There the mind grasps everything intuitively without any composition of parts—every magnitude in the mathematical point and the circle in its center—not as one thing is this and a second that, but as all things are one and are all.[9]

For Cusanus, this intuitive mode of understanding constitutes in fact the source of absolute truth:

> When someone in the manner just mentioned sees how Being is shared differently among all beings and then in the way we are discussing grasps intuitively and directly absolute Being itself beyond all participation and variety, such a person would certainly see everything beyond the determined necessity of connection which he saw in variety. And without it, in an utterly simple way he would see everything in absolute necessity, without number or magnitude or any otherness.

Gerda von Bredow concludes from this passage that the mind's intuitive knowledge is rooted in a mystical awareness of God's presence. In intuitive introspection the mind grasps itself as *image of God* and thus totally assimilates itself with its exemplar. In that vision all things appear as rooted in unity.[10] The mind recognizes its own oneness only when becoming conscious of its essential coincidence with its divine exemplar, that is, when recognizing its own symbolic nature. Since all knowledge ultimately depends on the unity and unifying power of the mind, *all* knowledge thereby becomes symbolic, not only of the mind but also of the mind's divine exemplar. As symbol of God's unity the mind attains some certainty in even the most conjectural knowledge while even its most certain knowledge remains, due to its removal from the aboriginal unity, conjectural.

Though God is the exemplar and transcendental condition of all knowledge, we possess no direct, but only a symbolic knowledge of Him. Already in *De docta ignorantia* Cusanus had declared: *"Cum ad divina non nisi per symbola accedendi nobis via patet"* (DDI, I, 11). In the well-known comparison of the making of a spoon in *Idiota de mente*, the text which describes God as the ultimate *mensura* of thinking, Cusanus avoids any simplistic exemplarism by denying the existence of an ideal prototype. The conception of the spoon occurs entirely in the human mind. Cusanus postulates a divine exemplar, not because the mind requires a Platonic model for practicing a craft, but because relations

---

9*Idiota de mente*, § 7, *Werke*, 1.255. *The Layman: About Mind*, trans. Clyde Lee Miller (New York, 1979), p. 65.

10Gerda Freiin von Bredow, "Der Punkt als Symbol," MFCG 12 (1977): 103-115.

and proportions require a supreme unity in which they are all enfolded. God grants the spoon carver no model, but He is the divine exemplar without which no knowing or judging would be possible. Conjectural structures remain the mind's own projections. This is particularly the case with all conjectures relating to the divine model. The *absolute maximum* constitutes the transcendental condition of all knowledge. Without participating in some way in the total coincidence of thought and reality of the *absolute maximum*, human ideas could never claim to be "true." Thus, the mind attains the object proper to its nature only by intending, beyond a specific object, the absolute *maximum*. The same occurs with respect to the object of desire: through and beyond it the mind seeks the fulfillment of an infinite aspiration. The question of truth, then, for Cusanus, depends on the existence of God. Yet one does not establish that ultimate ground of truth through "proofs," because all alleged arguments for the existence of God begin by considering the finite *independently* of God, an assumption which according to *Idiota de sapientia*, denies what the question itself presupposes. "God is the absolute presupposition of all the things that are presupposed in any way, just as the cause is presupposed in every effect." [11] Nor can discursive *reason* (as opposed to *intellectus*), which posits the principle of contradiction as an absolute, ever justify the presence of a Being in which all contraries coincide. Since the ultimate truth consists in the totality of all perspectives, *reason* which is itself perspectival, is unable to grasp such a totality. It universalizes from a particular perspective—and that is never God.

The source of rational knowledge, then, lies beyond rational knowledge. Only the non-discursive thought of the *intellectus* renders the mind conscious of God's presence. Though the mind cannot adequately name this unknown God, the knowledge that God's essence includes the multiplicity of which it constitutes the unity enables the mind to refer to God through the names of the creatures in which He is present. But since those names are inadequate, it is only through the *intentionality* of the naming act that the mind transcends the particularity of the divine names. The names themselves merely refer to the intrinsic dependence of all finite reality on the infinite. They remain *symbols* in the fullest sense of the term. Through them the mind expresses a presence that exceeds all expression. Nor are they "images" of God. Only the mind may be so considered. In its signifying activity the mind mirrors the divine source of that activity. *What* the mind articulates in symbols and names contains no direct information about God's essence. Still, they are needed for *expressing* the divine presence to the mind.

Already in *De docta ignorantia* Cusanus had insisted on negative nature of all speech about God (DDI, I, 26, § 86). In *Idiota de sapientia*, published ten years later, he shows how the very dialectic of affirmative theology moves it toward negation. In turn, the principles of negative theology drive it toward a new affirmation. The act of negating the content of all symbols is as much a finite activity as the symbolizing act itself. In the end, then, the negation itself must

---

[11] *Idiota de sapientia*, Bk. II, *Werke*, 1.227; *The Layman on Wisdom and the Mind*, trans. M.L. Führer (Ottawa, 1989), p. 42.

be negated. The same divine presence that induced the mind to create symbols and to deny their ultimate appropriateness with respect to God, forces it to move beyond its own negation. Ultimately the mind asserts the presence of the absolute *within* the relative:

> Inasmuch as [God] is beyond every affirmation and negation, there is a consideration of God in which the reply is the negation of affirmation, negation, and conjunction.... Consistent with the way of speaking that is above every affirmation and negation, the rejoinder must be that He neither is, nor is not, absolute entity, nor both together, but that He is beyond them.[12]

The key to this paradox lies in the coincidence of all qualities in God. Because of this coincidence God can be the exemplar of all things without being similar to any of them. This justifies the use of religious symbols. Cusanus concedes the inadequacy of God talk, while at the same time asserting a divine presence, not only to the mind's *being* but also to its symbolizing activity. Cusanus assumes that God dwells in the symbolizing act as well as in the finite entity which the mind uses as a symbol, since God constitutes its entire being. Our awareness of that presence stems from the over-reaching intentionality of the act, not from the nature of the object.

In *De Deo abscondito* Cusanus further develops this dialectic of affirmation and negation. In a dialogue between a Christian and a "Gentile," the Christian denies that God is anything we know. To the Gentile's conclusion, "Therefore, God is nothing," the Christian replies: "He is not nothing, for even this nothing has the name nothing... God is above nothing and something. The nothing obeys him, so that it becomes something." Cusanus repeats the paradoxes Eckhart had formulated in his commentaries on Exodus and on Wisdom. But he resolves them in his theory of the coincidence of opposites. This theory, the main subject of *De docta ignorantia* and one assumed in all the later works, implies that, despite God's total ineffability, God remains the *exemplar* of all finite reality of which He is the enfolded essence. This inherence of all things in the divine nature authorizes the mind to refer to that nature by ordinary symbols, since all *participate* in the divine reality. The justification for religious symbolizing lies, beyond similarity, in God's presence at the core of all things.

One might object: in the second book of *De docta ignorantia* Cusanus speaks of "a likeness of God and the world" (II, 5) and the very title of II, 4 announces a consideration of the universe as "a likeness of the Absolute." Yet *likeness* here does not refer to similarity of appearance—which Cusanus has repeatedly ruled out—but to the mind's ability to name the unknown God by comparing its *own experience of God* with the experience of the world. The mind's power to *experience God* is grounded in its participation in God's nature. Still, one might insist, how can one speak of the mind as image of God if one does not *know* the original? Does image not always presuppose *likeness* and

---

12*Idiota, Werke,* 1:228; *The Layman,* p. 43.

comparison with a *known* original? In a noteworthy essay Wilhelm Dupré has
shed new light on this question by an analysis of the *Excitationes*, Bk. VIII.[13]
Here Cusanus states that God cannot be adored unless we are *certain* of his
existence. This certainty we receive in the grace of faith, a grace that becomes
fulfilled in Christ.

Yet Cusanus also finds a natural source of certainty in the human desire for
God. That desire inspires us to name God by known objects of spiritual desire,
such as truth, justice, goodness and, ultimately, that unity in which all qualities
coincide. Even the sensible order may suggest appropriate names insofar as some
sensuous experiences, such as the experience of light, quite naturally symbolize
objects of spiritual desires. Cusanus' discussion of faith and desire as sources of
an affirmative speech reminds us of an often overlooked passage in *De docta
ignorantia:*

> The worshipping of God, who is to be worshipped in spirit and in truth,
> must be based upon affirmations about Him. Accordingly, every religion, in
> its worshipping, must mount upward by means of affirmative theology.
> [Through affirmative theology] it worships God as one and three, as most
> wise and most gracious, as Inaccessible Light, as Life, Truth, and so on.
> And it always directs its worship by *faith*, which it attains more truly
> through learned ignorance. It believes that He whom it worships as one is
> All-in-one, and that He whom it worships as Inaccessible Light is not light
> as is corporeal light.... And so, the theology of negation is so necessary for
> the theology of affirmation that without it God would not be worshipped as
> the Infinite God but rather as a creature. And such worship is idolatry.[14]

In this passage Cusanus emphasizes faith and worship, rather than desire (as he
does in the *Excitationes*). But in both cases the mind's authority to *name* the
unknown God is derived from an awareness of God's presence. The many facets
of this awareness account for the variety of names. Yet the unifying drive in that
experience compels the mind to collect this plurality within a single intentionality. In the end, then, the "likeness" and analogy of religious symbolism in no
way implies a likeness or analogy between God and the creatures, but between
our *experience* of God and the experiences from which we borrow the names to
refer to the unknown source of religious experience.

Of course, the experience of God is itself no more than an *image* of God; but
it is the highest, for in the religious experience God's presence becomes directly
manifest. We do not *know* God, yet we experience God's presence sufficiently to
name Him. The symbol, then, that grounds all religious symbols is the

---

[13]Wilhelm Dupré, "Das Bild und die Wahrheit," MFCG 18 (1989): 125-166.

[14]*De docta ignorantia*, Bk. I, ch. 26, § 86, in *Werke*, 1.34. *Nicholas of Cusa on
Learned Ignorance*, trans. Jasper Hopkins, 2nd ed. (Minneapolis, 1985), p. 84. On
the link between worship and affirmative theology, see Birgit Helander, *Die visio
intellectualis als Erkenntnisweg und Ziel des Nicholaus Cusanus* (Uppsala, 1988), pp.
128-132.

experience of God in faith, in desire, in worship. This implies that, for Cusanus, the basis of all positive knowledge of God is mystical, as Gerda von Bredow asserted. Yet, because of the intrinsic inadequacy of all religious symbols no single one or no single group can ever claim to be exhaustive. All symbols, even the idea of *God* itself, fall short in their attempt to name God. All religions rest on symbols, yet none succeeds in naming God so adequately as to exclude all others. Even the "revealed" Christian faith does not destroy the truth of other religious symbolizations. Nor does it render other forms of worship superfluous.

Cusanus perceived the practical consequences of his theory for an ecumenical dialogue. In *De pace fidei*, he investigated the compatibility of various faiths according to their implicit or explicit closeness to the dialectic of unity and relationality that lies at the heart of trinitarian monotheism. If each faith understood its own fundamental principles, he optimistically declares, religious strife would come to an end in the awareness that a single monotheism underlies all of them. If God creates all things in wisdom and if religious symbols express that wisdom, we may assume that God self *constitutes* "the wisdom of the created wisdom."[15] All genuinely religious symbols, then, refer to the same divine unity that inspired humans to conceive them. God constitutes the intentional core of each faith. "See therefore how you, the philosophers of various schools of thought, agree in the religion of the one God, whom you all presupposed in that which you as lovers of wisdom acknowledge" (DPF V, p. 343; Wertz, p. 238). This, of course, is not to say that all religions are equal, but only that the "revealed" religion does not exclude the others.

Still, if God is one, what truth can there be in the many forms of polytheism? They are all united in one divine divinity. Their multiplicity represents the various powers in which that divinity expresses Himself. Worship goes to the one God who is the single source of the many powers. The personification of these powers stems from the spontaneous veneration of persons who lived a deiform life and whom people invoke for *particular* needs. Their images reflect the infinite riches of the one God. Only if objects, animals, or persons are adored as if the finite form itself contained a divine force do symbols lose their symbolic character and does religion degenerate into idolatry (DPF VII, p. 345; Wertz, p. 241). But monotheism itself may become perverted in the opposite direction, if its followers fail to reduce the divine plurality of the Trinity to God's unity, or even if they identify the divine unity with the number one. God is neither three nor one, but, standing at the origin of unity and plurality, He remains beyond number. The symbol of the trinitarian plurality expresses the truth that God's unity is fertile as well as self-contained. According to Cusanus, the dogma of the Trinity mediates the strict monotheism of Israel and Islam with the polytheism of other religions—and justifies the foundation of one and the other:

---

[15] *De pace fidei*, § V, *Werke*, 1.343; *On the Peace of Faith* in *Toward a New Council of Florence*, p. 238. I refer to this edition, abridged as DPF, in Wertz's translation.

> That fecundity, which is also a trinity, brings it about that it is unnecessary to have several gods, which mutually support each other in the creation of everything for the one infinite fecundity suffices to create all that which can be created (DPF IX, p. 348; Wertz, p. 246).

Cusanus blames the literalist reading of religious texts as being principally responsible for religious division, since it excludes the broader, symbolic interpretation. Peter, one of the interlocutors in *De pace fidei*, attributes the Jews' rejection of Christ to a literal reading of the Bible. "Since they follow the literal sense, they do not want to understand" (DPF XII, p. 355; Wertz, p. 255). Cusanus here anticipates Pascal and Newman, both of whom considered literalism a source of heresy. A similar incapacity to move beyond the symbol drives polytheists from a veneration of divine powers to idolatry. The dialogue concludes with a plea for recognizing the pluralism of religious symbols and rituals, as necessary for expressing the inexhaustible spiritual riches of the mystery of one God:

> Where no conformity in the mode can be found, as long as faith and peace are preserved, one may indulge the nations in their devotions and ceremonies. Perhaps the devotion is even augmented by virtue of the diversity, since every nature will attempt to produce its rite more splendidly with zeal and diligence, in order to outdo the others therein and thus to obtain greater merit with God and praise in the world (DPF XIX, p. 366; Wertz, p. 271).

BEHIND THE SCENE:
THE CARTHUSIAN PRESENCE IN LATE MEDIEVAL SPIRITUALITY

Dennis D. Martin

I. Introduction

Strictly cloistered and contemplative religious orders took a back seat in western Christendom after the rise of the mendicant apostolate to the city streets and the emergence of semi-religious communities in the thirteenth and fourteenth centuries. In light of this, the last place one might be inclined to look for a powerful influence on popular spirituality and theology would be the strictly cloistered, ardently contemplative Carthusians.[1] Yet precisely from the fourteenth- and fifteenth- century charterhouses we find emanating a powerful, often but not exclusively indirect, influence on surrounding society. In many important instances, Carthusian "authors" "merely" translated or compiled preexisting materials and sent them on their way, usually into monastic channels of distribution, from which extended a wider dissemination outside the monasteries. Accustomed to value originality and direct influence, modern scholars have not always noticed how a particularly apt compilation caught on precisely because it met a real need in the "market" for spiritual and ethical guidance, how a "mere" translation served a wide public because it made the transition from Latin to the vernacular in a manner particularly useful to monastics (including lay brethren) *and* lay people. Taken separately, each of the three approaches to religious education and edification surveyed below may seem ambiguous and less than fully successful to the modern mind, accustomed as it is to valuing highly "direct" access to Scripture, to Scripture understood archeologically as a written text. Taken together, however, they suggest ways of envisioning *accessus* to the heart of Scripture that may not immediately register with today's students of late medieval religious history.

---

[1] A general history of the Carthusian Order is in process, under the direction of an international commission headed by Daniel Le Blévec, James Hogg and others and with informal cooperation from the order itself. The first of three volumes will appear in 2001, published by Éditions Honoré Champion. Until this history has been completed, the interested reader is directed to the articles "Certosine" (by a Carthusian nun) and "Certosini" (by Jacques Dubois) in the *Dizionario degli istituti di perfezione,* 9 vols. (Roma, 1974-), 2.771-822; "Chartreux" in *Dictionnaire de spiritualité,* 16 vols. (Paris, 1937-1995); Adam Wienand and Marijan Zadnikar, *Die Kartäuser: Orden der schweigenden Mönche* (Köln, 1983); E. Margaret Thompson, *The Carthusian Order in England* (London, 1930). Carthusian expansion increased dramatically in the later Middle Ages (more than one hundred houses founded during the 14th and forty during the 15th century, nearly half of the more than two hundred houses existing in 1500) when they began to enjoy patronage at the highest levels of western European society, from bishops, popes, kings, and princes of the various royal families, as well as burgher elites in major cities; see Dennis D. Martin, "'The Honeymoon Was Over': Carthusians between Aristocracy and Bourgeoisie," in *Die Kartäuser und ihre Welt: Kontakte und gegenseitige Einflüsse* (Analecta Cartusiana, 62.1; Salzburg, 1993), pp. 66-99.

We shall first survey in a brief introduction the astonishing range of topics on which Carthusian authors from the thirteenth through the fifteenth centuries wrote, translated, and compiled. Often at the request of individuals or institutions, Carthusians gave advice via handwritten and, by the late 1400s, printed treatises, on how to apply basic Christian principles to matters ranging from city and state government to agriculture to the more obvious topics of prayer and liturgical devotion, including some of the best Latin liturgical and hagiographical poetry written in the Middle Ages. Like Nicholas of Cusa, they regularly gave advice to Benedictines and others seeking to inaugurate or continue monastic reform, and the Carthusian Johann Rode of Trier (d. 1439), from Nicholas of Cusa's home region, became a leading Benedictine reform abbot. Like Cusanus, Carthusians brought sober discretion to bear on popular piety, e.g., in the controversy around the Wilsnack Bleeding Host devotion or on the question of abuses relating to indulgences.[2]

Having cast a brief glance over the Carthusian literary landscape, our attention in the present essay will focus on three of the most popular works of spiritual theology carried out by Carthusians during the fourteenth and fifteenth centuries: the *Vita Christi* of Ludolf of Saxony (d. 1378), well-known even today; the far less known but, in its own day, highly popular *Marienleben* of Philip of Seitz (fl. 1316); and the development and popularization of the meditative rosary devotion in the fifteenth century, originated by two members of the Carthusian house at Trier. All three of these works consist of meditations on the life of Christ and Mary, on the heart of the gospel, enlisting the imagination to help the Christian believer ponder and be moved by the central events in the origins of Christianity, which remain, despite Enlightenment attacks, utterly dependent on the facticity of crucial events that occurred in a specific time and specific place.

---

[2]Several authors could be cited here, but here we must be content with Johann Brewer of Hagen (d. 1475) at the Erfurt charterhouse, whose corpus of writings rivals in comprehensiveness the encyclopedic work of the much better known Denis the Carthusian. Johann of Hagen wrote the following treatises, many of them very brief: *Tractatus de visionibus, De visione Tundali et de aliis visionibus, De apparitione mulieris defunctae et de prodigiis varis, De futuris prodigiis et cognitione et causis eorum, De cognitione futurorum et somniorum, De discretione spirituum, Contra prophetias prophanas hujus temporis, De casibus contingentibus in quibusdam locis ratione miraculorum.* On the Wilsnack bleeding host miracle he wrote (very skeptically): *Tractatus continens multa dubia de quodam mirabili casu circa eucharistiam* and *Alius casus etiam de eucharistia, in quo fuit multus concursus populi,* and *De sanguine Iesu Christi et cruore in sacramento altaris.* He also wrote on relics: *De reliquiis et veneratione sanctorum* and against all superstition: *De arte magica.* On indulgences, he wrote: *De plenariis indulgentiis datis anno jubilaeo, De quibusdam dubiis, quae occurrunt de plenariis indulgentiis concessis Erffordiae; De indulgentiis contra Turcos; Super indulgentiis bullae Bonifacii papae de festo Visitationis gloriosae virginis Mariae.* For details, including codices at Oxford, Trier, Paderborn, and Weimer, see Heinrich Rüthing in *Dictionnaire de spiritualité,* 8.549, and Johannes. Klapper, *Der Erfurter Kartäuser Johannes Hagen: Ein Reformtheolog des 15. Jahrhunderts,* 2 vols. (Leipzig, 1960-1961), 1.83-95.

Carthusians in the late Middle Ages are generally well known for their contributions to contemplative and mystical theology, beginning with the classic work by Prior Guigo II of the Grande Chartreuse (d. 1178), *Scala Claustralium*, with its four stages of *lectio, meditatio, oratio*, and *contemplatio*.[3] Widely circulated under Bernard of Clairvaux's name, it only became recognized as a product of the Chartreuse early in the twentieth century.[4] The contemplative and mystical spirituality of Hugh of Balma (d. ca. 1305)[5] and its possible influence on the *Cloud of Unknowing* (whose author may have been a Carthusian[6]) and the writings of Guigo du Pont (d. 1297),[7] Denis the Carthusian (d. 1471),[8]

---

[3]Guigues II, *Lettre sur la vie contemplative (L'échelle des moines); Douze Méditations*, ed. Edmund Colledge and James Walsh, trans. "un Chartreux" (Sources Chrétiennes, 163; Paris, 1970); English translation in *The Ladder of Morris: A Letter on the Contemplative Life and Twelve Meditations* (Garden City, New York, 1978); Dariusz Dolatowski, "Die Methode des inneren Gebetes im Werk *Scala claustralium sive tractatus de modo orandi* des Guigo II. des Kartäusers," in *The Mystical Tradition and the Carthusians*, vol. 2 (Analecta Cartusiana, 130.2; Salzburg, 1995), pp. 144-167.

[4]André Wilmart, "Les écrits spirituels des deux Guigues," in Wilmart, *Auteurs spirituels et textes dévots du moyen âge latin: Études d'histoire littéraire* (Paris, 1932), pp. 217-260.

[5]Hughes de Balma, *Théologie mystique*, trans. Francis Ruello and Jeanne Barbet (Sources Chrétiennes, 408, 409; Paris, 1995, 1996); English translation by Dennis Martin in *Carthusian Spirituality: The Writings of Hugh of Balma and Guigo de Ponte* (Classics of Western Spirituality; Mahwah, New Jersey, 1997), pp. 69-170, with references to secondary literature at pp. 9-47; German translation by Harald Walach, *Notitia experimentalis Dei--Erfahrungserkenntnis Gottes: Studien zu Hugo de Balmas Text "Viae Sion lugent" und deutsche Übersetzung*, 2 vols. (Analecta Cartusiana, 98.1-2; Salzburg, 1994).

[6]*The Cloud of Unknowing*, ed. James Walsh (Classics of Western Spirituality; New York, 1981), pp. 1-97; *The Pursuit of Wisdom and Other Works by the Author of the Cloud of Unknowing*, ed. James Walsh (Classics of Western Spirituality; New York, 1988), pp. 68-73; J.P.H. Clark, "The *Cloud of Unknowing* and the Contemplative Life," in *Die Kartäuser und ihre Welt—Kontakte und gegeseitige Einflüsse*, vol. 1 (Analecta Cartusiana, 62.1; Salzburg, 1993), pp. 44-65.

[7]Guigo du Pont, *De contemplatione*, ed. Philippe Dupont 2 vols. (Analecta Cartusiana, 72; Salzburg, 1985); Italian translation by Emilio Piovesan as Guigo du Pont, *Della contemplazione* (Analecta Cartusiana, 45; Salzburg, 1979); English translation by Dennis Martin in *Carthusian Spirituality*, pp. 171-253, with references to secondary literature.

[8]*Doctoris ecstatici Dionysii Cartusiensis Opera Omnia*, 44 vols. (Montreuil, 1896-1913); Kent Emery, *Dionysii cartusiensis opera selecta*, vol. 1, *Prolegomena: Bibliotheca et manuscripta*, in 2 parts (Corpus Christianorum Continuatio Mediaevalis, 121A, 121B; Turnhout, 1991). Note also the use made of Denis the Carthusian as an exemplary late-medieval commentator on Scripture by David C. Steinmetz in *Luther in Context* (Bloomington, Indiana, 1986), pp. 102-104.

Jacob of Paradies (d. 1465),[9] Nicholas Kempf (ca. 1416-1497),[10] and Vincent of Aggsbach (d. 1464)[11] figure in most surveys of late medieval spirituality and have been studied in the context of Nicholas of Cusa's own mystical- contemplative and reform-conciliarist writings.[12] Usually not considered "mystical" writers, the Carthusians Ludolf of Saxony (d. 1378)[13] and Heinrich Egher of Kalkar (d. 1408)[14] have also received considerable attention. But all of this represents only one small arc of the immense circle of Carthusian literature during the late Middle Ages.[15]

---

[9]Incorrectly but commonly referred to as Jakob of Jüterbog; see Dieter Mertens, *Iacobus Cartusiensis: Untersuchungen zur Rezeption der Werke des Kartäuserpriors Jakob von Paradies* (Veröffentlichungen des Max-Planck-Instituts für Geschichte, 50 / Studien zur Germania Sacra, 13; Göttingen, 1976); Mertens, "Jakob von Paradies (1381-1465) über die mystische Theologie," in *Kartäusermystik und mystiker*, vol. 5 (Analecta Cartusiana, 55.5; Salzburg, 1982), pp. 31-46; Johann Auer, "Die *Theologia mystica* des Kartäusers Jakob von Jüterbog († 1465)," in *Die Kartäuser in Österreich*, vol. 2 (Analecta Cartusiana, 83.2; Salzburg, 1981), pp. 19-52.

[10]Dennis D. Martin, *Fifteenth-Century Carthusian Reform: The World of Nicholas Kempf* (Studies in the History of Christian Thought, 49; Leiden, 1992).

[11]For this figure, well known to most students of Nicholas of Cusa's life, see Edmonde Vansteenberghe's classic work, *Autour de la docte ignorance: Une controverse sur la théologie mystique au XVe siècle* (Beiträge zur Geschichte der Philosophie des Mittelalters, 14.1-4; Münster, 1913; reprint as Analecta Cartusiana 35.17; Salzburg, 1992). For additional literature, including various studies by Heribert Roßmann, see Dennis D. Martin, "Vinzenz von Aggsbach" in *Die deutsche Literatur des Mittelalters: Verfasserlexikon*, 2nd ed., ed. Kurt Ruh et al., 10 vols. (Berlin, 1978ff), 10.359-365.

[12]As evidence of Vincent's significance as an advocate of conciliarism (and opponent of Cusanus after the latter changed course on the issue), see Hubert Jedin's references to him in the first volume of his *History of the Council of Trent*, trans. Ernest Graf (St. Louis, 1957), pp. 37, 43-44, 46, 53, 117, 120.

[13]See section III, below.

[14]Earlier literature and editions are found in Henrich Rüthing, *Der Kartäuser Heinrich Egher von Kalkar, 1328-1408* (Veröffentlichungen des Max-Planck-Instituts für Geschichte, 18 / Studien zur Germania Sacra, 8; Göttingen, 1967), with Rüthing's updated summary in *Verfasserlexikon*, 2.379-384. See also A.P. Orbán, *Die Korrespondenz und der Liber Exhortacionis des Heinrich von Kalkar: Eine kritische Ausgabe* (Analecta Cartusiana, 111; Salzburg, 1984). Hendrina B.C.W. Vermeer, *Het tractaat "Ortus et decursus ordinis cartusiensis" van Hendrik Egher van Kalkar met een biographische inleiding,* Phil. diss., Leiden; printed at Wageningen, 1929, has been reprinted in *Die Geschichte des Kartäuserordens*, vol.2 (Analecta Cartusiana, 125.2; Salzburg, 1992), pp. 1-153.

[15]In the following summary, only a few outstanding names of writers are listed for each genre in the footnotes, for the most part without attempting to cite the literature on them. For bibliographical and other details, see my initial survey of late

Moreover, an understanding of the nature of early Carthusian spirituality has not been well served by a division into "mystical" or contemplative and "other" genres. The heart of the Carthusian world was the *propositum*, or firm intent and purpose,[16] to give oneself totally to God in one's inmost being by spending the rest of one's life steadily abiding in one's cell (a small cottage). If one studies the Carthusian statutes, one discovers that they were designed primarily to encourage such cell-sitting and to discourage leaving the cell either literally or spiritually.[17] Sticking to this *propositum* gives one distance from the world in order to know the world truly and deeply, and thereby to love the world more profoundly.[18] Carthusian spiritual writings from the first Carthusian century are set within the cell and the structured customs and activities that make such cell-sitting possible. Guigo II discovered his four-fold method while engaged not in meditation but in manual labor, i.e., copying of books, as mandated by the Carthusian statutes. Adam of Dryburgh (d. ca. 1212) wrote a major treatise on the Carthusian life titled *On the Fourfold Exercise of the Cell*[19] that is primarily a guide to meditative reading touching only briefly on contemplative prayer, then taking the reader back into manual labor at the conclusion. To the untrained modern eye it might seem a not very contemplative work. But Adam's apparent oddness was based on experience: the chief obstacles to contemplation are distraction and the temptation to abandon the cell. Learning to read meditatively

---

medieval Carthusian spirituality in the forthcoming general history of the Carthusian Order as described in note 1 above. In addition to articles on many Carthusian spiritual writers in the *Dictionnaire de spiritualité* (beginning with the Yves Gourdel and others in the entry "Chartreux") and the *Verfasserlexikon*, for the Low Countries a comprehensive survey was published by H.J.J. Scholtens, "De litteraire nalatenschap van de Kartuizers in de Nederlanden," *Ons geestelijk Erf* 25 (1951): 9-43.

16For this use of *propositum* as designating the Carthusian way of life, the Carthusian calling, see the *Consuetudines* of Guigo I, prologue sect. 3 and chapters 14.5, 20.3; 22.2; 25.2; 38.1; 41.2,4,5; 80.7,12 in *Coutumes de Chartreuse*, ed. un Chartreux (Sources Chrétiennes, 313; Paris, 1984).

17See Bruno Rieder, *Deus Locum Dabit: Studien zur Theologie des Kartäuserpriors Guigo I (1083-1136)* (Veröffentlichungen des Grabmanns-Instituts, Neue Folge, 42; Paderborn, 1997), esp. pp. 128-129, 177-231.

18Gordon Mursell, *The Theology of the Carthusian Life in the Writings of St. Bruno and Guigo I* (Analecta Cartusiana, 127; Salzburg, 1988); Marie-Charlotte (Soeur Bruno) Barrier, *Les activités du solitaire en chartreuse d'après ses plus anciens témoins* (Analecta Cartusiana, 87; Salzburg, 1981).

19Until the modern edition announced by Francesco Palleschi appears, one must use the seventeenth-century edition in PL 153.799-884. See also M.M. Davy, "La vie solitaire cartusienne d'après le *De Quadripertito exercitio cellae* d'Adam le Chartreux," *Revue d'ascetique et de mystique* 14 (1933): 124-145; André Wilmart, "Maister Adam Cartusiensis," in *Mélanges Mandonnet: Études d'histoire littéraire et doctrinale du moyen áge*, vol. 2 (Bibliothèqe Thomiste, 14; Paris, 1930), pp. 145-161; Barrier, *Les activités du solitaire.*

and tempering this with manual labor are in fact long-term keys to a steady
contemplative life in the Carthusian *propositum.*

Only later in the thirteenth century did a specific genre of treatises on
mystical theology emerge, inspired largely by the efforts to integrate the
writings of Pseudo-Dionysius into the Latin intellectual tradition beginning
especially with the twelfth-century Victorines at Paris and continuing through
the scholastics of the thirteenth century. Building on the work of the Victorine
Thomas Gallus of Vercelli (d. 1246),[20] Hugh of Balma made a major statement
on this topic, which, in turn, inspired many of the later medieval treatments of
the topic by Carthusians, Franciscans and others, leading, above all, to the
Tegernsee controversy over a purportedly anti-intellectual mystical ascent to
union with God, a controversy into which Nicholas of Cusa entered with his *De
visione Dei* and his letters to the Benedictines of Tegernsee.[21] Focusing on
mystical theology, however, obscures the more fundamental Carthusian
spirituality of meditative reading that, occasionally, rises up into *oratio* and
contemplatio. Unless one keeps in view the broader tradition of cell-sitting and
meditative reading, one will fail to understand how Ludolf of Saxony's popular
Vita Christi or the diverse handbooks on living the Christian life in various lay
states written by Denis the Carthusian and Johannes Brewer of Hagen could be
integrated into the Carthusian way of life, the Carthusian *propositum.* Losing
sight of the centrality of cell-sitting, one will be tempted to dismiss much of the
Carthusian literary output as at best eccentrically, even bizarrely, suited to the
Carthusian "contemplative" tradition.

Now, just what would one do while sitting sedulously in one's cell?
Contemplate, yes, and write treatises on contemplation, but also work with
one's hands at copying books, and compiling treatises about how to test a
vocation and enter monastic life,[22] and how to live a genuine monastic life and

---

[20]The best study remains the unpublished dissertation by James Walsh,
*'Sapientia Christianorum': The Doctrine of Thomas Gallus Abbot of Vercelli on
Contemplation,* (Roma, Gregorian University, 1957). James Walsh, "Thomas Gallus
et l'effort contemplatif," *Revue d'histoire de la spiritualité* 51 (1975): 17-42. For
additional literature, including the often difficult to access articles of G. Théry, see
Jeanne Barbet's article in *Dictionnaire de spiritualité*, 15.800-816, and Rosemary
Ann Lees, *The Negative Language of the Dionysian School of Mystical Theology: An
Approach to the "Cloud of Unknowing"* (Analecta Cartusiana, 107.1-2; Salzburg,
1983).

[21]In addition to the literature cited above in connection with Vincent of
Aggsbach, see *Nicholas of Cusa: Selected Spiritual Writings*, trans. H. Lawrence
Bond (Classics of Western Spirituality; Mahwah, New Jersey, 1997) regarding
Cusanus' *De visione Dei.*

[22]Nicholas Kempf, *Dialogus de recto studiorum fine ac ordine*, in Bernhard Pez,
Bibliotheca ascetica antiquo nova, 12 vols. (Regensburg, 1724-40, reprint
Farnborough, 1967), 4.258-492; Nicholas Kempf, *Tractatus de proponentibus
religionis ingressum de anno probationis usque ad professionem inclusive*
(unpublished), see Martin, *Fifteenth-Century Carthusian Reform*, pp. 276-82; Gerard

lead a monastic community with discretion,[23] or describing Carthusian specifics and vigorously defending the Carthusian Order against its detractors.[24] Then, again, one might assemble a variety of manuals on the vices and virtues in general or in particular,[25] write the lives of saints in verse or in prose,[26]

---

of Schiedam (d. 1442), *Tractatus de professione religiosorum* (unpublished), see H.J.J. Scholtens in *Dictionnaire de spiritualité*, 6.280-281), are only a few examples.

[23]One of the best surveys of Carthusian approaches to leadership is Heinrich Rüthing, *Der Kartäuser Heinrich Egher van Kalkar*. To illustrate only briefly the range of such writings: Johann Rode wrote for Benedictine abbots out of his Carthusian background, *De bono regimine abbatis tractatus*, published in Pez, *Bibliotheca ascetica*, 1.157-204; Nicholas Kempf wrote for monastic superiors in general, drawing on the rich monastic tradition, in *De discretione*, published in Pez, *Bibliotheca ascetica*, 9.379-582; Michael of Prague (d. 1401), wrote *Remediarium abiecti prioris*, published in Pez, *Bibliotheca ascetica*, 2.227-468, for a Carthusian prior who had been deposed. Johannes Hagen wrote a very specialized treatise on the power and authority of the vicar in a charterhouse, *De potestate vicariorum in ordine cartusiensium quoad absolutionem in foro poenitentiali et in confessione*, and Jacob of Gruytrode (d. 1475), wrote a general manual for all who are in authority: *Instructio principum et omnium qui in potentatu aliquo sunt.*

[24]Dirk of Haarlem (d. 1465), *Epistola de solitudine ac silentio Cartusiano*, see Scholtens, "Nalatenschap," p. 19; William of Hyporegia (d. 1320/25), presumed author of *Tractatus de origine et veritate perfectae religionis* (unpublished), see James Hogg, "Guillelmus de Yporegia: *De origine et veritate perfecte religionis*," in *Collectanea Cartusienia*, 2 (Analecta Cartusiana, 82.2; Salzburg, 1980), pp. 84-118; Hermann of Apeldorn (d. 1472), *Regimen breve et utile pro Cartusiensibus*, see Scholtens, "Nalatenschap," p. 22; Heinrich Egher of Kalkar, *Ortus et decursus ordinis cartusiensis*, ed. Vermeer as cited above; Nicholas Kempf, *De confirmatione et regula approbata ordinis Cartusiensis* (unpublished), see Martin, *Fifteenth-Century Carthusian Reform*, pp. 292-294; Peter of Doorlant (Dorlandus) (d. 1507), *Tractatus de mysterio seu spirituali habitus carthusiensis significantia cum remedio circa carnalem delectationem* (Louvain, 1514), L. Moereels on Doorlant in *Dictionnaire de spiritualité*, 3.1646-1651.

[25]From innumerable examples, one might consider the various works of Nicholas Kempf; see Martin, *Fifteenth-Century Carthusian Reform*, pp. 285-292, as well as Adam of Hinton (d. ca. 1400), *De patientia tribulationum* (London, 1520), originally written in English and printed ca. 1500; see M. Ilge in *Dictionnaire de spiritualité*, 1.195-196). See also Jacob of Paradies, *Tractatus de causis multarum passionum, praecipue iracundie, et remediis earundem*, published in Pez, *Bibliotheca ascetica*, 7.389-444.

[26]Perhaps most outstanding are the Latin hagiographic hymns, following the church calendar, of Konrad of Haimburg (d. 1360), prior at the monasteries of Seitz and Gaming in Austria, published, e.g., in *Conradus Gemnicensis/Konrads von Haimburg und seiner Nachahmer, Alberts von Prag und Ulrichs von Wessobrunn, Reimgebete und Leselieder*, ed. Guido Maria Dreves, (Analecta hymnica medii aevi, 3; Leipzig, 1888), pp. 1-102; Franz-Josef Worstbrock in *Verfasserlexikon*, 5.182-189. But countless other Carthusians wrote hagiography, including Heinrich Arnoldi of Alfeld (d. 1487), prior of the Charterhouse of Basel ; see Eugen Hillenbrand in *Verfasserlexikon*, 1.488-89, and L. Ray in *Dictionnaire de spiritualité*, 1.892-93; Giles Aurifaber (d. 1466), possible author of a widely-distributed miracle book and

compose passion meditations,[27] or busily extract the sweet blossoms from Scripture and spiritual writings to form *florilegia* and prayer manuals.[28] Or, one

---

exempla collection; see L. Ray in *Dictionnaire de spiritualité*, 1.1138-39; and Peter of Doorlant. Moreover, though the Carthusians rarely publicized their members as saints (*"Cartusia sanctos facit sed non patefacit"*), Beatrice of Ornacieux (d. 1310) wrote the life of her fellow Carthusian nun and fellow visionary, Marguerite d'Oingt (d. 1310). On both, see B. Gaillard in *Dictionnaire de spiritualité*, 10.340-343. See also Roland Maisonneuve, "Les visions mystiques de Béatrice d'Ornacieux (d. 1303?), moniale de la chartreuse de Parménie, première prieure de la chartreuse d'Eymeux," in *Kartäuserliturgie und Kartäuserschrifttum*, vol. 1 (Analecta Cartusiana, 116.1; Salzburg, 1988), pp. 53-68; Peter Dinzelbacher, "Marguerite d'Oignt und ihre Pagina Meditationum," in *Kartäuserliturgie und Kartäuserschrifttum*, 1.69-100; and Bernard McGinn, *The Flowering of Mysticism: The Presence of God* (A History of Western Christian Mysticism, 3; New York, 1998), pp. 289-292, summarizing Stephanie Paulsell, `Scriptio divina': Writing and the Experience of God in the Works of Marguerite d'Oignt, PhD dissertation, U. of Chicago, 1993.

[27] In addition to the Passion sections of Ludolf of Saxony's *Vita Christi*, studied in detail by Walter Baier (see section III, below) one finds, e.g., Boniface Ferrer (d. 1417), brother of Saint Vincent, prior of the Grande Chartreuse during the western Schism, *Tractatus de passione Domini*; Heinrich of Dissen (d. 1484), *Centum articuli de passione Domini* and *Expositio in passionem Domini, Oratio de passione Domini* (all unpublished), see H. Rüthing in *Dictionnaire de spiritualité*, 7.185-188); and Heinrich Egher of Kalkar, *Informatio meditationis de passione Domini*, ed. H. Lindemann, as "Een tractaat over de overweging van's heerenlijden aan Hendrik van Calcar toegeschreven," *Ons geestelijk Erf* 7 (1933): 62-88; Catherine Buls (d. 1438), a nun of the Charterhouse of Sint Anna at Westijne near Bruges wrote a *Tractaat ofte boecxken der selve Passie Christi genomen uyt de H. Schriftuur,* see Scholtens, "Nalatenschap," p. 17. Peter of Doorlant's *Aureum opus de opere amoirs et passione domininostri Christi* was published at Louvain in 1516, and Passion meditations by Heinrich of Coesfeld and Johann Rode of Hamburg (d. 1439, monk of Prague, not to be confused with Johann Rode of Trier, the Carthusian- Benedictine reformer) enjoyed circulation in German versions of their Latin originals. On Johann Rode of Hamburg, see Rudolf Ohlbaum, *Johann Rode aus Hamburg: Von deutschem Geistesleben in Böhmen um 1400* (Sudetendeutsches historisches Archiv, 5; Prague, 1943) and H. Rüthing in *Dictionnaire de spiritualité*, 8.655-657.

[28] Heinrich Egher of Kalkar wrote a manual on how to develop spiritually through prayer: *Scala spiritualis exercitii per modum orationis,* see Rüthing in *Dictionnaire de spiritualité*, 7.191. Several of Heinrich of Dissen's collections of *"Psalteria"* on the persons of the Trinity, the Blessed Virgin Mary, all the saints and angels etc., drawn from the writings of Hilary of Poitiers, Ambrose, Jerome, Augustine, Leo the Great, etc., were printed in the 1470s. See Rüthing in *Dictionnnaire de spiritualité*, 7.187. Heinrich Arnoldi of Alfeld also compiled important collections of prayers and meditations, see Hillenbrand in *Verfasserlexikon* as cited above. Jacob of Gruytrode's *Salutationes ad membra Christi et Mariae* continued an ancient Syriac form of prayer, perhaps mediated via the Celtic Christian "Lorica" prayers of the 9th century; see Gerard Achten, "Die Kartäuser, Meister des Gebetes im 15. Jahrhundert," in *Kartäuserliturgie und Kartäuserschrifttum*, vol. 4 (Analecta Cartusiana, 116.4; Salzburg, 1989), pp. 85-94.

might write poetry,[29] receive visions[30]—often based on one's thorough assimilation of the concentric daily, weekly, and seasonal liturgical cycles,[31] or research canon law and patristic and scholastic writings to answer questions posed by outsiders about how to live a Christian life as a town clerk, lawyer, doctor, knight, prince, or merchant[32] or even respond to questions about business contracts and coinage[33] and the physical and spiritual practice of

---

[29]See the anthology by Augustin Devaux, *La poésie latine chez les chartreux: Une Anthologie avec traduction Française* (Analecta Cartusiana, 131; Salzburg, 1997).

[30]A thorough study of visionary phenomena among Carthusians remains a major research desideratum. Apart from the well-known visions of Marguerite d'Oignt and Beatrice of Ornacieux and those related to the rosary (Adolf of Essen, Dominic of Prussia) as discussed in section IV below, we have the controversy surrounding Richard Methley at Mount Grace charterhouse in Yorkshire. See, in addition to several editions of Methley's writings, James Hogg, "Mount Grace Charterhouse and Late Medieval English Spirituality," in *Collectanea Cartusiensia*; 3 (Analecta Cartusiana, 82.3; Salzburg, 1980), pp. 1-43, at pp. 25-39, an expansion of Hogg's entry on Methley in the *Dictionnaire de spiritualité* and Michael Sargent, "The Self-Verification of Visionary Phenomena: Richard Methley's *Experimentum veritatis*," in *Kartäusermystik und Mystiker Dritter internationaler Kongress über die Kartäusergeschichte und Spiritualität*, vol. 2 (Analecta Cartusiana, 55.2; Salzburg, 1981), pp. 121-137). We also have a Carthusian advocacy of visions received by Birgitta of Sweden and Catherine of Siena. The Carthusian Stephen Maconi was a major promoter of the canonization cause of the latter; see Augustin Devaux in *Dictionnaire de spiritualité*, 10.55-56) on Jakob of Paradise, Vincent of Aggsbach and others; see Martin, *Fifteenth-Century Carthusian Reform*, pp. 13-14, citing work by Johann Auer and Dieter Mertens.

[31]On the centrality of the liturgical rhythm in Carthusian spirituality, see Hermann Josef Roth, "Kartäuserspiritualität," and Hubertus M. Blüm, "Die Kartäuserliturgie um 1500," in *Die Kölner Kartause um 1500: Aufsatzband*, ed. Werner Schäfke (Köln, 1991), pp. 213-224, 241-251.

[32]Jacob of Gruytrode wrote a series of *Specula* for all states of life that have been printed with the writings of Denis the Carthusian; see *Doctoris ecstatici Dionysii Cartusiensis Opera Omnia*, 42.657-817; see also Gerard Hoekstra in *Dictionnaire de spiritualité* 8.36-38). Less well known are the innumerable treatises along these lines by Johann Brewer of Hagen, e.g., *De regimine principum*, written for the Prince Elector Friedrich II of Brandenburg; *De regimine comitiis*, written for Duke Wilhelm II of Saxony; and *De officio cancellarii*, *De regimine civitatis et consulum*, *De regimine boni advocati*, *De regimine magistri camerae*, *De regimine medicorum et spirituali medicina*, *De negotiatoribus temporalibus et spiritualibus*, *De salario medicorum et aliorum operariorum*, *De venditione frumentorum*. See the most recent summary by Dieter Mertens in *Verfasserlexikon* 3.388-398,with references to the older study by Klapper.

[33]Johann of Hagen wrote at least three treatises *De contractibus* and *De moneta* (which complains about the depreciation of coinage, for which the princes are responsible, and which hurts the common people).

agriculture or draw up an introduction to the various branches of human learning and the natural sciences.[34] Carthusians would also prepare homilies and instructions to inaugurate monastic and clerical reform,[35] write commentaries on Scripture as well as manuals on how to interpret Scripture,[36] address thorny issues of monastic property,[37] write manuals on a proper health regimen for those living the religious life,[38] discern genuine popular piety from superstition and the proper use of indulgences from abuse (see n. 2, above), and draw up universal world histories.[39]

---

[34]For the last two topics see Johann of Hagen, *De agricultura corporali et spirituali et de agricolis*, *Tractatus contra pestilentiam*, *De ortu et origine scientiarum et de modo studendi*, and *De studio philosophiae*.

[35]Among the most prominent Carthusian writers in this regard are Johann Rode of Trier, see Petrus Becker in *Verfasserlexikon*, 8.128-135, gives references to Becker's various articles and monographs on Rode's reform work, Jakob of Paradies, Johann Brewer of Hagen, and Denis the Carthusian as described above.

[36]E.g., Johann Brewer of Hagen's *De commendatione sacrae Scripturae de multiiplici sensu ejusdem et de regulis exponendi eam* and *De modo exponendi et intelligendi divina eloquia sine exteriore et humano doctore*, along with a series of allegorical exegetical works devoted to the Virgin Mary and female Old Testament types (Judith, Esther); see Mertens in *Verfasserlexikon*.

[37]Heinrich of Coesfeld, *Tractatus de vitio proprietatis religiosorum*; Peter of Doorlant, *De enormi proprietatis monachorum vicio dialogus* (Louvain, 1513); Johann Brewer of Hagen, *De statu religiosorum et maxime quoad vitium proprietatis*, are only a few examples. See the *Verfasserlexikon* and *Dictionnaire de spiritualité* articles on these figures.

[38]Johann of Hagen, *De regimine sanitatis maxime spiritualium virorum*.

[39]James Hogg, "A Middle English Carthusian Verse Chronicle on the Foundation and Progress of the Carthusian Order," in *Kartäuserliturgie und Kartäuserschrifttum*, vol. 2 (Analecta Cartusiana, 116.2; Salzburg, 1988), pp. 109-118; James Hogg, "The Ways of God to Man; The Carthusian Chronicle of Universal History in Oxford Bodleian Library MS. E. Museo 160," in *Kartäuserliturgie und Kartäuserschrifttum*, 4.152-163; C.B. Rowntree, "A Carthusian World View: Bodleian MS E Museo 160," in *Spiritualität Heute und Gestern*, vol. 9 (Analecta Cartusiana, 35.9; Salzburg, 1990), pp. 5-72; Laviece Cox Ward, "Two Carthusian Histories: Their Authors and Audiences," in *Die Ausbreitung kartäusischen Lebens und Geistes im Mittelalter*, vol. 2 (Analecta Cartusiana 63.2; Salzburg, 1991), pp. 132-138, drawing from her University of Colorado dissertation on the popular world chronicle by the Carthusian Werner Rolevinck (d. 1502) of the Cologne Charterhouse.

II. Philip of Seitz and His Marienleben (Life of Mary)

On its face, Philip of Seitz's ten-thousand-line verse life of Mary[40] seems to offer little content for the life of Mary and Jesus not already found in the early thirteenth-century *Vita beatae virginis Mariae et salvatoris rhythmica*,[41] which was itself an effective compilation under clear headings of the various canonical and extra-canonical materials for the life of Jesus and Mary. Philip's *Marienleben* had a variety of competitors for the vernacular reading and listening public in the fourteenth century,[42] yet it stands out among them because of its uniquely effective integration of Marian and Christological doctrines (e.g., her sinlessness, Jesus' virginal conception) with a very human, affective portrait of the members of Jesus' entire clan network, from Joachim and Anna through Joseph and the family of John the Baptist. Drawing on what modern theologians dismiss as mindlessly superstitious, apocryphal accounts of the "hidden" years of Jesus, Mary, and Joseph, Philip shows a genius for bringing high theology to the masses[43] that deserves some real respect in an age of suspicion of elitism and

---

[40]The inadequacies of the edition by Heinrich Rückert, *Bruder Philipps des Carthäusers Marienleben zum ersten Male herausgegeben* (Bibliothek der deutschen National- Literatur, 34; Quedlinburg and Leipzig, 1853) are regularly complained of in the secondary literature, but producing a modern critical edition, a project long underway by Kurt Gärtner, has proved to be a complex undertaking. Gärtner's Habilitationsschrift, *Die Überlieferungsgeschichte von Bruder Philipps 'Marienleben'* University of Marburg, 1978, likewise remains unpublished. For a summary of the research up to the late 1980s, see Gärtner in *Verfasserlexikon*, 7.588-597.

[41]Or *Vita Beatae Mariae metrica*. A. Vögtlin, *Vita Beate Virginis Marie et Salvatoris Rhythmica* (Tübingen, 1888), remains, by default, the edition of choice, supplemented by Max Päpke, *Das Marienleben des Schweizers Wernher, mit Nachträgen zu Vögtlins Ausgabe der Vita Marie Rhythmica* (Palaestra: Untersuchungen und Texte aus der deutschen und englischen Philologie, 81; Berlin, 1913). See Kurt Gärtner, *"Vita beatae virginis Mariae et Salvatoris rhythmica,"* in *Verfasserlexikon*, 10.436-443, and Joze Mlinaric, "Das Epos `Vita Mariae metrica' als Unterlage für das Marienlied des Kartäusers Philipp von Seitz," in *Kartäuserliturgie und Kartäuserschrifttum*, 2.29-40. Joze Mlinaric's dissertation *Srednjeveski latinski epos `Vita Mariae metrica': Textnokriticna historiografska in literarna analiza*, University of Ljubljana, 1977, which remains difficult to access, apparently offers preliminary work toward a critical edition.

[42]For the literature on the main varieties of medieval German Marian poetry, see the articles on Konrad von Fußesbrunnen, Walther von Rheinau, Priester Wernher, Wernher der Schweizer, the *Vita rhythmica*, and the *Passional* in *Verfasserlexikon*, 5.172-75, 7.332-340, 10.436-443, 657-660, 903-915, 953-957, and the corresponding entries in the *Marienlexikon*, ed. Remigius Bäumer and Leo Scheffczyk, 6 vols. (St. Ottilien, 1988-1994).

[43]This was also the explicit purpose of the contemporaneous 100,000-verse *Passional;* see Hans-Georg Richert in *Verfasserlexikon* 7.334-35.

hierarchy and of advocacy of "theology from below."[44] The work was widely transmitted in northern Germany beginning as early as 1324 and remained very popular until the Protestant Reformation. Found in manuscripts of all types, from luxuriously illuminated showpieces to small copies for personal reading, its influence was not limited to direct transmission, since it was taken up in large measure into late medieval chronicles of world history.[45] In short, Philip's *Life of Mary* was understood to be historical reporting on the events that forever changed the history of the world, the history that forms the heart of Christian belief, and thus is a centerpiece for Christian edification.

What exactly did Philip the Carthusian[46] contribute to this particular life of Mary, which has survived in at least one hundred manuscripts?[47] The

---

[44]As Kurt Gärtner indicates in his *Verfasserlexikon* article on the "Driu liet von dem maget" by "Priester Wernher" (10.903-915), in one of the earliest German lives of Mary (written 1172), but one based on Pseudo-Matthew, the author directed his work toward lay people in general, assuring them that even if the book is simply kept in a house it will bring joy to the household which values it, but also especially to women approaching childbirth, assuring them that having it in hand as one goes into labor will ensure short labor and that Mary will preserve the child from deformities. All devout women are urged by the author to copy and disseminate the work.

[45]See, for example Norbert H. Ott, "Heinrich von München," in *Verfasserlexikon*, 3.827-837: Heinrich's world chronicle varies from 56,000 to 100,000 lines in various manuscripts. One Berlin manuscript incorporates nearly the whole of Philip's *Marienleben*, another has about half of Philip's *Marienleben* (5,000 lines), compared with 6,000 verses (six percent) of the *Passional* (which includes all of the life of Christ as well as the lives of saints). See also the fundamental study on which Gärtner is drawing, P. Gichtel, *Die Weltchronik Heinrichs von München in der Runkelsteiner Handschrift des Heinz Sentlinger* (Schriftenreihe zur bayerischen Landesgeschichte, 28; München, 1937), pp. 117-140. Gärtner has published a series of articles on the phenomenon of Philip of Seitz's life of Mary being incorporated into world chronicles.

[46]Despite explicit statements in the text, Joseph Haupt, in *Bruder Philipps Marienleben* (Vienna, 1871), esp. pp. 20-22, attempted to assign the work, at least in its most widely distributed version, to a low German author, interpreting "Seitz" as a reference to the Dutch Charterhouse of Zelem near Diest, or perhaps a reference to Silesia. The *Marienleben* is, however, now generally accepted to be the work of a Carthusian of the monastery of Seitz in Lower Steiermark (today's Slovenia) and Mauerbach in Lower Austria.

[47]Gärtner in *Verfasserlexikon*, 7.589-593. Twenty-two additional copies of a prose version are known. These numbers are far higher than those for the "Driu liet von der maget" by "Priester Wernher" of Augsburg (1172), mentioned in an earlier note, or the two later medieval Swiss versions of the *Vita rhythmica* by Wernher der Schweizer and Walther of Rheinau, comparable to the *Passional*. Both Philip's work and the *Passional* enjoyed dissemination through the network of the Teutonic Knights. In the absence of a thorough critical edition, the full scope of the dissemination of Philip's *Marienleben* cannot yet be assessed. In comparing a venacular work of this sort with a Latin text like the *Imitatio Christi* or the various

compilation of the data had already been done by the early thirteenth century in two main Latin sources, Pseudo-Matthew[48] and the *Vita Rhythmica*.[49] Unlike two other German vernacularizers, Walther of Rheinau and Wernher der Schweizer, who stayed fairly close to the *Vita Rhythmica*, Philip left half of his source unused and frequently freely changed the order of incidents, making a steady narrative out of choppy segments in his source.[50] For instance, the *Vita Rhythmica* describes at length Mary's rapid acquisition of skill at reading Scripture, including skill at applying the four senses of scriptural exegesis, interweaving this with her rapid acquisition of skill at embroidery and other textile arts, another main occupation of the group of young women who lived in the Temple at Jerusalem (*VR*, 603-30). The passage includes Mary's affective appropriation of Scripture, which she carried in "*cordis sui cella*" (cf. Lk 2:19). Philip omits most of the detail when he turns this section of the *Vita rhythmica* into German (*ML*, 585-95), including the comment about the "cell of her heart" but inserts this crucial point later when he describes her practice of the seven daily hours of prayer (*ML*, 767). One might think that Philip simply reflects his monastic setting here (treatises on how to participate in the Divine Office without becoming distracted abound in monastic libraries), but devout lay people were following various forms of the Divine Office at home or as visitors to monastic churches[51] and distractions may have concerned them as well. In most

---

Vita Christi texts, one must keep in mind that the Latin texts were useful internationally rather than restricted to one language area.

[48]Which served as the source for Priester Wernher's *Driu liet von der maget (Three Songs of the Maid*; 1172), Konrad of Fußesbrunnen's *Kindheit Jesu* (ca. 1200), and the 100,000-verse *Passional* (before 1350). The fundamental source, the 2nd-century *Protevangelium Jacobi*, was not known directly in the medieval west (it was first edited and made known by Renaissance scholars), but its contents were taken up into the Latin Pseudo-Matthew.

[49]This was the basic source for *Marienleben* by Walther of Rheinau (Swiss, 1278) and Wernher der Schweizer (Swiss, ca. 1370) as well as the one by Philip.

[50]Most lives of Mary include Mary's weaving of a seamless robe for her child, which grew as the child grew into adulthood. The *Vita Rhythmica* places this in Nazareth, after the return from Egypt, when Jesus was past infancy. Philip places the weaving of the robe during the exile in Egypt, when Jesus was still an infant (*Marienleben [ML]*, lines 3638-3669; *Vita Rhythmica [VR]*, lines 346-61), increasing the miraculous nature of the story but eliminating the need for Jesus to have worn a non-miraculous garment during his first years.

[51]See, for instance, Joseph Gribbin, *Aspects of Carthusian Liturgical Practice in Later Medieval England* (Analecta Cartusiana, 99.33; Salzburg, 1995), regarding frequent visitors present at the liturgy in the London Charterhouse. Most Carthusian churches were built with a screen nearly completely cutting off the monk's choir (which was usually in effect simply the first half of the church's single nave) from the lay brothers' area, occupying the rest of the nave, where laity might be present. See Marijan Zadnikar in *Die Kartäuser: Der Orden der schweigenden Mönche*, pp. 75-80, 126.

of the medieval lives of Mary, whether Latin or German, Mary follows a daily cycle of prayer as a young girl in the Temple (in some, also after Jesus' Ascension).[52] Out of his monastic choir office experience, Philip seems to have glimpsed an opportunity here to bring two elements together to serve his vernacular readership.

Above all, what Philip has done is to add humanizing (and sometimes humorous) elements, especially in the form of dialogue, to the third-person narrative of the *Vita Rhythmica*. For instance, in one of the Nazareth miracle stories (*ML*, 4536-4603; *VR*, 2802-2889), Philip inserted dialogue between Jesus and Mary that has all the earmarks of mother-child conversation. In another place, we find Jesus and other children playing on the Sabbath when a Jewish elder scolds them for Sabbath-breaking. Jesus, in effect, asks the old man to mind his own business, whereupon he destroys the fish weir that Jesus, like the other children, had constructed in the Sea of Galilee (*ML*, 4488-4511). The man instantly drops dead, and a hubbub arises, with people from the town accusing Jesus of practicing black magic learned in Egypt and of being in league with the Devil.[53] Hearing of the danger their son finds himself in, Joseph takes counsel with Mary, addressing her as "Frau" and she addressing him as "Herr," he referring to "her son" and "our child."[54] Though the *Vita Rhythmica* has dialogue between Joseph and Mary (*VR*, 2856-2861),[55] the forms of address and the nuanced labels for the child found in Philip's vernacular are missing from the Latin source. Mary and Joseph seek Jesus out and, upon finding him, Mary asks what happened. Jesus tells her, "that old man did me harm," to which Mary replies, "even if he did harm you, I ask you to restore him to life." Jesus obeys His mother.

Jesus is very childishly, yet sinlessly, human here—belying the claim that traditional Christian piety invariably offered a docetic, largely supernatural Jesus. Mary is also very human here—a mother teaching her child not to insist on strict justice (although anger at injustice is not sinful but meritorious), but to have pity and compassion alongside justice.

---

[52]The *Vita Rhythmica* sections on Mary's daily office circulated separately as the "Rule of Mary" and are known in twenty-three manuscripts. See Gärtner in *Verfasserlexikon*, 10.437.

[53]Notice that the accusations essentially mirror those of the New Testament opponents of Jesus. See, e.g., Mt 12:24, 27; Mk 3:22, Lk 11:15-19.

[54]"Jôsep sprach 'nu sage, vrouwe, / waz ist dîn rât daz wir nu tuon / umb unser kint und dînen sun?' / Marîâ sprach 'herr, ich daz râte / daz wir gên und suochen drâte / min liebez kint, swâ wir ez vinden, / swâ er sî bi andern kinden, / wan koment im die juden zuo, / ich vürht daz sî im leit tuon.'" (*ML*, 4577-4585).

[55]"Ad matrem ait pueri: 'Quid modo faciemus, / salvare nostrum puerum quomodo valemus?' / Maria dixit ad Joseph: 'Subito vadamus / atque meum filium ubi sit queramus, / hunc ne forte furientes inveniant Judei, / et ingerant in ira sua mali quicquam ei.'"

Or, we have the story of the finding of Jesus in the Temple at age twelve. Philip has Joseph first ask Mary whether they should take *her* son to Jerusalem for the feast. She, in turn, consults with Jesus, whom she addresses as her son and her Lord.[56] After the lost child has been found again, Jesus and Joseph talk privately, with Jesus revealing his salvific mission to Joseph, but doing so not directly and thus "supernaturally," but indirectly via a Christological reading of the prophets. Mary, ever the mother, asks Jesus where he had stayed overnight. He tells her he was taken in by Zacharias and Elizabeth (*ML*, 4880-4895). On the way back, when "the Savior" becomes tired, Joseph leads Jesus by the hand—suddenly Jesus is above all a child again, after having taught the elders and his own adoptive father about the messianic interpretation of the Scriptures.[57] Interaction between the Holy Family and the family of John the Baptist, by means of frequent visits by the latter to Nazareth, which gave the two boys a chance to play together, is another feature accented particularly by Philip (*ML*, 4176-4247), who sharply informs his reader that those who deny that Jesus ever met with John the Baptist before Jesus' baptism are lying (*ML*, 4248-4259).

We have only begun to probe the surface of the manner in which Philip creates a theologically astute interplay between the divine and the human, avoiding either a purely docetic or a purely humanized portrait of Jesus and his entire clan network. This is already present in germ in the New Testament. One can rightly interpret the patristic commentaries on the gospels as well as the extra-canonical life of Jesus and life of Mary materials as having established this general pattern—though the miracle stories rather than the human side have generally received most of the attention from scholars of this literature, especially since the Protestant Reformation and the Enlightenment. Yet the miracle stories are not the most significant theological aspect of this extra-canonical material in which the "hidden" years of Jesus' childhood and early manhood are imaginatively brought to light. These are precisely the periods of Jesus' life that naturally would readily describe the parameters of his humanness: childhood, with its dependence on parents, and early manhood, with its coming of age. Yet, though the patristic and extra-canonical sources set the switches for this humanizing element to counter a seemingly inevitable tendency toward docetism, when Philip of Seitz speaks in his own voice, he frequently elaborates the existing contribution of the extra-canonical materials toward a full-orbed incarnate Christ, both fully God and fully man.

56"Marîâ vrâgte Jêsum dô / unde sprach ze im alsô *f sage mir, sun und hêrre mîn,* / waz ist nu der wille dîn: / wildu zuo dem tempel varn mit uns?" (4762-4779; emphasis added). Jesus' response was very down-to-earth: "Dô sprach daz gotes barn / 'liebiu muoter, ich wil ouch / ze dem kirchtac varn mit iuch'" (4779-4782). This dialogue is not found in the *Vita Rhythmica*, which devotes only thirty lines to the entire "lost in the Temple" incident.

57"Dô gie von Jêrusalem / Jêsus mit sîner muoter heim. / Jôseph vuort in an sîner hant, / swenn müede wart der heilant" (4838-4841).

A few examples must suffice here. Yes, the infant Jesus, when he began to walk, walked perfectly from the beginning, and he spoke in full sentences when he began to talk.[58] This seems quite docetic. Next, Philip describes Jesus' perfect behavior as a child (*ML*, 3720-3725), which at first glance also seems docetic, since we all know how far from well-behaved children "normally" are! However, this need not be docetic at all. If, by "good behavior" one means a lack of willfulness and self-centeredness, one ought not immediately attribute this to human nature. After the Fall of Adam and Eve, all humans, children included, are indeed inclined toward willfulness and self-centeredness. But if Jesus was both divine and human, His human will would have been completely in conformity with His divine will (as clarified in the Monothelite controversy of the sixth century). He would therefore not have been self-centered or willful even as a child. We may find it hard to consider a will perfectly conformed to God to be "normal" and "human," but that only reveals how imprecisely we normally think about the Christian understanding of the human condition. Strictly speaking, perfect behavior would be a fully human characteristic of a human child unspoiled by the effects of original or actual sin.[59] What seems to us to be unrealistically superhuman, what seems docetic, is in fact a theologically nuanced characterization that does justice to the nature of sin and to the hypostatic union, but does so in terms common folk in a Christian culture that still believed in original sin could understand. But, one might ask, when Philip describes Jesus as perfectly well-behaved, would he not thereby have to be claiming that Jesus did not cry and was no trouble at all to his parents? Not at all. A child who cries because he is hungry is not misbehaving but behaving humanly and naturally. Not to realize this is child abuse, and modern scholars might trust at least some medieval parents to have had enough wit to make such distinctions.

The *Vita Rhythmica* and Philip's *Marienleben* agree in portraying the return from Egypt as an arduous journey "across forest, field and heath, also through many a wide waste" where "they seldom found water" but remained cheerful despite suffering from rain, frost, wind, snow, from hot sun by day and cold by night.[60] Yet unique to Philip's version is Joseph carrying Jesus on his back when the child was tired or Mary leading Him, "the Savior," by the hand, because the journey was very hard for Him. The miracle-working, allegedly docetic Jesus of much of the Egyptian exile becomes in Philip's account a

---

[58]*ML*, 3674-3703—note that this supernaturalizing material is also found in *VR*, 2486- 2509.

[59]Philip acknowledges this explicitly in lines 3929-3930 (quoted in context below): "Alliu kintlich werc er tete / diu ân sünde mugen geschên."

[60]"Sî vuoren walt, velt unde heide, / ouch durch mange wüeste breite. / Sî wurden oft und dicke müede, / daz vertruogen sî mit güete. / Sî heten michel ungemach, / von durst in ofte wê geschach, / wand sî vunden selten brunnen" (3828-3834).

palpably human, miracle-working child with lovingly human parents to take care of Him.[61]

Occasionally Philip becomes explicitly and didactically theological.[62] For instance, he describes the child Jesus playing with other children while, through great discretion (*wisheit*) keeping His divinity hidden as He endured sickness and fatigue and weakness lest He appear to be a *monstrum* (*Ungeheuer*) to those around Him and lest the Devil be tipped off to His true identity.[63] Yet even this belongs centrally to the gospel accounts, particularly in Mark, and to the patristic commentaries, in which Jesus' divinity remains a puzzle to most onlookers even though it is apparent to those with "ears to hear." All the children always wanted to play with Him, and they made Him the leader in their games—but would not a truly well-behaved child (not a priggishly "well-behaved" mama's boy) be the sort of people others, including other children, want to be around? That this seems so far-fetched to us might simply remind us that we have never encountered other humans entirely free of selfishness and self-centeredness, that what we consider "good behavior" is often a disguise for a very self-centered and manipulative self-righteousness.

Finally, when one of Joseph's apprentices cuts four boards too short, Jesus miraculously lengthens them, but not instantaneously. Instead, consistent with the principle of grace perfecting nature, Jesus takes hold of one end while the apprentice takes the other and pulls. The boards stretch to the correct length. All this is found in the *Vita Rythmica* as well as Philip's *Marienleben*. Philip, however, adds dialogue between Mary and Jesus: coming upon Him as He pulls on the lumber, she asks Him what happened. He explains laconically, naively,

---

61"Jêsum daz kint oft unde dicke / Jôsep nam ûf sînen rücke / und truog in als er müede was. / Dâ mite erzeigte er im daz, / daz er durch in was bereit / ze lîden alle arbeit. Dicke Marjâ ouch an ir hant / ir kint vuorte, den heilant, / und half im als er müede wart, / wan vil wê tet im diu vart. / Mit beiden henden zwischen in / daz kint vuorten etwenn hin / Jôseph und Marjâ diu reine: / ir beider arbeit was niht kleine" (3838-385).

62E.g., when he explains original sin and its eternal consequences apart from baptism in Christ's name, before asserting Mary's freedom from it in lines 350-368.

63"Etwenne er ze den kinden gie / und kindisch spil er ane vie: / durch grôze wisheit tet er daz, / daz sîn gotheit dester baz / dem tievel möht verborgen sîn, / und waer ouch vor den liuten schin / daz er rehter mensche waere, / sîn leben niemen möht verkêren. / Daz ist âne widerrede, / alliu kintlich werc er tete / diu ân sünde mugen geschên, / ân schame und âne schande ergên. / Dar umbe er nam dô an sich / unser vleisch / und wart menschlich. / Dô er enphie die krankeit, / gebresten unde bloedikeit / die man mac ân sünde getragen: / welhiu diu sîn, daz wil ich sagen. / Daz ist weinen und lachen, / ezzen trinken slâfen wachen, / daz ist kintlîchen gebâren / in den kintlîchen jâren. / Deist âne widerrede, / daz kint Jêsus daz allez tete, / wand het er des niht getân, / man het gehabt einen wân / ûf in daz er ungehiure / waer und ân mensches natiure. / Der tievel het ouch sich verstanden / daz er waer von gotes handen / von himel ûf die erde komen / im ze schaden, uns ze vrumen. / Umbe daz begie er kinde sîte, / daz er den tievel trüge dâ mite" (3920-3953).

yes, childishly: "The boards were too short, so *we* had to make them longer. At that he began secretly to laugh."[64]

In short, along the lines of the general assessments of Philip's contribution by Masser[65] and Gärtner,[66] we can attribute a remarkable achievement to this Carthusian: he has taken the choppy segments of the *Vita Rhythmica* and his other sources and worked them into a flowing narrative of the normal stages of human development for Jesus and His mother with remarkable character development and subtle theological acumen. Philip's Jesus, Joseph, Mary, Joachim, Anna and even some of the unnamed minor characters are recognizably human actors, with one of them also very much divine, though, true to the New

---

[64]"Jêsus muoter kom dar zuo, / dô daz kint diu hölzer zô. / Sî sprach `waz tuostu, liebez kint?' / Jêsus sprache `diu hölzer sint/ ze kurz, diu sul wir lenger machen.' / Dô begundes tougen lachen" (4328-4333).

[65]E.g., unlike Walther of Rheinau and Wernher der Schweizer, "Wenn es ihm richtig erscheint, folgt er seiner Quelle sehr genau; in anderen Fällen scheut er sich nicht vor größeren Abweichungen. Er kürzt, erweitert, bringt den Stoff in besserer Ordnung, oder er läßt ganze Abschnitte aus. Für ihn steht nicht die Einzelerzählung im Vordergrund, die er nachdichtet, ohne sich um die vorhergehende und die folgende zu kümmern. Er hat stets das thematisch Zusammengehörige im Auge und gestaltet aus dieser Sicht geschlossene Erzählkomplexe, in denen nicht länger wundersame Begebenheiten beziehungslos aneinandergereiht, sondern in denen die einzelne Episode, das einzelne Wunder dem Ganzen organisch eingefügt sind. Man kann Max Päpke nur zustimmen, wenn er sagt, daß Philipp die Kindheit Jesu `offenbar mit ganz besonderer Liebe behandelt hat.'" Achim Masser, Bibel, *Apokryphen und Legenden: Geburt und Kindheit Jesu in der religiösen Epik des deutschen Mittelalters* (Berlin, 1969), p. 264. Cf. pp. 268-269, where Masser describes how Philip deals with a seeming contradiction in the *Vita Rhythmica*: on the one hand, the Egyptians treated Mary like a goddess, on the other hand the Holy Family had a hard time simply surviving the seven years in Egypt. He first says that Joseph worked at his trade, while Mary contributed to the family income by her needlework. This permits him to portray the Egyptian women interacting with Mary as women, coming to admire the baby *and* to help them out materially. Then Philip can add that they called her a goddess and a queen of all virtues, tying it back to Mary's role as "queen" among the Temple maidens. Masser concludes: "Philipp verbindet also die beiden Berichte der *Vita Rhythmica*, glättet die Widersprüche und gibt einen abgerundeten Überblick über das Leben der heiligen Familie in der fremden Umgebung."

[66]Though Gärtner's comprehensive overview in his Habilitation thesis remains unpublished, apart from portions in various articles, we do have his concise assessment in his *Verfasserlexikon* article: "Philip geht sehr frei mit der `Vita' um und folgt ihr nur ganz selten einmal genauer (z.B. für das Soliloquium `Vita' 3450-3621 = `ML' 5082-5359)....Die beziehungslos gereihten Kapitel der `Vita' bringt er in einen geschlossenen Handlungszusammenhang, indem er sie aufeinander abstimmt und verknüpft durch redaktionelle Übergänge sowie durch Vor- und Rückblenden, die-- wie z.B. in der Marienregel...—den Inhalt des gesamten Werkes nochmals vergegenwärtigen....Auf diese Weise entsteht eine fortlaufende Darstellung der wesentlichen Ereignisse der neutestamentlichen Geschichte, die sich für die Aufnahme in die Weltchroniken besonders gut eignete...."

Testament gospels, confusingly so to many of those around Him, some of whom attribute His supra-human powers to the Devil.

III. Ludolf of Saxony

Ludolf of Saxony's *Vita Christi*, at first sight, appears merely to regurgitate patristic and scholastic treatments of the life of Christ, employing the various levels of the literal and spiritual senses of Scripture.[67] Yet a closer look at its structure, designed to facilitate the transition from reading and meditation to prayer and contemplation, with built-in pauses for wonder at the events in Christ's life, shows that Ludolf managed to create the framework for an imaginative and affective appropriation of the material read such that Christ Himself, in full theological dress, becomes present to the reader. In other words, he employed the same basic technique that had been established during the first Carthusian generations in the work of Guigo II and Adam of Dryburgh, following the *lectio*, *meditatio*, and *oratio* pattern, with a pause for a moment of *contemplatio*, which is really a pause for wonder at what one has read, meditated, and prayed. The method is not new; but Ludolf applied it systematically and thoroughly to a large and important body of material, producing a compendium of patristic explication integrated into a meditative structure—a ready-made *summa* for the practice of *lectio divina*. Written in Latin, it served, of course, the educated clerical and general public; but it and other handbooks like it[68] were

---

[67]On Ludolf in general, see Walter Baier in *Verfasserlexikon*, 5.967-977 and Baier, *Untersuchungen zu den Passionsbetrachtungen in der Vita Christi des Ludolf von Sachsen*, 3 vols. (Analecta Cartusiana, 44.1-3; Salzburg, 1977), with references to the work of Mary I. Bodenstedt and others. See also Lawrence F. Hundersmarck, "A Study of the Spiritual Themes of the Prayers of the *Vita Jesu Christi* of Ludolphus de Saxonia," in *Kartäuserregel und Kartäuserleben*, vol. 1 (Analecta Cartusiana, 113.1; Salzburg, 1984), pp. 89-121, a summary of his dissertation, *A Study of the Spiritual Themes in the Prayers and Passion Narration of Ludolphus De Saxonia's Vita Jesu Christi*, Fordham University, 1983.

[68]The best-known, of course, was the Pseudo-Bonaventurian *Meditationes Vitae Christi*, which experienced a number of vernacular adaptations, including the Carthusian Nicholas Love (d. 1410) with his *Mirror of the Blessed Lyfe of Christ;* see *Nicholas Love's Mirror of the Blessed Life of Jesus Christ: A Critical Edition based on Cambridge University Library Additional MSS 6578 and 6686*, ed. Michael G. Sargent (Garland Medieval Texts, 18; New York, 1992; new edition in process), pp. xiv-xx. The Pseudo-Bonaventurian *Mediationes* was taken up into what has become known as Michael of Massa's *Meditationes vitae Christi*. Walter Baier argued that Ludolf combined the Pseudo-Bonaventurian version with Michael de Massa's version to produce his *Vita Christi*. More recently, K.-E. Geith has convincingly argued that Ludolf took his material from Michael de Massa's version (although authorship by this 14th-century Augustinian Eremite has not been proven), while adding greatly to it, e.g., in one chapter adding eighty-percent more material. Significantly, Ludolf adds material serving particularly to encourage mediation on the spiritual sense of the historial events. See K.-E. Geith, "Ludolf von Sachsen und Michael de Massa zur

widely adapted in the vernacular.[69] Major spiritual authors of the fifteenth-eighteenth centuries in Germany, France, Spain, Italy and elsewhere, from Jean Gerson, Hendrik Herp, Bernardino of Siena and Johann Mauburnus (Mombaer) to Peter Canisius, Francisco de Osuña, John of the Cross, Theresa of Avila, and Alphonsus de Liguori all made use of it.[70]

Ludolf's *Vita Christi* aimed at stimulating imitation of Christ, and imitation of Christ serves one's liberation from sin by inspiring self-judgment; imitation illumines the follower, arouses compunction and the grace of tears as a gift from Christ to the one who clings to Him, assists one to make an exit from this life free of anxiety and so on and so forth.[71] Moreover, like the various lives of Mary, Ludolf's life of Christ explicitly links the life of Mary and the life of Christ. Mary is the foremost example of the sort of meditative practice Ludolf envisions his work will serve, as well as the foremost example of the life of the saints and apostles in heaven.[72] The person meditating must himself be in a state of grace and recollect himself so that all distractions and cares have been set aside. In meditating one thus becomes present to the words and actions of Christ in history, and Christ becomes present to him.[73]

As massive as the work may seem, precisely Ludolf's selectivity and shaping of what he selected made the work valuable. One has to consider what he was attempting: to take the vast patristic-monastic-scholastic body of commentary, extract the most fruitful meditative aspects from it, and arrange it according to a chronological framework derived from the canon tables harmonizing the gospels. For instance, his reference to the "*first* ejection of the merchants from the temple" (part I, ch. 26) indicates just how aware he was of the problems

---

Chronologie von Zwei Leben-Jesu-Texten," *Ons geestelijk Erf* 61 (1987): 304-336.

[69]See *Verfasserlexikon* 5.973-974 for a preliminary overview. The full extent of the reception of Ludolf's work in Latin and the vernaculars has not yet been studied, hence one cannot assess how it compares to, e.g., the hundreds of manuscripts and printed editions in various languages of the *Imitation of Christ*.

[70]Walter Baier lists these and other names, with cross references to related articles, in his summary of his own voluminous research in *Dictionnaire de spiritualité*, 9.1130-1138 at col. 1135-1136, cf. *Verfasserlexikon*, 5.972-76.

[71]*Vita Jesu Christi e quatuor evangeliis et scriptoribus orthodoxis concinnata per Ludolphum de Saxonia...*, ed. A.-C. Bolard, L.-M. Rigollot, and J. Carnandet (Paris and Rome, 1865), Prooemium, p. 1b-2a. No critical edition exists.

[72]Ludolf juxtaposes Mary the mother of Christ and the apostles and saints in heaven with Mary of Bethany: "Plane haec vita est vita beatae matris Christi, ipsi sedule ministrantis in annis pluribus, et famulantis. Haec est vita Apostolorum Christo familiariter adhaerentium, et cum eo fideliter perserverantium. Haec est vita civium supernorum Christo fruentium, et ejus opera mirabilia admirantium, et sibi reverenter assistentium in aeternum. Haec vita est optima pars, scilicet sedere ac pedes Christi, et audire verbum ejus." (Lk 10:42). *Vita Jesu Christi*, Prooemium, p. 2a.

[73]Walter Baier in *Dictionnaire de spiritualité*, 9.1136-1137.

involved in harmonizing the gospels as a single narrative. Likewise, he places the incident in the synagogue at Nazareth from Luke 4 in part I, ch. 65, after the Sermon on the Mount, the sending of the Twelve and the Seventy-Two, and after the miracles and parables reported up to the thirteenth chapter of Matthew.

A mind geared toward the *minutiae* of creating a harmony of the gospels might easily become trapped in details. Not Ludolf, who moves at a fairly rapid pace through early chapters, beginning theologically with the eternal generation of the Son and the divine salfivic purpose through Mary's conception, birth and betrothal, to the conception of John the Baptist. The Incarnation itself receives more attention, followed by the birth and circumcision of John the Baptist, Jesus' genealogy, and Joseph's struggle over whether to divorce Mary. Ludolf is hitting the highlights in historical sequence while at the same time including the essential theological signposts. He is doing systematic theology, catechism, and spiritual theology all at once. Remarkably, he catches the key themes of the synoptic gospels, precisely what modern scholars emphasize as major themes of Christ's early ministry: e.g., the emphasis on the hiddenness of Jesus' divinity characteristic particularly of Mark, which we have already seen in Philip's *Marienleben*. This was certainly not his invention; rather, he has read key patristic commentators[74] carefully, who, in turn, had read the New Testament carefully, despite the common modern assumption that patristic spiritual exegesis abandoned the literal and historical in favor of flights of allegorical fancy.[75] Theologically *and* pastorally aware, he included a disproportionately long section on the Sermon on the Mount (part I, ch. 33-40), which gave him a chance to expound the basic principles of Christian theology and practice. His chapter on "doing penance" (part I, ch. 20) is a good example of a strikingly fruitful compendium of patristic and monastic sources from Bernard of Clairvaux, Augustine, Chrysostom, and others on a topic equally fundamental to monastic and lay life. The chapter shows real construction and clearly belies the image of regurgitation and "mere compilation." Likewise, the meditations on Christ's passion (part II, ch. 52-66) are structured around the various hours of prayer, which were not merely monastic, but were also found in the cathedral office and were by no means unfamiliar to the laity.[76]

---

[74]In addition to the predictably heavy use of Augustine, Ludolf frequently employs John Chrysostom as well as Jerome, Ambrose, Gregory the Great, and Bernard of Clairvaux.

[75]For a refutation of this widespread canard, in addition to Henri de Lubac, *Exégèse Médiévale: Les quatre sens de l'Écriture*, vol. 1 (Paris, 1955), translated by Mark Sebanc as *Medieval Exegesis*, vol. 1, *The Four Senses of Scripture* (Edinburgh and Grand Rapids, 1998), see Denis Farkasfalvy, "A Heritage in Search of Heirs: The Future of Ancient Christian Exegesis," *Communio* 25 (1998): 505-519, and Paul M. Quay, *The Mystery Hidden for Ages in God* (New York, 1995), pp. 149-180.

[76]A distinct set of meditations by Ludolf for the seven canonical hours of the entire week circulated independently; see Walter Baier, "Flores et fructus arboris vitae Iesu Christi des Kartäusers Ludolf von Sachsen († 1378)—Ein Horologium des Lebens Jesu für alle Horen an den sieben Tagen der Wochen," in *Mysterium der Gnade:*

Walter Baier, the foremost authority on the sources of Ludolf's *Vita Christi*,[77] has subjected one chapter (part II, ch. 64), on Christ's sacred heart, to a particular examination of medieval *and* early modern contexts.[78] Bernard of Clairvaux's sermons on the Song of Songs provided a basic source on this theme for the author of the *Meditationes Vitae Christi*. Ludolf also regarded Bernard as a key source; but he used other texts, notably Mechthild of Hackeborn (d. 1299), though only after assessing her work against the entire tradition, and defusing the potentially undisciplined apocalyptic and visionary elements.

In Baier's summary estimation,

> Ludolph of Saxony, "the Carthusian," who wanted to create a *Summa evangelica*, first gathered together all the texts from the tradition of spirituality. With these in hand, he interpreted the scriptural texts and presented a work in the form of a harmony of the Gospels. In this way, like rays of light through a prism, he brought to a single focus all that had been said in the past and in his own time on the subject of devotion to the heart of Jesus, . . . and fashioned from it his wide-ranging reflections on the piercing (in *Vita Christi*, part II, chap. 64).[79]

In short, Ludolf sought the center, the time-tested, the well-proven heart of patristic-monastic-scholastic commentary on the life of Christ, in order to create a guidebook that would last and could serve as a basis for a variety of adaptations.

The *Vita Christi* is thus an excellent example of medieval Catholic reading of Scripture, namely a *guided* reading of Scripture. It assumes the basic medieval principle that the patristic commentators themselves belong to Scripture, as, for example, Hugh of St. Victor takes for granted in his *Didascalicon*[80]—his encyclopedic guidebook to reading, rather than reference research, as a way of

---

Festschrift für Johann Auer, ed. Heribert Roßmann and Joseph Ratzinger (Regensburg, 1975), pp. 321-341.

[77]Baier's *Untersuchungen*, though focused on the Passion portion of Ludolf's work, remains the most thorough study of Ludolf's sources.

[78]Walter Baier, "Key Issues in Medieval Sacred Heart Piety," in *Faith in Christ and the Worship of Christ: New Approaches to Devotion to Christ*, ed. Leo Scheffczyk, trans. Graham Harrison (San Francisco and Milwaukee, 1986), [originally published as *Christusglaube und Christusverehrung: Neue Zugänge zur Christusfrömmigkeit* (Aschaffenburg, 1982), pp. 81-99].

[79]Baier, "Key Issues," p. 90 (my translation). Baier points out that this is closely related to the tradition of devotion to the wounds of Christ.

[80]*Hugonis de Sancto Victore Didascalicon: De Studio Legendi*, ed. Charles H. Buttimer (Catholic University of America Studies in Medieval and Renaissance Latin, 10; Washington, D.C., 1939), English translation by Jerome Taylor as *The Didascalicon of Hugh of St. Victor* (Columbia Records of Civilization; New York, 1961), bk IV, ch. 1-2, 14, etc.

life.[81] Precisely Ludolf's guidebook, this *accessus* to Scripture's history of Jesus Christ as a person rather than to an archeology of the texts, was perhaps *the* late spiritual medieval "bestseller" (in an age when most of the bestselling books were devotional or religious books [82]) and the book that, in vernacular dress, helped convert Ignatius of Loyola.[83] The ancient canard that the Scriptures were kept from the people in the late Middle Ages runs aground on the popularity of Ludolf's *Vita Christi* and other works of its type. Of course, if one assumes that access to Scripture must always be direct and individual, Ludolf's guidebook would not count as "access to Scripture." But if one assumes that even the average medieval Latin-literate reader might find the Bible as a whole somewhat mystifying, at least from a chronological perspective, such a reader might find his access to the Scriptures improved by access to Ludolf's compendium.

Ludolf has taken the scholarly resources already developed from patristic times, e.g., harmonies of the gospels and canon tables, fleshed them out with the patristic commentary on the resulting sustained historical narrative,[84] and put it in the hands of the Latin-reading public. The *Vita Beatae Virginis Mariae et salvatoris rhythmica* and Philip of Seitz's *Marienleben* did the same thing for the canonical and extra-canonical Marian and Christ materials. Modern readers might be inclined to think these two collections are like apples and oranges, since Philip's *Marienleben* drew so heavily on extra-canonical sources. Yet Philip chose material from the extra-canonical materials that produced a portrait preserving both sides of the hypostatic union, a full-orbed depiction of *persons* fitting the doctrinal parameters of the canonical gospels.[85] For Philip, history is still a matter primarily of the story of the lives of real, acting persons rather than thearchaeology of texts, that came to dominate biblical studies with the rise of

---

[81]See the remarkable commentary by Ivan Illich, *In the Vineyard of the Text: A Commentary to Hugh's Didascalicon* (Chicago, 1993), regarding the origins of a bookish culture of reference-reading that replaced the monastic wandering through the text still characteristic of Hugh of St. Victor. See also Paul J. Griffiths, *Religious Reading: The Place of Reading in the Practice of Religion* (New York, 1999).

[82]See the testimonials to this effect in *Verfasserlexikon* 5.972-973. Kurt Ruh called it "the most widely distributed, most famous book of devotion of the century" in his *Bonaventura Deutsch* (Bern, 1957), p. 55, cited in *Verfasserlexikon*, 5.973.

[83]See, e.g., Emmerich Raitz von Frentz, "Ludolphe le Chartreux et les exercises de S. Ignace de Loyola," *Revue d'ascetique et de mystique* 25 (1949): 375-388.

[84]For an assessment of Ludolf's skill as an historian harmonizing New Testament history, see John J. Ryan, "Historical Thinking in Ludolph of Saxony's *Life of Christ*," *Journal of Medieval and Renaissance Studies* 12 (1982): 67-81.

[85]Thus his approach differs from that of contemporary biblical scholars who deny any real distinctions between orthodox and heretical materials or texts and thereby make the extra-canonical materials, without distinction, usable for biblical studies. See Helmut Koester, *Introduction to the New Testament*, vol. 2, *History and Literature of Early Christianity* (Hermanea series; Berlin and Philadelphia, 1982), pp. xxii, xxxiii, 1-70.

humanist philology, Protestant antipathy toward deutero- and extra-canonical books, and Enlightenment historicism. Philip's understanding of history, which was simply that of his age, permitted him to deploy his material skillfully to produce an attractive and theologically sound and sophisticated work, much as Ludolf returned again and again to the solid theological center.

IV. The Rosary of the Blessed Virgin Mary

Like Philip's *Marienleben* and Ludolf's *Vita Christi*, the rosary devotion brings together meditation on the life of Christ and the life of Mary. Its fifteenth century Carthusian form was not identical to that of the present day, but its purpose was the same: by summarizing the main mysteries of the Christian faith in a meditative form suitable to *lay people* as well as clerics it ensured a biblical, historical-doctrinal focus for common devotion.

Though repetitive salutations of the Virgin Mary have been practiced since the patristic era, the recognizable origins of the rosary lie in the twelfth and thirteenth centuries, with the Cistercians and others.[86] Generally speaking, before 1400 the *Ave Maria* was used primarily as a prayer of acclamation and salutation of the Blessed Virgin.[87] One very common form was the Psalter of the Blessed Virgin, consisting of one hundred and fifty salutations, divided into three units of fifty (each unit was referred to consistently as a *Rosarium*).[88] This *Psalterium* was employed as a substitute for reciting the entire Psalter, a famous monastic practice since the days of the Desert Fathers, and the *Aves* might be accompanied by a single-phrase reminder of the appropriate Psalm and its

---

[86]Andreas Heinz, "Die Zisterzienser und die Anfänge des Rosenkranzes," *Analecta Cisterciensia* 33 (1977): 262-309; Anne Winston, "Tracing the Origins of the Rosary: German Vernacular Texts," *Speculum* 68 (1993): 619-636; André Fracheboud, "Les antécedents cisterciens du Rosaire," *Collectanea Cisterciensia* 56 (1994): 153-170. For the history of the rosary in general, see André Duval, "Rosaire," in *Dictionnaire de spiritualité*, 13.937-980.

[87]E.g., the late 13th-century Carthusian Hugh of Balma recommended a series of *Ave Maria* salutations as an intercessory adjunct to examination of one's sins and contrition as preparation for meditation and contemplation; see Hugh's *Viae Sion lugent, Via Purgativa*, par. 14; 1.172-174; trans. Martin, *Carthusian Spirituality*, p. 80.

[88]Yves Gourdel, "Le Culte de la très sainte Vierge dan l'ordre des Chartreux," in *Maria: Études sur la Sainte Vierge,* ed. Hubert du Manoir de Juaye, 5 vols. (Paris, 1949-1964), 2.627-678 at p. 653.

antiphon.[89] The transformation of the Psalter of the Blessed Virgin into the fifteen-decade meditative rosary took place primarily during the fifteenth century.

Until the research of the Dominican Thomas Esser during the late nineteenth century[90] the rosary was thought to have been given miraculously to St. Dominic in the twelfth century. Esser discovered the Trier Carthusians Dominic of Prussia (d. 1460) and Adolf of Essen (d. 1439) but did not fully understand their relationship as pioneers of the meditative rosary. A scholarly consensus for Carthusian origins[91] persisted until the discovery by Andreas Heinz of a Cistercian manuscript from the Cistercian Abbey of St. Thomas on the Kyll in the diocese of Trier with ninety-eight Latin meditative *clausulae* and datable to 1300. A handful of vernacular German rosaries have been studied by Winston-Allen, who considers the question of Cistercian or Carthusian priority to be unresolved.[92] However, the thorough research of Karl Joseph Klinkhammer

---

[89]See Herbert Thurston, "Notes on Familiar Prayers: I. The Origins of the Hail Mary," *The Month* 121 (1913): 162-176 at pp. 174-176; Anne Winston-Allen, *Stories of the Rose: The Making of the Rosary in the Middle Ages* (University Park, PA, 1997), p. 15. Many of these *Ave*-Psalters are published in Guido Maria Dreves, *Psalteria rhythmica: Gereimte Psalterien des Mittelalters* (*Analecta Hymnica Medii Aevi*, 35-36; Leipzig, 1900, 1901; reprint Frankfurt a. M., 1961). German equivalents are found in Peter Appelhans, *Untersuchungen zur spätmittelalterlichen Mariendichtung: Die rhythmischen mittelhochdeutschen Mariengrüße* (Germanische Bibliothek, series 3: Untersuchungen; Heidelberg, 1970).

[90]Thomas Esser, "Beitrag zur Geschichte des Rosenkrantzes: Die ersten Spuren von Betrachtungen beim Rosenkranz," *Der Katholik* 77 (1897): 346-60, 409-22, 515-28; "Geschichte des englischen Grußes," *Historisches Jahrbuch der Görresgesellschaft* 5 (1884): 88-116; "Über die allmähliche Einführung der jetzt beim Rosenkranz üblichen Betrachtungspunkte," *Der Katholik* 30 (1904): 98-114, 192-217, 280-301, 351-373; 32 (1905): 201-216, 252-266, 323-350; 33 (1906): 49-66; *Unser lieben Frauen Rosenkranz* (Paderborn, 1889). At the same time as Esser's later publications, the Jesuit Herbert Thurston was publishing a series of articles on the topic in *The Month*: "Our Popular Devotions: II. The Rosary," *The Month* 96 (1900): 403-418, 513-527, 620-637; 97 (1901): 67-79, 172-188, 286-304; "Alanus de Rupe and His Indulgence of 60,000 Years," *The Month* 100 (1902): 281-99; "The Name of the Rosary," *The Month* 111 (1908): 519-529, 610-623; "Notes on Familiar Prayers". Denys Mézard responded to Thurston in *Étude sur les origines du rosaire réponse aux articles du Père Thurston S.J., parus dans le Month, 1900 et 1901* (Caluir [Rhône], 1911).

[91]For the Carthusian contribution, in addition to Esser and Thurston, see Gourdel, "Culte," pp. 648-675.

[92]Winston, "Tracing"; reprised in larger context in Winston-Allen, *Stories*. One of the four vernacular rosaries she studied includes a thirty-eight-point *Life of Christ* section. See *Stories*, pp. 20-22. In "Tracing," p. 627 she flatly denies that Dominic's claim to have invented the life-of-Christ meditative rosary can be sustained in light of Heinz's discovery. This seems to the present writer a considerable overstatement, in light of the existence of two isolated pre-fifteenth-century instances (one Latin, one German) compared to hundreds of copies of the Trier

published in 1972[93] convinces the present writer that the two Trier
Carthusians[94] were indeed responsible for fully integrating meditation on the life
of Christ with repeated vocal *Ave Maria* salutations, the integration which even
Winston-Allen agrees constituted the key step in the development of the modern
rosary.[95] Moreover, they accomplished this integration in an eminently
practicable and popular manner.[96] Indeed, before Dominic of Prussia died, he and

---

life-of-Christ rosary in existence within a few decades of Adolf of Essen's vernacular
Rosengertlin.

[93] Karl Josef Klinkhammer, *Adolf von Essen und seine Werke: Der Rosenkranz
in der geschichtlichen Situation seiner Entstehung und in seinem bleibenden
Anliegen: Eine Quellenforschung*, Frankfurter theologische Studien, 13 (Frankfurt a.
M., 1972); Karl Josef Klinkhammer, "Zur ursprünglichen Spiritualität des
Rosenkranz-Betens," in *Spiritualität heute und Gestern*, vol. 2 (Analecta Cartusiana,
35.2; Salzburg, 1983), 143-159.

[94]According to Charles Le Couteulx, the Carthusian contribution to the
development of the rosary began ca. 1366 with Heinrich Egher of Kalkar. The Blessed
Virgin appeared to him and asked him to recite fifty *Aves* daily in her honor, because
fifty is the number of jubilee. Other accounts indicate that Egher of Kalkar divided the
one-hundred- fifty-*Ave* Psalter of the Virgin into fifteen decades separated by
Paternosters and developed a series of meditative *clausulae*. See Gourdel, "Culte," pp.
635-36, 652, 656-57, based on Le Couteulx, 7.3, for the division into decades.
Klinkhammer denies any significant role to Egher of Kalkar (see *Adolf von Essen*,
pp. 82-85), insisting that Egher knew only the traditional salutative and
non-meditative Marian *Psalterium*.

[95]The principle was first enunciated by Thomas Esser, e.g., in *Unserer Lieben
Frauen Rosenkranz*, p. 5, cited by Thurston, "Our Popular Devotions, II: The Rosary,"
The Month 96 (1900): 403: "das eigenthumliche Wesen" of the rosary is the
meditation on the life of Christ, which is to the rosary what the heart is to a man. For
Winston-Allen, see "Tracing," pp. 621,632, etc., and *Stories*, pp. 15, 26-27.

[96]Winston-Allen concedes that Dominic's *Rosarium* was the first to have exactly
fifty *clausulae*, that it began with the Annunciation rather than with a series of scenes
from Mary's life before the Annunciation, as was the case with the Cistercian
ninety-eight- clause meditation, and that it "solved the major problem that had
plagued older forms of the devotion all along; namely, the difficulty of maintaining
one's concentration throughout the many repetitions." Yet she minimizes Dominic's
contribution by insisting that he solved this problem "serendipitously," since she
lightly dismisses Dominic's own account of how Adolf of Essen pioneered the
method and how Dominic received it from Adolf. See *Stories*, 26, citing the authority
of Rainer Scherschel, *Der Rosenkranz: Das Jesusgebet des Westens* (Freiburger
Theologische Studien, 116; Freiburg, 1979, 1982), p. 137.   On this basis,
Winston-Allen essentially denies any role at all to Adolf of Essen in the development
of the rosary. Despite her interest in *vernacular* origins of the rosary, she does not
engage Klinkhammer's edition of Adolf of Essen's *vernacular* rosary (*Rosengertlin*).
While it is true that the claim for Adolf's priority stems primarily from Dominic's
own account, we do have the corroborating evidence of Adolf of Essen's
Rosengertlin, with its embedded life of Christ meditation, and above all his life of
Margaret of Bavaria, in which Adolf explicitly recommends the combination of

his confrères at Trier had responded to more than a thousand requests from other Carthusians, Benedictines, and lay people for copies of their formula.[97] The Carthusians may even have been the first to add what modern Catholics know as the second half of the rosary, the invocation of Mary's intercession ("Holy Mary, Mother of God, pray for us sinners, now and at the hour of our death. Amen.").[98]

From the work of Klinkhammer, Esser, and others, it seems beyond doubt that the origins of the life-of-Christ meditative rosary can be placed around the year 1400 at the Trier charterhouse, where Adolf of Essen wrote for Margaret of Bavaria, duchess of Lorraine,[99] a German treatise recommending the vocal recitation of fifty *Aves* while at the same time silently meditating generally on the life of Christ.[100] For her convenience, he also wrote down a vernacular life of Christ, though whether it was drawn from that of Ludolf of Saxony as Gourdel asserted[101] remains unclear, since the treatise is now lost.[102]

---

salutation rosary and life of Christ meditation. Moreover, Winston-Allen ignores Klinkhammer's evidence for the existence in 1407 of a rosary confraternity in Düsseldorf employing Adolf of Essen's methods before Dominic of Prussia had even entered the Trier charterhouse, a rosary confraternity led by relatives of the duchess of Lorraine. See below.

[97]Klinkhammer, *Adolf von Essen*, 42, 111-112. Winston-Allen says this is Klinkhammer's claim (*Stories*, pp. 22-23), when in fact it stems from Dominic himself. The text from Dominic's *Libri Experientiae* is given in p. 349, n. 206. Klinkhammer's study of two hundred such copies, summarized pp. 198-271, makes Dominic's claim eminently credible. Though the contents of the fifty *clausulae* could vary from copy to copy, in details the main contours indicate a common source.

[98]This formula is definitely found in early 16th-century Carthusian printed breviaries. See Gourdel, "Culte," p. 635-636, who cites an unpublished study by his confrère, Amand Degand, prepared for a Marian conference in Rome in 1904 and Charles Le Couteulx, *Annales Sancti Ordinis Cartusiensis*, 3.528 and 4.233-35, referring to Carthusian breviaries and other manuscripts of the thirteenth and early fourteenth centuries that contain the full formula. A *Collectorium* manuscript of 1484 in the Archives of the Grande Chartreuse actually seen by Degand also has the full formula of today's rosary salutation and invocation.

[99]Adolf wrote a *Vita Sanctae Margaretae Ducissae Lotharingiae*, published in Klinkhammer, *Adolf of Essen*, pp. 118-130.

[100]*Unser Frauwen Marien Rosengertlin*, edited in Klinkhammer, *Adolf von Essen*, pp. 131-161, with a shorter Latin version pp. 162-171.

[101]Gourdel, "Culte," p. 661.

[102]Some elements of a *Vita Christi* meditation are found in Adolf's *Rosengertlin* treatise written for Duchess Margaret, lines 484-787. See Klinkhammer, *Adolf von Essen*, pp. 146-152. Klinkhammer speculates on the possibility that two extant Latin *Vita Christi* treatises, one originally from a Beguinage in Essen, might represent a Latin version of the now lost vernacular *Vita Christi* written for Duchess Margaret; see *Adolf von Essen*, p. 133.

Margaret of Bavaria was well connected. She was the daughter of Ruprecht of Bavaria, Elector Palatine, who replaced the deposed Wenceslaus, dissolute son of Charles IV of the house of Luxemburg, as King of the Romans, 1400-1410. She and her husband, Duke Charles II, were great patrons of the Carthusians in the Rhine and Moselle regions. Her sister, Anna, was married to Wilhelm, duke of Berg. Both of them were patrons well known to the Carthusian General Chapter;[103] and they were the first to enroll in the rosary- confraternity employing Adolf of Essen's method founded at Düsseldorf in 1407, the "Broederschafft der Freuden unserer Lever Frauen vor Susteren und Broederen des Rosen Krantz."[104] Duchess Margaret's effort to establish a charterhouse near a ducal castle at Sierck in 1415 failed, but her work with the Carthusians in the development of the rosary was, in the long run, far more significant.

We turn now to Adolf's protégé at Trier. Not unlike Nicholas of Cusa, Dominic Eloynus of Prussia was the son of a boatman, a fisherman from the Baltic coast at Elbing. After a profligate life as a student particularly of the sciences and alchemy at Kraków and as a vagabond, and after having been refused entry to the Prague charterhouse, he experienced a genuine conversion in the midst of what he expected to be a terminal illness and was admitted to the Trier charterhouse by Adolf of Essen in 1409. When Adolf left in 1415 to lead the aborted attempt to establish the Carthusians at Sierck, he took Dominic, now become infirmarian, with him as his vicar. Both returned in 1421 to Trier, where Dominic remained until his death, apart from brief periods spent in Mainz and Cologne. In giving spiritual direction to this recently converted recruit, Adolf of Essen recommended that, if he wished really to make progress in amendment of his life, he recite fifty *Aves* each day and meditate daily on the mysteries of the life of Christ. Dominic of Prussia found the two together formidably distracting, so he broke up Adolf's (now lost) *Vita Christi* meditation into a series of fifty German *clausulae*.[105] Adolf and others requested copies,[106] and Dominic's *Clausulae de vita Christi* proved highly practical and much sought-after,

---

[103]Klinkhammer offers detailed accounts of the interconnections between Berg, Lorraine, Cologne and other Rhenish-Moselle political events, all against the background of conflicting loyalties in the western Schism of the late 14th century and within the Carthusian order, pp. 26-35, 43-47, 50-76, etc.

[104]Klinkhammer, *Adolf von Essen,* pp. 105-106, 111.

[105]Gourdel, "Culte," pp. 661-662; Klinkhammer, *Adolf von Essen*, pp. 8-9, 39-41, 198-203, 278. The text of the surviving *clausulae* in Latin is given on pp. 198-203, followed by variations on them, pp. 203-225.

[106]Adolf initially requested a copy of Dominic's *clausulae* to give to Duchess Margaret of Lorraine. Within a short time, other nobles at her court were reporting enthusiastically about Dominic's method. Indeed, Adolf of Sierck, father of Jacob of Sierck, who succeeded Otto of Ziegenhain as Archbishop of Trier in 1430, rode to Trier to consult with Dominic; see Klinkhammer, *Adolf von Essen*, p. 41-42, citing Dominic's report of the incident in his *Libri Experientiae* (Klinkhammer gives the text in notes on pp. 310 and 359).

resulting in the thousand copies mentioned above. They were transmitted both in Latin and German.[107]

Dominic has left us a moving account of his conversion[108] and of his insights, visions, and contemplations between 1439 and 1458, in his *Libri experientiae*, intended to encourage others to persist in the spiritual life through all its difficulties and adversities.[109] In this he was, like Adolf of Essen, heavily influenced by the *Liber spiritualis gratiae* of Mechthild of Hackeborn.[110] He wanted to develop a simple, even puerile method by which the soul could be united to God by following the path of Jesus and Mary, and by emphasizing spiritual poverty as the fruit of a heroic act of abandonment.[111] In Dominic of Prussia, then, the *Vita Christi* of Ludolf, boiled down to a memorable essence by Adolf of Essen, was integrated with the much older practice of the *Ave Maria* salutation to produce something we now recognize as the rosary devotion.

Dominic did not stop with his *clausulae* of the life of Christ for the fifty-part *Rosarium* devotion. He also developed a *Pallium Mariae*, a series of rhymes for the protection of a Christian beneath the mantle of Our Lady; a *Corona gemmaria Beatae Virginis Mariae*, comparing Mary to seventy-seven precious stones (fifty gems in the German version), all coordinated with the life of Christ and undoubtedly reflecting his study of the natural sciences; a one-hundred-

---

[107]Klinkhammer, *Adolf von Essen*, pp. 198, 222.

[108]Afraid, given his dissolute life, to make a general confession to Adolf of Essen, Dominic made the confession (required for entry at the Charterhouse of Trier) to a Carmelite, who wept deeply. This, in turn, deeply affected Dominic—if another person is so affected by my sins, why am I not so moved? As masters of the spiritual life frequently noted, if one is unable to arrive at sorrow for one's sins, one can at least begin with being sorry that one has no contrition. This spark was precisely what Dominic apparently needed, and the fountain of tears within him began to flow. The Carmelite left him alone for an hour to calm himself; returned, gave him the recitation of ten Psalters as a penance, absolved him, and recommended to Adolf of Essen that he receive him into the charterhouse. See Karl Josef Klinkhammer, "Die 'Libri Experientiae' des Trierer Kartäusers Dominikus von Preußen," in *Kartäusermystik und mystiker*, vol. 2 (Analecta Cartusiana, 55.2; Salzburg, 1981), pp. 34-55 at p. 43. See Karl Josef Klinkhammer and A. Triller,, "Jugenderinnerungen im Werke des Kartäusers Dominikus von Preußen," *Zeitschrift für Geschichte und Altertumskunde Ermlands* 31/32 (1968): 41-58; 33 (1969): 9-40.

[109]They survive in three Trier manuscript volumes and have remained unpublished; see Klinkhammer, "*Libri Experientiae*." Excerpts are found in *Ab anno 1084 ad Annum 1429,* ed. Charles Le Couteulx, 8 vols. (Monstrorh, 1887), *Annales ordinis Cartusiensis*, 7.422, 552-557.

[110]See Klinkhammer, "*Libri Experientiae*," p. 39 and *Adolf von Essen,* pp. 38-39, 98, 108-109, 134-135.

[111]Anselme Stoelen in *Dictionnaire de spiritualité*, 3.1540-41.

fifty-clause *Psalterium Mariae*; and a *Planctus Mariae* celebrating the Marian lamentations, the *Compassio Mariae* so popular in the late Middle Ages.[112]

One of the stories related by Dominic in his *Libri experientiae* involves a visit to him by the archbishop of Trier, Otto of Ziegenhain (well known to students of the life of Nicholas of Cusa) shortly before the archbishop's death in 1430. The bishop poured out his heart to Dominic, relating his fears over the future of his troubled diocese.[113] After his death, Otto of Ziegenhain once more appeared to Dominic and led him to the cell's prayer chamber, where they together recited the *Rosarium*.[114] The archbishop enters into the story in yet another manner. Under his influence, Adolf of Essen had been elected abbot of several Benedictine houses in the region as part of the emerging effort to reform Benedictine monasticism in the 1420s in the wake of the Council of Constance. Adolf refused to accept these positions, but this trajectory was later taken up by Johannes Rode of the Charterhouse of Trier. Karl Joseph Klinkhammer attributes the surprisingly large number of copies of the Trier version of the rosary *clausulae* to this Carthusian-Benedictine connection.[115]

With the aid of Johann Rode[116] the texts of the new meditative rosary were copied and recopied in Benedictine reform circles emanating from the Rhine and Moselle valleys and in the Bavarian-Austrian Melk Benedictine reform to which Cusanus' devoted followers at Tegernsee[117] adhered. The duchess of Lorraine encouraged it among lay circles. Alanus de Rupe (Alain de la Roche), a Breton Dominican, became a tireless, even fanatical[118] champion of a somewhat meditative one-hundred-fifty-*Ave Psalterium* of the Blessed Virgin, developed after contact with the Trier Carthusians, and seems to have been responsible for

---

[112]See Klinkhammer, *Adolf von Essen*, pp. 225-238.

[113]His fears were more than realized during the decade of the 1430s, with the disputed archepiscopal appointment (Jacob of Sierck and Ulrich of Manderscheid), well known to students of the life of Nicholas of Cusa; see Klinkhammer, *Adolf von Essen*, pp. 61-64, etc. The decade concluded with a severe plague epidemic, which took the life of Adolf of Essen as well as Johann Rode; see *Adolf von Essen*, pp. 72-76 for Dominic's role nursing members of the Trier charterhouse.

[114]Gourdel, "Culte," p. 641, citing the *Libri experientiae* manuscript.

[115]Klinkhammer, *Adolf von Essen*, pp. 55-59, 260-271.

[116]Petrus Becker, *Das monastische Reformprogramm des Johannes Rode, Abtes von St. Matthias in Trier: Ein darstellender Kommentar zu seinen Consuetudines* (Beiträge zur Geschichte des alten Mönchtums und des Benediktinerordens, 30; Münster, 1970), and "Erstrebte und erreichte Ziele benediktinischer Reformen im Spätmittelalter," in *Reformbemühungen und Observanzbestrebungen im spätmittelalterlichen Ordenswesen,* ed. Kaspar Elm (Berliner historische Studien, 14 / Ordensstudien, VI; Berlin, 1989), pp. 23-34; Becker in *Verfasserlexikon*, 8.128-35.

[117]Klinkhammer, *Adolf von Essen*, pp. 264-271, on Tegernsee's role.

[118]See Thurston, "Alan de Rupe," pp. 283-284 and *passim*.

the now apparently ineradicable legend that the Blessed Virgin had appeared to St. Dominic in the twelfth century to instruct him in the rosary. In 1475 an immensely popular, Dominican-sponsored, indulgenced rosary confraternity was founded at Cologne in an effort to storm heaven so that Cologne might be spared the sort of brutality that Charles the Rash, duke of Burgundy, was inflicting on the town of Namur. A division into fifteen decades separated by *Paternosters* became common and made the full one-hundred-and-fifty *Aves* more maneagable for the masses, whose meditation on the mysteries became more minimal, as they flocked into the Dominican-sponsored confraternities across western Europe.[119]

The complexities of four hundred years of development should not be permitted to obscure the important Carthusian contribution, one fully in keeping with the emphasis on *lectio, meditatio, oratio,* and *contemplatio* found already in Guigo II and Adam of Dryburgh and developed by Hugh of Balma with his aspirative affective prayer.[120] The two Carthusians of Trier shortened and adapted to a lay public the same basic materials found in the compendium of patristic-monastic commentary assembled by Ludolf as well as in the canonical and extra-canonical materials on the interrelated lives of Mary and Christ assembled in the *Vita Rhythmica* and enlivened and vernacularized in Philip of Seitz's *Marienleben*. Dissemination in monastic circles thus actually and ultimately served the lay public.

In Klinkhammer's view, Adolf of Essen's imaginative, synthetic mind drove him to find ways to bring home to people the biblical-doctrinal and the contemplative-ascetic contents of the mystery of Christ's incarnation in their entirety. Adolf's *Rosengertlin* tract is an original reworking of traditional contents to better serve and guide the biblical education and edification of the Christian laity. He seems not to have fully achieved his goal and he seems to have realized he had not, for he instantly saw in Dominic's pragmatic adaptation (growing out of Dominic's very lack of a synthetic imagination for the whole) the final pedagogical reworking he had been seeking.[121]

V. Conclusion

Study of the Carthusian contribution to popular piety thus establishes an important backdrop against which the life of Nicholas of Cusa can be better understood. What we glimpse here is a living, breathing, graphic, and pedagogically-astute transmission of an historical record for the lives of Christ and his mother, *as persons*, designed to inspire and nourish a powerful, affective

---

[119]See Klinkhammer, *Adolf von Essen*, pp. 91-113; Duval in *Dictionnaire de spiritualité*, 7.946-959.

[120]See Martin, *Carthusian Spirituality,* pp. 35-38, regarding the origins of aspirative prayer in the *Conferences* of John Cassian (d. 435).

[121]See *Adolf of Essen*, pp. 134-135.

meditative life for those with ears to hear. During the next century, some Christian reformers would substitute this rich, variegated, affectively-inspiring body of material for shaping one's spiritual life, accessible in layered stages from learned elites to anyone capable of learning the *clausulae* of the rosary, with a direct reading of Scripture that in fact was indirect and dependent on vernacular translations made by learned reformers whose philological assumptions led to theological revision, indeed, theological truncation.[122] The absence of *guided* reading of Scripture initially led to an explosion of charismatic sectarians that frightened the learned reformers into locking interpretation of Scripture into an elitist philological straitjacket, in the process transforming the Pauline "gift of tongues" into university-acquired knowledge of Greek and Hebrew.[123] Concomitantly, the richness of the patristic tradition of scriptural interpretation, for the most part, went by the boards. Of course, Protestants eventually restored a humane, living, breathing, rhetorical, and pedagogical *accessus* to Scripture via children's Bible story books and various adaptations and abridgements, but in doing so they were conceding the Catholics' point: the average reader frequently does not make it very far reading through the Bible verse by verse. He often gets lost in the genealogies and ritual legislation and finds himself easily confused about the historical sequence. Modern Scripture scholars attempt to restore a chronological and historical sequencing via new *accessus* guidebooks ("introductions to the Bible" and Bible encyclopedias or dictionaries), but these

---

[122]According to Alister McGrath's account, humanist graecists discovered the strictly forensic connotations of *dikaiosyne,* employed by the Septuagint translators for the Hebrew *tzedek* (righteousness); Augustine, ignorant of Greek, did not realize that the forensic Greek *dikaiosyne* and its verb form *dikaioun* would not support the "becoming righteous" connotations of Augustine's verb form, *justifacere,* a term that had no classical Latin track record. The reformers felt compelled to return to the "true" biblical meaning, which they assumed had to be purely forensic because of the strictly forensic secular usage of the Septuagint Greek terms. What the reformers failed to realize is that the Septuagint employed this terminology for Hebraic realities that clearly included becoming righteous rather than merely being acquitted of sin and, having employed it, after several centuries of use of the Septuagint in Jewish and Christian circles completely immersed in the "becoming righteous" assumptions of Hebrew religion, the Septuagint's terminology would certainly have taken on new meanings not found in secular Greek literature of the ancient world, namely precisely the *justifacere* connotations that Augustine and the other church fathers took for granted. See Alister McGrath, *Iustitia Dei,* 2 vols. (Cambridge, 1986; new edition, 2000), 1.4-23 (1986 edition), and McGrath, "Do We Still Need the Reformation," *Christianity Today* (December 12, 1994): 28-33. For a discussion of related issues in Syriac and Greek patristic circles that is more sensitive to the ways religious concepts are received in new languages, see Robin Darling Young, "Philoxs of Mabbugh and the Syrian Patristic Understanding of Justification," *Communio* 27 (2000): 688-699.

[123]Dennis D. Martin, "Schools of the Prophets: Shepherds and Scholars in New England Puritanism," *Historical Reflections/Réflexions Historiques* 5, no. 1 (Summer, 1978): 41-80.

are consulted by relatively few "average Christians." The imaginative pedagogical guides provided by Philip of Seitz, Ludolf of Saxony, and Dominic of Prussia, taken in hindsight, deserve reconsideration.

However, the question remains: exactly what part of these three major contributions to late medieval spirituality on a wide, popular level was really a specifically *Carthusian* contribution? Alanus de Rupe and the Dominican network made it possible for the rosary devotion really to take off in the sixteenth century. The world chronicles in which Philip of Seitz's life of Mary had perhaps their greatest impact were, for the most part, not compiled by Carthusians. His *Marienleben* itself was "marketed" primarily by the Teutonic Knights. Ludolf of Saxony's *Vita Christi*, though one of the "bestsellers" of the later Middle Ages, was only one of several such meditative lives of Christ. His own fellow Carthusian, Nicholas Love, chose a Franciscan life of Christ rather than Ludolf's when he decided to vernacularize (very successfully) this form of devotion in England.[124] Hugh of Balma's *Viae Sion* manual on mystical theology had its greatest impact via Franciscans in the Netherlands and in Spain.[125]

The Carthusians did contribute to the fourteenth- and fifteenth-century spiritual landscape something genuinely Carthusian, growing out of three centuries of sedulous cell-sitting. The Carthusian *propositum* was not a particular set of theological or psychological doctrines, but a finely-tuned sense, growing from long experience, for what worked spiritually. They developed, over time, an acute ear and sharp eye for compiling, choosing, assembling, and reassembling to meet the needs of the present, all guided by faithfulness to the Christian and Catholic tradition, a faithfulness stemming from a careful monastic formation. One must beware of exaggerating, of course, but the Carthusians did work out, in the twelfth century, a constitutional structure that balanced autonomy of houses with centralized supervision[126] and put in place a

---

[124]See Elizabeth Salter, "Ludolphus of Saxony and His English Translators," *Medium Aevum* 33 (1964): 26-35 at p. 26. As noted above, Ludolf's *Vita Christi* did enjoy widespread Latin and vernacular adaptation in Spain and elsewhere.

[125]Martin, *Carthusian Spirituality*, pp. 12-14.

[126]See Léo Moulin, "L'Assemblée, autorité souveraine dans l'Ordre des Chartreux," *Res publica* 12 (1970): 7-67; Johannes Simmert, "Zur Geschichte der Generalkapitel der Kartäuser und ihrer Akten," in *Festschrift Hermann Heimpel zum 70. Geburtstag am 19. September 1971*, vol. 3 (Veröffentlichungen des Max-Planck-Instituts für Geschichte, 36.3; Göttingen, 1972), pp. 677-692. James Hogg, *Die Ältesten Consuetudines der Kartäuser* (Analecta Cartusiana, 1; Berlin, 1970), carries the history of the legislation up to 1222. In anticipation of a synthetic three-volume study of the entire Carthusian legislation over the centuries, to be titled, *The Evolution of the Carthusian Statutes*, Professor Hogg has published the texts of legislation from the 1120s to 1971 in Analecta Cartusiana, 99, Documents, parts 1-13, under the collective title *The Evolution of the Carthusian Statutes: Documents* (Salzburg, 1989ff). A good summary in English of the medieval developments is found in E. Margaret Thompson, *The Carthusian Order in England* (London, 1930), pp. 86-130. For the visitation system, see Heinrich Rüthing, "'Die

means of formation that kept the order on track when most other orders were dissolving into laxity and dividing over efforts to reform themselves. [127] That the Carthusians were clearly the most popular religious order for patrons at the highest level in the late Middle Ages indicates that they were good at what they set out to do, at their *propositum*. By sticking to their original vision of cell-sitting, which was simple enough to be clear, yet flexible enough to permit constant development and practical adaptation, they became attractive to devout nobles like Margaret of Bavaria and her clan and court, as well as to activist members of other orders (Alanus de Rupe, Ignatius Loyola, Peter Canisius), even to world explorers and movers-and-shakers at the highest level of the temporal realm.[128] The Carthusian meditative rosary caught on and thrived; even in its most widespread form, the rosary retains a meditative quality—not, to be sure, the same meditative quality suited to the Carthusian cell, but one suited to people active in the world, bringing the mysteries of the life of Christ home to pious Catholics for centuries. It has fallen out of favor in recent decades, dismissed by many modern Catholics (in Protestant terms) as "vain repetition" and devoid of contextualized biblical content. One suspects, however, that those most critical of it are now among those least familiar with its practice and practicality. Perhaps the present consideration of its origins, within the context of two other important forms of *accessus* to Scripture's mysteries developed by late medieval Carthusians, can open a new window for understanding how Christian history and doctrine, as history and doctrine of persons rather than of mere texts, was made available to both professional religious and *amateurs* (in the root sense of the word) in the devout life in the later Middle Ages.

Wächter Israels': Ein Beitrag zur Geschichte der Visitationen im Kartäuserorden," in Zadnikar and Wienand, *Die Kartäuser: Der Orden der Schweigenden Mönche*, pp. 169-183.

[127]For orientation, see Heinrich Rüthing, "Die Kartäuser und die spätmittelalterlichen Ordensreformen," in *Reformbemühungen*, pp. 35-58, together with the articles on other orders in this volume.

[128]Christopher Columbus corresponded with a Carthusian prior, considered a Carthusian vocation, and was initially buried among the Carthusians at Seville. Gregor Reisch of the Freiburg im Breisgau charterhouse served as confessor to Emperor Maximilian I, etc.

CANONISTS IN CRISES CA. 1400-1450:
PISA, CONSTANCE, BASEL

Thomas E. Morrissey

The universities, and especially the canonists and theologians teaching at these institutions, were sorely pressed by the problems and questions that the Great Western Schism had created and which lasted through the first half of the 15th century. These pressures went back to the outbreak of the Schism in 1378, when lines were drawn and various writers were called upon to render an evaluation, legal advice or just a proclamation of support for one of the sides. Try as they might, this was not one of those situations or issues where it was easy to "sit this one out." Very early in the Schism, the famed canonist Johannes de Lignano produced at Bologna a tract in defense of Urban VI; and, as R.N. Swanson remarked two decades ago, Lignano's treatise, when joined with what another canonist, Baldus de Ubaldis, wrote at the same time, provided the basis for the Romanist case and were the foci of discussion and debate over the next decades.[1]

Almost a century ago, Franz Bliemetzrieder, an indefatigable researcher and editor of texts from the era of the Schism, put out a series of articles presenting the variety of views in the first years of the Schism. He continued later with a number of works that reflected the developing opinions that appeared in the 1390s.[2] During that critical decade, a shift had occurred and a good deal of the controversy had moved northward and been centered at the University of Paris. This dispute, naturally enough, took the form of debates much more between theologians than canonists, not least because Paris was far more noted for philosophy and theology than canon law. Paris was also a focal point at this time because of the debates over and the actual withdrawal of obedience by France from the Avignon claimant, Benedict XIII.[3] This withdrawal by the French church, at the instigation of its political ruler, obviously had to be justified and defended by its proponents and vigorously attacked and repudiated by Benedict XIII's adherents.

---

[1]R.N. Swanson, *Universities, Academics and the Great Schism* (Cambridge Studies in Medieval Life and Thought, 3rd series, vol. 12; Cambridge, 1979), pp. 16, 25.

[2]A listing of the many works by Franz Bliemetzrieder can be found in Thomas E. Morrissey, *Franciscus de Zabarellis (1360-1417) and the Conciliarist Traditions,* unpublished Ph. D. dissertation, Cornell University, Ithaca, New York, 1973, pp. 649-652. See also Ansgar Frenken, *Die Erforschung des Konstanzer Konzils (1414-1418) in den letzten 100 Jahren* (Annuarium Historiae Conciliorum, 25. Jahrgang, Heft 1-2; Paderborn, 1993).

[3]Howard Kaminsky, *Simon de Cramaud and the Great Schism* (New Brunswick, 1983); *Simon de Cramaud De subtraccione obediencie* (Cambridge, Massachusetts, 1984); "The Politics of France's Subtraction of Obedience from Benedict XIII, 27 July 1398," *Proceedings of the American Philosophical Society* 115 (1971): 366-397; Michael Nordberg, *Les ducs et la royauté: Études sur la rivalité des ducs d' Orléans et de Bourgogne (1392-1407)* (Uppsala, 1964).

In this era, then, a great deal of time, energy, ink and paper were devoted to the controversy by scholars from Paris and Italy, while the major part of western Christendom was wrapped up in its own problems. For example, in England we note the disputes over the power and claims of Richard II, the aftermath of the Peasants Revolt of 1381 and, one must not forget, the ongoing dispute over the ideas and criticisms of John Wyclif, the Lollards, and, finally, the uprising against, the deposition, and replacement of Richard II by Henry IV, who then had his own revolts to deal with.[4] Within the Holy Roman Empire, discontent with Wenceslaus had led to a revolt and his displacement by Ruprecht of the Rhine Palatinate in 1400,[5] while there continued the disputes of the Teutonic Knights with Poland and Lithuania.[6] There was a rising tide of discontent of the Czechs with what appeared to them to be the oppressive Germanic presence in their domain. As events would later show, this took a very heightened form at Prague

---

[4]*The Reign of Richard II: Essays in Honour of May McKisack,* ed. F.R.H. DuBoulay and Caroline M. Bynum (London, 1971); Peter McNiven, "Legitimacy and Consent: Henry IV and the Lancastrian Title, 1399-1406," *Medieval Studies* 44 (1982): 470-488; Lynn Staley, "Gower, Richard II, Henry of Derby, and the Business of Making Culture," *Speculum* 75 (2000): 68-96; Christopher Philpotts, "The Fate of the Truce of Paris 1396-1415," *Journal of Medieval History* 24 (1998): 61-80.

[5]Bruno Gebhardt, *Handbuch der deutschen Geschichte,* vol. 1: *Frühzeit und Mittelalter* (Stuttgart, 1954), pp. 520-523. Among the charges alleged against Wenceslaus were that he had not fulfilled his duty to "enrich and not to impoverish his realm," F.R.H. DuBoulay, *Germany in the Later Middle Ages* (London & New York, 1983), p. 40; that he had granted Gian Galeazzo Visconti, the ruler of Milan, the imperial title of duke in exchange for money, p. 44; that he insisted on living in Bohemia outside the German kingdom: Geoffrey Barraclough, *The Origins of Modern Germany* (New York, 1946; reprint 1957), p. 357; that he did not bring peace but rather "war was everywhere and no one knew before whom he should seek justice": H.S. Offler, "Aspects of Government in the Late Medieval Empire," in *Europe in the Late Middle Ages,* ed. John Hale, et al. (London, 1965), p. 226. It is ironic that Ruprecht of the Rhine Palatinate, who replaced Wenceslaus in 1400, is described simply as "the king without power" in *Deutsche Geschichte,* vol. 5: *1378-1517,* ed. Heinrich Pleticha (Gütersloh, 1982-1983), p. 37. There was, of course, the other accusation, that Wenceslaus was drunk too often to accomplish anything. See also: Michel de Boüard, "L' empereur Robert et le Grand Schisme d' Occident (1400-1403)," *Melanges d' archéologie et d'histoire* 48 (1931): 215-232, and Anton Eitel, "Zur Kritik der Approbationsverhandlungen Papst Bonifaz IX. mit König Ruprecht von der Pfalz," *Historisches Jahrbuch* 35 (1914): 59-85.

[6]Karl August Fink, "Zum Streit zwischen dem Deutschen Orden und Polen auf den Konzilien zu Konstanz und Basel," in *Reformata Reformanda. Festgabe für Hubert Jedin zum 17. Juni 1965* ed. Erwin Iserloh and Karl Repgen (Münster, 1965), 1:74-86; Stanislaus Belch, *Paulus Vladimiri and His Doctrine Concerning International Law and Politics,* 2 vols. (The Hague, 1965); Hartmut Boockmann, *Johannes Falkenberg, der Deutsche Orden und die polnische Politik* (Veröffentlichungen des Max-Planck-Instituts für Geschichte, 45; Göttingen, 1975); Thomas Wünsch, *Konziliarismus und Polen* (Paderborn, 1998).

with the disputes there which, in time, led to the withdrawal of many German faculty and students from the "Charles-University" to Leipzig, where, in 1409, they founded a new university.[7] At the same time, the increasing complaints at Prague would find their voice in John Hus, who would become a center of conflict and tragedy in the years before, at and, even more so, after the Council of Constance.[8] Finally, an example of what the Schism was doing to Europe's intellectual elites could be seen in the controversies at the University of Heidelberg, recently begun in 1386, and at the University of Vienna, founded only a few years later, where the quarrels imported from Paris and the division between Roman and Avignon supporters made for some bitter disputes.[9]

Then, as the fifteenth century began, the central point for proposals and theories about the Great Western Schism and how it could be dealt with shifted back to Italy. It was there, and especially at its universities, that the pace of claim and counterclaim, argument, and refutation of arguments really accelerated. It was there also that the political vacuum made the idea of action or pre-emptive strike most enticing.[10] There had been the complex disputes, alliance systems and wars that had accompanied the rise to dominance of Gian Galeazzo Visconti of Milan and the precipitous collapse of this regime with his sudden and unexpected death in September 1402.[11] A series of wars and shaking out then followed, with Venice moving to consolidate its holdings on the mainland of Italy, a process marked by its absorption of Padua in 1405-1406, and Florence,

---

[7]Swanson, *Universities, Academics and the Great Schism,* p. 170.

[8]Howard Kaminsky, *A History of the Hussite Revolution* (Berkeley, 1967) and the many studies by F. Smahel, F. Seibt, M. Spinka, et al.

[9]The universities in this era not only had to choose between the conflicting claims of papal obedience, Roman or Avignonese, and then later Pisan as well, but also to consider what the local ruling lords wished, and, finally, in faculties of philosophy and theology whether they would follow the paths of the *moderni* or the *antiqui.* It is no wonder then that Swanson, *Universities, Academics and the Great Schism,* pp. 216-217, gives a list of universities founded in this era of division and notes how many did not survive by the end of the Great Schism: out of twenty-two that began, twelve were soon gone.

[10]Swanson, *Universities, Academics and the Great Schism,* p. 31, reports at the outset of the Schism the persecution in the Spanish kingdoms of Spaniards who wished to remain loyal to the Roman papal claimant, and similar reactions in France; see *Universities,* pp. 34, 36, 40-41. He also reports at pp. 46-48 that, in general, universities did not support the *via facti,* which was proposed as one way of settling the Schism: whoever was left in power was the valid pope. This obviously implied use of force or military intervention to decide the question.

[11]Paolo Brezzi, "Lo Scisma d' Occidente come Problema italiano," *Archivio d. R. Deputazione Romana di Storia Patria* 67 [n.s. 10] (1944): 391-450; also D.M. Bueno de Mesquito, *Giangaleazzo Visconti Duke of Milan (1351-1402): A Study in the Political Career of an Italian Despot* (Cambridge, 1941), pp. 279-294.

in its turn, carving out a sphere with the taking of Pisa in 1406.[12] The intransigent and unmalleable Boniface IX—some have applied other and less flattering adjectives to this pontiff[13]—passed away; and he was replaced by Innocent VII (1404-1406), who initiated a flurry of activity in the short two years of his pontificate with missions aimed at peace and the restoration of church unity.[14] Meanwhile, in south Italy, Ladislaus of Naples was gathering his forces to make what capital he could out of the chaos and uncertainty that beset Italy at this time, while, as in the north, Venice had picked up the pieces left by Gian Galeazzo Visconti's death and the disastrous intervention by the emperor-elect, Ruprecht of the Rhine Palatinate. His supposed triumphal march as a successful warrior-emperor had earlier turned into a fiasco after an ignominious defeat at the hands of Visconti in 1402, leaving him to skulk ingloriously back to Germany.[15]

In this perplexing situation, Baldassare Cossa had intervened as papal legate in Bologna to set up his own safe zone, a power base of stability and order from which some hope for a solution would appear. Cossa would later enjoy a somewhat unsavory reputation as Pope John XXIII and, at Constance, would suffer deposition and removal to a more or less honorable retirement, brief as it was, after his unacceptable action of fleeing from the very Council of Constance that he himself had convoked.[16] Still, at this early stage, Cossa stimulated a burst of activity by canonists, whose opinions and ideas he himself personally

---

[12]Benjamin G. Kohl, *Padua Under the Carrara 1318-1405* (Baltimore, 1998), pp. 318-325, 329, 333-336; Hans Baron, "A Struggle for Liberty in the Renaissance: Florence, Venice and Milan in the Early Quattrocento," *American Historical Review* 58 (1953): 265-289, 544-570; Attilio Simioni, *Storia di Padova dalle origini all fine del secolo XVIII* (Padova, 1968), pp. 529-568.

[13]Arnold Esch, "Simonie-Geschäft in Rom 1400: 'Kein Papst wird das tun, was dieser tut,'" *Vierteljahrschrift für Sozial- und Wirtschaftgeschichte* 61 (1974): 433-457.

[14]Thomas E. Morrissey, "Peter of Candia at Padua and Venice in March 1406," in *Reform and Renewal in the Middle Ages and Renaissance: Essays in Honor of Louis Pascoe, S. J.* ed. Thomas M. Izbicki and Christopher M. Bellitto (Leiden, 2000), pp. 155-173.

[15]Kohl, *Padua Under the Carrara 1318-1405*, pp. 318-320.

[16]Walter Brandmüller, *Das Konzil von Konstanz 1414-1418*. vol. 1: *Bis zur Abreise Sigismunds nach Narbonne* (Paderborn, 1991), pp. 308-311, and Thomas E. Morrissey, "'More Easily and More Securely': Legal Procedure and Due Process at the Council of Constance," in *Popes, Teachers and Canon Law in the Middle Ages: [Festschrift for Brian Tierney]*, ed. James Ross Sweeney and Stanley Chodorow (Ithaca, New York, 1989), pp. 238-239.

solicited in several cases.[17] It is not surprising then that in reply to the question from this wily man of action as to what was the legal situation in those years and what could be done to bring about church unity, a number of the most prominent canonists of that generation delivered their personal and professional opinions. Needless to say, they did not all agree; but it is out of this ferment that what became known as the basic tenets of conciliar theory took their classic form.

A look at three canonists, Petrus de Ancharano, Johannes de Imola and Franciscus de Zabarella, gives a rapid overview of how their ideas had evolved and took form in these critical years when the Council of Pisa took place and was followed by that of Constance, and what shifts these historical and historic events induced in their ideas and outlook. This might then provide a basis for a quick look at a similar critical moment a generation later, when the Council of Basel forced Giuliano Cesarini, Nicolaus de Tudeschis (Panormitanus) and Nicholas of Cusa to reexamine their own views on some comparable fundamental questions.

We start with Ancharano, who was an active participant in the daily events both in the religious sphere and in the urban secular concerns of his day.[18] In the 1380s, he had lectured on canon law at Bologna, served as a judge for the *podestà* there, and served as a consultant to the Doge of Venice in 1387, while also teaching at the revived University of Siena in 1387-1390. He was in Venice again in 1390 and 1392. Sometime in these years he was at Padua but then back to Bologna in 1396. In 1402-1405, he was at Ferrara before returning to Bologna, where he remained until his death in 1416. Certainly in those years Ancharano could not avoid the question of the Great Western Schism, since it was at the heart of the crises afflicting both Church and state in north Italy in his lifetime. Surprisingly, as John Sawicki noted, in Ancharano's canonistic commentaries, that were apparently written in the 1390s, there is virtually no reference to the Schism. In Sawicki's view, Ancharano was writing in the abstract about the normal situation and not concerning a crisis situation. Even in some of his *Consilia* composed in the years 1405-1409, Ancharano still displayed the viewpoint of what we might call a "high papalist," who wished to

---

[17]Swanson, *Universities, Academics and the Great Schism,* pp. 150, 154; Dieter Girgensohn, "Francesco Zabarella aus Padua. Gelehrsamkeit und politisches Wirken eines Rechtsprofessors während des grossen abendländischen Schismas," *Zeitschrift der Savigny-Stiftung für Rechtsgeschichte, Kanonistische Abteilung* 79 (1993): 232-277.

[18]John J. Sawicki, *The Ecclesiological and Political Thought of Petrus de Ancharano 1330?-1416,* unpublished Ph. D. dissertation, Cornell University, Ithaca, New York, 1977, gives details on the missions that Ancharano took on for Baldassare Cossa in these years, pp. 3-4: to Rome for the coronation of Gregory XII in 1406, to Venice in 1407, to Livorno and Florence in 1408 and to the Council of Pisa in 1409. In the discussion of Ancharano's ideas that follows I rely heavily on Sawicki's study.

end the Schism and restore a strong papacy. [19] Ancharano presented the pope as
one able to change the law, especially any law that seemed an obstacle to the
exercise of his power. The pope could resign his position but not weaken it. In
one of the most critical texts that would soon come to the fore in the drive to
define the limits of papal authority, the well-known text that spoke of the pope
as acting with the consultation of the cardinals, Ancharano's language was that it
would be "fitting" (*decet*) for the pope so to act but he did not bring in the word
"ought to" or "must" (*debet*). In regard to another key phrase, which spoke of
the *status ecclesiae* as a limiting force in the papal plenitude of power,
Ancharano used this in a very restricted sense and very sparingly.[20]

There is an interesting string of verbs that appears in Ancharano's treatment
of the papacy in relation to the Church at large, which we do not have time to
explore in depth but which should be mentioned, since Ancharano spoke of:
"what was allowed to the pope" (*quod papae licet*), "what was fitting for a pope"
(*quod papae decet*), and "what would be expedient [or beneficial] for a pope to do"
(*quod papae expedit*).[21] One gets the strong impression that, in this earlier stage,
before the final crisis years that would lead to the Councils of Pisa and
Constance, Ancharano placed his major emphasis on the first of these questions:
what was allowed to the pope. And yet, by the time of the Council of Pisa in
1409, Ancharano would be a leading spokesman for the authority of that council.
One might say the crisis had forced his hand.[22]

A brief look at one of Ancharano's contemporaries, Franciscus Zabarella,
reveals some similarites and some startling differences in their views and in the
evolution of their ideas. Like Ancharano, Zabarella's entire adult life and,
certainly, his professional life was dominated by the fact of the Great Western
Schism, which neither lived to see the end of, since Ancharano died in 1416 and
Zabarella in 1417. Zabarella has been seen by different viewers in various
lights. For some he was a radical; for others, an obstructionist. But, like the

---

[19]See Sawicki, *Petrus de Ancharano,* pp. 7, 12, 20 on Ancharano as a high
papalist with no mention of the Schism in his commentaries. Sawicki points out that
Ancharano wrote *Consilia* in those years, 1405-1407 for Cossa and other cardinals.
Significantly, Sawicki, *Petrus de Ancharano,* p. 58, notes that Ancharano did not
accept the view of the famed earlier canonist Hostiensis on the obligation of the pope
to govern with the cardinals, a point that played a major role in the views of his
contemporary, Franciscus Zabarella.

[20]Sawicki, *Petrus de Ancharano,* pp. 24-25 (pope could change any law), 28
(pope could resign his office but not weaken it), 39 (Ancharano's use of *decet* as
opposed to *debet*), and 46 (Ancharano's virtual non-use of the phrase *status
ecclesiae*).

[21]Sawicki, *Petrus de Acharano,* p. 62.

[22]As Swanson pointed out in *Universities, Academics and the Great Schism,* pp.
180-181, Ancharano had been chosen to write the official defense of the actions of
the cardinals in assembling the Council of Pisa for 1409.

other great canonists of that era, his views in actuality were more nuanced, more carefully refined and crafted than such simple tags can adequately report.

Let me illustrate what these questions meant in a concrete way. The great question of Zabarella's lifetime was what to do about the papacy. This took specific form in the further question: who really was the true pope; and, if this question were hotly disputed (as indeed it was), then what could be done to settle this question? How could the Schism be resolved; and who, if anyone, had the authority to act in this crisis, especially if, as it appeared, neither of the two, and then later three, claimants were able to settle the matter? But for Zabarella, all of these questions and their answers could only be phrased in a context in which the powers and prerogatives of the papacy were carefully defined. Furthermore, any solution, if it were not to upset the order of the Church (*status ecclesiae*) and thus create new and equally pressing problems, had to include a recognition of these powers and prerogatives as they had been spelled out in a long legal tradition. It had been crafted by generations of canonists who themselves had been, and were, relying on centuries of church law, decrees of councils and decisions issued by popes. Thus Zabarella was caught in a bind. To solve the problem of the Schism he had to be radical; but, to propose a doable and acceptable solution that would stand up to scrutiny, he had to exercise restraint and practice realism. He would have to demonstrate what a writer several generations ago described well as "the romance of orthodoxy." He would have to be a conservative revolutionary. To save the papacy, he would have to stand up to and challenge its current occupants; and, to preserve the powers of the papacy, he would have to remove the ones exercising those powers if and when they were not acting for the good of the Church universal.[23]

It is not surprising then to find strong papalist statements in Zabarella's various writings: "The pope is the one to whom no one is allowed to ask 'why do you act in this way?'"; "No judge can discuss an action by the pope because it is sacrilege to dispute about actions of the pope." The pope's freedom of action and decision is so wide because his will is taken as law. But, at the same time, this line of thought consistently comes back to qualification on papal authority: the pope ought to act with complete justice, since his decision makes law.[24] It

---

[23]How Zabarella carried out this delicate balancing act in both his writings and in his actions before and at the Council of Constance has been shown in a number of studies: Dieter Girgensohn, "Francesco Zabarella aus Padua"; also Thomas E. Morrissey, "The Decree 'Haec Sancta' and Cardinal Zabarella: His Role in its Formulation and Interpretation," *Annuarium Historiae Conciliorum* 10 (1978): 145-176; Morrissey, "'More Easily and More Securely'," pp. 234-247.

[24]These expressions are found throughout Zabarella's legal commentaries and other public writings. I cite the following early printed editions: *Cardinalis Zabarella, Super libris decretalium*, I-II (Venice, 1502), III-V (Venice, 1602); Franciscus Zabarella, *In Clementinarum volumen commentaria* (Venice, 1602), and his *Consilia* (Milan, 1515), henceforth noted as *Comm. ad X, In Clem.*, and *Consilia*. Thus that no one can question the pope, *Comm. ad X*, I.7.2, fol. 208rb; sacrilege to

was quite true that no prelate or bishop beneath the papal authority, but only the pope himself, could create a statute that contradicted canon law. The reason for this wide-ranging freedom of papal prerogatives was that the pope can establish a general law and is above the law. All of this could be summed up in the traditional phrase that the fullness of power resided in the papacy and was exercised by the pope.[25] This line occurred many times in the legal commentaries of Zabarella; and, by this time, had a long history of generations of canonistic commentaries that went with it. We have a sign of his significant reaction to the excesses of his day, When Zabarella was composing, in the critical years 1403-1408, his tract *De scismate,* in his final version and perhaps in frustration over the two papal contenders at that time, Gregory XII and Benedict XIII, he was led to write that even though Peter was the prince of the apostles (*princeps apostolorum*) the fullness of power nevertheless was not in him alone.[26] But, even before this, Zabarella had been led to comment that, even though the pope was capable of taking action as above the law, nevertheless, he must proceed according to the law.[27] At one point in his commentary, Zabarella addressed the question about the power of the pope to act or decide a case contrary to the mandate of the law, since he was above the law. Zabarella, at this point, briefly alleged an important distinction between the situation where the pope was acting according to an absolute power (*de potestate absoluta*) and where it was according to his ordinary or ordained power (*de potestate ordinata*), in accord with which the pope wished to preserve the laws. This line was complemented by other statements: the pope was acting in the place of God; the pope acted in God's stead on earth; and the pope was functioning not on the purely human level but on the part of God.[28] These were commonplace expressions by Zabarella's time.

But we must note how often Zabarella clearly introduced, apposed and stressed qualification and limitations on the power of the papacy. One example is in an address Zabarella delivered during the first decade of the fifteenth century for the awarding of the doctorate at Padua to two brothers from a prominent Venetian family, Petrus and Fantinus Dandulo, who had studied with Zabarella. He took this occasion to point out a reality, and his address went this way: that day was an opportunity to recognize two brothers. This led Zabarella to reflect on the idea of brotherhood and what it meant. He moved to an example of brotherhood, that of the cardinals, who were called the brothers of the pope from

---

dispute over papal action, *Consilia* #143, fol. 72va; papal will made law, *In Clem.* II.12.2, fol. 94rb; therefore, the pope should render just decisions, *Consilia,* #142, fol. 72va.

[25]*Comm. ad X,* I.4.5, fol. 89va, I.1.2, fol. 12vb; *In Clem.,* I.3.2, fol. 16ra.

[26]Zabarella's tract *De scismate* was incorporated into the early printed editions of his legal commentaries as an appendix, *Comm. ad X,* I.6.6, fol. 119vaff.

[27]*Comm. ad X,* III.8.4, fol. 59va.

[28]*In Clem.,* V.1.1, fol. 166ra.

their role in the general running of the Church.[29] In another address of welcome, for the visit of Peter Philargus of Candia as papal legate in Venice and Padua in early 1406, Zabarella again had emphasized the role of the cardinals as brothers of the pope, who thus functioned in some way as a limiting force upon papal action.[30] When he deemed it necessary, Zabarella expressed forcefully the duties incumbent upon the pope to act not just as he pleased. Significantly, he used the word "ought to/must" (*debet*) in his comment that the pope, more than others, ought to be especially concerned about decency and equity in rendering a decision.[31] In a *Consilium* dated to 1401, Zabarella even said that the ordinary gloss was wrong when it said that the pope could take away a benefice or depose a bishop without cause.[32] Zabarella demanded that this only be done if based on a legitimate cause. In that same text, Zabarella had pointed to a decision given by Pope Boniface IX, which, he said, was done with the counsel of his brothers, the cardinals, and from the fullness of apostolic authority; and so clearly Zabarella saw no mutual exclusion in these two expressions.[33] Zabarella noted in another place (*Consilium* #137) that the provisions and collations done by Pope Celestine V, since they had been done without the counsel of the cardinals, were revoked by his successor.[34]

Looking very briefly at the third canonist, we see that Johannes de Imola composed a tract on the Schism sometime in 1408 and that he wrote it while in

---

[29]The address which remains in manuscript form exists in several codices: Zeitz, Stiftsbibliothek, 2o Ms. 48 fol. 214r; Pommersfelden, Schlossbibliothek, Ms. 168, fol. 142v-143v; Stift S. Paul [Lavantthal] Ms. 31/4, fol. 124v-125r; and Vienna, Österreichische Nationalbibliothek, Cod. Lat. 5513, fol. 170r-v. I am citing here the Zeitz codex, fol. 214r: "sic fratres pape dicuntur cardinales ex universalis regiminis officio."

[30]Morrissey, "Peter of Candia at Padua and Venice in March 1406," pp. 155-173.

[31]*Comm. ad X,* III.8.4, fol. 59va "quod licet papa possit supra ius, tamen debet procedere secundum ius"; and again his *Consilia* #142, fol. 72va: "papae...qui debet iudicare omnino iuste, cum eius sententia facit ius."

[32]*Consilia* #142, fol. 72ra: "Item non est verum quod glosa dicat in c. per venerabilem quod sine ausa possit papa auferre beneficium vel deponere episcopum. Immo debet intelligi cum causa sicut et alibi dicit glosa quod papa potest dividere episcopatus ex causa."

[33]*Consilia* #142, fol. 71va: "De fratrum suorum consilio et apostolice plenitudine potestatis."

[34]*Consilia* #137, fol. 66vb: "debet ardua de consilio cardinalium tractare adeo quod sine ipsis gesta non observantur per successorem ut notabiliter dicit Iohannes Monachus...ubi refert quod collationes abbatiarum episcopatuum et superiorum dignitatum facte per Celestinum sine consilio cardinalium fuerunt revocate per successorem."

Padua.[35] In this tract, Imola showed himself, in that year, to be a strong protagonist for the position and rights of Gregory XII at a time when many were abandoning him.[36] Only a few years later, however, in 1413, Johannes de Imola spoke out as an advocate of the Pisan popes. But then, by 1413, Imola was in Bologna which was the old stomping ground of Baldassare Cossa, who had become John XXIII and, in fact, was resident in Bologna. Perhaps a discrete conversion of views had taken place in Imola's thinking.[37]

Thus we have seen three canonists who, in the early years of the 15th century, were being pushed by the force of events, the exigencies of their times and the disputes that swirled around them to define their views in a more outspoken fashion. We are not surprised then to learn of the key roles that each played in the critical events of the succeeding years, Ancharano especially with the influence of his ideas at the Council of Pisa, and then Zabarella at the Council of Constance.

A generation later, in the 1430s and 1440s, another group trained in canon law found themselves in a parallel dilemma. Nicholas of Cusa, Cardinal Cesarini and Nicolaus de Tudeschis (Panormitanus) came out of the same canonistic tradition as Ancharano, Imola and Zabarella. They too faced a crisis of the relationship between the papacy and the Church at large, and so they also had to make a decision.[38] To speak of them as having to choose a side is a gross over-

---

[35]The strong connection between these three canonists reveals itself clearly when we note that Johannes de Imola was a student of Ancharano and, in 1406, came to Padua to teach where Zabarella was a leading figure. Swanson, *Universities, Academics and the Great Schism,* p. 212. The major studies on Johannes de Imola with details on his life, career and ideas are: Dino Staffa, "De Iohannis ab Imola vita et operibus," *Apollinaris* 10 (1937): 76-104 and Staffa, "Tractatus Johannis ab Imola super schismate occidentis," *Rivista di storia della chiesa in Italia* 7 (1953): 181-224.

[36]Swanson, *Universities, Academics and the Great Schism,* p. 161. We can note that Zabarella had spoken out for the conciliarist position in his own tract, *De scismate,* which he completed in 1408, after the cardinals of the Roman obedience had requested advice from Ancharano (which he gave in his *Consilia # 66*) in October, 1407; see Sawicki, *Petrus de Ancharano,* p. 113. Sawicki mentions other canonists who were writing at this time, Paolo de Castro, Antonius de Butrio, Mateo Matasselanis, *Petrus de Ancharano,* p. 121, but notes that Ancharano was still hesitant, even at this late date to speak of an "obligation" [*debet*] on the part of the pope and of any resort to a council, see p. 127. The definitive break now occurred when neither Gregory XII nor Benedict XIII would take that definite step to cooperate to end the Schism. This pushed Ancharano into the "conciliarist camp," see *Petrus de Ancharano,* p. 137.

[37]Swanson, *Universities, Academics and the Great Schism,* p. 185.

[38]Our earlier trio had to deal with the uncertainty of who was the real pope (and if there was, at that time, in fact a valid pope) and how to determine this question and so bring unity to the Church while advancing reform. In contrast to this, the later genera

simplification, since each in his own way was fighting to preserve the papacy and the Church from what he saw as great threats to their survival, while, at the same time, they struggled to fulfill the mandates each brought to Basel. These were themselves quite distinct: a delegate from the pope (Cesarini), a proctor from a claimant to be bishop (Cusanus), and a spokesperson for a king (Panormitanus).[39] Just as we do not find a simple party line espoused by the canonists of the earlier generation, we should not be surprised by divergent views in the reactions of these men to the crisis that the split between Eugenius IV and the Council of Basel provoked. Their world had been, for several generations and in differing voices, calling for unity and reform in Church and society. Over and again it had appeared that the one seemed to preclude the other. In the months just before the death of Zabarella at Constance in September 1417 and right down to the final compromise which had set up a conclave representing both the council and the cardinals, which brought unity with the election of Martin V, the question had been bitterly contested whether the move to elect a new pope and so restore unity meant an indefinite postponement of reform measures.

Each of the three men of this later generation of the Council of Basel had to confront this dilemma of unity and/or reform and work it out. We know that it led to critical decisions at that council, for example, the decision to invite the Hussites to discuss and debate issues. Later at that council, which had by then moved to Florence, the Greeks joined the Latin West for the first time in generations in a common effort at reunion and discussions of faith and reform.[40]

---

tion had to wrestle with the problem of a growing disagreement between a council and a valid pope, who had come to his office from the very process that Pisa and Constance had initiated to achieve unity and reform but now appeared to be blocking the very measures that these councils had set up to preserve unity and advance reform. This was a wholly new problem that required new lines of thinking.

[39]Cardinal Cesarini came to Basel as a representative of Eugenius IV. Nicholas of Cusa was there to protect and defend the rights and claims of the dean of the cathedral chapter of Cologne. Ulrich von Manderscheid, to become the archbishop of Trier, sent Cusanus with his suit to the council at Basel. Finally Nicolaus de Tudeschis (Panormitanus) was part of the official delegation for the King of Aragon. Their perspectives then were both alike—all three had a background of studies in canon law—and radically different at one and the same time. For Cesarini's assignment at Basel, Gerald Christianson, *Cesarini: The Conciliar Cardinal, The Basel Years, 1431-1438* (St. Ottilien, 1979), esp. pp. 10ff.; for Panormitanus, see Kurt Wolfgang Nörr, *Kirche und Konzil bei Nicolaus de Tudeschis (Panormitanus)* (Forschungen zur kirchlichen Rechtsgeschichte und zum Kirchenrecht, Bd. 4; Köln, 1964), p. 4; for Cusanus among the vast library of works, I mention only: Paul Sigmund, *Nicholas of Cusa. The Catholic Concordance* (Cambridge, 1991), "Introduction" pp. xi-xxxix. For the Basel events in general, see Johannes Helmrath, *Das Basler Konzil 1431-1449: Forschungsstand und Probleme* (Kölner Historische Abhandlungen, 32; Köln, 1987).

[40]The Council of Basel-Florence was acting in an innovative way since in the search for a "consensus," a term very dear to the heart of Nicholas of Cusa, it really did desire dialogue and a search for ways to achieve agreement. Thus, at least in this area, it avoided the high-handedness of the Council of Constance in the latter's

We know also that the initial decision to be open and creative was only the first step; and, difficult as this may have been, it was far easier than the agonizing steps that Cardinal Cesarini had to take as Basel's factions split wide apart, referred to in shorthand as papalists versus conciliarists. Cesarini strove desperately to hold the polarities together, but it was not to be.[41] Nicholas of Cusa wrote his great *De concordantia catholica* in the midst of this crisis and wrestled with the problems he saw. As we well know, in the long run Cusanus sided with Pope Eugenius IV, not least because he saw this side as offering the greater possibility of preserving unity and re-uniting the divided Greek and Latin churches.[42] Panormitanus, on the other hand, joined with John of Ragusa and others in the Council of Basel who saw it as preserving the true spirit of canon law and the gospel.[43] For centuries the position of this latter group was labeled as wrong, and they were portrayed as adherents of a lost and misguided cause. But the question these three men, like their predecessors Imola, Ancharano and Zabarella, had to face is not one so easily dismissed; nor should it be.

At Basel, a question was raised which was studied in an excellent work a generation ago by Arnulf Vagedes, *Das Konzil über dem Papst?*. Vagedes presented the carefully nuanced arguments of Panormitanus and Cusanus in the dispute between the adherents of Basel and those of Eugenius IV as raising a fundamental question.[44] This question could be phrased in language drawn from

---

treatment of John Hus and Jerome of Prague. Basel struggled to defend the faith, heal divisions and advance reform at the same time. Eugenius IV's great victory in getting the Greeks to come to Florence in a sense sealed his victory over Basel even if in other ways it was a hollow victory in that reform was set back for generations; see Karl August Fink, "Papsttum und Kirchenreform nach dem grossen Schisma," *Tübinger Theologische Quartalschrift* 126 (1946): 110-122. Helmrath has shown that Eugenius IV sold out the cause of reform for the sake of personal advantage; see *Das Basler Konzil,* pp. 97-98, 102.

[41]As early as 1431, Pope Eugenius IV had acted to destroy the council by unilaterally closing it or transferring it, and so had undermined the position of his own legate at Basel (Cesarini); see Christianson, *Cesarini,* pp. 27ff. The invitation to the Hussites was not received well by Eugenius IV, and he ordered the council's dissolution; see Christianson, *Cesarini,* p. 31. By early 1432, [Christianson, p. 45], Cesarini had been forced to resign his position as president of the council (a status he had held as legate for Eugenius IV); however, the two sides were now growing farther apart, and there was little hope of reconciliation. Cesarini, however, continued to try.

[42]Helmrath, *Das Basler Konzil,* pp. 375, 377, 382-383.

[43]Nörr, *Kirche und Konzil,* p. 112. It is no accident that, in one section cited by Nörr, *Kirche und Konzil,* p. 113, Panormitanus used the same phrasing concerning the location of ecclesiastical authority that was to be found in Zabarella's *De scismate:* "tota potestas ecclesiastica est in ecclesia tamquam in fundamento, Petrus autem recepit tanquam principalis minister."

[44]Arnulf Vagedes, *Das Konzil über dem Papst?: Die Stellungnahmen des Nikolaus von Kues und des Panormitanus zum Streit zwischen dem Konzil von Basel und Eugen IV,* 2 vols. (Paderborn, 1981), 1:282-297. Joachim W. Stieber, *Pope Eugenius IV,*

the *Credo* known to all and in words made famous by Pope Boniface VIII in *Unam Sanctam:* "one holy Church." What if unity/oneness meant absence of or a failure to reform and so meant not to be holy, while holiness meant to cut off and exclude the sinner/the brother or sister who failed to meet the high standard demanded by any particular group? In that context, which would one prefer, which should one prefer: unity or holiness? This is a question that has come back over and again to confront the Christian communities through history and, presumably, always will, since it asks a question to which no canonist then or now can really be expected to give a definitive answer.[45]

---

the *Council of Basel and the Secular and Ecclesiastical Authorities in the Empire: The Conflict Over Supreme Authority and Power in the Church* (Studies in the History of Christian Thought, 13; Leiden, 1978), p. 340, has pointed out how bitterly many clergy in the north of Europe viewed the papacy as having become the principal opponent of reform.

[45]An interesting and very recent discussion that develops further implications of this line of thinking is to be found in Bradford E. Hinze, "Ecclesial Repentance and the Demands of Dialogue," *Theological Studies* 61 (2000): 207-238. Hinze takes up some of the questions raised by the actions in recent years of Pope John Paul II and his call for the Roman Catholic Church to repent. There is no clear agreement on what this would mean, and strong disagreement on what it would entail. Most relevant to the earlier debate in the fifteenth century is the quotation from Vatican II which taught that the Church was "simul sancta et semper purificanda"; see Hinze, "Ecclesial Repentance," p. 221. Clearly discussions of future ecumenical development will very much focus on the concept of the Church that is called both to be "one" and "holy" and how these attributes are to be interpreted and reconciled.

PART TWO

CUSANUS: PREACHER, BISHOP, THEOLOGIAN

NICHOLAS OF CUSA'S EARLY SERMONS ON THE INCARNATION: AN EARLY RENAISSANCE PHILOSOPHER-THEOLOGIAN AS PREACHER

Lawrence Hundersmarck and Thomas M. Izbicki

Nicholas of Cusa (d. 1464) is well known for his important treatises on ecclesiastical, philosophical, and theological topics. Except for a few studies, his sermons have not been the object of extensive analysis.[1] This is due in no small part to the lack of a modern critical edition of the sermons, which, until recently, appeared only in manuscripts or in excerpts in the *Libri excitationum*,[2] and to the fact that scholarly efforts in the 20th century have been devoted more to the philosophical and theological treatises of Cusanus.[3]

This paper seeks to examine some of the fundamental characteristics of Nicholas of Cusa's early preaching on the Incarnation through a study of four of his pre-1441 sermons. Three of them were preached at Koblenz while Cusanus was dean of St. Florin in that city and chancellor of Ulrich von Manderscheid,

---

[1] Use of Cusanus' sermons in a discussion of his theology can be found in Rudolf Haubst, *Die Christologie des Nikolaus von Kues* (Freiburg, 1956) and James E. Biechler, *The Religious Language of Nicholas of Cusa* (Missoula, 1975); Ray C. Petry, "Emphasis on the Gospel and Christian Reform in Late Medieval Preaching," *Church History* 16 (1947): 75-91 at pp. 88-90; Walter A. Euler, "Does Nicholas of Cusa Have a Theology of the Cross?," *The Journal of Religion* 80 (2000): 405-420. Nicholas' sermons are considered briefly within the context of Renaissance political life and thought by John W. O'Malley, *Praise and Blame in Renaissance Rome: Rhetoric, Doctrine, and Reform in the Sacred Orators of the Papal Court* (Durham, NC, 1979).

[2] A critical text of the sermons is being published by the Heidelberg Academy as Volumes 16, 17, 18 and 19 of the *Opera Omnia* edited by Rudolf Haubst et al. The Roman numeration assigned these sermons is used in this article together with the paragraph numbers in the published texts (¶); these citations are followed by "h", the volume, fascicle and page numbers. For the *Excitationum libri decem*, see Nicolaus Cusanus, *Opera omnia* (Paris, 1514; Frankfurt, 1962), vol. 2., fol. viir-clxxxviiiir. For translations of sermons, see *No Uncertain Sound: Sermons That Shaped the Pulpit Tradition*, ed. Ray C. Petry (Philadelphia, 1948), pp. 289-294; Peter J. Casarella, "*His Name Is Jesus*: Negative Theology and Christology in Two Writings of Nicholas of Cusa from 1440," in *Nicholas of Cusa on Christ and the Church: Essays in Memory of Chandler McCuskey Brooks for the American Cusanus Society*, ed. Gerald Christianson and Thomas M. Izbicki (Leiden, 1996), pp. 281-307.

[3] See Morimichi Watanabe, "The Origins of Modern Cusanus Research in Germany and the Foundation of the Heidelberg *Opera omnia*" in *Nicholas of Cusa in Search of God and Wisdom: Essays in Honor of Morimichi Watanabe by the American Cusanus Society*, edited by Gerald Christianson and Thomas M. Izbicki (Leiden, 1991), pp. 17-42, and Thomas M. Izbicki, "Nicholas of Cusa: The Literature in English Through 1988," in *Nicholas of Cusa in Search of God and Wisdom*, pp. 259-281. The latter is updated in *Nicholas of Cusa on Christ and the Church*, pp. 341-353 and in the Appendix to this volume.

who claimed the archbishopric of Trier:[4] a 1430 sermon on John 1:1 (Sermon I); a 1432 sermon on the feast of the Assumption (Sermon XIII); and a 1432 or 1435 homily entitled *Gloria in excelsis Deo* (Sermon XVII). The fourth was preached in Trier on Christmas Day 1440 (Sermon XXII). Cusanus, following his shipboard vision on the return voyage from Constantinople and the completion of *De docta ignorantia*, was representing Eugenius IV before the princes and prelates of Germany during his struggle with the Council of Basel and its pope, Felix V. This sermon reflects the ideas which Nicholas advanced in *De docta ignorantia*; and, even more than most of the evidence for Cusanus' preaching, it shows signs of reworking from notes for the pulpit into a detailed exposition of its speculative theme, nearly submerging the spoken in the written word.[5] One later sermon, the fifth discussed here, was preached at a synod in Rome during 1458 over which Nicolas presided as legate for Pius II, who was absent at the Congress of Mantua. It too will be considered because it stands in the tradition of Nicholas' early sermons in content, if not always in style (Sermon CCLXXXVII).

The aim of this study is to set forth a number of controlling conceptions that are fundamental to the structure and content of Cusanus' preaching. An examination of this material reveals the activity of a philosopher-theologian who used the sermons as a vehicle to express his Neo-Platonic world view, as well as his concerns with more traditional themes of Christian piety. While the ideas set forth in Cusanus' sermons were known to the Middle Ages, indeed, in some respects were quite common, a reading of these early Renaissance homilies leaves the unmistakable impression that one has taken, to some extent, a step away from the medieval world of the schools and the preaching of the friars. Unlike so many medieval sermons calculated to arouse the emotions and to move the will to holy action, these early sermons of Nicholas are offered to inform and lift the intellect. Rather than a biblical homily, in which each word triggers a set of associations, the Cusanus sermon is ordered and arranged in a clear hierarchy of ideas from an apex of God to the multiplicity of the creation. This approach survives Cusanus' stylistic shifts from the traditional idioms of most of his earliest preaching to a reflection of the style of his speculative treatises and even the more rhetorical style of his synodal sermon.

A pyramidal structure characterizes the sermons because this was basic to Cusanus' understanding of the universe; and, as such, it is quite different than the excessively rigid divisions one finds in, for example, Aquinas' few surviving sermon texts. With Nicholas, attention is directed to the activity of the Trinity in creation and redemption rather than to the imaginative representation of the

---

[4]Morimichi Watanabe, "The Episcopal Election of 1430 in Trier and Nicholas of Cusa," *Church History* 39 (1970): 299-316.

[5]*Nicholas of Cusa on Learned Ignorance: A Translation and an Appraisal of De docta ignorantia*, tr. Jasper Hopkins, 2nd ed. (Minneapolis, 1985); Thomas M. Izbicki, "The Church in the Light of Learned Ignorance," *Medieval Philosophy and Theology* 3 (1993): 186-214.

life of Jesus, Mary, and the saints. For Cusanus, illumination of the mind is the goal of preaching. Thus, he carefully sets forth his ideas with the care and precision of a philosopher-theologian. Questionable examples of holy lives or deeds offered to fuel the pious imagination are carefully avoided in these sermons. (When they do appear in Nicholas' sermons, they are noted in a perfunctory manner, as if irrelevant to the preacher's real interests.[6]) Modern scholars such as Rudolf Haubst have judged his preaching not to be "popular" but, rather, "aristocratic."[7] We also have evidence that the people of his day complained that Cusanus' sermons were over their heads, evidence that he had carried his intellectual interests into the pulpit, instead of inserting these themes later in his study.[8]

This does not mean, however, that Cusanus lacked a sense of drama. Instead of *exempla*, he used allegorical dramas, like the legal pleadings of Truth and Justice, Mercy and Peace before God recorded in Sermons I and XVII which culminated in the decision to send the Son into the world to save sinful man. Elsewhere in his early sermons, Nicholas describes the dramatic entry of Mary into heaven (Sermon VIII).[9] In the same sermon, Cusanus also described how the Christian went into the desert to find Jerusalem; the Church; his entry into the holy city; and the arms and armor given him for his climb to Mount Sion to appear before the Father.[10] Here Cusanus' sense of symbolism and drama, Janus-like, looks back to Hildegard's *Scivias*, a copy of which is in the library at Kues,[11] and forward to the rhetorical tastes of preachers of the later Renaissance.[12] This device can be found too in the later sermons, like the imaginary dialogue with his audience in the synodal sermon, which defends his finding inspiration in a chance glance at the introit for that day's mass.

The pyramidal structure of these sermons is what needs to be examined first, for in the pattern of movement of the ideas lies the key to Cusanus' preaching. In these five sermons Nicholas sets before his audience the highest reality, which

---

[6]The same *exempla* concerning the punishment of blasphemy appear in two early sermons, Sermon XVIII (h XVI/3, 13) and Sermon XXI (h, XVI/3, 14).

[7]Rudolf Haubst, *Studien zu Nikolaus von Kues und Johannes Wenck* (Münster, 1955), p. 136.

[8]Biechler, *Religious Language*, pp. 110-111.

[9]Sermon VIII, h, XVI/2, 30-31.

[10]Sermon VIII, h, XVI/2, 34-43.

[11]Jakob Marx, *Verzeichnis der Handschriften-Sammlung des Hospitals zu Cues bei Bernkastel a./ Mosel* (Trier, 1905; reprint Frankfurt, 1966), pp. 69-70: MS 63.

[12]O'Malley, *Praise and Blame*, pp. 98-101, notes the emphasis on the speculative and remote, except where obedience is emphasized. The lack of *exempla* might be tied to their potential for urging the listener to action, rather than contemplation.

sustains and gives identity to all reality. In his sermon on the opening verse of St. John's gospel, the flow of discussion begins with the simplicity of divine nature, then the Trinity, and the expression of that Trinity in the creation and redemption. By this descent of God, humanity is called to ascend back to its God. In his 1432 sermon on the feast of the Assumption, he explicates Revelation 11:19-12:1 (the covenant scene in the temple and the woman clothed with the sun) as descriptions of the perfect ideal of the Church intended from all eternity. The theme of *Gloria in excelsis Deo* (Sermon XVII) also focuses on divine activity presented with Anselmian tones at the end of one of his allegorical dramas:

> A final sentence was handed down that the Lord of infinite piety, justice, truth, mercy and peace, the Creator, the Word of God should assume human flesh, descend from heaven, assume humanity, make satisfaction and, having pacified justice, should lead man back to his fatherland (XVII, h, XVI/3, 3).[13]

The later synodal sermon at Rome keeps the listeners' attention directed toward the holiness of God, a holiness expressed in the Son as ought to be the case with the priests who are sent by Christ to express God's own holiness. To develop this theme Cusanus, who had been a papal legate in Germany,[14] drew on the canon law of legations:

> Thus, if the pope can send a legate with the fullness of Papal power, certainly he shares the nature of the pope [as office holder], is no different in essence [of office] and is no less by nature, rather there is one and the same dignity, authority and individual papal office [shared] by both, which cannot be multiplied in its fullness, although the sender and the sent are different persons... (Sermon CCLXXXVII).[15]

The mind of Cusanus moves from the one to the many, from that point of unity which gives to the multiplicity of the creation its source and end. As often noted by scholars, this is the characteristic Neoplatonism of Nicholas of Cusa as

---

[13]This sermon, like Sermon I, reports a lawsuit heard before God, with justice and truth pleading against mercy and peace, a version of a medieval literary device for presenting the Anselmian justification for the Incarnation; see Moshe Lazar, "Satan and Notre Dame: Characters in a Popular Scenario," in *A Medieval French Miscellany: Papers from the 1970 Kansas Conference on Medieval French Literature*, ed. Norris Lacy (Lawrence, KS, 1972), pp. 1-14.

[14]Donald Sullivan, "Nicholas of Cusa as Reformer: The Papal Legation to the Germanies, 1451-1452," *Mediaeval Studies* 36 (1974): 382-428.

[15]This sermon is cited from a typescript kindly supplied by Dr. Heinrich Pauli through Professor Peter J. Casarella.

well as the tendency of the age.[16] We may take his Christmas sermon of 1440, *Dies sanctificatus*, as an excellent example of this tendency. This sermon seeks to present the creation as the dynamic gift and self-expression of the Father. The Father is that *unitas* from which all things proceed and return.[17] Eternal unity precedes all things (Sermon XXII, h, XVI/4, 20). Thus, God is like the eternal artist who has all forms within himself (Sermon XXII, h, XVI/4, 26), for the production of anything proceeds from the conceiver and the conceived (Sermon XXII, h, XVI/4, 29). Thus, all things insofar as they exist, proceed from and participate in different degrees to the unity which is God (Sermon XXII, h, XVI/4, 11), for just as every stone is but a part of the total tower, so too all beings are but a part of the total universe (Sermon XXII, h, XVI/4, 29). From his sermon on John 1:1 we read:

> Every form then flows from the form of God, every being from the divine Being, every good from the divine Good and every truth from the divine Truth. And such a flow we call creation (Sermon I, h, XVI/1, 13).[18]

Cusanus, standing in the Neo-Platonic tradition of Augustine (d. 430) and Proclus (d. 485) would favor in his preaching images that capture the downward movement from the one to the many. This movement is seen in his sermon of August 15, 1432. Here he uses the image of the woman clothed with the sun and her head crowned with twelve stars (the twelve apostles) with the moon under her feet to discuss the Church in its original purity with the feet representing the present age and its difficulties. To trust in the moon is to trust in the instability

---

16See Biechler, *Religious Language*, pp. 74-81, 92-103. Biechler puts it this way: "*Unitas* language, together with its explication in more complex mathematical symbols appears as a direct accommodation of religious language to the scientific predilections of the times. If *felicitas* is to be found in *sapientia*, *unitas* is the principle of all knowledge. To know a thing in its unity is to know it in its totality for not only is unity the source of all being and motion but also the goal..." (p. 98).

17"And because we attribute all names to God in comparison to creatures, it follows that, as we aid our self with creatures we ascend to the Trinity. There is nothing we do not receive. We see in anything what is one thing, discreet and connected; these things are found to be in essence every being. And that unity means lack of division, discreet existence and connection. If, therefore, we find that Being in every participating being, we see contracted unity, in which things participate, not to be unless it is triune" (Sermon XXII, h, XVI/4, 17).

18This is why diverse names for God all point to the same one absolute (Sermon I, h, XVI/1, 5) as did the ancient Greek philosophers (Sermon I, h, XVI/1, 5). These passages contain the germ of Cusanus' *De pace fidei*; see *Nicholas of Cusa on Interreligious Harmony: Text, Concordance and Translation of De pace fidei*, ed. James Biechler and H. Lawrence Bond (Lewiston, New York, 1990), p. 234 n. 69.

of what passes rather than the stability of the more noble sun (Sermon XIII, h, XVI/3, 5).[19] So:

> from the nature of the moon and its instability, its influence and its vulnerability to the sun and to eclipse etc., one can learn how our sins are opposed to God etc., if we wish, therefore, to serve and reform in the ark and the Church, we, who are feet, ought to walk in the way of equity and justice, and receive the influx of motion and sensation from those who are above us and who have excelled in sanctity; and it is fitting that we direct the lunar soul to conjunction with the sun, so that, having attained that conjunction, the soul may be moved ever into the full moon of eternal glory (Sermon XIII, h, XVI/3, 5-6).

There is also in other sermons the use of light as an image for dynamic downward movement (Sermon I, h, XVI/1, 11; XXII, h, XVI/4, 23). For God is the light of all men that shines in the darkness of their ignorance (Sermon XXII, h, XVI/4, 29; I, h, XVI/1, 23). Elsewhere the holiness of God is compared to heat which, when received by a cold object, is made warm so pleasantly that it cannot sufficiently praise the heat that liberated it from the cold (Sermon CCLXXXVII). Another favored image is that of water. God, he writes, is "overflowing" goodness (Sermon I, h, XVI/1, 14). Christ, we are told:

> ...poured out the water of saving wisdom in His eloquence, like dew from heaven...the Clean cleanses; the Living gives life; the Wise Teacher teaches wisdom; and, therefore, the Word of God cleanses like cleansing water (Sermon CCLXXXVII).

In his sermon on the opening of John's gospel, he refers to the Incarnation with the image of clouds dropping justice as dew, allowing the earth to be opened and thus bud forth a savior (Sermon I, h, XVI/1, 25).

As useful as these images of light and water are for Nicholas in his preaching, they are not as central as is the *logos* image. For him, God is He who reveals Himself from above in His words, words that are heard by those below. God's words have been revealed by the patriarchs, prophets, apostles, and saints (XVII, h, XVI/3, 10), but made flesh in Christ. God sends His Word for He is faithful to His promises (Sermon I, h, XVI/1, 21; I, h, XVI/1, 23). Although Cusanus does not ignore the mercy of God, his concerns are more directed to the absolute wisdom and intellect of the divine. The infant Son of Mary comes to illuminate us (Sermon I, h, XVI/1, 1) with a word not sensible but intellectual (Sermon I, h, XVI/1, 8). This word is that by which God creates (Sermon I, h, XVI/1, 12). In another sermon we read:

---

[19]Here the downward movement of head to feet and sun to moon ties with the theme *ante omnem pluralitatem est unitas.*

See that He is the light which has shone on us.   How has He shone however? For, although He is a hidden God, He reveals Himself. Thus, while the mental Word is hidden from you, for this, so that He is revealed to you, He takes a voice; and, under a voice, which is His sign, the hidden mind is made apparent, so that the hidden eternal Word assumed flesh, so that He would be visible (Sermon XXII, h, XVI/4, 39).

Committed as he was to the rational and ordered structure of the universe, *sapientia* language was very important for Cusanus.[20] God as *logos* or absolute reason is the very center of every intellectual being. Thus, Christ preached and illuminated, for He communicated light to the disciples without diminution of His light, thus "making us participants in His Wisdom" (Sermon XXII, h, XVI/4, 39). This theme, so fundamental to Christianity, is seen by Nicholas to have particular soteriological importance because the fall of humanity was occasioned by the deception of the snake, [the devil], in the Garden of Eden. While he notes the element of pride in Adam and Eve (Sermon I, h, XVI/1, 16), it is their intellectual failure to comprehend the falsehood and deception of the tempter that led to their demise (Sermon I, h, XVI/1, 19; I, XVI/1, 20). More deeply, what is at issue for Cusanus is that, in sin, humanity fails to know that its true end is God (Sermon I, h, XVI/1, 14; I, h, XVI/1, 17). The most damning error is that man thinks he can be equal to God (XVII, h, XVI/3, 3). Adam is thus condemned because of his crime of treason (Sermon I, h, XVI/1, 17; XVII, h, XVI/3, 3) in the tradition of Psalm 5:7 and Revelation 22:15:

Oh God, have you not hated the worker of inequity? And so you condemn all who spoke lies! And these are outside your kingdom, the dogs, the poisoners, the shameless, the killers, those who serve idols, and all who love and live lies (Sermon I, h, XVI/1, 14).

For Cusanus, to overcome this falsehood by revealing the truth about humanity's true end is a most fundamental goal of the Incarnation (Sermon XXII, h, XVI/4, 3). The wise are wise to the extent they know God (Sermon CCLXXXVII).[21]

Cusanus as preacher addresses the intellect. He wishes to inform his audience about things eternal and as such offer them wisdom. This impulse emerges from his theological and philosophical assumptions regarding the structure and order of being and the supreme value of divine revelation. These preoccupations lead him also to celebrate the human mind and its potential throughout these sermons. In the intellect, human beings find that spirit which enfolds within the

---

[20]See Biechler, *Religious Language*, pp. 105-138.

[21]To those at the 1459 synod Cusanus preaches: "See how God is the end of all His work. He confers holiness, so that it might be displayed. He teaches so that he may be understood. He justifies so that His justice may be displayed. He illuminates so that His light may be reflected back" (Sermon CCLXXXVII).

self the natures of all things (Sermon XXII, h, XVI/4, 17). The dynamic intellect aspires to transcend all finite realities, hence its restlessness and its desire to know God, the first principle of all things (Sermon XXII, h, XVI/4, 39). The mind as it turns to beings seeks the absolute Being in all things (Sermon I, h, XVI/1, 12). So we find Cusanus praising the dynamic impulse of the intellect to his congregation at Koblenz:

> Oh, if any contemplative should ascend here (to reflect on the Trinity) what sweet speculations he would find! Truly, no infidel, no proud man, miser, lecher or anyone involved in other sordid sins can grasp this sweetness. Nor is anyone so hard that, if he enters upon this way of contemplation, he would not be satisfied (Sermon I, h, XVI/1, 14).

Humanity has its final end in the beatific vision of God where alone are all "treasures of knowledge and wisdom" (XVII, h, XVI/3, 5). For Nicholas of Cusa "...the intellect, which is the king of kings (the intellect is the ruler, reigning truly over all things) wishes to know more nobly and better..." (Sermon CCLXXXVII).

At this point, one note of caution should be offered. These sermons do not see the purpose of the Incarnation as only for the illumination of humanity, although that is, as we have seen, an important emphasis in these homilies. Cusanus repeats the Anselmian idea that satisfaction needs to be offered to the Father for Adam's fall (Sermons I and XVII). He does not, however, sustain the argument in the tradition of *Cur Deus homo?*. Rather, another important soteriological idea appears closer to his heart, that is, when God enters into human nature, nature itself is changed. This serves as a corrective to an exclusively "gnostic"" reading of the Incarnation whereby the wisdom of God only teaches correct knowledge. In his Christmas homily of 1440 he calls his audience to keep in mind that in Christ's human nature, human nature is perfected (Sermon XXII, h, XVI/4, 36) for now humanity is most united with divinity. So he preaches:

> See here how human nature in Christ puts on immortality by union to the word...see here the error of all who expect salvation without Christ (Sermon XXII, h, XVI/4, 38).

This union of divinity and humanity makes Christ the "substantial intimacy" with persons, for He is humanity's "plenitude and perfection" (Sermon XXII, h, XVI/4, p. 37).[22]

---

[22]Cusanus' Christology has been too little studied, but see the work by Haubst cited in n. 1 and H. Lawrence Bond, "Nicholas of Cusa and the Reconstruction of Theology: The Centrality of Christology in the Coincidence of Opposites," in *Contemporary Reflections on the Medieval Christian Tradition: Essays in Honor of Ray C. Petry*, ed. George H. Shriver (Durham, NC, 1974), pp. 81-94.

Scholarship on Cusanus has often noted that he defies easy and systematic classification. At first glance, these early sermons offer a clear hierarchical universe with an emphasis on the ascent of the intellect to the ultimate source and end of all things. This dynamic, so influential to Cusanus' preaching style, is not the whole of his world-view. God, for Nicholas, cannot be reached by the intellect alone, for God surpasses all finite intellects (Sermon CCLXXXVII). God surpasses every opposition as the absolute infinite cause (Sermon XXII, h, XVI/4, 10), thus, all names which are imposed by comparison and reason fail to grasp the simple and infinite God (Sermon XXII, h, XVI/4, 16-17).

Cusanus' insight, that insight is not enough, brings this early Renaissance thinker back to the well-traveled themes of medieval preaching. He, like so many preachers before him, calls his audience to deeper faith in and obedience to God.[23] Do not be, he cautions, like gentiles who trust in the subtlety of human reason; but rather seek Christ with simplicity, purity, charity, and prayers (Sermon XXII, h, XVI/4, 42). Elsewhere, in his Christmas sermon entitled *Gloria in excelsis Deo*, we read regarding the Incarnation that it is a union beyond wonder "...which no one apprehends except by faith, that, because Adam strove to apprehend by knowing, [consequently] he fell" (XVII, h XVI/3, 9). It remains unclear how one reconciles this last statement with the condemnation of Adam for having false knowledge. Nicholas of Cusa would not be the first preacher, nor the last, to tolerate logical difficulties in the sermon. Nicholas, when speaking of the life of Christ in his 1432 sermon on the feast of the Assumption (Sermon XIII), chooses to highlight themes fundamental to a great many medieval homilies: patience and obedience (Sermon XIII, h, XVI/3, 7). He tells his audience that if a cause brought against you by a superior is unjust, "you will merit all the more by obeying him" (Sermon XIII, h, XVI/3, 7). On that day Cusanus left his listeners with the following words:

> And God rested among the obedient. Christ entered Bethany, that is, the house of obedience. Where obedience dwells, there is the love of God. The love of God makes a man pliable, and obedient, like melted wax. And note this: if you wish to know in whom God's love can be found, look at His obedience, because obedience is better than sacrifices (Sermon XIII, h, XVI/3, 7).

Therefore, the homiletic material we have examined reflects the complexity of its author. We have on one hand, with Cusanus, a preacher who presents a sermon

---

[23]This has caused modern scholars some distress. For example, Biechler writes in his *Religious Language*, "Cusanus' appeal to obedience, often couched in language which stands in direct contradiction to his customary language of reason, understanding and freedom, stands out as a foreign body in his thought as if to call attention to an irreducible inconsistency or a dangerous psychological insecurity" (p.152). Perhaps this is too strong. Nicholas may only be giving attention to basic medieval, indeed Christian, virtues, especially the virtue of faith, based on revelation. For an example of this emphasis in Cusanus' preaching, see Sermon CCLXXXIV, cited here from a typescript kindly provided by Dr. Heinrich Pauli.

in the style of a learned systematic theological treatise. Influenced by the re-emergence of Neoplatonic thinking in his age, his homilies have a structure and order that proceeds from the one to the many, from that which is above to that which is below. For him, the sermons, like all his other writings, have as their goal to help make the unintelligible more intelligible, to offer light to the darkness.[24] On the other hand, Cusanus, in his respect for authority[25] and his attention to issues of traditional piety, demonstrates in his preaching that he also stands in a medieval world, already in his day quickly disappearing. We hear in these sermons not only the speculative thinker but also the future cardinal of the Roman Catholic Church.[26]

---

[24]In his study of the Lenten sermons of Cusanus (Sermons XXVIII XXVIII, CXXII, CLIV, CCLXXVI and CCLXXXVIII), Euler ("Theology of the Cross") argues that the supreme vehicle of revelation for Nicholas was the cross of Jesus. What becomes intelligible through the cross is the full truth of obedience to God's will, as well as the meaning of loving God and neighbor.

[25]In our sermons Nicholas refers by name to Augustine (Sermon I, h, XVI/1, 1; Sermon XXII, h, XVI/4, 18; Sermon XXII, h, XVI/4, 20); Nicholas of Lyra (Sermon I, h, XVI/1, 7); Basil (Sermon I, h, XVI/1, 10); Robert Grosseteste of Lincoln (Sermon I, h, XVI/1, 13); Lactantius Firmianus (Sermon I, h, XVI/1, p. 11); Ambrose (Sermon XVII, h, XVI/3, 2); Hilary (Sermon XXII, h, XVI/4, 23); and Athanasius (Sermon XXII, h, XVI/4, p. 35).

[26]In his synodal sermon of 1459, he spoke of the role of the papal legate as one who is completely under the authority of the pope (Sermon CCLXXXVII).

PROCLAMATION OF CHRIST IN SELECTED SERMONS
FROM CUSANUS' BRIXEN PERIOD*

Walter Andreas Euler

Josef Koch was the first to direct attention to the fact that, as he put it, the sermons of Cusanus can be easily divided into three large groups: first, the sermons prior to being elevated to the cardinalate (1431-1448); second, the sermons of the papal legation (1451-1452); and, third, the sermons he delivered as bishop of Brixen and in other places in his diocese (1452-1457). To this one can add a sermon in Bruneck (1458) and four sermons he delivered in 1459 as papal visitator to the clergy of Rome.[1] Incidentally, the Bruneck sermon definitely belongs, pace Koch, to the sermons from the Brixen period since it was delivered by Cusanus in his capacity as bishop of Brixen in a city of his diocese. The last extant sermon of Cusanus from 1463, delivered in the monastery of Montoliveto, also has to be added to Josef Koch's listing.

Each of these groups is marked by important distinguishing characteristics. In the words of Josef Koch: "Before 1450 Nicholas appeared as a homilist almost exclusively for holidays. The Christmas season, Holy Week and Easter, Pentecost, Trinity Sunday, and Marian feasts are the principal opportunities at which he spoke."[2] The sermons from the legation trip have a unique purpose, namely, that of the legation itself. From these sermons we possess little more than short notes since the cardinal found neither sufficient time nor leisure during the trip to draft comprehensive sermon outlines.

A basic change takes place in Brixen. From the beginning Cusanus saw the proclamation of faith during the sermon as an essential task of his office. While only four sermon outlines remain extant from Cusanus' first year in Brixen and it is possible that Nicholas reverted to previous outlines,[3] very intensive preaching activity took place in the four-year period spanning June 29, 1453 and June 29, 1457, which is suddenly interrupted by Cusanus' escape to Buchenstein. Sermons CXXVI-CCLXXXVII stem from this period, in other words, a total of 162 sermons (or about forty per year). If one also takes into account the first four Brixen sermons and the last one in his diocese, from Bruneck of September

*This article was delivered at the Sixth Biennial Gettysburg Conference on the Works of Nicholas of Cusa, "The Sermons: An Introduction," held at Gettysburg Lutheran Seminary, Gettysburg, Pennsylvania, October 20, 1996. I thank the organizers of the conference for their invitation, and I especially thank Peter Casarella of the Catholic University of America, Washington, D.C., for his efforts in translating my article into English.

[1] *Vier Predigten im Geiste Eckharts,* ed. Josef Koch (Sitzungsberichte der Heidelberger Akademie der Wissenschaften, philosophisch-hist. Klasse, Jg. 1936/37, 2. Abh.; Heidelberg, 1937) (= Cusanus-Texte [hereafter cited as CT] I, 2-5), p. 185.

[2] *Vier Predigten,* p. 185.

[3] Sermones CXXII-CXXV (h XVIII 1, 1-19) according to Haubst's numeration, which will also be employed in what follows; see Rudolf Haubst, "Conspectus enumerationis nostrae novae et Indicis a Josepho Koch editi" (h XVI, pp. XLVII-LV).

8, 1458 (Sermo CCLXXXVIII), then the sum total of sermons which Nicholas of Cusa delivered in his capacity as bishop of Brixen comes to 167. In other words, more than half of all of Cusanus' extant sermon outlines (we possess a total of 293 Cusan sermons) came from his time as bishop of Brixen.

In the vast majority of cases, we have relatively complete drafts and, by contemporary standards, unusually comprehensive outlines, which document the significance which Nicholas attached to his sermons. Incidentally, the delivery of a sermon normally took one or sometimes even several hours,[4] and the edition of sermon outlines from the Brixen period will certainly include well over a thousand pages in the Heidelberg edition. It is noteworthy that in the years between 1454 and 1457, the most intensive period of Nicholas' activity as a preacher, no philosophical or theological works whatsoever were composed. *De beryllo* was supposed to be finished in the year 1453, which we know from Nicholas' correspondence with the monks of Tegernsee;[5] however, it was not completed until 1458, during his so-called exile in Buchenstein. In other words, he devoted his time for written work between 1454 and 1457 solely to the preparation of sermons.

These texts show us Cusanus as an enthusiastic shepherd and pastor of the faithful entrusted to him. In the words of Josef Koch, he exerted himself to provide them with instruction in the basic truths of salvation and to do every-thing in his power for their religious renewal.[6] Cusanus preached in his Brixen cathedral just like any pastor, not only on the solemn feasts of the hurch cyear or the Brixen calendar but often on normal Sundays and the feast days of saints. Outside of Brixen, Cusanus preached mostly at ordinations and visitations or on special occasions.[7] The particularity of the Brixen sermons in the context of the entire corpus of sermons illustrates an uninterrupted catechesis to a circle of independent and relatively similar audiences. This fact can be documented in these sermons and is not present in this manner in the earlier sermons.

***

In accordance with the character of the Brixen sermons as a comprehensive proclamation of faith, Cusanus naturally addresses a multiplicity of themes in these sermons dependent on the occasion and the biblical text of the daily Mass.

---

[4]P. Niederkofler, "Über die Predigtweise des Kardinals Nikolaus von Cues," *Priester- Konferenzblatt* 75 (1964): 119-125 at p. 120.

[5]Edmond Vansteenberghe, *Autour de la docte ignorance: Une controverse sur la théologie mystique au XVe siècle* (Münster, 1915), p. 120.

[6]CT I, 2-5, p. 185.

[7]For example, Niederkofler, "über die Predigtweise,"; Alois Trenkwalder, "Zur Geschichte der Predigt in der Diözese Brixen," *Konferenzblatt für Theologie und Seelsorge* 95 (1984): 147-165 at pp. 148-149; Heinrich Pauli, "Die geistige Welt der Brixener Predigten des Nikolaus von Kues," MFCG 22 (1995): 163-186.

But he returns over and over again to one central point. The kernel and favorite topic of his proclamation is the person of Jesus Christ. In his great synodal sermon before the clergy of his diocese on May 2, 1457 (Sermon CCLXXX), Nicholas offers a concise description of the chief task of ecclesiastical proclamation: *evangelizare Christum*, "to preach Christ as the good news." There he writes:

> Therefore, if Christ is known, then all things are known in Him. If Christ is possessed, then one possesses all things in Him. It is our task to preach Christ as the good news (*evangelizare Christum*) so that He may be known because salvation and life exist in His name or in knowing Him. Nor is there another name or knowledge other than the one which heals a nature endowed with understanding and living off knowledge. Whence Christ is the truth which is sought and recognized by every intellect. When one possesses this truth, then one possesses the final goal of every desire. The joy about every desired truth is eternal life.[8]

This passage summarizes *in nuce* several essential aspects of Cusan christology. Nicholas regarded as the central task of the preacher to develop the inner truth of what is sketched out programmatically in this statement. He himself made almost countless attempts, which are reflected in almost every sermon of the Brixen period. It is not a coincidence that Cusanus indicates in *De aequalitate* that he tried ever anew in his diverse sermons to explain the *summa evangelii*, the kernel or inner concept of the good news, which is Christ. In his own words:

> It came to me first vaguely as I began and was a deacon, then more clearly as I rose to the priesthood, and finally it appeared to become even more complete when I exercised the office of bishop in my church in Brixen and was active with my apostolic legation in Germany and elsewhere.[9]

Since it is impossible to discuss in one article every detail in this extensive body of literature concerning Cusanus' proclamation of Christ, I will limit myself in the first main part (I) to presenting the main themes of the Cusan image of Christ in the Brixen sermons and in the second main part (II) to laying out some general characteristics of his proclamation of Christ. In both sections I will make reference to selected examples, which—*pars pro toto*—are somewhat representative of Cusanus' thought according to my examination of the corpus of the Brixen sermons.

---

[8]Nikolaus von Kues, *Textauswahl in deutscher übersetzung,* 4: *Vom rechten Hören und Verkündigen des Wortes Gottes Sermo XLI [Prothema] und Sermo CCLXXX,* Hören Wolfgang Lentzen-Deis (Trier, 1993), p. 20; #7.

[9]Nikolaus von Kues, *Philosophisch-theologische Schriften,* ed. Leo Gabriel, 3 vols. (Wien, 1964-1967; reprint Wien, 1982), 3:416; Rudolf Haubst, *Streifzüge in die cusanische Theologie* (Münster, 1991), p. 302.

I

The question concerning the reason for God's incarnation (*Cur Deus homo?*) can be approached from several angles. The most comprehensive and foundational way to discuss it takes place when it is connected to the question about the reason for creation. This way of looking at the question, which considers the mystery of Christ from the viewpoint of a theology of creation and revelation, is of fundamental significance to the sermons of the Brixen period and can be demonstrated from numerous texts.

In response to the question of why God created the world, Nicholas answers in harmony with the tradition: God, the best creator, created the world with the best purpose, that is, He created it for His own sake and to communicate His own glory (*gloria*).[10] The purpose of creation is thus the *ostensio* or *manifestatio gloriae Dei*, the self-disclosure or self-manifestation of the Creator in creation. Nicholas sketched out this thought in many sermons. He develops it most intensively in Sermon CCIV, a sermon from September 29, 1455 on the feast day of the Archangel Michael, whose theme is *gloria Dei*. Nicholas accordingly names this sermon a *sermo ... primus omnium atque fundamentalis*, a sermon of absolutely primary and fundamental significance.[11] The "kingdom" of God's "glory," which Nicholas mentions often in connection with Romans 9:23 and Philippians 4:19, can in principle be grasped in creation only by rational creatures, but their capacity to recognize the divine archetype of creation is diminished. Therefore, the divine itself must enter into creation in order that God's glory becomes visible without limitation. This train of thought, which is developed in detail in Sermon CCIV, is summarized by Cusanus in Sermon CLIV from Palm Sunday 1454 as follows:

> God, who is the purest intellect, intended to communicate and announce His riches. Man is thereby the goal of creation since he possesses an intellect, which is capable of knowing whom God created so these matters could be understood. The more learned someone is, the more willing he will be to communicate his teaching. The more well-known the glory of the king, the more glorious is the king. An unknown king cannot be distinguished from a non-existent king (*ignotus rex non differt a non-rege*).[12] Man was not able to attract a God who is invisible to him; therefore, if one can see neither him nor his form or hear his voice (as Christ says in the fifth chapter of the gospel of John [5:37]), then the goal of creation is a man, who is the Son of God. The Son is the Son of the Father as the word of the [divine] intellect. The living word, since it is a concept of the intellect, proceeds from the

---

10Sermon CCIV, #5 (h XIX/1, 3-4). "Hic ergo est finis creationis, scilicet ostensio gloriae creatoris" (#6 [h XIX/1, 4]).

11#1 (h XIX/1, 1).

12Sermon CCIV, #5 (h XIX/1, 3).

intellect and knows (*scit*) whence it proceeds and recognizes (*cognoscit*) the intellect. Likewise, the word, which is hidden in the written work of a teacher, would know its Father and reveal Him with a living voice if it were alive like the intellect ... Should God not have created such a man, whose spirit was elevated to union with the divine spirit, God would have remained unknown. Therefore, every creature exists for the sake of such a man since He is the goal.[13]

The Son reveals the Father. This is made visible in the created order through the incarnation. Christ is, as Nicholas writes from time to time with lapidary brevity, the *ostensor Patris*[14] and also the *finis creaturae*, the purpose of the creature as well as the *perfectio creationis*, the completion of creation.[15] Without the man who is joined to the Creator in hypostatic union, the creation itself would be incomplete. Indeed, creation could not endure, for the purpose of creation is identical with the purpose of the incarnation of the Son. *Finis igitur creationis et incarnationis est gloria Dei Patris*, he states in Sermon CCLXXXIII, the sermon at the Vigil Mass of Corpus Christi 1457.[16]

The well-known idea of Christ as the point of unity of the universe, the medium and goal of creation, from the third book of *De docta ignorantia*[17] occupies a significant place in the Brixen sermons and is often presented by Cusanus with pregnant conciseness. It is not surprising that he admits in these sermons even without qualification the absolute primacy of Christ before creation and postulates that the incarnation of the Son is predetermined *ab aeterno* from the Father, for example in Sermon CCIII.[18]

The fact that Christ assumed human nature a long time after the creation of the world does not make his mediation of creation and ontological primacy questionable. "Jesus," as the cardinal formulates it in Sermon CLXXI, delivered on the feast of Epiphany 1455,

---

[13]Sermon CLIV, #21 (h XVIII/2, 165-166); Rudolf Haubst, *Die Christologie des Nikolaus von Kues* (Freiburg i. Br., 1956), p. 180; Pauli, "Die geistige Welt," p. 184.

[14]Sermon CCLVIII (Città del Vaticano, Biblioteca Apostolica Vaticana, Codex Vaticanus latinus 1245 [hereafter cited as V2], fol. 200rb); Sermon CCLXXX, #27 (Nikolaus von Kues, *Textauswahl in deutscher übersetzung*, 4.52).

[15]Sermon CXXIX, #7 (h XVIII/1, 41).

[16]Sermon CCLXXXIII (V2, fol. 270va).

[17]Haubst, *Die Christologie*, pp. 138-192.

[18]Sermon CCIII (V2, fol. 118ra): "Creavit autem Deus omnia propter se ipsum ad ostensionem gloriae suae. Ideo dicit Salomon, quod Dei sapientia delectatur esse cum filiis hominum, quia filii hominum sunt creati a Deo, ut sint capaces sapientiae, ut in Dei sapientia videant gloriam illius, qui omnia creavit tam sapienter et ordinate, et in causatis causam contemplentur. Et quoniam sapientia in se manens se transfert in animas sanctorum, tunc perfectissimum opus complere volens statuit ab aeterno in humanam naturam descendere."

is nothing more than the chamber of the whole building (of the world), in which as in a great palace the Son of the King rests,... The rational creature is the palace,... That chamber is the last one prepared even if everything exists for its sake. And the purpose of the chamber is the rest of the Word.[19]

Throughout these reflections it becomes clear that Nicholas understands the incarnation strictly speaking as, to employ an expression from contemporary theology, the self-communication of God, of the Father.[20] The incarnation of the Son is the inner notion of the divine revelation, to which in the end all divine proclamation (and the entire creation is God's proclamation) is oriented. The self-communication of the Father in the incarnated Son signifies that God does not simply make any old announcement in Christ, for example, certain commandments, prohibitions, information, or models for conduct. Rather God discloses in Him the divine life itself. Christ is, as Nicholas presents it in different sermons, the *Deus revelatus*, the revealer of the hidden Father. For example, in Sermon CCLX on the feast of the Lord's Circumcision (January 1, 1457), he writes: *Jesus igitur est apparitio absconditi Dei seu revelatio sive ostensio.*[21]

Because he is the infallible revealer of divine truth and the actual embodiment of divine wisdom, as Nicholas writes literally in Sermon CCX[22] and in a similar manner in numerous other sermons,[23] Christ is also the inner notion of true religion. He speaks about God not only like a prophet would, as a reality distant from and ultimately unfathomable to man, but as someone who knows him—to speak metaphorically—from the neighborhood, just as the Son knows the Father. He is not just a witness whose testimony we must believe. He is the presence of the divine itself in this world. In Sermon CCXVI, the highly speculative sermon from the feast of the Epiphany in 1456, Nicholas explains in broad strokes the unique significance of the person of the God-man for the concept of religion. There he treats religion as the path to the perfection and completion of human life:

---

[19]Sermon CLXXI (V2, fol. 66rb); Haubst, *Die Christologie*, p. 179; Rudolf Haubst, *Vom Sinn der Menschwerdung: "Cur Deus homo"* (München, 1969), p. 163.

[20]Karl Rahner, *Grundkurs des Glaubens: Einführung in den Begriff des Christentums* (Freiburg-Basel-Wien, 1976), pp. 122-132.

[21]Sermon CCLX (V2, fol. 204ra); Sermon CCXLVI (V2, fol. 181ra; see n. 29); Sermon CLXXI (V2, fol. 68rb).

[22]Sermon CCX, #4 (h XIX/1, 32).

[23]Sermon CXLIII, #2 (h XVIII/2, 100); Sermon CXLIV, #22 (h XVIII/2, 166); Sermon CCLVIII (V2, fol. 200ra); Sermon CCLXII (V2, fol. 209rb).

One must also include among the arts religion based upon divine authority and revelation [meant are the human gifts of discovery which are expressed in, among other things, the handicrafts, ed.]. Religion leads man to obedience before God through fear of Him and through love for Him and neighbor, in the hope of reaching friendship with God, the giver of life, so that we accrue a long and peaceful life in this world and a happy and divine one in the next. But in contrast to all forms of religion which deviated significantly from true life, the way to eternal life through Jesus, the Son of God, has been revealed to us. He has informed us about the heavenly life which the children of God possess. He also tells that we can attain divine childhood and the manner in which [it is to be pursued]. For just as the art of living rightly in this world is presented diversely by diversely-gifted people and just as this art is more complete the more clearly one has reflected upon it beforehand, so too is religion. Religion is presented in diverse ways when it touches upon eternal life and directs the present life to the future through prophets who foresaw a future life from a distance. Because all of them saw the future life only in a preliminary fashion, only the one who came into our nature from God or from the heavenly life which lies in our future could inform us completely about religion or the way to the heavenly life.[24]

Were religion to actually attain its goal, namely, establishing a binding relationship to God, then it must take its point of departure from God Himself. He must show Himself so that we see Him and can recognize Him. This speculative justification for a christological notion of religion makes sense in light of Cusan epistemology, whereby purely human knowledge of the absolute (and this even includes what the prophets[25] and great philosophers know) can never be more than *coniectura*, conjecture.[26] This obviously does not mean that the teachings of the prophets and philosophers are arbitrary and worthless, but they do not make it possible in the end to ground a secure binding relation. Religion promotes such a tie and only the God-man Jesus Christ can communicate it, for he is the one whom Cusanus identifies in Sermon CLXXI as *rex omnium religionum*[27] and in Sermon CCLXXVII as *rex religionis divinae*.[28]

---

[24]Sermon CCXVI, #13 (h XIX/1, 87-88).

[25]Sermon CLXXXIX (V2, fol. 95va-95vb): "Jesus vero est nuntius seu legatus Dei, in quo verbum Patris, in omnibus aliis nuntiis verbum de verbo Dei. Alii nuntii et prophetae locuti sunt quo modo audiverunt. Nam nemo eorum vidit Deum ut unigenitus revelavit, Jesus vero quo modo vidit."

[26]Sermon CCLIV (V2, fol. 194va).

[27]Sermon CLXXI (V2, fol. 68rb).

[28]Sermon CCLXXVII (V2, fol. 246rb).

***

The problem of religion marks the transition from the viewpoint of a theology of creation and revelation to the anthropological and soteriological dimension of the Cusan proclamation of Christ, which is theologically closely related to the first aspect of the mystery of Christ discussed above. Nicholas himself connected both facets with one another in different places in his Brixen sermons. For example, in Sermon CCXLVI from September 29, 1456 (Michaelmas Day), he writes:

> A face signifies knowledge. We recognize people through their faces. Seeing the face of the Father signifies for an intellectual nature understanding the source of its life or arriving at knowledge which he provides.... Nothing is sweeter and more delectable to an intellectual nature. But this seeing takes place through the showing of the Son of God. Only the Son knows the Father, and everyone else knows Him through the revelation of the Son. The Father lies in hiding, as the Son says. Therefore, the Word or the Son of God is the mediator to all minds endowed with reason. Through Him each one of them arrives at the goal of their desires or the final blessedness.[29]

Because He is the complete, pure image (*imago*) of the Father, the incarnated Son of God is the mediator of divine sonship (*filiatio Dei*) for those persons created according to the Genesis account (1:27 sec. Vulg.) *ad imaginem et similitudinem Dei*. In other words, man is created for the image of the Son and finds his perfection, ultimate happiness, by assimilating himself to Him. Nicholas discussed this connection in *De visione Dei*, the writing on mystical theology, which appeared in 1453 in Brixen.[30] The sermons preached that year yield similar results. In Sermon CCXLIX, delivered on the day before All Saints' Day in 1456, he developed this thought very beautifully. Drawing upon the request Jesus made to the Pharisees, "Show me the coin!" (Mt 22:19), Cusanus transfers the image of a coin in an allegorical manner to man and God:

> It is striking that our nature is the coin of God. We are what we are in accordance with the image of God and therefore the likeness (*similitudo*) of the Son of God, who is the image (*imago*) of the living God, receives within us the imprint of His being from God the Father, who formed us equal to the Son. And because we through sin are enslaved to the prince of this world, this image of ours became stained and was made unrecognizable by rust and

---

[29]Sermon CCXLVI (V2, fol. 181ra); also Sermon CCXI, #8 (h XIX/1, 43-44).

[30]*DVD*, XXV, #118 (h VI, 89): "Omnes autem alii spiritus intellectuales sunt illo spiritu mediante similitudines, et quanto perfectiores, tanto huic similiores. Et quiescunt omnes in illo spiritu, ut in ultimitate perfectionis imaginis dei, cuius imaginis assecuti sunt similitudinem et gradum aliquem perfectionis." See also Klaus Reinhardt, "Christus, die 'absolute Mitte,' als der Mittler zur Gotteskindschaft," MFCG 18 (1989): 196-220 at p. 207.

through the Son of God, the true image of God, is purified and renewed. He saves us and leads us out of the realm of enslavement to sin into His Kingdom so that we might be heirs of God and co-heirs with Him.[31]

Christ leads people back to divine sonship by liberating them from the context of entanglement provoked by the sins of the first parents. The objection that Nicholas overlooked the problematic of sin, which is raised again and again even among contemporary theologians,[32] is not supported by an examination of his sermons as bishop. It is in any case correct that sin is not the most important theme of his proclamation, but I do not believe that one must criticize Nicholas on this basis. Likewise, it is correct that Cusanus viewed the problematic of sin predominantly from the angle of the ignorance conditioned by sin. In Sermon CCLXXI from the Lenten season in 1457, Nicholas identifies *ignorantia originis*, i.e., the incapacity of man to understand his divine origin on his own, as the natural consequence of man's original sin. Since the loss of immediacy with God in paradise, the intellect is no longer able to recognize its primal origin on its own even though it is the image of God.[33] In another sermon the cardinal compares post-lapsarian man with a prince who lives among farmers, no longer has an inkling of his stature, and therefore pays no attention to what his Father the King, i.e., God, says.[34] The Son of God who became man, who remains unafflicted by sin, bestows liberation from this ignorance by revealing divine truth.[35]

In everything which Jesus did and taught, He gave testimony to the truth, as Cusanus states many times with reference to John 18:37. Nicholas also views Jesus' death on the cross from this angle. He sees Christ's offering of His own life as the ultimate proof for the credibility of His message of acting benevolently for the sake of others so that an unsurpassable expression of readiness to obey the will of the Father, i.e., obedience to the truth, is esteemed more valuable than one's own existence. In Sermon CLIV from Palm Sunday 1454, Cusanus similarly refers to the liberation from doubt concerning whether the spirit of error or the spirit of truth was in Jesus as the fruit of Jesus' death.[36] In Sermon CCLXXVIII from 1457 (the last Good Friday sermon which Cusanus delivered in Brixen), a fictitious dialogue takes place among the church of

---

[31]Sermon CCXLIX (V2, fol. 186vb); see also Sermon CCLI (V2, fol. 188ra-189rb).

[32]Albert Dahm, *Die Soteriologie des Nikolaus von Kues: Ihre Entwicklung von seinen frühen Predigten bis zum Jahr 1445* (Münster, 1997), pp. 2-6.

[33]Sermon CCLXXI (V2, fol. 227va).

[34]Sermon CLII, #2 (h XVIII/2, 145).

[35]Also Sermon CLXXXIII (V2, fol. 84va-84vb); John W. O'Malley, *Praise and Blame in Renaissance Rome: Rhetoric, Doctrine, and Reform in the Sacred Orators of the Papal Court, c. 1450-1521* (Durham, NC, 1979) pp. 97-142.

[36]Sermon CLIV, #10 (h XVIII/2, 162).

Brixen, the Virgin Mary, and the apostle and evangelist John in which the reasons for Jesus' death on the cross are given.[37] Nicholas has John the evangelist utter the following words:

> Because Christ intended to display every proof for love of God and of neighbor by His own example, He chose death even though He was innocent. He wanted to show how much He loved God by dying out of obedience to Him and how much He loved humanity by entering into death for the sake of our salvation. All divine mysteries are thus enfolded (*complicata*) in the crucifixion of the innocent Christ. God is to be loved by the whole power of the soul so that one judges everything, even life itself, as nothing when it comes to showing His glory. One must love the salvation of the soul of one's neighbor so much that one would think nothing of the most shameful temporal death for the sake of such a good. The death of the completely innocent Christ procured eternal life which is justifiably given to Him since He alone suffered death for the sake of love of God and neighbor, but not to cleanse Himself of sin since He had none in Him.... One should glorify the great goodness of the Father, who created man in order to show him His glory and who did not spare His Son but offered Him up for the liberation of man. The goodness of the Son should also be glorified since He committed himself to humanity by appearing as God's Son.[38]

***

In the above treatment of the Cusan understanding of the person of Christ as the revealer of the Father and the Savior of mankind, it was quite clear in more than one case that Cusanus accorded great significance to the humanity of Christ. This aspect of his image of Christ merits special attention because it represents a major theme in Cusan proclamation. For Nicholas, both sides of the dogmatic definition of the Council of Chalcedon, i.e., that Christ is true god and true man, serve as guiding principles of his christological thought, and he can be hardly reproached for neglecting the humanity of Christ, an objection which occurs with great frequency in the history of theology.[39]

Cusanus understands the expression "true man" from the statement of Chalcedon in the twofold sense of the phrase. Christ was an actual man; He did not possess only the appearance of a body. Christ is at the same time absolutely a human being. He is what a human being should be, in fact, the *true* human being. If each human being is created according to the image of God, then the

---

[37]Haubst, *Streifzüge*, pp. 416-429.

[38]Sermon CCLXXVIII (V2, fol. 248rb-248va); Walter Andreas Euler, "Does Cusanus have a Theology of the Cross?," *Journal of Religion* 80 (2000): 405-420 at pp. 412-416.

[39]Reinhardt, "Christus, die 'absolute Mitte'," pp. 210-211.

one who reached oneness with God must be labelled the complete man since He is *the* image of God who remains unrestrictedly open to God's fullness of life. This means that in Cusanus' understanding the most human man is at once the most divine man. Thus, Christ is identified in Holy Scripture as the Son of man because the human race in its completeness and purity is enfolded and summed up in Him. This conception is found as early as the first Brixen sermon from Good Friday 1452,[40] in which Christ is identified as *veritas hominis.*[41] Almost five years later in Sermon CCLXVII, Cusanus summarizes the thought as follows:

> I conclude that Christ is the man who designates man in an absolute sense, the man of men (*homo hominum*) as it were or the king of men. He is also the Son of man, as if in Him were contained the completeness and purity of human nature in the original state of this nature, in which everyone participates. Human nature in Christ attains [the status of] the first, the pure, and the complete, not only in the sense that a purer or more perfect man never was or will be, but also in the sense that one more perfect could not even exist. In Him the purity and completion of every possible man is enfolded (*complicatur*) so that He alone is the highest, and the sun in the kingdom or heaven of humanity, or the sole king.[42]

As the enfolding fullness of the human race and thereby also the prototype of every single human individual, Christ is at once the model for each person to imitate and the teacher of life as such. *Omnis Christi actio nostra est instructio* ("Every action of Christ serves for our instruction"), Cusanus repeats several times in the sermons of his period as bishop.[43] Because he is a complete man, Christ is also the inner notion of virtue, the *virtus virtutum*, viz., *virtus ipsa*,[44] even the perfection, *consummatio* in an absolute sense.[45] Nicholas never tires of finding new ways to show his audience the different aspects of the human "maximality" of Christ. The basic idea which spurred him on was later emphasized in the pastoral constitution of the Second Vatican Council, *Gaudium*

---

[40]Sermon CXXII, #13 (h XVIII/1, 8-9).

[41]Sermon CXXII, #2-9 (h XVIII/1, 2-6).

[42]Sermon CCLXVII (V2, fol. 219va-219vb).

[43]Sermon CLXIX (V2, fol. 64va); Sermon CCXXI, #3 (h XIX/2, 117); Sermon CCXLV (V2, fol. 179ra).

[44]Sermon CCI (V2, fol. 115rb); Sermon CCLXXX, #10 (Nikolaus von Kues, *Textauswahl in deutscher übersetzung,* 4.24-26); see also Haubst, *Die Christologie,* pp. 270-271; Albert Dahm, "Christus - 'Tugend der Tugenden'," MFCG 26 (2000): 187-202.

[45]Sermon CCXXVII, #6-10 (h XIX/2, 157-158).

et Spes, with equally simple and clear words: "Whoever follows Christ the perfect man will also become himself or herself more human."[46]

In Sermon CCLXXX, the great synodal sermon from 1457, Cusanus admonishes the clergy of his bishopric to proclaim Christ through the "door of humanity" (*ostium humanitatis*), for, to cite him literally:

> when we look upon what Christ accomplished as a man, we find in this man a divine excellence (*virtus divina*) which surpasses every man. On account of this, we believe in Him when He stated that He is Son of God and sent from the Father. In other words, He provided a very effective and certain evidence so that no one who employs reason can have doubts in this matter.[47]

In later passages of this sermon, whose theme is the "good shepherd," he adds:

> There is surely only one good shepherd, who is the wisdom of God the Father. He does not err and is man in such a way that out of his weakness he may discern how to send out to pasture those who are themselves weak.[48] ... As an example of His teaching, Christ presented us with His humanity so that we could take their orientation from Him and find a place to graze through word and example.[49]

II

After a necessarily detailed outline of the main theological themes of the Cusan image of Christ, we shall now discuss in a much shorter section some general characteristics of the proclamation of Christ in the Brixen sermons.

It is characteristic of Cusan theology in general and in particular for his christology that metaphysical speculation and faithfulness to the core assertions of Holy Scripture and church doctrine are connected with one another. This is especially true of his sermons. The necessity of a theandric revealer of the hidden God as well as a theandric mediator to men of divine sonship is demonstrated by Cusanus in one of two ways. Either he developed them speculatively and then checked against the Bible, or he took the scriptural passage from the daily mass as the point of departure of a speculative investigation and meditation.

The cardinal's image of Christ in this regard is taken primarily from the gospel of John, which conceives of the incarnate Son as *the* absolute revelation of the Father who lies beyond: "No one has ever seen God. Only the one who is God and who is at the Father's side has revealed Him," states John 1:18, for

---

46#41.

47Nikolaus von Kues, *Textauswahl in deutscher übersetzung*, 4.22, #8.

48Nikolaus von Kues, *Textauswahl in deutscher übersetzung*, 4.34, #16.

49Nikolaus von Kues, *Textauswahl in deutscher übersetzung*, 4.42, #21.

example. If one followed the original Greek text, then one could say that the Son interpreted the Father for us[50] and would thereby have recalled a key idea of Cusanus introduced above. Besides John, Nicholas also shows a preference for citing Paul, whose statement in Romans 9:28, *verbum abbreviatum faciet Dominus super terram* (cf. Is 10:23), is often applied to Christ as the "abbreviated Word" of the Father and becomes the point of departure for christological speculation.[51] In a short marginal notation to Sermon CCLXXX, it becomes clear that the cardinal treasures the Johannine and Pauline approach to Christ more than that of any other writing of the New Testament, but he also employs a theological harmonization of all revealed texts: "Consider carefully that Christ is knowledge, that is, knowing (*scientia*) or coming to know (*cognitio*) God, and you will be able to understand the gospel of John and Paul and others."[52]

***

The speculative and biblical orientation of the Cusan sermons recalls the christological proposals of his major philosophical and theological works, for example, *De docta ignorantia* III, *De pace fidei*, *De visione Dei*, and *Cribratio Alcorani*. To be sure, Cusanus does not present a different christology in the sermons than in the writings just named, as the main themes of his proclamation of Christ make clear, but the form of presentation is distinct.

In place of lengthy justifications we find shorter, often more concise, and from time to time even more intellectually convincing outlines, augmented by images, of which Nicholas in any case makes only cautious and sparse use, such as through references to the real world, the realm of experience of his listeners. When it came to the theological substance of his teaching, he made no concessions at all to his audience. Neither can the sermons be thought of as a haute vulgarisation or a merely primitive version of Cusan thinking, as one assumed for a long time without precise knowledge of their content. Rather, they must be taken seriously as original developments of his central ideas. There is another characteristic which follows from this. If considered both in terms of the level of education of his time, when many of the faithful were no doubt illiterate, and in terms of an average sermon in a church today, the proclamation of the cardinal was extremely demanding. In Sermon CCLXXIV, delivered on the feast of the Annunciation in 1457, Cusanus addressed head on the objection of which he had caught wind that his sermons were too difficult. In defense of his manner of preaching, he invoked explicitly the model of Jesus, whose encounter

---

[50]Heinrich Fries, *Fundamentaltheologie*, 2nd ed. (Graz-Wien-Köln, 1985) p. 263.

[51]For example, Sermon CLIV, #22 (h XVIII/2, 166); Sermon CCLVIII (V2, fol. 200ra); Haubst, *Die Christologie*, pp. 180-181.

[52]Nikolaus von Kues, *Textauswahl in deutscher übersetzung*, 4.54, #28.

with the Samaritan woman at Jacob's well (John 4) was depicted in the daily gospel reading:

> Some are in the habit of grumbling (*murmurare*) that I often preached to you simple people about lofty matters, just like here the apostles were astonished that Christ spoke to a woman about lofty matters. If everyone tried to pay attention to this poor, wretched woman (*muliercula*), who was a sinner and a Samaritan, and the only one to hear the highly mysterious and very profound things He revealed in such a fecund manner, then you would excuse me. For I speak to a great number of men and hope that there are some among them who understand more than that woman.[53]

Nicholas was aware that he made great demands upon his listeners, especially since he never tried to rope them in with the cheap effects and shrill public rhetoric which late medieval preachers were often wont to relish.[54] His efforts to deliver a reflective proclamation adequate to the existential meaning of faith is an expression of his obedience to Christ's will that he carried out in himself and that he preached to the faithful, as the office of bishop demanded of him. Likewise, he preached in the same Sermon CCLXXIV:

> All the apostles acted upon the will of Christ and nothing else because they were sent by Christ, as Christ was from God the Father. Likewise, we too who bear the burden of the episcopal office through life and serve in this position should make an effort to carry out Christ's will. As servants of Christ you too should carry out the will of Christ, which consists of being holy. The work of the bishop must be this: he makes you holy and purifies you through God's Word. Your work is to remain obedient and prepare to accept the purification.[55]

Evangelizare, "preaching the good news," is, as Nicholas writes in Sermon CLII, "the greatest and highest task of the preacher."[56] Such a proclamation means participating in the work of Christ and can only succeed through conformity to

---

[53]Sermon CCLXXIV, #3 (CT I, 2-5, p. 118).

[54]Pauli, "Die geistige Welt"; O'Malley, *Praise and Blame*, p. 97; Edmond Vansteenberghe, *Le cardinal Nicolas de Cues (1401-1464): L'action - la pensée* (Paris, 1920; reprint Frankfurt/M., 1963), p. 164: "On pourrait caractériser d'un mot la prédication de Nicolas de Cues, en disant qu'elle fut, avant tout, sincère et positive. Le 'docteur très chrétien', comme on l'a appelé, a moins cherché à détruire qu'à édifier. Il a prêché ce qu'il a aimé; et il a aimé par-dessus tout Dieu, tel qu'il s'est révélé à nous dans son Christ."

[55]CT I, 2-5, p. 144, #24.

[56]Sermon CLII, #9 (h XVIII/2, 148): "Maximum igitur et altissimum officium est evangelizare atque in hoc mundo christiforme et apostolicum."

Christ.[57] Therefore, the cardinal continues, all priests possess the authority to consecrate, but only the best priests, the ones more virtuous and in apostolic succession, i.e., the bishops, are permitted to preach.[58]

***

By way of conclusion let us recall Sermon CCLXXX in which Nicholas of Cusa orders his priests to preach Christ as the good news: "If Christ is known, everything will be known in Him. If one possesses Christ, then one possesses everything in Him."[59] Probably no one can say of himself that he has understood the mystery of the theandric person of Christ completely. Even Nicholas never made that claim. However, as a Christian, a philosopher, a theologian, and with particular intensity as a bishop commissioned with the proclamation of the good news, he strove unremittingly to grasp more and more profoundly this unique man in whom faith contends that God encounters us—and thereby to understand better his own human existence, the entire creation, and the nature of the absolute. In Him, Cusanus maintains, all destruction and division ends, for these represent in the end nothing other than the outflow of the division of creation and creator. Christ is, as Nicholas states in Sermon CCXII, the *pax pacificans seu uniens*, the peace-making and unifying peace,[60] by which everything which appears to the limited mind of man as gloomy and dark will become bright and enter into the shining light of divine truth.

---

[57]Wolfgang Lentzen-Deis, *Den Glauben Christi teilen: Theologie und Verkündigung bei Nikolaus von Kues* (Stuttgart-Berlin-Köln, 1991), pp. 154-155.

[58]Sermon CLII, #10 (h XVIII/2, 149).

[59]See n. 8.

[60]Sermon CCXII, #17 (h XIX, 1, 63); see also *Sermo* CCLXXIV (CT I, 2-5, p. 140).

MEISTER ECKHART IN NICHOLAS OF CUSA'S 1456 SERMON:
Ubi est qui natus est rex Iudeorum?

Clyde Lee Miller

I stumbled into this topic out of ignorance. I expected that Josef Koch's book, *Vier Predigten im Geiste Eckharts*,[1] would be a selection of Cusan sermons modeled after Eckhart's wondrous German sermons. But Koch had other purposes —he was concerned to show that Nicholas, though not directly influenced by Eckhart before the late 1440's, was definitely reading Eckhart by the early 1450's. So he picked four sermons where Cusanus took material directly from Eckhart's Latin treatises (not even Eckhart's Latin sermons!).[2]

Koch's effort was and is edifying, of course, for those tracing Nicholas' relation to or defense of Meister Eckhart. Yet the upshot is that this sermon of 1456 is definitely not "in the spirit of" Eckhart's German sermons, in the sense of Eckhart's literary style. But what Nicholas says accords with the teaching Eckhart propounded in his Latin commentaries on John's Prologue and on Genesis. Cusanus' sermon is *secundum mentem Magistri Eckardi* in substance and often repeats his words verbatim. His further explanations and proposals are particularly interesting as he expounds the Meister in Cusan fashion.

Ubi est qui natus est rex Judeorum? Following Eckhart's commentary on John 1:38, Nicholas indicates (#4) that this utterance of the magi from Matthew's gospel need not be taken as a question. Instead, it can be read as a statement or declaration, as if it said that the where or place of everything is God, the one born king of the Jews. Jesus is "'where' or 'place' in the absolute sense."[3] The next ten sections of the sermon expand on and interpret this idea.

---

[1]Josef Koch, *Vier Predigten im Geiste Eckharts* (Cusanus-Texte: Predigten 2/5; Heidelberg, 1937). When we read these four sermons, we have to sympathize with Nicholas' hapless listeners, who, I hope, quickly fell asleep until he was finished. Koch remarks that the first two of the four sermons undoubtedly have little to do with what Nicholas said in the pulpit.

[2]By 1959 Koch's own student, Herbert Wackerzapp, proved that Nicholas was reading Eckhart at least a decade earlier than Koch believed in 1937. See Herbert Wackerzapp, *Der Einfluss Meister Eckharts auf die ersten philosophischen Schriften des Nikolaus von Kues (1440-1450)* (Münster, 1962). I am grateful to Prof. Elizabeth Brient for her comments on my original presentation to the American Cusanus Society. Her recent assistance has helped me correct further blunders and oversights in what I originally wrote.

[3]All translations from Nicholas' Latin are my own. See below for my translation of the whole sermon. The Latin text is that of the Heidelberg critical edition, XIX/1, Sermo CCXVI; I give the Heidelberg section numbers in the text. A German version can be found in Koch, *Vier Predigten*, pp. 84-116; Koch's commentary is on pp. 173-184. See also Rudolf Haubst, "Nikolaus von Kues als Interpret und Verteidiger Meister Eckharts," in *Freiheit und Gelassenheit*, ed. Udo Kern (München and Mainz, 1980), pp. 75-96, esp. pp. 83-86 for this sermon; and Donald F. Duclow, "Nicholas of Cusa in the Margins of Meister Eckhart: Codex Cusanus 21," in *Nicholas of Cusa in Search of God and Wisdom*, ed. Gerald Christianson and Thomas M. Izbicki (Leiden, 1991), pp. 57-69.

Cusanus draws on Eckhart, Augustine and the Aristotelian tradition about things having a "natural place" where they tend and where they are at rest. He applies this to Christ's divinity by pointing out that everything that has being receives its being from God, the one Being who is the source and goal of every being. This means that God can count as the resting place of all things, though "beyond the mode [of speaking or thinking] of our feeble concept" (#4). What Cusanus means is that "place" here is used metaphorically to propose conjecturally rather than to describe literally God's relation to created beings. God is their source and their goal, and, properly speaking, creatures should be considered as somehow "in" or encompassed by God.

This is a familiar move in the Neoplatonic Christian tradition of Dionysius, Eriugena, Eckhart and Cusanus. In this "God's eye" view of created things, we are encouraged to speculate "principially," to think through participation from the viewpoint of the imparticipable principle rather than from that of its participants. As so frequently happens, Eckhart and Cusanus change our typical standpoint. They lead us to realize that we have not thought through the idea that God is related to all things as their "where" or *ubi* until we make sense out of this metaphor from God's perspective, as it were. From that putative viewpoint, God is not in all things; instead, all things are in God both as their ultimate resting place, their destiny, and as their present ontological location while they are temporal and spatial. Even in the sermon we find the traditional *caveat*: "In this way of speaking, however, one must always take care not to believe the terms are exact when we are speaking of the unspeakable" (#8). Being encompassed by the infinite God must ultimately stagger the human mind and tongue.

Nicholas moves out from this ontological beginning to find parallels and correspondences. As in his theoretical writings, he sees time as properly located within eternity, movement or motion only making sense in terms of rest, numbers really encompassed by and so located in the one, reasoning processes finding their proper place or rest in the truth. These examples—Being and beings, time and eternity, motion and rest, number and the one, reasoning processes and true judgment—are classic Cusan instances of *explicatio* and *complicatio*. That Cusan metaphorical couple, though only implicit in the sermon, is supposed to remind his readers and hearers that we cannot think unfolding apart from enfolding, creatures apart from creator. Enfolding and unfolding, thought together, provide the Cusan dialectical "dissimilar similarity" we require in order never to think creatures apart from God.

What Nicholas wrote in *De visione Dei* 11 is appropriate here: "*Cum te reperio virtutem complicantem pariter et explicantem, intro pariter et exeo*— when I discover you, the power which at once enfolds and unfolds, I go in and equally I go out [the door of your Word]." Creatures cannot be properly conceived in their own right without understanding that at each moment they represent the dynamic creative outflow from and the simultaneous return to the God who encompasses or enfolds them. That is why God is indeed the "location" of each thing in its "going in and going out."

But this may interpret the "where" of God in too narrowly philosophical terms. Cusanus' sermon proceeds to recall our religious status as pilgrims or wayfarers—our spiritual journey or way and its goal are the clearly the same, for "the unlimited way is called the place of the wayfarer and is God" (#9). This turns anyone familiar with the Christian gospels to the metaphors there associated with Christ or God as the way. Being on the way is also being in the way that is Jesus, and thus to be such a wayfarer is already to have arrived, for on this way movement is at once rest and homecoming. Jesus Christ is also door or gate or entry to this way that is truth and life, a way illuminated by his example and his grace, a divine life beyond created nature and thus a place of rest in a further sense. "Jesus is the place where every movement of nature and grace finds rest" (#14).

In these several observations and proposals, Cusanus has given us an extended philosophical and religious reading of what Eckhart wrote succinctly, commenting on John 1:38:

> God is properly the place and "where" of all things for three reasons. First, all things are restless outside their proper place. Second, individual things seek out and return to their proper place. Third, because they are protected in their proper place, there all things are safe and at rest. All three of these considerations properly befit God (#200).[4]

Nicholas' teaching in this sermon is thus a further explication of what Eckhart had written, remarkable not just because Nicholas turns to Eckhart's writings, but because he finds the way of thinking in those writings so congenial to his own ideas.

The next section of the sermon (#15-20) interprets the question in the gospel text as a question, though not about the location of the newly-born Christ child. Rather Nicholas says that he is taking *Ubi est*? as a question about where Jesus is "according to his divinity" (#15). In response, Cusanus again turns directly to Eckhart's *Commentary on John* 1:38, which he quotes or paraphrases through this part of the sermon.[5] We can, in fact, better see where God is not—not in any physical place, not in any privation or negation. Nicholas quotes one of Eckhart's favorite formulations, "proper to him and him alone is the negation of negation" (#16). This riddling phrase recalls what Eckhart says in his commentary on the book of Exodus:

> Everything that is less than God, since it is less than existence, is [both] being and nonbeing, and some kind of existence is denied to it since it is below and less than existence. And so negation is a part of it. But to existence itself no existence is denied, just as to the genus animal no particular animal, such as a lion, is denied. Therefore, no negation, nothing

---

[4]My translation is from Meister Eckhart, *Expositio Sancti Evangelii Secundum Johannem*, #300, in *Die lateinischen Werke*, ed. Karl Christ and Josef Koch, 5 vols. (Stuttgart, 1936) [hereafter LW], 3.168-169.

[5]Eckhart, *Exp. Johannem*, #206-209, LW 3.173-177.

negative, belongs to God, except for the negation of negation which is what the One signifies when expressed negatively (#74).[6]

Nicholas concludes by citing Eckhart's *Commentary on John* practically verbatim:

> *Unde Deus est in omnibus et in nullo. In quolibet enim est, ut ens est, in nullo vero, ut hoc ens est* (Therefore God is in everything and in no thing. For he is in each insofar as it is being, but in none insofar as it is *this* being) (#16).

Nicholas expounds this rather paradoxical formulation (which he repeats often in his dialogues and treatises[7]) by appealing to three further considerations, all of which derive from and exemplify Christian Neoplatonic thinking: 1. God is the form of forms giving form or being to all else; 2. God is the being of beings just as oneness is the being of every number; 3. God's being is to the being of creatures as the being of whiteness is to the being of white things. All three proposals are implications of the paradigmatic, nonreciprocal relation of images or participants to original or participated exemplar. All any reality Y has that renders it an image of X derives from the original X. Whatever Y is or has of reality apart from this dependent imaging is not due to X. Moreover, images have no reality as images and make no sense as images without their originals, while originals make perfect sense and stand on their own without being imaged. Therefore, both image and original have to be recognized and acknowledged if justice is to be done to the way things are. Take away the original and the image disappears; take away the image and the original continues undisturbed. That is the relation of whiteness to the white things that are its images. Oneness and the numbers are connected in the same way—no less are creaturely forms dependent on their independent divine maker, the form of forms.

Nicholas' summary of this matter is perfectly apt and quite eloquent in this sermon, recalling his similar proposals in *De docta ignorantia* 2.4 and *De possest:*

> I also think there is no difference between saying that all things which are, insofar as they are, exist in the being that God is, and saying that God who is being itself is in all things which exist insofar as they exist. For how could they exist if being itself were not in them? But the being, which is in all things that exist, is in each thing that exists without being restricted to this

---

6Meister Eckhart, *Expositio Libri Exodi* in *Die lateinischen Werke*, vol. 2, ed. Herbert Fischer, Josef Koch and Konrad Weiss (Stuttgart, 1954), p. 77. The translation is by Bernard McGinn in *Meister Eckhart, Teacher and Preacher*, ed. Bernard McGinn (New York, 1986), p. 68.

7For further references and a full account, see Klaus Kremer, "Gott—in allem alles, in nichts nichts. Bedeutung und Herkunft dieser Lehre bei Nikolaus von Kues," MFCG 17 (1986): 188-219.

or that, so that all things which are, are that which they are through it. . . . Thus it [being] is in everything and in nothing: in all things insofar as they exist, and in no one of them contractedly, insofar as it is this [being] (#19).

The thrust of this passage is to remind Cusanus' hearers that God and creatures must be thought together, but in a dialectical way that does not lose sight of either. Answering the question: "Where is God?" means discovering God in all things without restricting God to their finitude, while realizing that each and all of them *at the same time* exist most truly in God! That is why God is everywhere and nowhere while remaining the ultimate *locus omnium*. We have to realize that Eckhart's negation of negation requires a dialectical thinking of God and creatures, of encompassed and encompassing, of original and image without cancelling or omitting either.

What Nicholas does next (#21-25) is perhaps the most remarkable section of this sermon. Nicholas takes up the *quaestio vulgata,* "Where was God before He created heaven and earth?" At first glance this recalls Augustine's classic discussion in Book 11 of his *Confessions.* But as Nicholas proceeds it is clear, as Josef Koch noted over sixty years ago,[8] that he is responding to the charges made in the condemnation of Eckhart. Thus the first three articles in the Bull *In agro dominico* read as follows:

> The first article. When someone once asked him why God had not created the world earlier, he answered then, as he does now, that God could not have created the world earlier, because a thing cannot act before it exists, and as soon as God existed He created the world. The second article. Also, it can be granted that the world has existed from eternity. The third article. Also, in the one and the same time when God was, when he begot his coeternal Son as God equal to Himself in all things, He also created the world (McGinn translation).[9]

What had Eckhart himself written? One characteristic text occurs in his *Commentary on Genesis:*

> . . . the "beginning" in which "God created heaven and earth" is the first simple now of eternity. I say it is the very same now in which God exists from eternity, in which also the emanation of the divine Persons eternally is, was and will be. Moses said that God created heaven and earth in the very first beginning in which He himself exists, without any medium or time interval. So when someone once asked me why God had not created the world earlier, I answered that He could not because He did not exist. He did not exist before the world did. Furthermore, how could He have created earlier when He had already created the world in the very now in which He was God?

8Koch, *Vier Predigten,* pp. 50-53.

9*Meister Eckhart, the Essential Sermons, Commentaries, Treatises and Defense,* trans. Edmund Colledge and Bernard McGinn (New York, 1981), pp. 77-78.

It is false to picture God as if He were waiting around for some future moment in which to create the world. In the one and the same time in which He was God and in which He begot His coeternal Son as God equal to Himself in all things, He also created the world (#7).[10]

What Cusanus does in his own sermon explains further how to understand what Eckhart taught in a way that would make utterly good sense, though uncommon sense, and thus hardly be grounds for condemnation. The key to his explanation and to Eckhart's original passage is to recall that the grammar of temporality and creatures does not fit that of eternity and the Creator. Our language and thought and imagination need both a transformation and a kind of training in refusing the temptations posed by our ordinary ways of speaking. Eckhart (and Cusanus following him) sees creation from God's standpoint, not from a standpoint that can be given an earthly date and location. Our minds are most comfortable in moving around in time. We find it difficult enough to think from time to eternity. Worst of all, we simply are not accustomed to moving from eternity to time—to put our quandary spatially, we need to work, as it were, from outside in and this turns our normal habits of thought inside out!

Nicholas' first question is transitional (#21). He has discussed how God is the ultimate where or *ubi;* he has shown how God is that Being *cui nullum esse potest abesse* by explaining how God is everything and nothing. Now he considers a further *ubi* question: "Where was God before or prior to creating heaven and earth?" His tactic is to refuse the question since it embodies the mistaken presupposition that there is a time ("before") and place ("where") which can be specified for God—as if time and place were not co-created with heaven and earth. It is this false picture in the imagination evoked by the normal grammar of "where" and "before" that makes the question not just a "wifebeater" but worse—confused and confusing. Of course, one can interpret the "before" as an ontological, not a temporal priority, but then the question needs changing to something like: "In what sense is God prior to God's creation?" Of course, one can turn "where" into what is meant by God's metaphorical place or God's relation to all else that is; but Nicholas has already discussed these possibilities in this sermon.

So Nicholas proceeds to consider Eckhart's dramatic way of refusing the question, one which the bull condemning him (*In agro dominico*) notes he never retracted: "Where was God before creating?" Eckhart replies: God did not exist —*non fuit!* Nicholas notes that this answer refuses the question by proposing an answer which embodies its false assumption, namely that God's existence is to be understood in some sort of hyper-time where we imagine God (to quote Eckhart again) "as if He were waiting around for some future moment in which to create the world." In this imagined hyper-time *fuit* refers to a hyper-past. Eckhart denies that God had that hyper-past—*non fuit!*

---

[10]Meister Eckhart, *Expositio Libri Genesis,* in *Die lateinischen Werke*, vol. 1, ed. Konrad Weiss (Stuttgart, 1936), p.189; *Essential Sermons*, p. 85.

Cusanus explains more tactfully that Eckhart's response was not *absona responsio* because of the implication in the initial question that there was a time before time was created in which God would be placed if "He did exist" were taken as tensed expression. Cusanus compares it to another *fatua quaestio:* "Where was eternity when time did not exist?" This query is silly or foolish "because it implies the contradiction that eternity is not eternity since it is temporal" (#21).

Nicholas proceeds (#22) to educate our misleading tongues and ears and errant imaginations by tossing five other questions into the same trash bin where God is imagined as operating in some sort of hyper-time and hyper-place. Here are the questions: "What did God do before the creation of the world? Why did God not create before He created the world?" (Both are queries Augustine had rejected centuries before.) Did not God exist before the world? Why did God not create time beforehand or earlier? Where was God before the world? In all these cases Cusanus points out, the questioner is committed to two assumptions: first, *extra esse est esse:* being exists outside of being; second, *extra Deum est increatus locus [et tempus],* outside of God there exists uncreated place [and time]. On this basis the questions are to be rejected.

Nicholas takes up (#23) another point mentioned in the bull condemning Eckhart, namely, the proposal that the world has existed from eternity. Here he considers various ways of construing that proposal. One might consider the God's eye view in which God's eternal existence encompasses all creaturely existence. Then, of course, it will be true that both world and God exist in that "now" which is eternity. "From eternity" does not measure the extent of created time but places the causal beginning of the world in the atemporal now that is God or eternity itself. It is worth emphasizing that the eternal now is not the instantaneous now we understand in temporal terms as the current point in time or instant dividing past from future. Rather, the now of eternity is the point-source or ontological present or presence from which flows out or emanates all that is created into a kind of radial fullness, the unfolding and unfolded whole. We need to rework the Cusan spatial metaphor of God as center and circumference of the created universe in temporal terms so that we do not think God's eternity is merely timeless absence. Rather, it is the boiling life of the Trinity Eckhart described so dramatically. As Nicholas puts it: "the temporal world exists and always was from eternity, that is, from God." The issue is one of the world's source, not of its duration. Even if we focus on the words "always was," this expression simply means there is no time apart from the world, let alone that the world had some other source—time is coextensive with the created being of the world. Eckhart himself had this in mind when he wrote (in the passage already quoted) "the 'beginning' in which 'God created heaven and earth' is the first simple now of eternity."

On the other hand the notion that the world existed from eternity can be misconstrued to mean the world is itself eternal—that it is "atemporal and without an origin." Here the misunderstanding is based on the mistaken idea that "what is temporal and originated (*temporale et principiatum*) is not such. If Cusanus first explained how to avoid a temporal interpretation of "from eternity," which might reduce God to creaturely conditions, here he is working to cut off mistaking what is temporal and created from what is divine and eternal. In both cases, the temptation is to short-cut the differences between God and creatures by either placing God in hyper-time or taking creatures out of time altogether. But God's eternal now is not a moment in hyper-time; and "from eternity" does not describe or refer to some relatively endless, quasi-eternal stretch of creaturely duration in the fashion of such biblical and liturgical expressions as "forever and ever" or "world without end." To say it again, the expression "from eternity" is not temporal at all, as are such common phrases as "from the founding of the country," "from the discovery of America," "from time immemorial."

Once again the challenge is to keep time temporal and created and to keep eternity atemporal and uncreated, yet not to lose sight of the connection between them. The latter point leads Nicholas to state: "Between eternal being and temporal being no time-period falls or intervenes. This is the same as saying: nothing mediates between the being of God and the being of the world" (#23). In the Neoplatonic tradition that established this sort of thinking about time and eternity, we know that time and eternity make one topic, not two—they are bound together, no less than the ultimate divine source and all that emanates from and returns to it.[11] For Plotinus, for instance, eternity and time are two manifestations of one life, each bound up with the other like mirror-image and original.[12] Eternity stands as the intensification or enfolding of the order or *ratio* or intelligibility that unfolds in time and this means that God's presence touches temporal duration in such a way that the latter is never eternity, but neither is it nothing but time.

Nicholas rounds off his considerations by taking up three final questions associated with the charges against Eckhart and his defense: (1) "How is it said by the wise that the temporal world always existed?;" (2) "If the world always existed, why is it said that it is not yet seven thousand years since it began?;" (3) "Was God able to create the world earlier?" Rather than rehearse the answers in his sermon, it is worth noticing how he adverts to the fact that all these questions are based on misleading images. Moreover, what is misleading is that each image involves our entertaining a picture which involves some quantity or extension, while the greatness of God is beyond the sort of quantification with which human imagination ineluctably must operate. We can always imagine a greater quantity or extent—more than seven thousand years, earlier than a given point on a time-line. But such imaginings are merely that—misleading picture-thinking—when it comes to understanding eternity over against time, let alone infinite creative power or capacity as opposed to created capacities, however great. Nicholas recalls for us that "imagination does not get beyond quantity"—

---

11 I am indebted to conversations with Peter Manchester for these ideas. See his "The Religious Experience of Time and Eternity," in *Classical Mediterranean Spirituality*, ed. A.H. Armstrong (New York, 1986), pp. 384-407; and his "Time and the Soul in Plotinus III.7 [45]," *Dionysius* 11 (1978): 101-136.

12 Plotinus, *Enneads* 3.7. See also Andrew Smith, "Eternity and Time," in *The Cambridge Companion to Plotinus*, ed. L.P. Gerson (Cambridge, 1996), pp.196-216.

imaginationem non exire quantitatem and this should warn us that our imaginings about time and its extent or duration will be inadequate to eternity.[13]

It may seem ironic to hear these warnings against misleading imaginative pictures from the man who insisted in *De docta ignorantia* that we should fruitfully use imagination on geometrical diagrams by extrapolating, then transforming and transcending their quantitative aspects. Perhaps we should distinguish speculative imagination from ordinary picture-thinking. When it comes to Cusan speculation and conjecture, I would judge that it is precisely our speculative capacities of imagination and thought to transcend any quantitative limit that become crucial when we are considering God or eternity. To eliminate false imaginings and misleading pictures is not to give up on imagination, but to eschew picture-thinking. If we are to discard the quantitative or extensional constraints intrinsic to human imagining and human language, we are not to forget what extrapolation or transcending comes to in human thinking. We are to think time and eternity together as a dialectical whole; but, if we cannot transcend our own temporality as finite creatures, we have no dialectical whole to think. It will always remain true that God remains *supra modum conceptus nostri infirmi* (#4); but both Eckhart and Cusanus press us to use every resource of thought and imagination, of metaphor and language to work towards a better answer to the question the text of this sermon raises: *Ubi est qui natus est rex Iudeorum?*

Let me end with some proposals for comparing Eckhart and Cusanus. I do not believe this sermon, or indeed any of the four Koch edited and translated, are really comparable to what we experience upon reading Eckhart's German sermons. They are more comparable to many of Eckhart's Latin sermons and treatises and even more comparable to sections of Cusanus' own writings. This particular sermon affords us a fascinating explanation and justification by a Roman cardinal of misunderstood teachings for which Meister Eckhart had been officially, though unjustly, condemned. It is the ease and obviousness of Cusanus' reading that stand out, even while he does not mention explicitly the controversy about Eckart's teaching on which he is drawing. One might wish Meister Eckhart had had readers of such sympathy and understanding during his own lifetime.

Be that as it may, where the two thinkers' minds are at one should be clear from what I have already said. They both employ a kind of dialectical Neoplatonism that allows them to think from God to creature or from creatures to God without either distorting or separating the two. This is finally, in my estimate, because neither was afraid to push reason and imagination, to conjecture beyond the settled teachings and usual formulas and formulations, beyond the conventional wisdom and scholastic truisms that they both knew had to be discarded to capture the Christian truth beyond all telling. Nicholas knew the excesses to which too great a separation or too great an identification of God and creatures could lead. But, like Eckhart, he rethinks the balanced picture we

---

[13]For a brief summary of Nicholas' thought on time and eternity, see Hans G. Senger, "Die Zeit und Ewigkeitverständnis bei Nikolaus von Kues im Hinblick auf die Auferstehung der Toten," MFCG 23 (1996): 139-164, esp. pp. 140-142.

find in the *Summae* of high Scholasticism. We have to imagine, think and live in the faith and understanding that God and creatures, no less than eternity and time, are inseparable.

Nicholas of Cusa could think through a traditional text of Scripture or a name for God and come up with startling insights which even now challenge our own images and conceptions of the divine. That is why I will end by quoting from Nicholas' sermon the list of scriptural citations he cribbed from Eckhart[14] about where God is to be found or at least sought. I believe that this can be read as a kind of source list for some favorite Cusan metaphors explored in his other writings:

> Returning, then, let us say: "Where is God or where does He dwell?" For in this question to be and to dwell coincide in God. Or rather God is said to dwell in the highest places, "I dwell in the highest places" (Sir 24:7). He dwells in heaven as the psalmist says: "To you who dwell in heaven have I lifted up my eyes" (Ps 122:1); and in the midst: "He dwells in the midst of them" (Ex 25:8). He dwells in the mist or darkness: "Moses went to the dark cloud wherein God was"(Ex 20:21). He dwells in the holy places, according to the psalmist, "But you dwell in the holy place, the praise of Israel"(Ps 21:4). "He inhabits light inaccessible" (1 Tim 6:16) (#26).

14Eckhart, *Exp. Johannem*, #209, LW 3.176-177.

APPENDIX

NICHOLAS OF CUSA'S SERMON
FOR THE FEAST OF EPIPHANY, 1456

Translated by Clyde Lee Miller

Ubi est qui natus est rex Iudaeorum? Where is he that is born king of the Jews?

1. Beyond what I have written about this feast in other sermons, when I was preaching on this day in various places, I would now like to add an explanation of its theme.

The wise men had no doubts that the king of the Jews was born, but they made inquiries where he might be. That nation had the king of kings "who dwells in heaven" (Ps 2:4) in place of a king. He ruled the Jewish people through Moses and the prophets. Then He who was speaking to the people through the prophets said: "Here I am" (Is 58:9). And "He was seen upon the earth and conversed [with men]" (Bar 3:38), just as He had predicted that He would come. And so the magi, [realizing] from the star that the one who was to come was now born, without hesitation asked where He was.

2. Some who treat of religious sects say that these events could have been foreseen from the important and rare conjunctions of the planets, especially of Saturn and Jupiter. Among the religions, they call the Christian group which deals with occult wisdom that of Mercury. For it is possible that the conjunction signifying a sect take place in the house or natural constellation of a planet. Accordingly, religions arise so that one is the religion of Saturn, another of Venus. For they say the Jewish religion belongs to Saturn, the Arabic to Venus and the Christian to Mercury, etc. [They say] the magi could have foreseen from the direction of the great conjunction that the king and leader of a religion was born and in what region, but not exactly in what town or in what house. Thus Messahala writes that the elders had observed that at the first appearance of Virgo a virgin would appear nursing a son whom the nations would adore. And, according to them, these astrologers came to see Him on earth with their own eyes, since they had already seen His constellation in the east from where they had come.

3. Yet we should not bother with these conjectures, but notice that the magi were led by a visible sign that went before them in the form of a star. In that sign they were made certain that He was born. From Him [comes] all wisdom; He is to be sought out, recognized, and adored by all the wise men of this world.

4. The words of our theme which must now be expounded, can first be understood "dispositively" in accord with Meister Eckhart's *Commentary on*

John,[15] so that it may be said that the King of the Jews, who is born, is "where" or "place" in the absolute sense. It is just as if the wise had said: "The king who is born is God who is the place of all things." For thus all the wise saw that God is place. For all things are at rest in their place and outside that place all are restless, because they are not where they seek to be. Just as Solomon saw that all rivers return "to the place from which they go out" (Ecl 1:7), so all things return to the place from which they have gone out.

All things, however, insofar as they exist, are from being (*essentia*), just as white things are from whiteness, good things from goodness and true things from truth. So the being from which all things which exist have proceeded is the place which all things seek. For, from the fact that all things are restless outside their proper place and that all seek and return to their proper place and that everything is protected and secured and at rest in its proper place, it follows that God is not unfittingly said to be place—only not in the way in which the meaning of the word is understood, but beyond the mode of our feeble concept. In this way, in the Apocalypse John says the Word of God has said: "I am the Alpha and the Omega, the beginning and the end" (Apoc 1:8, 22:13). But "end," "rest," and "good" are the same.

In many places the psalmist acknowledges that God is the place of the soul, as do Augustine throughout the discourse of his *Confessions* and others, too.

But, because God exists, from whom all things receive their being—because He calls to Himself the things that do not exist so they may be, yet because it is being to which all things are called in order to exist, and outside of being they are restless (for things that do not exist desire only to be where they are at rest)—therefore being, the source of everything which exists, is the goal, place and rest of all things. Just so, we see how all the things which are made by art or nature thereupon come to rest in being. For, when a house is brought into being by art, it stands and rests unchangeably. If it needs to be colored or painted, even though as a house it stays unchanged, it is still changed to be that which it lacks, namely colored. Once it has this it rests, and every preceding change ceases.

5. Attend to the fact that the place of time is eternity or the now or the present, and the place of movement is rest, and the place of number is oneness, and so on. For what being appears in time except the present? For time flows and its flow is only from being to being. This being is the present or the now. It is said that of time we possess only the now; and there are not many nows, but only one. For the now does not pass into the past, nor can now be said of the future. The now, therefore, from which and to which all time flows is the essence or being of time. We name it today or eternity or now because it always stands without moving. Therefore the now of eternity is eternity itself or being itself, in which exists the being of time. And it is the eternal God who is His eternity. For we call eternity the origin and goal of being itself, and likewise the place of time.

---

[15]LW 3.168-186.

6. I believe that when we look at movement we find no being in motion except rest. For every moving thing moves from rest to rest just as time moves from now to now. Nor are there many rests around which motion takes place, just as there are not many nows. Rest is therefore the stable essence of motion. And so everything that is moved is moved from being at rest to being at rest. However, this stable and eternal being of motion is rest, which is God. Anyone who pays attention to the coincidence of source and goal, and to the fact that in the absolute limit the terminus from which and the terminus to which coincide, sees the truth of this matter.

7. Matters stand thus regarding number. For number proceeds from one to one, and no other being of number is found except the one. Nor are there many "ones," but there is one "one." Oneness, therefore, which is also entity or essence, is one. It is the source and goal and place of all beings or of every countable number. Therefore, God, as He is the essence of countable beings, is said to be entity or oneness or one God, who is His own oneness.

8. Thus reasoning is the movement of the rational spirit from truth to truth. There is but one truth and God is called truth because [God is] rest or the place of reason's rational processes or intellectual discourses.

   Conceptualize similarly other matters and you will discover in the variety of terms nothing but the same God, the place and rest of everything, who is the source that coincides with the goal of all creatures. In these ways of speaking, however, one must always take care not to believe the terms are exact, since we are speaking of the unspeakable.

9. Now Paul said that we exist and move in God, for we are wayfarers. But a "wayfarer" is named and is a wayfarer from "way." Therefore a wayfarer who walks or moves on an unlimited way, if asked where he is, is said to be "on the way." If some one asks where he moves, the answer is "on the way." If someone asks from where he moves, one says "from the way." If someone asks where he is heading, one says "from the way to the way." And in that manner the unlimited way is called the place of the wayfarer and is God.

   Hence the way, outside of which no wayfarer can be found is the Being without beginning or end from whom the wayfarer exists and possesses all that makes him a wayfarer. But the fact that a wayfarer begins to be a wayfarer on the way adds nothing to the unlimited way and causes no change in the perpetual and unchangeable way.

10. Therefore notice how the Word of God calls Himself the way. You can understand this because a really living intellect is a wayfarer on the way or in the Word of life. From that way he exists and is called a wayfarer and on it he moves. For if to move is to live, then the way of movement is life. Thus it is the living way of the living wayfarer. A living wayfarer possesses from the living way that which makes him a living wayfarer, and the living way is his place, and he moves along it and from it, through it, to it. Therefore, the Son of God rightly calls Himself the way and the life.

11. Now notice that this way which is life is also truth. For the living wayfarer is a rational spirit and takes living delight in its own movement; for it knows where it is tending. For it knows that it is on the way of life. But this way is truth. For truth is the most delightful and undying food of its life. For the living wayfarer is fed by Him from whom He has being.

Therefore, the living way that is also truth is the Word of God who is also God and is the light of men walking on the way. For the one who walks needs no other light lest he walk in darkness as does someone who knows not where he is going. But the way that is life and truth is also the light that illuminates; and that light is alive, because it is the light of life making itself manifest.

12. Now everyone has one entrance into this world, but not all men live in an equal way. For even though men are born naked, like the other animals, still they are clothed by men's art of weaving so they may live in a better state. They use cooked foods and shelter and horses and many such things which art has added to nature for better living. We possess these arts as a great service and gift or favor from their inventors.

And so, when many live wretchedly and in sadness and in prisons and suffer much, but others lead lives of abundance joyfully and nobly, we rightly infer that a human being can, with some favor or art, attain more of a peaceful and joyful life than nature grants. Many have discovered the various arts of living better by their own talent or with divine illumination, as those who discovered the mechanical arts and the arts of sowing and planting and doing business. And others have gone further, as those who wrote the rules of political life and of economic activity, and those who discovered the ethical life of habituating oneself through mores and customs even to the point of taking delight in a virtuous life and thus of governing oneself in peace. Nonetheless, all these arts do not serve the spirit but hand on conjectures how, in this world, a virtuous life worthy of praise can be led with peace and calm.

13. Thereupon religion based on divine authority and revelation is added to these arts. It prepares a person to obey God out of fear of Him and from love of Him and one's neighbor. Our hope is to attain the friendship of God, the giver of life, so that we may attain a long and peaceful life in this world and a joyful and divine life in the world to come. Nonetheless, among all the ways of religion which fall too short of true life, a way to eternal life has been revealed to us through Jesus, the Son of God. He taught us what the heavenly life is that the sons of God possess and that we can reach divine sonship and how to do so.

Just as the art of living well in this world has been handed over in different ways by different talented men and is more perfect when drawn from clearer reasoning, so too religion, which looks toward future life and orders the present to the future, has been propounded in different ways by prophets, who foresaw the future from a distance. Since no one sees the future life except in a conjecture, for this reason He alone who came into our nature from God, that is, from the heavenly life that is our future, could perfectly hand over religion or the way to that life. This is our Jesus, who came from heaven so that we might have life and might live more abundantly through Him than through nature. He is the one who "began to do and teach" (Acts 1:1) how this might be accomplished and said: "He who follows me walks not in darkness, but shall have the light of life" (Jn 8:12). He was, therefore, the way of attaining grace, the one who was also the way of nature.

14. Therefore, Jesus is the place where every movement of nature and grace finds rest. The word of Christ or His teaching and His command or the paradigm of His behavior is the way to vision or the obtaining of eternal life which is the life of God who alone is immortal. It is a more abundant life than the life of a created nature. Therefore, no one can reach on his own the way of grace that leads to the Father, but must proceed to that way through the gate.

Christ, however, says that He is the gate that is also the way. A Christian, that is, one who is faithful with a faith acting through love, has gone in through the gate and is on the way. The gate is faith; the way is love. So the formed faith in Christ is equally gate and way. Therefore, the Word of God the Father calls [creatures] from non-being to being and finally to the sort of being that lives with intellectual life because it understands that it exists. However, the Word made flesh calls this intellectual being through grace to fellowship with Him so that he might taste in the paternal font the sweetness of His own divine life which is shared with the sons of God.

15. We may understand the words: "Where is He who is born?" in another way, as a question, so that the wise men sought the boy king in order to adore Him as God and to see Him as man. So we may ask first: "Where is He, namely God become man, where according to His divinity?" And, first of all, we know that God is the one whose "greatness has no end" (Ps 144:3) and that, as Solomon says (2 Kings 8:27), "the heavens of heavens cannot contain Him," He is therefore not to be located in any place.

16. However, since we wish to track down where He is, we may note first, according to Meister Eckhart, [16] that we can see better where He is not. We may say that He is not in anything "that includes defect, deformity, evil, privation or negation." For these expressions take away and deny that anything exists, even though they also posit that something exists besides what they take away or deny. They posit that God is Himself that full being from whose fullness all the things that exist receive so they may be. For God is being itself, apart from whom no being can exist, just as nothing white can be apart from or lacking in whiteness.

"And so God is not some part of the universe" but "prior to and above the universe." For the being of the other parts is lacking to any part of the universe. Therefore, "no negation or privation fits" God, "but proper to Him and to Him alone is the negation of negation. This is the marrow and apex of the purest affirmation, according to the line in Ex 3:14, "I am who am," but neither can He deny Himself, according to 2 Tim 2:13. However, He would deny that He is

---

[16]LW 3.173.

being itself, if something were lacking to Him or He were lacking to something. Therefore God is in every thing and in no thing. For He is in each insofar as it is being, but in none insofar as it is this being.

17. I think this is nothing else than that God is, as it were, the form of forms, the absolute form or essence, which gives being to forms. Thus Moses calls Him the one who formed heaven and earth. For God is not heaven or earth or anything of this sort. For the heaven has its proper form which gives it heavenly being and this form has being from the form of forms. Thus God who forms everything is the essence giving being to all forms and they give being this or that. But God is not able to be the form of heaven, which is constituted by the differences of heaven from what is not heaven. Therefore, being is not present to the form thus constituted through differences and did not constitute it. But no being is lacking to the absolute essence that is God.

Therefore, God is the being of every being, just as the being of oneness is the being of every number. But as oneness is neither two nor three, so God is neither heaven nor earth. Oneness is the source and term of two. For two finds its limit in oneness; and, if oneness is taken away, two ceases to be. So God is the beginning and end of all things, namely, the end that has no end, that is, the infinite end.

18. If, therefore, God does not exist except in being, then Meister Eckhart[17] says that He is not in time, or in division, or in the continuum, or quantity, or in anything which has more or less or in what is distinct or in any created thing insofar as it is this or that or in anything proper to something, even though He is in all things insofar as they are beings. Just so, whiteness is in all (white) things insofar as they are white and whiteness is not in them insofar as they are temporal or quantified or distinct or this or that, namely sticks, stones and so on. For God is "He who is" and "being" is His name, and He is that being which everything desires.

19. I also think there is no difference between saying that all things that are, insofar as they are, exist in the being that God is and saying that God who is being itself is in all things that exist insofar as they exist. For how could they exist if being itself were not in them? But the being, which is in all things that exist, is in each thing that exists without being restricted to this or that, so that all things which are, are that which they are through it. For if being itself were in the sky in a contracted way, namely in the sky as sky, it would not be in the earth. And how could the earth exist without being? Thus it is in everything and in nothing: in all things insofar as they exist and in no one of them contractedly, insofar as it is this [being].

The sky, however, is this and not that because it is not absolute being, but contracted and limited. For if it were uncontracted and unlimited, infinite, it would no more be this than that, but would enfold the being of everything

17LW 3.174.

equally as the power of being all things which exist or can exist. God is everywhere and nowhere, as Augustine [18] said of Truth in *De vera religione*. He is everywhere, namely, in every place, but not in a localized or contracted way. But while He is in every place, He remains independent of every place because He exists in every place in a non-localized way.

20. For He exists in the being of a place since the being of the place is in Him and He is not in the place although He is not apart from the being of the place, just as, so to speak, the being of the hand exists in the being of all the fingers. For all the fingers take up their being from the fullness of the hand's being and unless the being of the fingers was in the being of the hand, they would not exist. For a finger separated from the being of the hand is not a finger. The hand is not a finger but the being of the finger has being from the being of the hand. Therefore, the being of the hand is not in a finger as finger or in the thumb as thumb or in the index finger as index finger. For if the being of the hand were in the thumb as thumb, the index finger would not exist from the being of the hand. For the being of the hand would not enfold the being of all the fingers if it were contracted to the thumb. And so in order that the being of the hand can provide being to all the fingers, it is not limited to any one of them. From this example of the being of the hand, you can help yourself by going beyond it to the being of the universe, and from that to the cause of its being. It is just as if you moved from the being of the hand to its cause, namely the intellect, you would see that it is the source and goal of the hand.

21. You can help yourself in many ways with this likeness as regards the common question, which asks: "Where was God before or prior to creating heaven and earth?" The question has a false assumption, namely that "where" or place existed when it did not and that time existed before it did. For since time and place do not exist before creation or before heaven and earth, the question has a false assumption.
   Therefore, if one were to answer the question "Where was God before He created heaven and earth?" by saying that He did not exist, one would mean that if He had existed, He would have existed in time, for "He did exist" refers to some time which did not yet exist. "He did not exist" would hardly be an absurd response. For it is similar to asking: "Where was eternity when time did not exist?" It is a silly question because it implies the contradiction that eternity is not eternity since it is temporal. For, if eternity had been somewhere, it would have been in place and time, which do not comprise the immense and eternal and which did not exist before heaven and earth.

22. Thus to the question: "What did God do before the creation of the world?" (a question Augustine [19] treats in Book 11 of the *Confessions* as well as the question: "Why did God not create before creating the world?"), one can respond

---

18CCSL 32.227.

19CCSL 27.200-203.

that the question has a false assumption, namely that there was a "before" when
the world did not exist. For without time "before" does not exist, since before
and after are temporal distinctions. And because there was no "before," He,
therefore, did not create before He created.

If one says: "Did not God exist before the world?," one answers: "If 'before'
is a difference of time, the question implies a contradiction." So too the
question: "Why did God not create time beforehand?" presupposes a real
contradiction, namely that time existed and did not exist. Thus, if someone were
to ask: "Where was God before the world?," this has a false assumption, namely
that being exists outside being and that there exists an uncreated place outside of
God.

23. Even if someone were to say: "Did the world exist, then, from eternity?,"
one can respond in one way, that God and world have existed in the same now of
eternity. For the world did not begin in some other now of eternity but in the
same one in which God is. For that now is without origin and goal and is God.

And one can say that because God is eternity itself, just as from eternity time
exists, so also the temporal world exists and always was from eternity, that is
from God. And it always was, that is, for all time. Indeed, it was never true to
say that it was not. For in all the time when it could be said that the world did
not exist, then it did exist. And the "did exist" is from eternity; but it is not
eternal, because it is time. It is false imagining [to think] that some period
intervenes between the now of eternity from which time flows and time itself,
because for a time-period to exist without time implies a contradiction. Between
eternal being and temporal being no time-period falls or intervenes. This is the
same as saying: nothing mediates between the being of God and the being of the
world. If you consider it correctly, the question whether the world existed from
eternity implies a contradiction, for it presupposes that what is temporal and
originated can be atemporal and without an origin.

24. You might say: "The temporal world is not eternal, even though it issues
from the eternal." How then is it said by the wise that it always existed? One
may answer: Because "always" is understood as "for all time." You might say:
"Did time, therefore, always exist?" I answer: "Yes." For this is to say nothing
else than that time existed for all time or that time was always time.

You might say: "If the world always existed, why is it said that it is not yet
seven thousand years since it began?" One may answer that "always" is not
eternal and not without quantity, because it is not without time and its measure
is said to be taken by so many revolutions of the sun.

You might say: "I imagine that more years have existed." I say that
imagination does not get beyond quantity, nor can there be a quantity than which
no greater could be imagined. But, just as imagination errs when the vault of
heaven is imagined as extension, namely thus, that one sitting over the vault
could extend his arm [beyond], in the same way I call it false imagining when
someone imagines that the universe could be larger. For one thinks that there
could be some intermediate [magnitude] between the magnitude of God that has
no limit and the limited magnitude of the world, and that is false.

In the same way I say it is false imagining by which you imagine that there is a time before "always" and that before time there was motion, which cannot exist except in time. Therefore, the prophet who spoke of a determinate amount of time from the past made clear to us that the imagined picture of time exceeding that extent is mistaken.

25. You might ask: "Was God able to create the world earlier?" I say your question implies a contradiction, just as the others you proposed, namely, that before creation a creature could exist. Therefore, just as any quantity you wish does not exhaust unlimited magnitude, so neither does time exhaust eternity. Therefore, God's infinite and eternal power that can do what he wishes is not correctly conceived when such a question is formulated. For the question presupposes that an omnipotent being cannot do all that He wishes and that God is not God. Hence the prophet answered the question correctly: "As He wished, so has He done" (Jon 1:14), and in prayer we acknowledge that His will be done in heaven and on earth. Therefore, you may respond thus: "Had he wished it, He could have done it."

Thus, if one continuously asks: "Why did He not earlier will to create?," you will say that the question implies a contradiction. For it presupposes that free will is not free. Therefore, there is no other response except this: "The will of God is free and His liberty answers in place of a reason."

Regarding these questions see Book XI of Augustine's *Confessions*.[20] They should be set aside, because they are not constructive.

26. Returning, then, let us say: "Where is God or where does He dwell?" For in this question, to be and to dwell coincide in God. Or rather God is said to dwell in the highest places: "I dwell in the highest places"(Sir 24:7). He dwells in heaven, as the psalmist says: "To you who dwell in heaven have I lifted up my eyes" (Ps 122.1); and in the midst, "He dwells in the midst of them" (Ex 25.8). He dwells in the mist or darkness, "Moses went to the dark cloud wherein God was" (Ex 20:21). He dwells in the holy places, according to the psalmist: "But you dwell in the holy place, the praise of Israel"(Ps 21:4). "He inhabits light inaccessible" (1 Tim 6.16).

27. "Where is He who is born king of the Jews?" Let us speak now of its moral sense. From what has been said we may draw an answer. For graced being imitates natural being to which it is added and which it further adorns, just as art imitates nature as much as it can. First, God does not exist in time. Therefore, those who embrace temporal and passing things, as though the God whom all things desire were in them, are deceived. Thus both everything divided in itself and everything continuous, whether corporeal extension or an image that does not escape the limits of quantity, and anything inhering in them (all of which admit of more or less), do not possess God who is infinite and free from all the limitations of these things. But one who desires to reach God must seek Him

---

[20]See above n. 5.

"in the heights or highest places, in heaven, in the midst, in what is secret, namely in darkness and mist." And one must become holy and separated from earth and earthly affection, holy and a son of Israel—one who dwells in the light by rejecting the works of darkness.

28. Tuscanello[21] speaks to this point in a sermon for this feast whose theme is what we mentioned earlier, namely, that each bodily creature, since it is finite, has a place in which it is kept safe, as a plant in the ground, a rose on a thorn-bush, fish in water, birds in air. But a spiritual creature does not exist in place because it is neither restricted nor kept safe by a place—understand this refers to bodily location. Even if there were not a corporeal universe, a spiritual creature could still exist. Eternal beings, such as the Father, Son and Holy Spirit, do not exist in place but encompass and embrace all places because, just as a thing in place is kept safe by the place, so place is kept safe by God.

29. But God is said to be in place on account of some of the effects that He brings about there. Thus He is in the world for the training of wayfarers, in hell for the punishment of the damned, in heaven for the joy of the blessed, and in the soul for the consolation of His friends. Hence He is said to be in the world. What is originated cannot exist without its source. The branch does not bring forth fruit without the root. A bodily member has no movement without the power of the heart. The bright heavenly bodies do not give light without the sun. In this way no creature can act without God. "Without me," says God's Son: "you can do nothing" (Jn 15:5). And John says: "Without Him was made nothing" (Jn 1:3). In this way, then, to give efficacy to the actions of creatures, is He said to be in the world. "He was in the world and the world was made by him" (Jn 1:10).

30. He is in hell for the punishment of the damned, but one who acts from divine power is not afflicted by the fire. For it is the instrument of His justice as judge and there is no aptitude for suffering from that fire in anyone unless he is guilty, just as the servants of a judge have power only over malefactors. So the fire of hell only acts against sin, and the punishment corresponds to the offense. In any offense there are three fires: the passion of sin to which corresponds the fire, the stench of sin to which the brimstone corresponds, and the disorder to which corresponds the storm of punishment. The psalmist speaks of these three: "Fire and brimstone and storms of winds, and so on" (Ps 10:7).

31. In heaven there is always the joy of the blessed, and unless they saw God through His essence, they would not possess the glory of blessedness. So all their happiness consists in vision. St. Peter says that the angels desire to look

---

21The Heidelberg edition (h 19.1.95) refers to a manuscript copy of a sermon by Aldobrandinus de Tuscanella on the text *Ubi est qui natus est rex Iudaeorum* in Cod. Seminarii maioris Brixiensis R 1 fol. 26vb-28ra.

upon Him (1 Pt 1:12). And of this joy Christ says: "And your joy no man shall take from you" (Jn 16:22).

32. Likewise, God is in the soul for the solace of His friends. For even though friends stand together in a kind of equality, nonetheless the Son of God, who was exalted in His majesty, emptied and humbled Himself and became lowly in His humanity (Phil 2.6-7). Wherefore He says, "I will not now call you servants but friends" (Jn 15.15). But friends associate with one another. Thus the Son of God associates with us both by dwelling in the flesh and by bringing peace of mind. And His "conversation has no bitterness" "nor tediousness, but joy and gladness" (Wis 8:16).

MEISTER ECKHART AND NICHOLAS OF CUSA ON THE "WHERE" OF GOD

Elizabeth Brient

Cusanus "Translating" Eckhart

In 1937 Josef Koch edited and commented on four sermons by Nicholas of Cusa from the years 1453-1457, *Vier Predigten im Geiste Eckharts*, in which Cusanus makes explicit use of Meister Eckhart.[1] It was Koch's thesis at the time that the earliest influence of Meister Eckhart on Nicholas of Cusa dated to Cusanus' acquisition of his Eckhart manuscript (Codex Cusanus 21), which was written in 1444, four years after the composition of *De docta ignorantia* (1440). He saw evidence for this position in the fact that Cusanus interprets and defends Eckhartian ideas in these four sermons by way of "translating" Eckhart's thoughts into the language of *De docta ignorantia*. Koch reasoned that, since Cusanus felt the need to translate Eckhart's thoughts in these sermons into his own conceptual language, the language of *De docta ignorantia*, then that implied that *De docta ignorantia* was not itself written under the influence of Eckhart. Koch later changed his view; and his doctoral student, Herbert Wackerzapp, was able to demonstrate that, on the contrary, Cusanus was already well acquainted with Eckhart before 1444 and that Eckhart's influence was already at work in the composition of *De docta ignorantia*.[2]

While Koch's initial dating of the beginning of Eckhart's influence on Cusanus was mistaken, his analysis of the four sermons as "translations" of Eckhartian ideas into the language and conceptual framework of *De docta ignorantia* is still very much to the point. In this article I will examine one of these four sermons, *Ubi est qui natus est rex Iudaeorum?* (1456),[3] and raise the question: to what extent is this sermon indeed conceived "in the spirit" of Meister Eckhart?[4] That is to say, I will ask the question: to what extent does

---

[1]Nicholas of Cusa, *Vier Predigten im Geiste Eckharts*, ed. Josef Koch (Cusanus-Texte I, Sitzungsberichte der Heidelberger Akademie der Wissenschaften; Heidelberg, 1937).

[2]Wackerzapp's thesis was revised and expanded and published as *Der Einfluss Meister Eckharts auf die ersten philosophischen Schriften des Nikolaus von Kues, 1440-1450* (Münster, 1962). See also Josef Koch, "Nikolaus von Kues und Meister Eckhart," *Mitteilungen und Forschungsbeiträge der Cusanus-Gesellschaft* 4 (1964): 164-173; Rudolf Haubst, "Nikolaus von Kues als Interpret und Verteidiger Meister Eckharts," in *Freiheit und Gelassenheit: Meister Eckhart heute*, ed. Udo Kern (München and Mainz, 1980), pp. 75-96; and Donald F. Duclow, "Nicholas of Cusa in the Margins of Meister Eckhart: Codex Cusanus 21," in *Nicholas of Cusa in Search of God and Wisdom*, ed. Gerald Christianson and Thomas M. Izbicki (Leiden, 1991), pp. 57-69.

[3]Nicholas of Cusa, Sermo CCXVI (h XIX/1, 82-96).

[4]Clyde Lee Miller asked this question when he presented an earlier version of his paper on Cusanus' 1456 Sermon, included in this volume, at the Sixth Biennial

this process of "translation" result in a faithful rendering of the Eckhartian ideas and to what extent does it represent a departure from Eckhart? There is no question that this sermon makes extensive and detailed use of Eckhart's *Commentary on John* 1:38 (*Ubi habitas?*).[5] Indeed, Cusanus' sermon is itself a very close and careful reading of that text. Throughout his own sermon, Cusanus directly quotes from and paraphrases Eckhart's discussion, and elaborates on Eckhart's meaning by situating it within the conceptual framework of *De docta ignorantia*. Cusanus even devotes a sizable piece of his sermon (nn. 21-25) to a defense of Eckhart's views on the eternity of creation, views which had been condemned in the papal Bull *In argo dominico*.[6] In this sense, then, there is no doubt that Cusanus wrote, and intended to write, his sermon "in the spirit" of Eckhart. I will argue, however, that if we compare Eckhart's commentary with Cusanus' sermon, we will see a significant difference in emphasis, tone, and trajectory. While Cusanus' appropriation of the content and substance of Eckhart's ideas is indeed faithful, his incorporation of those ideas into the intellectual landscape of *De docta ignorantia* shifts their contextual meaning in significant new directions.

Since Clyde Lee Miller has provided a translation and a commentary on Cusanus' *Ubi* sermon, both of which are included in this volume, I will confine my own remarks on Cusanus' sermon to an analysis of the shift in tone and trajectory between the Eckhart and Cusanus texts. In order to effectively make this contrast I will begin by providing an overview of Eckhart's *Commentary on John* 1:38, being sure to highlight in particular the passages Cusanus himself commented on in the marginalia of his own copy of Eckhart's text.[7] I will then turn to Cusanus' sermon and focus on the shifts in Cusanus' text as seen against this backdrop.

Gettysburg Conference on the works of Nicholas of Cusa in 1996. My own remarks, here, are an elaboration on the response I gave to his paper at that time.

5The critical edition of the works of Meister Eckhart is *Die deutschen und lateinishen Werke* (Stuttgart and Berlin, 1936-); the Latin works will be cited as LW and the German as DW. Eckhart's *Commentary on John* 1:38 appears in LW 3 (*Expositio sancti Evangelii secundum Johannem*), ed. Karl Christ, Bruno Decker, Josef Koch, Heribert Fischer, Loris Sturlese, and Albert Zimmermann (Stuttgart and Berlin, 1936-1989), pp. 168-186, nn. 199-222.

6The first three of the condemned articles are expressions of Eckhart's teaching on the eternity of creation. The first and third are drawn from Eckhart's *Commentary on Genesis* (n. 7) and the second from his *Commentary on John* (n. 216). For a text of the condemnation see M.-H. Laurent, "Autour du procès de Maître Eckhart: Les documents des Archives Vaticanes," *Divus Thomas* Ser. 3, 13 (1936): 435-446.

7For a very helpful discussion of Cusanus' marginalia to his Eckhart manuscript in general see Duclow, "Nicholas of Cusa and Meister Eckhart," pp. 57-69.

Meister Eckhart on the "Where" of God: Ubi habitas?

Eckhart begins his *Commentary on John* 1:38 (*Ubi habitas?*, "Teacher, where are you staying?" or "Teacher, where are you dwelling?") by remarking that the text can also be read, with a different intonation, as a statement: "'Teacher you inhabit the where,' as if he wanted to say: you are the where (*ubi*) and the place (*locum*) of all things."[8] Indeed, Eckhart points out, this insight can be brought to the reading of several similar passages. For example, the question of the Psalmist (42:3), "Where is your God?" can be read as a statement with the emphasis on the "where": "*Where* is your God," that is to say, "God *is* your where." Similarly the question posed by the wise men seeking the newborn king in Matthew 2:2 ("Where is he who is born?") reveals a deeper meaning if read as the statement, "*Where* is he who is born," as if to say, "He who is born according to the flesh, is 'the where' according to his divinity."[9]

Eckhart goes on to argue that God is the where or the place of all things for three reasons: 1) all things are restless outside their (proper) place, 2) all things strive to return to their (proper) place, and 3) in their proper place all things find shelter and peace. Eckhart is clearly drawing here on the Aristotelian conception of natural place and motion, and goes on to apply this physical principle metaphorically to the relationship between God and the soul.[10] He begins by citing various authorities in order to illustrate these three points and focuses in particular on Augustine who in his *Confessions* had so vividly described God as the place of the soul, outside of which it is perpetually restless. Indeed, the soul is driven by a natural longing to return to God and rest in God.[11]

Eckhart goes further, however, and insists that God must be understood not only as the place of the soul but, quite in general, as the place of *all* things. He goes on to give an argument for this general claim which Cusanus noted with interest in his own copy of the text.[12] First, Eckhart says, God is Himself the being (*esse*) and principle or origin (*principium*) of all things. They all receive being, insofar as they are, from him immediately; for there is no medium between being (*esse*) and a being as such (*ens ut ens*).[13] Further, being is that outside of which all beings are restless; it is that which they all seek, and it is

---

[8]*Comm. Jn.,* n. 199, p. 168.

[9]*Comm. Jn.,* n. 199, 6-7, p. 168. Eckhart refers, here, to his discussion in the prologue to his second commentary on Genesis, concerning the multiplicity of literal readings of scripture (LW 1, Par. Gen, n.2).

[10]See for example, Aristotle's *Physics*, IV.4, 210b34-211a6; and *On the Heavens* IV.3, 510a20-23.33.

[11]Augustine, *Confessions* 1.1.1 and 10.40.65.

[12]Nicholas of Cusa in marg. C: "rationem ponit probantem deum locum omnium, quia est esse omnium in quo quiescit omne ens."

[13]*Comm. Jn.,* n. 205, 12-14, p. 172.

also sought by whatever is not in order that it may come to be. And again it is that in which all individual beings (come to) rest.

This can be seen to be true, Eckhart goes on to explain, of all beings in nature and in art. All things in motion move and strive from not-being to being, striving to realize some potential for being. Once a thing in motion attains being it rests unmoving insofar as it has achieved being. He goes on to give an example, noted with interest by Cusanus,[14] of the building of a house.[15] Once the house is complete and possesses its being as a house, the building process comes to an end and the house rests in its being as a house. No further process of becoming, no further transformation, generation or change can aim at its becoming a house. It can, of course, change in other ways. It can, for example, be painted. The painting process aims at transforming something lacking color into something possessing color. But once the house becomes colored, once it has achieved *this* being, i.e. being colored, then the teleological transformation comes to an end, and again the house, now as colored house, rests in its being *as* a colored house.

Since God is the being of all beings, Eckhart argues, He is the teleological end of all their motion, the goal of all particular beings, and can thus be understood as the "natural place" toward which all things strive and in which all things come to rest.

The next section of Eckhart's exposition considers the phrase, "Where do you [God] dwell?" as we would normally read it, namely, as a question. In seeking to answer the question of where God dwells and can be found, Eckhart says, it is best to begin by clarifying where God is *not,* and only then turn to the question of where God *is.* In the spirit of apophatic theology Eckhart insists that:

> This is proper to God, that our understanding of what and where God is not, is truer than our understanding of what and where God is.[16]

Eckhart goes on to list seven things in which God is not to be found. God is not in time, not in division, not in anything continuous or quantitative. God is nowhere where there is a more or a less. God is not in anything that is distinct or in any creature insofar as it is this or that, or in anything proper to something.

Eckhart then goes on to explain, as Cusanus noted in the margin of his copy of the text, "how it is that God is in everything and nevertheless in nothing"[17]:

---

[14]Nicholas of Cusa in marg. C: "exemplum."

[15]See also Aristotle, who gives this example of the process of the building of a house as the actuality of the potentially buildable in *Physics* III.1 201b 7-11.

[16]*Comm. Jn.,* n. 206, p. 173.

[17]Nicholas of Cusa in marg. C: "quomodo deus in omnibus et tamen in nullo."

Indeed, God is in each being insofar as that being is, but in none insofar as it is this being; indeed God is in all beings insofar as those beings are, but outside of all and in none of them insofar as they taste of those things mentioned above: time, division, continuous quantity, the more or less (also of degree), distinction, this and that, characteristic property (*proprium*), and in short generally: [God is] not in anything that includes defect, deformity, evil, privation or negation.[18]

This is because there is no limitation or negation in God, and all these terms signify a deprivation or a negation of some particular being: "even though they also posit some other being besides the being which they negate."[19] That is to say, all these particular and limited ways of being are particular and limited, because they lack the fullness of the being which is denied them insofar as they are this and *not* that, exist now and *not* then, etc. Each entity is only a part of the totality of all beings and is what it is precisely because it is *not* what all the others are. Only God has, or rather is, perfect fullness of being (*esse plenum*), lacking nothing.

Hence God is not a part of the totality of all beings. He "is not a part of the whole, but outside, or better, prior to and above the whole."[20] God is not a being among beings, but rather the source of their being. Insofar as they exist at all, creatures participate and share in God's being, but His perfect fullness of being is received by no particular entity, and each particular entity is *this* particular through the negation or privation of its being. But there is no privation or negation in God:

Moreover, the negation of negation is proper to Him and to Him alone, [and the negation of negation] is the marrow and apex of the purest affirmation, according to the line in Exodus 3: "I am who am," as I explained thoroughly in my commentary on Exodus.[21] But [according to] Timothy 2: "He can not

---

18*Comm. Jn.*, n. 206, 4-10, p. 174.

19*Comm. Jn.*, n. 207, 11-12, p. 174.

20*Comm. Jn.*, n. 207, 3-4, p. 175. Cusanus elaborates on this passage in Sermo CCXVI, n. 16 by adding: "For the being of a part of the whole lacks the other parts" (h XIX/1, 89).

21See LW 2, *Expositio libri Exodi*, n. 16 and LW 2, *Expositio Libri Sapientiae*, n. 147-148. See also *Expositio Libri Sapientiae*, n. 148: "The term 'one' signifies Existence [esse] Itself in itself along with the negation and exclusion of all nonbeing, which [nonbeing], I say, every negation entails. Every negation denies the existence of a thing whose very existence bespeaks privation. The negation of negation (which the term 'one' signifies) denotes that everything which belongs to the term is present in the signified and everything which is opposed to it is absent. This is necessarily the One. It is impossible for any being or nature to be multiplied unless something of its nature is either lacking to a second being or there is something added to the second being from another source, or both together, that is,

deny Himself."[22] However, He would deny that He Himself exists, if
something were lacking to Him or He were lacking to something.[23]

Indeed it is precisely because God is infinite fullness of being, lacking nothing,
that He both transcends all creatures and is immanent in them. He transcends all
limited, distinct beings by virtue of His absolute indistinction. Each creature
exists as a distinct this or that through negation. In contrast, God, as the
negation of negation, is the utterly "in-distinct." At the same time, however, it
is by that very indistinction that God is immanent in all things as the source of
their being.[24]
Eckhart continues in a similar vein to show how what has been said of God's
fullness of being, God's absolute indistinction, can also be said of God as
absolute unity. For "God is One" (Gn. 3:20) and in the One there is no more or
less, no this and that, no distinction, and so on.[25]   The One "is the negation of
negation" because it negates division, number and multiplicity.
From this Eckhart draws a moral lesson. It is precisely those people who
scatter themselves in the multiplicity of created things in whom God does *not*
dwell:

> For insofar as someone understands and loves temporal things, insofar as he
> is divided in himself, insofar as he is attached to continuous quantity and
> corporeal imagination, insofar as there is a more or less for him, God does
> not dwell in him. . . . Thus it is clear that those who love what is proper to
> them, what is theirs (Phil. 2:21), further those who do evil and love
> creatures, in which there is privation, this and that and multiplicity, such
> people are those in whom God does not dwell.[26]

---

there is both lack and addition." Translated in *Meister Eckhart: Teacher and Preacher*,
ed. Bernard McGinn et al. (New York, 1986), pp. 167-168 (hereafter TP).

[22] Tim 2:13.

[23]*Comm. Jn.,* n. 207, 5-9, p. 175.

[24]See LW 2, *Expositio Libri Sapientiae*, n. 154-155. On Eckhart's dialectic of
identity and difference, see Bernard McGinn, "Meister Eckhart on God as Absolute
Unity," in *Neoplatonism and Christian Thought*, ed. D.J. O'Meara (Albany, 1982),
pp. 132-134. See also Donald F. Duclow's discussion in "Nicholas of Cusa and
Meister Eckhart," pp. 67-68. Duclow notes that, "Cusanus recalls this Eckhartian
dialectic when he includes 'indistinct distinction' among the *Apologia's* paradoxical
descriptions of God" (p. 67). See *Apologia doctae ignorantiae*, p. 49 (h II, 10); and in
a Trinitarian context, p. 58 (h II, 24).

[25]See LW 4:263-270 for Eckhart's Sermo XXIX on "God is one."   For a
discussion of Cusanus' keen interest in this Sermon, see Duclow, "Nicholas of Cusa
and Meister Eckhart," pp. 62-64. See also LW 2:481-494, for his commentary on Ws
7:27a, "And since it is one, it can do all things."

[26]*Comm. Jn.,* n. 208, pp. 175-176; and n. 208, 5-7, p. 176.

It is our love of and attachment to the particular as such that keeps us far from God.[27] Here we recognize the familiar Eckhartian theme of detachment and self-negation: we must be completely emptied of self and all things if we are to be filled with God. Perfect loving and knowing is no more or less than the love and knowledge of God Himself. It is quite literally God's loving and knowing which is at the same time His simple unity of being. Radical negation of self and all particular being makes "divinization" possible.[28]

Having concluded his discussion of where and in whom God does not dwell, Eckhart turns to a brief consideration of where and in whom God *does* dwell. He first cites scripture and authorities in giving a list of eight "places" in which God dwells: in the heights, in heaven, in the midst, in darkness or in a cloud, in the holy places, in inaccessible light, and finally everywhere and nowhere.[29] This is followed immediately by the moral admonition:

> Hence you should also be in the heights, in the highest heights, in heaven, in the midst, namely in your most inner [being], in the dark and in the cloud. . . . You should be holy, separated from earth, that is separated from earthly affection.[30]

And just as God is everywhere and nowhere, Eckhart writes:

> So also you should nowhere fix earthly affection, you should be in the same spirit everywhere, then God dwells in you.[31]

Eckhart goes on to give a telling illustration from Hugh of St. Victor: he who is attached to his homeland is weak; he who is at home everywhere is strong; but

---

[27]In his *Commentary on Exodus*, Chapter 16, verse 18 Eckhart writes in a similar vein: "There is no 'greater' or 'less' in God nor in the One; they are below and outside God and the One. And thus someone who sees, seeks, and loves what is more or less is not as such divine" (LW 2, n. 91, p. 94, TP p. 75).

[28]See, for example, Predigt 40 (DW 2:278) where Eckhart cites Augustine's teaching that a soul becomes like what it loves, and becomes God in loving God. On divine knowing see, for example, *Von dem Edeln Menschen* (DW 5:116) and Predigt 3: "Because the soul has the potentiality of knowing all things, it never rests until it comes to the first image where all things are one. There it rests, there in God. . . . [God] is a pure abiding within himself, where there is no this or that; for whatever is in God *is* God" (DW 1:55; TP, p. 246).

[29]See Ps 112:5, Eccli 24:7, Ps 122:1, Ex 25:8, 3 Kg 8:12, Ex 20:21, Ps 21:4, 1 Tim 6:16, Jer 23:24, Wis 7:24. On God as everywhere and nowhere, Eckhart cites Augustine's *De vera religione* c. 32 n. 60, PL 34, 149; and Gregory's *Hom. in evang. II hom.* 28 n.1, PL 76.1211. See also Peter Lombard, *Sent.* I d. 37 c.5 n. 344.

[30]*Comm. Jn.*, n. 209, 4-5 & 7-8, p. 177.

[31]*Comm. Jn.*, n. 210, 1-2, p. 178.

only he, to whom the whole world is foreign, is perfect.[32] Eckhart elaborates by adding that the first person has fixed his love on the world, the second person scattered his love around, and the third person has extinguished it. The hierarchy, here, is striking insofar as Eckhart does not equate the person who is at home everywhere with the person who is at home nowhere. Indeed, someone who is at home everywhere and loves all worldly things alike and without distinction is morally laudable. Such a person has overcome the moral weakness of loving someone or something in particular, of a love which shows partiality. Nevertheless, the person who is at home nowhere, who has extinguished love for the world *as such* is superior. Such a person can be present everywhere as a "foreigner," that is, perfectly detached, at home nowhere but, as we shall see, in God himself.

Having now explained how God is present in the world (in what sense everywhere and in what sense nowhere) Eckhart reiterates the question: "Where does God dwell?" He is still unsatisfied with the answers given so far. This is because the most proper answer to the question, as already intimated above, is not that God dwells in creation, but rather, that God dwells in Himself. Hence, Eckhart concludes his commentary with a consideration of God as He is "in Himself," insofar as He is metaphysically *prior* to creation. When we use our imagination in trying to think about God in Himself "prior" to creation, however, we are apt to fall prey to a number of erroneous assumptions. Eckhart aims at combating these false assumptions by a careful consideration of three (misguided) questions: 1) Where did God dwell before the creation?; 2) What was He doing at that time?; 3) What was His life like and how blessed was it before there were any creatures to serve Him?

In answer to the first question: "Where did God dwell before the creation?", Eckhart gives the Augustinian answer: the question is based on a false assumption, namely that there was a time "before" God created time. The world always "was," because time and world are co-extensive. Hence there was no time in which the world was not or during which the world was not yet. "The world was from eternity,"[33] Eckhart writes, and:

> God could not have made it earlier. Because God made the world in the first now of eternity, in which God Himself is and in which He is God.[34]

It is false to imagine some interval of time, some duration, between the now of eternity in which God is and the creation of the world and time. Time flows out

---

[32]*Comm. Jn.,* n. 211, 3-5, p. 178. See *Didascalicon* III c. 20, PL 176:778.

[33]*Comm. Jn.,* n. 216, p. 181. Eckhart's doctrine of the eternity of creation, here, was condemned in the Papal Bull, *In agro dominico*. Cusanus wrote "cave" next to the condemned proposition in his copy of the Eckhart text. But Eckhart is giving a defensible reading of Augustine, whom he cites in support of his position; see *Confessions* 11.10-13.

[34]*Comm. Jn.,* n. 216, 7-9, p. 181.

of eternity immediately, without interruption. This question is also misguided because it imagines that creation is something "outside" of or next to (*extra*) God, which gets added alongside God "after" creation, as though God and creation were two distinct entities. But God is not a being among beings. He is rather the Being of beings, and nothing at all *is* outside of Being.

From what has already been said, we can easily see the erroneous assumption behind the second question: "What was God doing before creation?" Again, there was no "before," no time, when the world was not yet. And if there is no time before creation, then we cannot ask what God was doing "then." Eckhart cites Augustine at length here in order to make this point and to clarify the distinction between time and eternity. There is no future or past in eternity, in which nothing passes away but all is present at once. God does not precede time and the world *in* time but "in the eminence of ever-present eternity."[35]

Again, from what has already been said, the answer to the third question: "What was God's life like before there were any creatures to serve Him?" is clear, for there was no time in which there was no creature. This question is also erroneous because it implies that God was somehow better off or more blessed after having made creatures to serve Him. This is false. The cause, which is superior, receives nothing from the effect, which is inferior. The creature does not confer any added blessedness on God. Quite the opposite. Apart from God, the creature is nothing. Apart from God, there *is* no blessedness.

Having rehearsed the relationship between God and creation in this way, Eckhart is in a position to give his final answer to the question: "Where does God dwell?" While it is true to say that God dwells in all beings, and truer still that He dwells in the heights, in heaven, in the most inner, and the like; nevertheless, in the most proper sense, we must answer that God dwells in Himself. Eckhart draws on the Platonic conception of participation in order to explain his meaning. True, God dwells in beings insofar as they exist, i.e., insofar as they participate or share in being. And, indeed, the freer they are of defect, privation and negation, the more truly they participate in being. Hence, we say correctly that God dwells in the heights, in heaven, in the most inner, etc. But most properly speaking, if we are seeking absolute being, we must turn from an entity which participates in being to being itself. For where, Eckhart asks, could it be nearer and truer to being than in being itself? And God is being.

Eckhart uses the example of the relationship between a wise man and Wisdom in order to explain. A man, insofar as he is wise, shares in the nature or being of Wisdom itself. He is wise in and through Wisdom. Hence he can be said to dwell in Wisdom. Insofar as he is not wise, there is no Wisdom in him and he does not dwell in Wisdom. Similarly, for the just man and Justice itself:

> One finds justice only in it itself and not in that, which is something other than Justice, something foreign and different from Justice. Who would seek, find and recognize A in B or, the reverse [B in A]? Who could find and know

---

[35]Augustine, *Confessions*, 11.13. *Comm. Jn.,* n. 218, p. 183.

a man in the intelligible species of a lion or Martin as Martin in the image of Peter? Who could seek or find grapes in thorns or figs in thistles? . . . So Justice is only to be found and known in itself. Thus also God according to His own essence is, in the proper sense, nowhere to be found and known but in Himself.[36]

This is what Augustine means, Eckhart explains, when he turns to God in the tenth book of the *Confessions* and says: "Where did I find you and come to know you, if not in you above me?"[37] Every knower, says Eckhart, is capable of completely turning back to its essence, the divine Logos. As long as it does not stop in something other than the divine essence, this return can be complete. He goes on to invoke the familiar analogy to the just man who, insofar as he is just, shares in the same nature and being as "begotten Justice" (i.e., the Son). Begotten Justice, in turn, derives the whole of its being from begetting Justice (i.e. God the Father). Still the Son is not less than the Father, for He is the same being as the Father, and "where there is equality of being there is no lesser."[38]

It will be helpful at this point to underscore the overall trajectory of Eckhart's commentary. He begins by reflecting on God as the place of all things, as the Being of all beings. He then emphasizes that God is not present wherever there is defect, deformity, evil, privation or negation. God does not dwell in time, division, continuous quantity, nowhere where there is a more or less, not in anything that is distinct, in no creature insofar as it is this or that, or in anything that is proper to something. From this he draws the moral lesson: as long as a man is divided in himself, attached to the world in its particularity, God does not dwell in him. Just as God dwells in the heights, in heaven, etc., so also the person in whom God dwells is detached from the earthly in all its thisness. Just as God is present everywhere (as the absolute being of all things) and nowhere (in no being insofar as it is *this* being), so also the perfect man should have earthly attachments nowhere. He should be present everywhere and to everything without distinction, not, however, as someone who is at home everywhere, but rather, as someone to whom all places are equally foreign. Such a soul has extinguished his love for the world *as* world and yearns to rest in God as He is in Himself, in the immediacy of God's eternal being, in the eternal now in which God is and from which all things flow.

Thus the overall movement of Eckhart's commentary is *from* a consideration of God's omnipresence in the world as the being of beings, *to* a consideration of God as He is in Himself, insofar as He transcends all finite created beings in their temporal and spatial thisness. The moral lesson is a call to detachment: by becoming like God, the just man creates the condition for the possibility of the

---

[36]*Comm. Jn.*, n. 222, 1-8, p. 186.

[37]Augustine, *Confessions,* 10.26.

[38]*Comm. Jn.,* n. 222, p. 186.

birth of the Son in the highest part of his soul. Insofar as he *is* just, he is one and the same nature as unbegotten Justice Itself. He is one in God and with God.

In contrast, as we shall see, Cusanus begins and ends his sermon with the *incarnate* Christ in conversation with men in the world. For Cusanus, God is the source and goal of all things; but He is also—as Christ—the infinite way or middle. It is in the centrality of this emphasis on the incarnate Christ as the *link* between the infinite God and finite creatures that Cusanus most departs from Eckhart in his own analysis of the place of God.

Nicholas of Cusa: Christ as the "Infinite Way"

Nicholas of Cusa gave the sermon *Ubi est qui natus est rex Iudaeorum?* for the feast of the Epiphany on January 6, 1456 in Brixen. It is a commentary on the meaning of Matthew 2:2 and, in its skeletal outline, closely follows the structure of Eckhart's *Commentary on John* 1:38. After a preliminary introduction (nn. 1-3), he takes the Matthew text as a statement about God as "the where" of all things or place in an absolute sense (nn. 4-14). He then considers the text as a question, asking where God is to be found (nn. 15-27). This question, "Where is God?" is first considered in terms of where God is not (nn. 16-20), leading into a defense of Eckhart's insistence that God was not somewhere or doing something "before" creation (nn. 21-27), and concluding with a brief discussion of where God *is* to be found (nn. 26-27). Thus the bulk of Cusanus' sermon (nn. 4-27) consists of a close interpretive reading of Eckhart's *Commentary on John* 1:38 and follows the broad outline of that text. Cusanus concludes his own sermon, however, with an additional consideration of God's omnipresence from the point of view of His efficacy and activity in the world and in the soul (nn. 28-32). Although Cusanus bases his sermon on the skeletal framework provided by Eckhart, I hope to show in what follows that the way in which he frames the sermon with its introductory (nn. 1-3) and concluding remarks (nn. 28-32), and indeed the way in which he fleshes out the basic Eckhartian structure in the bulk of his text, serves to fundamentally re-orient Eckhart's own discussion.

Cusanus begins his sermon by pointing out that: "The wise men had no doubts that the king of the Jews was born, but they made inquiries where he might be."[39] That is, Cusanus explains, the wise men had no doubts that God, "the King of kings" who "dwells in heaven," was *born* in accordance with the prophecy: "He was seen upon the earth and conversed [with men]."[40] The magi, Cusanus explains, were certain that he had been born from a visible sign, the star which appeared before them to guide them, and so they made their inquiries. In the same way, he urges, "all wise men of this world" should seek the

---

[39]Nicholas of Cusa, Sermo CCXVI, n.1 (h XIX/1, 82); translation by Lee Miller included in this volume, above. Hereafter, citations to this sermon will be given in the body of the text by section number. All English translations are Miller's.

[40]Ps 2:4; Is 58:9; Bar 3:38.

incarnate God (n. 3). As we shall see, these introductory remarks are not simply an occasional and convenient entry into the more general metaphysical and spiritual question of the "place" of God. When Cusanus asks with the wise men, "Where is he who is born?," his emphasis—in contrast to Eckhart—really is on the "where" of a God incarnate.

God as the "Where" of Creation (nn. 4-14)

For a first "dispositive" understanding of the text at hand, Cusanus turns to Eckhart's *Commentary on John* and says that we should read Matthew 2:2 in accordance with the Meister's interpretation of God as "place" or "where" in an absolute sense, "just as if the wise had said: 'The king who is born is God who is the place of all things'" (n. 4). Cusanus goes on to summarize Eckhart's argument that God—as the being of beings—is the natural place of all things, the place outside of which all things are restless, and the place toward which all things strive and in which they all find rest.[41] God is being, "the source of everything which exists," and as such, "the goal, place and rest of all things" (n. 4). All this is a fairly straightforward and faithful rendering of Eckhart's discussion of God as the place of all things in general.[42] Nevertheless, it is striking that Cusanus does not orient his own exegesis around Eckhart's gloss on Matthew 2:2 (*Ubi est qui natus est rex Iudaeorum?*): "He who is born according to the flesh *is the where according to his divinity.*"[43] Indeed, whereas Eckhart goes out of his way in this text to distinguish Christ's human nature ("is born") from his divine nature ("is the where"), Cusanus associates the "where" of the world with the *incarnate* God. Cusanus' orienting gloss reads: "The king who is born is God who is the place of all things." Jesus, as God and man, the "absolute maximum" joined to the "maximum individual" (in the language of *De docta ignorantia*), links God and creation. Indeed it is this intimate *connection* between God and world which is the underlying theme of the first major section of Cusanus' sermon (nn. 5-15).

Cusanus concludes his summary of Eckhart's demonstration that God is the place of all things (n. 4) on a very Eckhartian note: God, as the source and being of all things, is the place from which all things flow and to which they all return. He is the goal, place and rest of all things. Cusanus goes on, however, to elaborate in an interesting and typically Cusan manner:

---

[41]Following Eckhart, Cusanus notes that the psalmist and also Augustine describe God as the place of the soul; but, like Eckhart, he focuses his discussion on the ontological point that God (as being) is the place, not just of the soul, but of all things in general.

[42]Eckhart, *Comm. Jn.,* nn. 199-205; See also Miller, above pp. ; Koch, *Vier Predigten*, pp. 175-179; and Francis Bertin, *Nicolas de Cues: Sermons Eckhartiens et Dionysiens* (Paris, 1998), pp. 201-203.

[43]Eckhart, *Comm. Jn.*, n. 199, 6-7, p. 168.

Attend to the fact that the place of time is eternity or the now or the present, and the place of movement is rest, and the place of number is oneness, and so on. For what does being in time mean except the present? For time flows and its flow is only from being to being. This being is the present or the now, as is said, because of time alone do we possess the now, nor are there many nows, but only one. For the now does not pass into the past nor can now be said of the future. The now, therefore, from which and to which all time flows is the essence or being of time (n. 5).

Cusanus relies here on his understanding of Infinite unity as the enfolding (*complicatio*) of all things, and of the created universe as the unfolding (*explicatio*) of this unity in multiplicity, temporality and motion. In Book II of *De docta ignorantia*, Cusanus describes unity as the enfolding of number, rest as the enfolding of motion, and the present as the enfolding of all (present) times. Motion he thus defines as rest ordered in a series, number as the unfolding of unity in the number series, and time as the unfolding of the present in ordered succession.[44]

Thus, the relationship between time and eternity, for example, is one of enfolding and unfolding, where the "now of eternity" (the present) is grasped as the essence or "being" of time (and similarly, rest as the being of motion and unity as the being of number). Each present moment in time must thus be seen to be a contracted image of eternity. This present moment in time is not the same as a previous moment in time, just as the sky is not the earth. But the *being* of the sky and the earth is the same. In each case the being is contracted to *this* particular entity through a difference of participation. Similarly the *being* of this moment in time is the same as the *being* of a previous moment in time. The being of time is eternity. But as the unfolding of eternity, each moment participates in the "now of eternity" in a contracted and limited way. There are not many nows strung together composing time. There is only the one now of eternity, which is the being of each finite moment, in that finite moment.

Similarly, Cusanus goes on, there are not many resting points around which motion takes place. Each motion progresses from rest to rest. There are many

---

[44]"In the like manner, if you consider [the matter] carefully: rest is oneness which enfolds motion, and motion is rest ordered serially. Hence, motion is the unfolding of rest. In like manner, the present, or the now, enfolds time. The past was the present, and the future will become the present. Therefore, nothing except an ordered present is found in time. Hence, the past and the future are the unfolding of the present. The present is the enfolding of all present times; and the present times are the unfolding, serially, of the present; and in the present times only the present is found. Therefore, the present is one enfolding of all times. Indeed, the present is oneness. In like manner, identity is the enfolding of difference; equality [the enfolding] of inequality; and simplicity [the enfolding] of divisions, or distinctions" (*De docta ignorantia*, II.3.106 [h I, 69-70]); translation by Jasper Hopkins in *Nicholas of Cusa On Learned Ignorance: A Translation and an Appraisal of De Docta Ignorantia* (Minneapolis, 1985), pp. 93-94.

motions but not many rests. Rest is the being or essence of motion. God is rest in the absolute sense, the source and goal of all motion (n. 6). In the same way, Cusanus explains, number "progresses from one to one." Oneness is the source, goal, and essence of every countable number. There are many numbers but not many ones. Oneness is the being of numbers. Furthermore, God, the essence of all countable beings, is both absolute being and absolute oneness (n. 7).

In the same way, Cusanus continues, Reasoning is the movement of the rational spirit from truth to truth. And "God is called truth because [God is] rest or the place of reason's rational processes or intellectual discourses" (n. 8). Again we find this idea vividly illustrated in Book I of *De docta ignorantia,* where Cusanus compares the relationship between the rational processes of a finite intellect and Truth to a many-sided polygon inscribed in a circle. The circle, Truth, acts as measure and goal of all human knowing, the absolute limit of an infinite approach:

> Hence the [finite] intellect, which is not truth, never comprehends truth so precisely that truth cannot be comprehended infinitely more precisely. For the intellect is to truth as [an inscribed] polygon is to [the inscribing] circle. The more angles the inscribed polygon has the more similar it is to the circle. However, even if the number of its angles is increased *ad infinitum,* the polygon never becomes equal [to the circle] unless it is resolved into identity with the circle.[45]

Cusanus' explication here of the relationship between time and eternity, motion and rest, unity and number, truth and the process of reasoning, is clearly in harmony with Eckhart's Neoplatonic conception of the relationship between the one and the many. And yet as Cusanus takes up these Eckhartian themes his reading undergoes a significant shift, not so much in content, as in the overall orientation which gives the content its broader significance. When Eckhart describes God as the "where" or "place" of all things, the overriding emphasis is on God as source and goal of all created beings. The person who seeks God must take leave of all time, movement, and number and seek rather their source (in Eternity, Rest, Oneness).[46] The emphasis is clearly on moving *beyond* time, movement, number, etc. *to* the eternal, *to* rest, *to* the One. Eckhart's orientation is always directed towards the principle which is the origin and goal of all things. He is much less inclined than Cusanus to underscore the fact that we can recognize the eternal *in* time (as its essential being), rest *in* movement (as its essential being) or oneness *in* number (as its essential being). And nowhere in

---

[45]*De docta ignorantia* I, 3.10 (h I, 9); Hopkins translation, p. 52.

[46]This is a prevalent theme of both Eckhart's Latin and German works. See, for example, Predigt 10: "Everything temporal is far from God and alien to him. In considering time, even if one takes it in the smallest amount, in a now, it is still time and exists in itself. As long as one has time and place, number, multiplicity, and amount, things are not right with him and God is far from him and alien" (DW 1:169, 8-11; TP, p. 264). See also Predigt 69 (DW 3:159-180).

Eckhart do we find Cusanus' situating of finite rational processes in an unending *approach* to truth as their *limit* and measure.

Whereas Eckhart tends to think about the relationship between the finite and the infinite in terms of the procession *from* and the return back *to* the principle or source of being, Cusanus places equal emphasis on the way in which the finite exists *through* the infinite. (Time exists through the now of eternity, etc.) Indeed, Cusanus is particularly concerned to understand the connection between time and eternity, the connection between movement and rest, between oneness and number, and between finite rational processes and truth. This connection, for Cusanus, as the locus of the enfolding and unfolding of Infinite unity, is of course Christ. Christ is the door, the connection, the place of this enfolding and unfolding.[47] Christ is the "joint" in which the infinite absolute and the finite processes of unfolding meet. Christ is the joint between the One and the many. It is not that this is at variance with Eckhart's understanding of the relationship between the One and the many. Cusanus certainly follows Eckhart in conceiving of the divine One as Infinite and so rethinks, along with Eckhart, the traditional Neoplatonic understanding of the immanence of the One in the many as the immanence of the infinite in the finite.[48] Nevertheless, it is the case that Eckhart does not focus on the joint the way Cusanus does here and in his work in general.

Indeed, it is by focusing on Christ as the joint (the door, the Gateway), between finite and infinite that Cusanus develops something like a "limit concept," to use a mathematical metaphor. That is, Christ is thought of as the "limit" which relates the order of process, of becoming, of being what is always underway and in a state of "more or less," a state of "better or worse," to the order of absolute being, of perfection and plenitude, of infinite unity. For Cusanus, Christ is the doorway in which both orders meet, as the focal point of enfolding and unfolding.

The next major section of Cusanus' sermon (nn. 9-14) takes as its theme Christ, as the "unlimited way" of all wayfarers moving through life seeking truth, and has no equivalent in Eckhart's *Ubi* text. "We exist and move in God,"[49] Cusanus begins, "for we are wayfarers." What follows is a vivid image of the simultaneity of divine transcendence and divine immanence. The spiritual journey to God is unending and no finite movement is capable of traversing the

---

[47]See especially *De visione Dei* 11, 46. See Miller, above p. .

[48]See Eckhart's Sermo XXIX, on "God is one" (LW 4:263-270). See especially n. 296: "God is infinite in his simplicity and simple by reason of His infinity. Therefore, He is everywhere and everywhere entire. He is everywhere by His infinity, but entire everywhere by reason of His simplicity. God alone flows into all created beings, into their essences; nothing of other beings flows into anything else. God is in the inner reality of each thing and only in the inner reality. He alone 'is one' " (TP, pp. 223-224).

[49]Acts 17:28.

distance.[50] But at the same time God Himself is the way or path of our journey, for the infinite way is the being of God without beginning or end. The wayfarer exists and possesses all that makes him a wayfarer from the unlimited way which is the place of his intellectual and spiritual life and motion:

> Therefore a wayfarer who walks or moves on an unlimited way, if asked where he is, is said to be "on the way." If someone asks where he moves, the answer is "on the way." If someone asks from where he moves, one says "from the way." If someone asks where he is heading, one says "from the way to the way." And in that way the unlimited way is called the place of the wayfarer and is God (n. 9).

Hence Jesus Christ, the perfection of human nature joined to God, is rightly called the living way (n. 10) and the truth[51] (n. 11) of the wayfarer.[52] Christ is the "limit" in which and through which the unending journey of finite human nature, the "living intellect" of the wayfarer, has its measure and comes to rest in the absolute infinity of God.

This idea of Christ as the limit at which these two orders meet is especially evident in Cusanus' discussion of the ethical and religious life which follows (nn. 12-14). The art of living well is also a process, which admits of degrees of more and less, better and worse. All human beings enter the world in the same way, born naked like other animals. We do not, however, all live equally. Indeed, human beings practice various practical or mechanical arts so that we may "live in a better state," e.g. the art of weaving, building, farming, doing business, and

---

[50]Koch notes, "Wenn ich die Stelle recht verstehe, will Cusanus mit dieser Lehre von dem unendlichen Weg der Erdenpilger dasselbe für unser religiöses Leben sagen, was er mit dem Prinzip 'Infiniti et finiti nulla est proportio' für das Verhältnes Gottes zum Geschöpf überhaupt ausdrückt" (*Vier Predigten*, p. 183).

[51]See in this context DDI III.4.206 (h I, 131-132): "For since the intellect of Jesus is most perfect and exists in complete actuality, it can be personally subsumed only in the divine intellect, which alone is actually all things. For in all human beings the [respective] intellect is potentially all things; it gradually progresses from potentiality to actuality, so that the greater it [actually] is, the lesser it is in potentiality. But the maximum intellect, since it is the *limit of the potentiality of every intellectual nature* and exists in complete actuality, cannot at all exist without being intellect in such a way that it is also God, who is all in all" (Hopkins translation, p. 135). By way of illustration, Cusanus returns to the metaphor of the inscribed polygon, which he had used in Book One to describe the relationship between the (human) intellect and Truth. Now the polygon figures human (intellectual) nature and the circle divine (intellectual) nature. Christ is thought of as the limit in which the two coincide. While the human intellect is potentially all things (in thought), the divine intellect *is* actually all things (as their very Being). Christ is here conceived of as the perfect coincidence of thought and Being, or absolute Truth.

[52]Christ as "the way, the truth and the life" (Jn 14: 6) is also a main theme of Cusanus' Sermo XXII, "Dies sanctificatus" (h XVI, 333-357).

so on, arts which add to what nature provides. "We possess these arts as a great service and gift or favor from their inventors," who discovered them by their own talent or with divine illumination. Others have gone further, and discovered the rules of political, economic and ethical life through which a more peaceful and joyful life of virtue can be attained. Nonetheless, Cusanus notes, all these arts, mechanical, political and ethical, "do not serve the spirit, but hand on conjectures how in this world a virtuous life worthy of praise can be led with peace and calm" (n. 12).

The religious life is added to these arts and goes still further in securing a better life in this world and a divine life in that to come. But just as the art of living well in this world "has been handed over in different ways by different men of genius," and just as that art which derives from clearer reasoning is more perfect, so too the religious life has been handed down in different ways by prophets who foresaw a divine future from a distance. Hence all the many ways of religion also fall short, insofar as these religious prophets are only able to glimpse the future life as "a conjecture." Our limited vision of the best life, that of divine sonship, would inevitably leave us in the realm of the more or less, better or worse, if Christ had not come into our human nature from God. "He handed over to us what the heavenly life is which the sons of God possess, and revealed that we can reach divine sonship and how to do so" (n. 13). In the incarnation, the divine life is disclosed to us by teaching and example.

Hence Christ is the entrance or gate to that "unlimited way," and is the way itself, which constitutes the perfection of human life. Christ is the limit at which this conjectural movement from one way of life to the next, each increasingly "better" but none attaining the fullness of life which is its perfection, finally finds its end and rest. Human and divine, Christ both leads the perfect human life and the most divine life. Indeed, for Cusanus, the most human man, the maximum individual, is at the same time the most divine man, the perfect image or son of God.[53] Cusanus concludes this section of his sermon with a reference to the magi who sought the incarnate God "in order to adore Him as God and to see Him as man" (n. 15). And we recall his introductory admonition, that in the same way all wise men should seek the incarnate God, who is the place in which the divine life is disclosed to us. As the "unlimited way" of the wayfarer, Christ is "the place where every movement of nature and grace finds rest" (n. 14).

Where is God? (nn. 15-27)

Having concluded his discussion of the incarnate God as the place or "where" of all things, Cusanus proceeds in the next major section of his sermon (nn. 15-27)

---

[53]On the centrality of Cusanus' Christology in the sermons of the Brixen period in general, see Walter Andreas Euler, "Proclamation of Christ in Selected Sermons from Cusanus' Brixen Period," a presentation to the Sixth Biennial Gettysburg Conference on the Works of Nicholas of Cusa, on October 20, 1996, printed in this volume   (pp.   ). On Christ as the true man, see especially pp.   .

to consider the text, "Where is he who is born?" as a question. He begins by asking, with something closer to Eckhart's emphasis, "Where is He, namely God become man, where according to His divinity?" (n. 15) Following Eckhart, he replies to the question first in terms of where God is not (nn. 16-20), then by responding to the question: "Where was God before creation?" (nn. 21-25), and finally with a few remarks indicating where God *is* to be found (nn. 26-27).[54]

In Cusanus' exegesis of where God is not there is an interesting back and forth, as he first gives a summary of Eckhart's answer (nn. 16, 18) and then subtly shifts the emphasis in his own interpretations of the Eckhartian themes (nn. 17, 19). The content of sections 16 and 18 is taken directly form Eckhart's text.[55] But the overall trajectory and emphasis in Cusanus' appropriation reveals interesting and important differences.

Eckhart, we recall, began his discussion with the list of seven things in which God is not to be found (time, division, continuous quantity, etc.). He then goes on to explain that God is in all things insofar as they are beings, but "outside them all and in none of them"[56] insofar as they exhibit one of the seven characteristics mentioned. In short, Eckhart concludes, God is "nowhere where there is defect, deformity, evil, privation or negation."[57] Cusanus, on the other hand, having just expounded in detail on the way in which God or eternity is the being of time, Oneness the being of number, and so on, does not begin as Eckhart did, by listing time, division, number, etc. as that precisely where God is *not*. Rather, he begins by restating Eckhart's more general conclusion: "We may say [with Eckhart] that [God] is not in anything 'that includes defect, deformity, evil, privation or negation'" (n. 16). He goes on to explain that these words negate or deny existence in its fullness and summarizes Eckhart's discussion of the distinction between God and creatures in these terms. Cusanus then restates Eckhart's explanation of how it is that God is in everything and nothing: "he is in each insofar as it is a being, but in nothing insofar as it is this being" (n. 16).

What follows (n. 17) is a "translation" of this Eckhartian theme into the language of *De docta ignorantia*: "I think this is nothing else than that God is, as it were, the form of forms, the absolute form or essence, which gives being to forms." Not, to be sure, as contracted to this particular form, constituted through its difference with other forms, but as "the essence giving being to all forms which give being to this or that" (n. 17).

54Notice that this is a different ordering from Eckhart, who began with a discussion of where God is not, followed with a discussion of where God is, and then turned to the question concerning God's priority to creation. This difference in the order of topics reflects the different trajectories in the two texts.

55Eckhart, *Comm. Jn.,* nn. 106-107, pp. 174-175.

56Eckhart, *Comm. Jn.,* n. 206, p. 174.

57Eckhart, *Comm. Jn.,* n. 206, p. 174.

Finally Cusanus does note (n. 18) that Meister Eckhart had insisted in his *Commentary* that, since God does not exist except in being, God is:

> . . . not in time or in division or in the continuum or quantity or in anything which has more or less or in what is distinct or in any created thing insofar as it is this or that or in anything proper to something, even though He is in all things insofar as they are beings . . . (n. 18).

He goes on (nn. 19-20), however, to contextualize Eckhart's assertion within the framework of *De docta ignorantia*, and in doing so shifts the emphasis and trajectory of Eckhart's text. Eckhart's discussion of where God is not to be found aims at moving thought away from a consideration of particular beings in their negativity and towards an understanding of God as He exists in Himself. Cusanus, in contrast, directs his own discussion back towards God's immanence in the world. He focuses on the fact that God's being is not contracted to this or that particular being *so that* God can be the being of all beings equally:[58]

> [God] is in each thing without being restricted to this or that, so that all things which are, are that which they are through it. For if being itself were in the sky in a contracted way, namely in the sky as sky, it would not be in the earth (n. 19).

God is in everything and nothing: in all things insofar as they exist and in nothing contractedly insofar as it is this thing opposed to that, *so that* God can provide being to each of them. God is everywhere but not in a localized or contracted way: "But while he is in every place, he remains utterly free of every place because He exists in every place in a non-localized way" (n. 19).[59]

The next thematic unit of Cusanus' sermon (nn. 21-25) considers the misguided question: "Where was God before or prior to creating heaven and earth?" and other related pseudo-questions. Cusanus' response is a reading and defense of Eckhart's doctrine of the eternity of creation as presented in Eckhart's *Commentary on John* 1:38 (nn. 213-220) and in his *Commentary on Genesis* (n. 7), and takes the form of an extended meditation on the relationship between

---

[58]This is not an idea that is at odds with Eckhart's understanding of the relationship between God and creatures, between absolute Being and being this and that. In *Comm. Wis.* n. 145 he writes, for example, that "God is existence. It is clear that existence is indistinct from everything which exists and that nothing exists or can exist which is distinct and separated from existence" (LW 2:483; TP, p. 166).

[59]Cusanus illustrates beautifully with an analogy to the relationship between the being of the hand and the being of the fingers. All the fingers have their being from the being of the hand. The being of the hand exists in the being of each finger but not as the thumb or as the index finger. "For if the being of the hand were in the thumb as thumb, the index finger would not exist from the being of the hand. For the being of the hand would not enfold the being of all the fingers if it were contracted to the thumb. And so in order that the being of the hand can provide being to all of the fingers, it is not limited to any one of them" (n. 20).

time and eternity. I will not attempt to provide a detailed reading of Cusanus'
fascinating discussion here,[60] but will focus instead on his shift in emphasis,
and the role that his discussion plays in the overall trajectory of his sermon.

In order to elucidate the manner of God's "priority" to creation, we recall
Eckhart had considered three misguided questions; 1) Where did God dwell before
creation?; 2) What was He doing at that time?; and 3) What was God's life like
and how blessed was it before there were any creatures to serve Him? All three
questions are based on a common false assumption, namely, that time existed
"before" God created time. The first question further implies the false assumption
that creation exists somehow "alongside" or "outside" of God, while the third
question also falsely assumes that creatures add something to the blessedness of
God. Eckhart counters these false assumptions with a lengthy discussion of the
way in which time flows out of eternity immediately and without interruption,
and by emphasizing the nothingness of creatures apart form God.

Cusanus, for his part, picks up on Eckhart's first two questions but
interestingly ignores the third. He also adds a discussion of related questions of
the same sort, but his explanation of their erroneous character focuses
exclusively on the false assumption that there was a time "before" God created
time.[61] He does not pick up on Eckhart's emphasis on the nothingness of
creatures apart from God. But he is especially keen to underscore Eckhart's
insistence that time flows out of eternity immediately and without interruption
or interval.[62]

Further, Eckhart and Cusanus' respective discussions of the relationship
between time and eternity play strikingly different roles in the overall trajectory
of their two *Ubi* texts. Eckhart's discussion is situated within the context of his
concluding argument that the most proper answer to the question: "Where does
God dwell?" is simply to say that God dwells in Himself. Hence the most correct
answer to the question: "Where was God before creation?"—once the "before" is
properly understood as the expression of God's metaphysical priority—is that
God "was" ("will be" and "is") there where He is now, namely, in Himself,
because God is sufficient in Himself.[63] In contrast, Cusanus' discussion of the

---

[60]See Miller, above pp. ; Koch, *Vier Predigten*, pp. 181-182; Bertin, *Sermons
Eckhartiens*, pp. 216-224, 276-281, 300-315.

[61]The only exception is in the answer he gives to the last two questions he
considers: "Was God *able* to create the world earlier?" and "Why did He not earlier *will*
to create?" Here he not only points out the erroneous assumption of a time before
creation but also notes that the questions imply a failure to grasp the nature of God's
omnipotence and freedom (n. 25).

[62]"It is false imagining that some period intervenes between the now of eternity
from which time flows and time itself. For to have a time-period without time implies
a contradiction. Between eternal being and temporal being no time-period falls or
intervenes. This is the same as saying: nothing mediates between the being of God
and the being of the world" (n. 23). See Eckhart, *Comm. Jn.,* n. 216.

[63]Eckhart, *Comm. Jn.,* n. 214.

nature of time and eternity serves—within the overall context of his sermon—as a further illustration of the way in which an infinite God is the being of all beings, and eternity is the essence of time. Eternity enfolds all times, and time is the quantitative unfolding of eternity. And: "just as any quantity you wish does not exhaust unlimited magnitude [i.e. the absolute greatness of God], so neither does time exhaust eternity" (n. 25).

The last part of Cusanus' sermon to draw on Eckhart's *Commentary* begins with a concise recapitulation of Eckhart's initial positive answer to the question where God is or dwells: in the highest places, in heaven, in the midst, in the mist or darkness, in the holy places, in light inaccessible (n. 26).[64] This is followed by a short precis of Eckhart's moral interpretation of his *Ubi* text (n. 27). Here Cusanus nods briefly to Eckhart's list of things in which God is not to be found, but he contextualizes Eckhart's assertions within the context of his metaphysics of contraction. God does not exist in time, Cusanus says, so anyone seeking God in temporal and passing things will be deceived. Also, things divided in themselves, and things restricted to quantity or to an image which does not escape the limits of quantity, of the more or less, do not possess the infinite and unrestricted God. Cusanus' emphasis here is not on God's absence from the finite as finite, as it is in Eckhart's text, but rather on the fact that a finite, contracted being is unable to fully possess or exhaust God's unrestricted, infinite nature. Cusanus concludes by quoting Eckhart:

But all those who desire to reach God must seek him "in the heights or highest places, in heaven, in the midst, in what is secret, namely in darkness and mist." And they must become holy and separated from earth and earthly affection, holy and a son of Israel--one who dwells in the light by rejecting the works of darkness (n. 27).[65]

God's Effective Presence in Creation (nn. 28-32)

Cusanus does *not* go on, however, as Eckhart did, from this exhortation to detachment from everything earthly, to a reflection of God as He exists in Himself. Indeed, Eckhart's concluding and favored answer to the question where God dwells—that He dwells in Himself—has no counterpart at all in Cusanus' sermon. Instead, Cusanus goes on to supplement and balance his interpretive reading of Eckhart's *Ubi* text with some additional remarks taken from a sermon given by Tuscanello for the same feast day (n. 28). Here he continues the theme stressed in the preceding section (nn. 26-27), that finite creatures are unable to fully contain or exhaust God's infinite nature, by adding the complementary point that it is God who contains all finite creatures in His infinite and un-restricted fullness. Tuscanello provides a beautiful image by way of illustration.

---

[64]Eckhart adds "everywhere and nowhere," counting eight places where God dwells. See *Comm. Jn.,* nn. 209-210 and 212.

[65]Eckhart, *Comm. Jn.,* n. 209, p. 177.

Cusanus summarizes: ". . . each bodily creature, since it is finite, has a place in which it is kept safe, as a plant in earth, a rose on a thorn-bush, fish in water, birds in air." God does not exist in place, but rather limits and embraces all places and, "just as a thing in place is kept safe by the place, so place is kept safe by God" (n. 28).

Cusanus follows up on this image of the world cradled and kept safe in God by adding that: "God is said to be in place on account of some of the effects which He brings about there" (n. 29).[66] Cusanus then concludes his sermon with reflections on God's animating and effective presence in creation:

> What is originated cannot exist without its source. The branch does not bring forth fruit without the root. A bodily member has no movement without the power of the heart. The bright heavenly bodies do not give light without the sun. In this way no creature can act without God (n. 29).

God is in the world to give it life, movement, fruit, light and actuality, to give efficacy to the actions of creatures. God came into the world, as we have already seen, for the instruction of wayfarers. He is in hell for the punishment of sinners (n. 30), in heaven for the joy of the blessed (n. 31), and in the soul for the consolation of His friends (n. 32).

Eckhart, we recall, had concluded his *Ubi* text with the complete return of the detached man to God. Where is the seeker to find God? Ultimately in God above self. The just man, insofar as he is just, shares in the same being and nature as begotten Justice (i.e. the Son), who in turn shares in equality of being with begetting Justice (i.e. God the Father). Cusanus, in contrast, concludes by reflecting on God's effective presence in the soul of the wayfarer:

> God is in the soul for the solace of His friends. For even though friends stand together in a kind of equality, the Son of God, who was exalted in His majesty, still emptied and humbled Himself and became lowly in His humanity (Phil 2:6-7). Wherefore He says: "I will not now call you servants but friends" (Jn 15:15). But friends associate in mutuality (n.32).

It is striking that both Eckhart and Cusanus end their respective reflections on the "where" of God with a "kind of equality" and mutuality between the human soul and God through the mediation of the Son. But while Eckhart stresses a movement away from our human nature toward God, Cusanus locates the

---

66Koch has pointed out that Cusanus no doubt is drawing on Peter Lombard's discussion of God's omnipresence in his *Sentences*. According to Lombard, God is in created things according to His presence, essence and power. See for example *Sent.* I d. 37 c. 1 n. 333. Cusanus nods to this distinction and his concluding remarks in nn. 29-32 fill out his previous discussion which, like Eckhart, had focused on God's presence *per essentiam et praesentiam*. See Koch, *Vier Predigten*, pp. 176-178.

"where" of this meeting in the incarnate God, in the descent of the divine to humanity.[67]

> Thus the Son of God associates with us both by dwelling in the flesh and by bringing peace of mind. And His "conversation has no bitterness" "nor tediousness, but joy and gladness" (n. 32).[68]

With these words Cusanus concludes his sermon on the "where" of God just as he began: with an incarnate God in conversation with human beings.

Conclusion

What conclusions can be drawn from this analysis of Cusanus' transformative reading of Eckhart's *Commentary on John* 1:38? First of all, it would be wrong to conclude from this comparison that Eckhart does not have a robust theology and metaphysics of the incarnation.[69] Indeed, for Eckhart the incarnation is the eternal source of our divine sonship. Eckhart had already emphasized this point earlier in his *Commentary on John* 1:14 ("The Word was made flesh and dwelt among us.")[70] He writes there, for example, that:

> the first fruit of the Incarnation of the Word, who is the natural Son of God, is that we should be God's sons through adoption. It would be little value for me that "the Word was made flesh" for man in Christ as a person distinct from me unless He was also made flesh in me personally so that I too might be God's son.[71]

The Word of God, Eckhart holds, assumed human nature in general and not simply the nature of a particular man. In doing so "He bestowed the grace of sonship and adoption on all men." [72] Whenever God's word is born in us, then the Word made flesh dwells in us, and the eternal event of incarnation takes

---

[67]This is not to say that there are not other texts in Eckhart's corpus in which he writes eloquently about God's loving descent into human nature. See especially Predigt 22 in DW 1:377, 4 - p. 379, 4. See also *Von Abgeschiedenheit*, DW 5:540.

[68]Wis 8:16.

[69]See Bernard McGinn's discussion in his "Theological Introduction" to *Meister Eckhart: The Essential Sermons, Commentaries, Treatises, and Defense*, ed. Edmund Colledge and Bernard McGinn (New York, 1981), pp. 45-46 [hereafter EE].

[70]Eckhart, *Comm. Jn.,* nn. 116-121.

[71]Eckhart, *Comm. Jn.,* n. 117, p. 101, 12 - p. 102 2; EE, p. 167.

[72]Gabriel Théry, "Édition critique des pièces relatives au procès d'Eckhart contenues dans le manuscrit 33b de la Bibliothèque de Soest," *Archives d'histoire littéraire et doctrinal du moyen âge* 1 (1926): 231; EE, p. 46. See *Comm. Jn.*, n. 106; and Predigt 5b in DW 1:85, 6 - p. 88, 5.

place.[73] In this event we are "formed, informed and transformed" into the same image in which Christ is the Son of God.[74]

It is nonetheless striking that in his subsequent exegesis of John 1:38, devoted to a consideration of the "where" of God, in his long list of scriptural references to the dwelling places of God, Eckhart never once makes mention of John 1:14, "The Word was made flesh and dwelt among us." Again, this has everything to do with the general trajectory of Eckhart's thought. God dwells in human nature so that we may become adopted sons of God. The incarnation, or the birth of the Word in the soul, is essentially an eternal event which Eckhart immediately assimilates to the eternal creation of the world and the eternal generation of the Trinity. If is for this reason that Eckhart speaks of the incarnation as the mid-point between the intra-divine emanation of the Trinity and the creative production of creatures.[75] But again, Eckhart's emphasis here, and in general, is consistently on God as the source and goal of creation; and the significance of the incarnation is in its role in the return of humanity to God.

Of course, it is equally true for Cusanus that God is the source and goal of all created things, and that the incarnation has its central significance in filiation. But Cusanus places special emphasis on God as the infinite Way of journeying wayfarers, and the centrality of his Christology in his corpus has its more general metaphysical correlate in his keen focus on the specific dynamics of divine enfolding and unfolding. Christ is the locus or "place" of this enfolding and unfolding. Christ is the joint or limit between two orders of infinity: the absolute infinity of God and the privative infinity of creation. Whereas Eckhart never tires of contrasting the two orders, Cusanus makes metaphysical speculation of their dynamic inter-relation a focal point—if not the focal point—of his thought.

---

[73]"John says therefore, 'The Word was made flesh' in Christ, and 'dwelt among us' when in any one of us the Son of God becomes man and a son of man becomes a son of God" (*Comm. Jn.,* n. 118, p. 103, 12-14; EE, p. 168).

[74]Eckhart, *Comm. Jn.,* n. 119, p.104, 11; EE p. 169.

[75]Eckhart, *Comm. Jn.,* n. 185.

MAXIMUM CONTRACTUM ET ABSOLUTUM:
THE MOTIVE FOR THE INCARNATION IN
NICHOLAS OF CUSANUS AND HIS PREDECESSORS

Bernard McGinn

In 1964 I was teaching religion in a Catholic high school on Staten Island—a challenging task, though the challenges were not always intellectual. One day, in a sophomore class devoted to salvation history, a student's hand shot up. Questions in that class were often more of a test of the instructor's ability to discern when he was being set up than of what he might know about his subject, so I had learned to be prepared for anything. This student's query, however, surprised me. He asked, "Would Christ have become incarnate if Adam had not sinned?" Where did this come from, I thought? Had the student been prompted by one of my colleagues? It did not seem likely. Had he been reading Thomas Aquinas and Duns Scotus for recreation? Even less likely. The only conclusion was that he had independently hit upon a theological problem implicit in the Christian message of redemption, one that had exercised the minds of theologians for centuries—the issue that historians of scholasticism have called the question of the absolute predestination of Christ, that is, whether the Incarnation was divinely foreordained independently of Adam's sin.[1]

I am afraid that the answer that I gave to the student was not a very successful one. I recall murmuring something about the disagreement of theologians, and saying that Thomas Aquinas (in 1964 Catholic high school students would have been expected to know who he was) argued against the position that the Word would have become human had not Adam sinned. I may even have mentioned the name of Duns Scotus. This small incident, however, is for me a proof that the issue his question raised is a real one. The motivation for the

---

[1]Little seems to have been written on this question in recent decades, but there were important treatments in the 1950s and 1960s. Among these were Gustave Martelet, "Sur le Motif de l'Incarnation," in *Problèmes actuels de Christologie* (Paris, 1965), pp. 35-80; and Rudolf Haubst, *Vom Sinn der Menschwerdung: Cur Deus homo* (Munich, 1969), developing concepts first laid out in his article, "Das hoch- und spätmittelalterliche 'Cur Deus homo?'," *Münchener theologischen Zeitschrift* 6 (1955): 302-313. In addition, three Christological papers of Karl Rahner touch upon the issue, without ever making it their central focus; see "Current Problems in Christology"; "The Eternal Significance of the Humanity of Jesus for our Relationship with God"; and "Christology within an Evolutionary View of the World." These can be found in *Theological Investigations,* trans. Cornelius Ernst, 23 vols. (New York, 1974-1992), 1.149-200, 3.35-46, 5.157-192. Several older surveys remain helpful. Among these pride of place must be given to the magisterial article, "Incarnation," written by A. Michel for *Dictionnaire de Théologie Catholique,* 16 vols. (Paris, 1905-1972), 7/2.1445-1539. Of special significance are the sections "IV. Possibilité, Convenience, Necessité" (cc. 1462-82), and "V. Cause finale" (cc. 1482-1507). See also J.-M. Bissen, "De Motivo Incarnationis: Disquisitio historico-dogmatica," *Antonianum* 7 (1932): 314-336; and "La tradition sur la Prédestination absolue de Jésus-Christ du VIIe au XIVe siècles," *La France Franciscaine* 22 (1939): 9-34. For a rich bibliography and treatment of the scriptural evidence, see Jean-François Bonnefoy, *Christ and the Cosmos* (Patterson, 1965).

Incarnation is a central issue of Christology, a key that helps unlock central features of a theologian's view of God, world, and of the destiny of humanity.

Like most such issues, the question of the motive for the Incarnation— *Cur Deus homo?*—is rooted in the Bible, specifically in the variety of ways in which the New Testament speaks of the Word's taking flesh. One set of texts is unambiguous in tying the Incarnation to overcoming the effects of the Fall. Among these soteriological passages are Luke 19:10 ("The Son of Man has come to seek out and save what was lost"); 1 Timothy 1:15 ("Christ Jesus came into the world to save sinners"); and Titus 2:13-14 ("We await the blessed hope, the appearance of the glory of the great God and our savior Jesus Christ, Who gave Himself for us to deliver us from all lawlessness..."). Commenting on the Lucan passage, Augustine provided a crisp formulation for those who privilege the soteriological side of the biblical message about the Incarnation: *Si homo non peccasset, Filius hominis non venisset.*[2]

Other biblical texts, however, emphasize broader anthropological and cosmological dimensions of the Incarnation, claiming that the deification of humanity and the perfection of the universe provide the reasons for God becoming man. Prominent among these is the Christological hymn in the first chapter of Colossians, which speaks of Christ as "The image of the unseen God, the first-born of all creation [see Wisd 7:26], for in Him were created all things in heaven and on earth....He exists before all things, and in Him all things hold together" (Col 1:15-17). Other frequently cited texts include Ephesians 1:3-10 and 4:10, Hebrews 2:10, 1 Peter 1:18-20, and Romans 1:4, which most Vulgate manuscripts read as *qui praedestinatus est Filius Dei in virtute,* and was thus responsible for introducing the terminology of "predestination" into the debate over the motivation of the Incarnation.[3]

Another scriptural basis for later discussion is to be found in the Prologue to John's Gospel, specifically in how the creation of all things in the Word (*omnia per ipsum facta sunt,* v. 3) is to be related to the Word's taking on flesh (*et*

---

[2]Augustine, Sermo 174.2 (PL 38.940). A text from Augustine's Sermo 175, commenting on 1 Tim 1:15, that entered into the *Glossa ordinaria,* was equally important: "Nulla causa fuit veniendi Christo domino, nisi peccatores salvos facere" (PL 38.945). See also Ambrose, *De Incarnationis dominicae sacramento* 7.56 (PL 16.832).

[3]The majority of Vulgate texts read praedestinatus, reflecting the Greek *prooristhentos.* Modern critical editions of the Greek prefer the reading *horisthentos* ("declared, proclaimed"), which Nestle-Aland (*Novum Testamentum Graece et Latine,* 27th ed.) render as *constitutus.* The other texts mentioned, in the Vg reading: a) "...sicut elegit nos in ipso [Christo] ante mundi constitutionem, ut essemus sancti et immaculati in conspectu eius in caritate...." (Eph 1:4); b) "Qui descendit, ipse est et qui ascendit super omnes caelos, ut impleret omnia" (Eph 4:10); c) "Decebat enim eum, propter quem omnia et per quem omnia, qui multos filios in gloriam adduxit...." (Heb 2:10); d) "...redempti estis...pretioso sanguine quasi Agni incontaminati et immaculati Christi, praecogniti quidem ante constitutionem mundi...." (1 Pt 1:18-20).

Verbum caro factum est, v. 14). Stressing an inner connection between these two actions of the Word was a potent source for theories of an Incarnation that was predestined independent of Adam's sin. Finally, we can note that even the Nicene Creed, the universal symbol of the faith of East and West, hints that the Incarnation was meant for more than overcoming sin when it says of Christ: *Qui propter nos homines et propter nostram salutem descendit de caelis et incarnatus est.*

The task of any Christology, of course, is not so much to choose between the more soteriological and the more universalistic texts as to seek to reconcile them in some coherent way. In so doing, however, important differences emerge in the understanding of the primacy of Christ, the God-man, in both the macrocosm of the universe and the microcosm of humanity. Today, the predestination of Christ, the rubric under which medieval theologians discussed the issue of the motivation and meaning of the Incarnation, is an unusual, perhaps even antiquated, way of framing the meaning of Christ's primacy. (It is also, I will argue, a wrong way.) But a look at the history of the question is necessary in order to see *why* absolute predestination misconceives the question, as well as to suggest a more fruitful approach to the relation between Christ and cosmos. Since the motivation of the Incarnation was most intensely discussed in the thirteenth century, and since the divergent viewpoints on the issue have often been presented as a clash between Thomas Aquinas and Duns Scotus (or at least between Thomists and Scotists), we can get some sense of the issues involved by a brief sketch of the position of these two thinkers. After that review, I will turn to Nicholas of Cusa's view of the *Cur Deus homo*? to open up another option, a "third option" that witnesses to a tradition of Christological ontology whose representatives are found in both eastern and western Christianity.

The Motive for the Incarnation in Thomas Aquinas and Duns Scotus

In comparing the positions of Thomas and Scotus it is important to note that differing views on the issue of Christ's predestination was not a matter of a contrast between Dominicans and Franciscans. Thomas' teacher, Albert the Great, admitted that the issue was doubtful, but said that the *pietas fidei* favored the view that the Son of God would have become man even if Adam had not sinned.[4] Some early Franciscan masters, notably Odo Rigaux, were against absolute predestination.[5] Bonaventure's position was complex. In his *Commentarius*

---

[4]Albert the Great, *In III Sent.* d. 20, a. 4, in *Beati Alberti Magni Opera Omnia,* ed. Auguste Borgnet, 38 vols. (Paris, 1890-1899) 28.360ff. Consult Donald Georgen, "Thomas Aquinas and Albert the Great on the Motive of the Incarnation," *The Thomist* 44 (1980): 523-538.

[5]Odo Rigaux's "Quaestio de motivo incarnationis" is edited by Bissen in "De Motivo Incarnationis," pp. 334-336. There is some dispute over the position of Alexander of Hales; see the discussion in Bissen, "De motivo incarnationis," pp. 317-323.

in Libros Sententiarum he distinguishes a *iudicium rationis,* which would support absolute predestination, from the "foremost reason" argued by the *pietas fidei* that the Word took on flesh to rescue humanity from sin.[6] But in his late *Collationes in Hexaemeron* the centrality of Christ presented in the first collation could be interpreted as leaning in the direction of the *iudicium rationis.* It was only in the latter part of the thirteenth century that the absolute predestination view became standard among Franciscans like Matthew of Acquasparta, John Pecham, William de Ware, and, of course, Duns Scotus. Most of those who considered the question, with the exception of Scotus, realized that the divergence of views made definitive statements risky. Bonaventure put it this way:

> Which of these modes of speaking may be more true, He who deigned to be incarnated for us knows. It is difficult to see which of them is to be preferred, because each mode is catholic and upheld by catholics, and each arouses the soul to devotion according to different considerations.[7]

Thomas Aquinas shared this caution. His answer to the question "Whether, if man had not sinned, God would nonetheless have been incarnated?" in the *Summa theologiae* IIIa, q. 1, a. 3 is in the negative, but expressed with qualifications that are often overlooked. (It is also worth noting that Thomas had changed his mind, or at least his emphasis, since in his early *Sentence* commentary, probably following his teacher Albert the Great, he held that either position was tenable.)[8] Thomas' answer is rooted in his distinction between truths that are available to rational proof or disproof and the strictly supernatural

---

[6]For Bonaventure's view, see *In III Sent.* d. 1, aa. 1-2, especially a. 2, q. 2, "Quae fuerit incarnationis ratio praecipua?" in *Sancti Bonaventurae Opera Omnia,* 10 vols. (Quarrachi, 1882-1892), 3:21-28), one of the most detailed thirteenth century discussions. Another very full treatment of the arguments on either side is that of Robert Grosseteste in his treatise, *De cessatione legalium* (c. 1230-1235), and elsewhere. Grosseteste argues for Christ's universal primacy but is unsure about the hypothetical issue of whether Christ would have become man if Adam had not sinned. Grosseteste's texts have been edited and studied by Dominic J. Unger, "Robert Grosseteste, Bishop of Lincoln (1235-1253), on the Reasons for the Incarnation," *Franciscan Studies* 16 (1956): 1-36.

[7]Bonaventure, *In III Sent.* d. 1, a. 2, q. 3, conc. in *Opera Omnia,* 3.24b: "Quis autem horum modorum dicendi verior sit, novit ille qui pro nobis incarnari dedignatus est. Quis etiam horum alteri proponendus sit, difficile est videre, pro eo quod uterque modus catholicus est et a viris catholicis sustinetur. Uterque etiam modus excitat animam ad devotionem secundum diversas considerationes."

[8]See *In III Sent.* d. 1, q. 1, a. 3. Georgen discusses this text in "Albert the Great and Thomas Aquinas on the Motive for the Incarnation," pp. 530-533. A similar case may be argued for the treatment of the fittingness of the Incarnation in *Summa contra Gentiles* 4.54. Though it does not give explicit attention to the question "If Adam had not sinned...," four of the eight arguments advanced there for the fittingness of the Incarnation do not depend on the condition of human sinfulness.

truths which revelation alone makes known to us, though "fitting reasons" can be discerned for why God chooses to act in such a way. The Incarnation is, of course, a supernatural mystery for Thomas. Hence, although he notes that there have been divergent views on the matter, he concludes:

> Since everywhere in sacred Scripture the reason for the Incarnation is assigned to the first man's sin, it is more fittingly (*convenientius*) said that the work of the Incarnation was ordained by God as a remedy for sin, so that had sin not existed, the Incarnation would not have happened. Still, God's power is not limited to this: even without sin, God could have been incarnated.[9]

It is important to note that Thomas does not deny that there is some "fittingness" to God's taking on flesh even apart from man's sin, an issue he had explored in III[a], q. 1, a. 1 on the basis of the Dionysian teaching *bonum est diffusivum sui*. He obviously thinks, however, that this fittingness is not sufficient to give a positive response to the hypothetical question framed in article 3, especially in the face of the scriptural witnesses.[10]

In considering the issue of what is possible for God as contrasted with what is seen as "more fitting" in terms of revelation, it is interesting to observe Thomas' replies to the five objections he cites against his position in article 3. He makes short work of the objection drawn from the word *praedestinatus* found in Romans 1:4. Since predestination implies foreknowledge, he notes, divine "predestination" of the Incarnation is a way of speaking about God's "foreseeing" Adam's sin. The most interesting objection is the second, which summarizes an oft-cited argument for the universal necessity of the Incarnation, stating that divine omnipotence requires the manifestation of an infinite effect for the perfection of the universe: "In such a work the universe would seem to be perfected in the greatest degree, in that the final creature, that is humanity, is joined to the first Principle, namely God."[11] Thomas' response is curiously brief and once again based on his view of the relation of reason and faith. God's infinite power is well-enough displayed in creation from nothing, says Thomas; and the perfection of the universe is sufficiently obvious in the natural ordering of creatures to God to obviate any argument *from reason* that the Incarnation was universally necessary.

---

[9]III[a], q. 1, a. 3c: "Unde, cum in sacra Scriptura ubique incarnationis ratio ex peccato primi hominis assignetur, convenientius dicitur incarnationis opus ordinatum esse a Deo in remedium peccati, ita quod, peccato non existente, incarnatio non fuisset. Quamvis potentia Dei ad hoc non limitetur: potuisset enim, etiam peccato non existente, Deus incarnari."

[10]Thomas makes the same point in two other brief discussions representing his mature view; see *In Epistolam ad Timotheum*, lect. 4; and *De veritate* q. 29, a. 4, ad 5.

[11]III[a], q. 1, a. 3, obj. 2: "In quo etiam opere maxime videtur perfici universum, per hoc quod ultima creatura, scilicet homo, primo principio coniungitur, scilicet Deo."

But could an argument be made from revelation that the Incarnation was more than soteriologically necessary? Aquinas' remark that "everywhere in sacred Scripture the reason for the Incarnation is assigned to the first man's sin" leads one to ask what the Angelic Doctor makes of the cosmological and universalizing texts about the God-man found in Paul and implied in John's Prologue. The Dominican does not neglect them. Indeed, the primacy of Christ is a central theme of his Christology, and he bases it precisely upon these passages. The Incarnation is the cause of the perfection of human nature (IIIa, q. 1, a. 6); Christ's grace makes him the *caput omnium hominum* (IIIa, q. 8, a. 3); and Christ's predestination is the exemplar and cause of our own (III, q. 24). However, Thomas always considers the scriptural texts about Christ's primacy under the aspect of final causality, that is, as indicating Christ's role in humanity's return to God.[12] In a fallen world, *reditus* to God is possible only through the Incarnate Word, as the very structure of the *Summa theologiae* with its three parts makes clear. While the *Verbum increatum* as one of the Persons of the Trinity is the creator of the universe, the three Persons act as a single principle in creating, according to Aquinas. Hence, there is no distinctive role for the *Verbum* precisely as *Verbum* in what we can know about the production of all things from nothing. Even less, according to Thomas, can we say that creation, understood as the *exitus* of all things from God, has some indissoluble link to the *Verbum incarnatum,* the Word made flesh. Christ is head, center, and goal of the world in its *return* to the divine source, but not in its procession.

Thomas' position on this point bears comparison with that of Bonaventure. Although the Seraphic Doctor's theology of creation, unlike Thomas', is centered on the *Verbum increatum* as the *similitudo expressiva* of the Father, he agrees with Thomas in seeing the *Verbum incarnatum* as essential only for the *reditus,* not for the procession of all things from God. A famous text from *De reductione artium ad theologiam* puts it clearly:

It is necessary to establish a center in the going forth and the return of all things. But the center in going forth should be more on the side of the one producing, while the center in the return is more on the side of the one returning. Therefore, just as things went forth from God through the Word of God, so it is necessary for a complete return that the Mediator of God and humans be not only God but also man to lead humans back to God.[13]

12For a brief summary of Thomas' teaching on these passages, see John H. Wright, "Christ and the Order of the Universe," in *The Order of the Universe in the Theology of St. Thomas Aquinas* (Roma, 1957), pp. 177-184.

13Bonaventure, *De reductione artium ad theologiam* 23 (*Opera Omnia* 5.325a): "Necesse est etiam ponere medium *in egressu et regressu* rerum; sed medium *in egressu* necesse est, quod plus teneat se a parte producentis, medium vero *in regressu,* plus a parte redeuntis; sicut ergo res exierunt a Deo per Verbum Dei, sic ad completum reditum necesse est, Mediatorem *Dei et hominum* non tantum Deum esse, sed etiam hominem, ut homines reducat ad Deum."

Duns Scotus, writing a generation after Thomas Aquinas, twice took up the question of the predestination of the God-man in commenting on the seventh distinction of the third book of Peter Lombard's *Libri Sententiarum.* [14] Scotus treats the issue of the motive of the Incarnation within the context of a discussion of the predestination of Christ based on Romans 1:4, unlike Thomas who separated the two issues (III[a], q. 1, and q. 24). Also unlike Thomas, Scotus' argument is based upon an analysis of the meaning of *praedestinatio,* not a distinction between what can be known by reason and what is available only through revelation. "Predestination," says Scotus, "is the preordination of something that can be glorified to glory and to the things ordered to glory." [15] The core of the Franciscan's argument rests in his appeal to the axiom, "Universally, someone willing in an ordered way is seen first to will what is closer to the goal intended." [16] On the basis of this premise, he argues that the divine will's first intention outside itself is directed to the glory ordained for Christ:

> In the first place the highest glory is preordained for Christ, then the union of [human] nature to the Word, through which He can attain to such great glory, because universally what is first in intention in effecting all things is the last in execution. [17]

Scotus goes on to provide several lists of the *signa,* or logical "moments," in the divine decree according to this teleology. In the first moment God preordains the Son of God to become man; in the second man is predestined to be the Son

---

[14]The longer of the two treatments is found in the *Ordinatio* (*Opus Oxoniense*), traditionally dated ca. 1300, *In III Sent.* d. 7, q. 3, in *Joannis Duns Scoti Opera Omnia,* ed. Luke Wadding, 26 vols. (Paris, 1891-1895), 14.348-360. The question is also treated in the *Reportata Parisiensia* of ca. 1302-1303, *In III Sent.* d. 7, q. 4 (*Opera Omnia* 23.301-304). For treatments of Scotus' position, see K.M. Balic, Duns "Skotus' Lehre über Christi Prädestinatio im Lichte der neuersten Forschungen," *Wissenschaft und Weisheit* 3 (1936): 19-35; J.-M. Bissen, "De Praedestinatione absoluta Christi secundum D. Scotum expositio doctrinalis," *Antonianum* 12 (1937): 3-36; and M. Caggiano, "De mente D. Scoti de motivo incarnationis," *Antonianum* 32 (1957): 309-334. There is a recent summary in Richard Cross, *Duns Scotus* (New York-Oxford, 1999), pp. 127-129.

[15]*Rep. Par.* 3.7.4 (23.301b): "...praedestinatio est preordinatio alicujus glorificabilis ad gloriam, et ad ordinata ad gloriam...." The same definition occurs in *Ord.* 3.7.3 (14.349a).

[16]*Ord.* 3.7.3 (14.354b): "...universaliter autem ordinate volens prius videtur velle hoc quod est fini propinquius...." On this principle, see Bissen, "De Praedestinatione absoluta Christi," pp. 11-16.

[17]*Rep. Par.* 3.7.4 (23.302a): "...et sic primo praeordinatur gloria summa Christo, deinde unio naturae ad Verbum, per quam potest attingere ad tantam gloriam, quia universaliter primum in intentione in omnibus exequendis est ultimum in executione...."

of God. The third moment falls upon the union of nature with the Word; the fourth on the merits of the elect; the fifth on the fall of the evil; the sixth on redemption through the Mediator.[18] One of these lists is especially noteworthy for its emphasis on the centrality of God's love as the source of the pre-destinating will. Scotus says:

> God first loves Himself; secondly, He loves Himself in the other [Persons of the Trinity], and this is chaste love. Thirdly, He wishes Himself to be loved by another who can love Him to the highest degree, speaking of the love of an extrinsic person; and fourth, He foresees the union of that nature which ought to love Him in the highest degree, *even if no one had fallen* [my italics].[19]

From this foundation, the Subtle Doctor argues against the traditional view that the Fall of man is the necessary reason (*ratio necessaria*) for this predestination. He announces: "I say that the Fall was not the cause of Christ's predestination; rather, even if an angel had not fallen, nor man, Christ would still have been predestined in this manner; even if no one else were to be created but Christ alone."[20] Scotus then offers a series of three arguments why the traditional view is not *verisimile*—even going so far as to say that it is *irrationabile!*[21] Of course, Scotus does not wish to exclude redeeming sin as a *secondary* motive for the Incarnation, insofar as the Word takes on flesh in a fallen world. Thus, the traditional Augustinian tag, "Had not Adam sinned, God would not have become incarnate," does have a meaning—it expresses the *manner* in which the Word has actually become incarnate, that is, in suffering flesh for the redemption of the

---

[18]*Rep. Par.* 3.7.4 (23.302b). For another list, see *Ord.* 3.19.un. (*Opera Omnia* 14.714a).

[19]*Rep. Par.* 3.7.4 (23.303b): "Dico igitur sic: Primo deus diligit se; secundo diligit se aliis, et iste est amor castus; tertio vult se diligi ab alio, qui potest eum summe diligere, loquendo de amore alicujus extrinseci; et quarto praevidet unionem illius naturae, etsi nullus cecidisset." For more on Scotus' view of the *ordo amoris,* see *Ord.* 3.32.un. (*Opera Omnia* 15.433a).

[20]*Rep. Par.* 3.7.4 (23.303a): "Dico tamen quod lapsus non fuit causa praedestinationis Christi, imo si nec fuisset Angelus lapsus, nec homo, adhuc fuisset Christus sic praedestinatus, imo, et si non fuissent creandi alii quam solus Christus."

[21]These arguments, as summarized in *Ord.* 3.7.3 (14.355a) are: "...(1) nec est verisimile tam summum bonum in entibus, esse tantum occasionatum, scilicet propter minus bonum; (2) nec est verisimile Deum prius praeordinasse Adam ad tantum bonum quam Christum, quod tamen sequeretur; (3) imo ulterius sequeretur absurdius, scilicet quod Deus praedestinando Adam ad gloriam, prius praevidesset ipsum casurum in peccatum quam praedestinasset Christum ad gloriam, si praedestinatio illius animae tantum esset pro redemptione aliorum, quia redemptio non fuisset, nisi casus et delictum praecessisset." Cf. *Rep. Par.* 3.7.4 (23.303ab).

world.[22] Finally, it is worth noting one other aspect of Scotus' defense of the absolute predestination of Christ, namely, its independence of any consideration of the perfection of the universe and destiny of humanity as grounds for the necessity of the God-man.

The abstract character of Scotus' solution, as well as its independence from the scriptural witness, has been a source of concern even for those who have defended it against Thomas' view.[23] So, if the Angelic Doctor's position leaves some interpreters with the sense that the universal and cosmological dimensions of the Incarnation have been slighted in relation to the soteriological ones, the Subtle Doctor's position seems to have reduced soteriology to an afterthought in an abstract schema of divine predestination.

The possibility of going beyond both these contrasting positions by investigating Christ's primacy from a perspective not based on hypothetical questions and artificial attempts to explore logical moments in the hidden will of God has been explored in our own century by a number of theologians, perhaps most notably Teilhard de Chardin and Karl Rahner.[24] My task here, however, is not to explore these modern options, but rather to point to the fact that they have a long and distinguished lineage in both eastern and western Christology, not least in Nicholas of Cusa.

Cusanus on the Motive for the Incarnation

The clash between absolute and conditional views of the necessity of the Incarnation continued to attract theological attention during the later Middle Ages. The prolific lay theologian, Ramon Llull (d. 1312), was one of the most ardent proponents of the absolute predestination position,[25] while Thomists, like John

---

[22]On the relation between Christ's absolute predestination and Adam's sin, see Bissen, "De Motivo Incarnationis," pp. 27-34.

[23]For a survey of the debate, see Haubst, *Vom Sinn der Menschwerdung,* pp. 164-177.

[24]For a survey of Teilhard's Christology, see J.A. Lyons, *The Cosmic Christ in Origen and Teilhard de Chardin: A Comparative Study* (Oxford, 1982). Rahner several times asserts that his own Christology involves an attempt to escape the artificial divide between Thomists and Scotists on the motive of the Incarnation, and he thought that Teilhard's views lay in the same direction. See Rahner, "Current Problems in Christology," pp. 164-165, 184-185, 199; "Christology within an Evolutionary Perspective," pp. 177-178, 184-187. The necessity for achieving a higher synthesis of the best insights from both perspectives was also stressed by Martelet, "Sur le motif," pp. 43-46, 77-79; and Haubst, *Vom Sinn der Menschwerdung,* pp. 177-210.

[25]Llull's texts on the Incarnation are conveniently collected in Samuel al Algaida, "Christologia Lulliana seu De motivo incarnationis doctrina B. Raymundi Lull," *Collectanea Franciscana* 1 (1931): 164-183.

Capreolus (d. 1444), stuck close to their hero's view. Many nominalist theologians, rejecting Scotus' speculative analysis of the moments of the divine decree of pre-determination, held that the debate was an empty one.[26] But the motive for the Incarnation was too important an aspect of Christology to be totally neglected; and the example of Nicholas of Cusa proves that a third way, one representing a broad and ancient tradition, was alive and well in the late Middle Ages.

Cusanus' Christology is too rich to be exhausted in a single essay. A number of his treatises, such as the *De pace fidei,* the *Cribratio Alcorani,* the *De coniecturis,* and the *De visione Dei,*[27] contain discusssions of Christology. The cardinal's sermons provide a wealth of evidence for his view of the God-man. In what follows I will concentrate on Cusanus' most extensive treatment of the God-man in *De docta ignorantia* III, as well as on a few sermons, arguing that these two sides of his writings need to be taken together as complementary in order to appreciate his full position.[28]

The structure of the *De docta ignorantia,* with its three books exploring the three manifestations of the *maximum,* makes it one of the most systematic of all Neoplatonic theological *summae.*[29] Within the dialectical development of Neoplatonic metaphysics, book one's analysis of the *maximum absolutum,* God as one and three, necessarily leads to a consideration of the universe as the *maximum contractum* in book two. In turning to the investigation of the

---

[26]See Ernst Borchert, *Die Einfluss des Nominalismus auf die Christologie der Spätscholastik* (Beiträge zur Geschichte der Philosophie und Theologie des Mittelalters 35.3-4; Münster, 1940).

[27]For the treatments not considered here, see *De coniecturis* II, 14; *De pace fidei* 19; *Cribratio Alcorani* III, 19; and *De visione Dei* [hereafter DVD] 21.

[28]Rudolf Haubst's methodology (see *Die Christologie,* pp. 191-192, 307-308), which tends to separate the two, considering the first four chapters of *De docta ignorantia* [hereafter DDI] as as "an apriori-hypothetical introduction to the mystery of Christ" and the sermons as the real meat of Cusanus' scriptural Christology, not only is contradicted by the text of the DDI, but also by Haubst's own practice. See, for example, the description of DDI III, 1-4 found on p. 192, n. 137: "...dass die apriorisch-hypothetische Hinführung zum Christusgeheimnis zu Anfang des III. Buches der Docta Ignorantia vom kosmologsichen Erwägerungen *ausgeht* und dass darin eine hervorstechende Besonderheit des cusanischen christologischen Denkens liegt." This approach also makes it easy for Haubst to see Cusanus as closer to Thomas Aquinas than he really was, although he is careful not to describe Nicholas as a Thomist: "Sein [Thomas] Einfluss reicht jedoch auch positiv bis in die Grundstruktur der cusanischen Christologie hinein, allerdings bei weitem nicht so, dass man den Kardinal als einen Thomisten ansprechen dürfte" (p. 307).

[29]The organization is first laid down in DDI I, 2, 5-7. I will cite the *editio minor, Nicolai de Cusa: De docta ignorantia, Libri I-III,* ed. Paul Wilpert (Hamburg, 1964-1977). I will generally use the *Nicholas of Cusa: Selected Spiritual Writings,* trans. H. Lawrence Bond (New York, 1997), unless otherwise noted.

maximum simul contractum et absolutum in book three, Cusanus makes it quite clear that he, like Anselm and other scholastics, is conducting an exercise in faith seeking understanding. This is evident in the prologue to the book, where Cusanus begins by expressing belief in "the maximum that is both absolute and contracted, Jesus, the ever blessed."[30] So, although the first four chapters of book three may involve setting up hypotheses, these are always rooted in faith. Indeed, the all-important chapters three and four are so grounded in belief that they can be considered a commentary on the Christological hymn of Colossians 1—the text of which is cited five times.

Cusanus' argument in book three proceeds from the understanding of the universe laid out in book two, an approach that emphasizes the importance of the cosmological role of the Incarnation, though never to the neglect of other aspects of the mystery. The details of the argument of III, 1-2 need not delay us here. Basically, Cusanus tries to show that in the created universe as the contracted maximum nothing can equal God, the Absolute Maximum, or even any other thing, since all things are distinguished by degrees. Nor can any genus, species, or individual be considered as maximally perfect or imperfect by attaining the limits assigned to it, since these always admit of more or less. The cardinal then explores the possibility that the Absolute Maximum could be contracted to a genus or a species, showing the entailments, as well as the logical paradoxes, of such a union that, if it existed, "would surpass all our understanding" (DDI III, 2, 190-194). Should such a union of "creator and creature without confusion and without composition" ever exist, the transcendental conditions for its possibility, as explored in chapter three, show that it would have to be realized in "the being that is more common to the whole company of beings," that is, in man, because humanity is "the middle nature which is the means by which the lower and the higher natures are united."[31] At this point, Cusanus returns to the evidence of Scripture, showing how biblical teaching about man and the God-man fulfills the *ratio hypothetica* that faith has encouraged him to lay out.

Because humanity, as "raised above all the works of God and made a little lower than the angels" (Heb 2:7, 9), embraces all created things, Cusanus argues that one true human (humans exist only as individuals) could ascend to God and "be a human in such a way as to be God and God in such a way as to be

---

[30]DDI III, prol., 181 (ed., p. 2). After the introductory three chapters, Cusanus makes the same point at the beginning of c. 4: "Quoniam quidem ad hoc indubia nunc fide his talibus ratiocinationibus provecti sumus..." (ed., p. 26). See also the comments on *fides quaerens intellectum* in III, 11, 244 (ed., p. 74), where Cusanus says: "Intellectus autem est fidei explicatio," as well as the concluding Letter to Cardinal Giuliamo Cesarini (III, 12, 264). For another treatment of *fides quaerens intellectum,* see *De filiatione Dei* I, 54 (h IV, 40-41).

[31]DDI III, 3, 197 (ed., p. 20): "Quapropter natura media, quae est medium conexionis inferioris et superioris, est solum illa, quae ad maximum convenienter elevabilis est potentia maximi infiniti dei."

human." This human being "would be the perfection of the universe, holding primacy in everything" (see Col 1:18).[32] It is important to note that as he approaches the heart of his argument about the necessity of the God-man, Cusanus does not frame it in light of the scholastic question about the absolute predestination of Christ. Rather, he utilizes the whole of the treatment of *De docta ignorantia* regarding God as the *maximum absolutum* and the universe as the *maximum contractum* to contend that Jesus Christ as *this human being* (and not just in his eternal state as the *Verbum increatum*) is the reason for both the *exitus* and the *reditus* of all things. He expresses the point as follows:

> Through this human being all things would receive the beginning and the end of their contraction, so that through this human, who is the contracted maximum, all things would *come forth* from the absolute maximum into contracted being and would *return* to the absolute through the same intermediary, so to speak, through the one who is the beginning of their emanation and the end of their return [my italics].[33]

Thus, for Cusanus, unlike Thomas Aquinas, creation is inherently Christological *both* in its beginning and its end—cosmogenesis is Christogenesis.[34]

In the light of this faith-inspired hypothesis, all things, insofar as they exist in God absolutely, exist contractedly in the God-man, who would be "the most perfect work of the maximum...in which no deficiency is possible; otherwise there would be neither Creator nor creature."[35] Finally, in the fourth chapter of the third book of the *De docta ignorantia,* Cusanus moves from the level of theological hypothesis to that of concrete affirmation, showing how this model

---

[32]DDI III, 3, 199 (ed., p. 20): "...et hic certe ita esset homo quod deus, et ita deus quod homo, perfectio universi, in omnibus primatum tenens...."

[33]DDI III, 3, 199 (ed., p. 20): "...per quem cuncta initium contractionis atque finem reciperent, ut per ipsum, qui est maximum contractum, a maximo absoluto omnia in esse contractionis prodirent et in absolutum per medium eiusdem redirent, tamquam per principium emanationis et per finem reductionis." The same primacy in *exitus* is highlighted in III, 3, 202 (ed., pp. 22-24) where Cusanus analyzes three logical moments in God's production, in a manner similar to Scotus' determination of *signa* first, God, as creator; second, God as both God and human; and third, the production of all things into contracted being.

[34]This position, as we shall see below, is similar to that of Maximus the Confessor, whose thought on this is summarized by Eric D. Perl as follows: "...the incarnation of God [is] not only the purpose but the very content and meaning of creation itself." See Perl, "Metaphysics and Christology in Maximus the Confessor and Eriugena," *Erigena East and West,* ed. Bernard McGinn and Willimien Otten (Notre Dame, Indiana, 1994), p. 260. In another formulation, Perl notes that for Maximus, "the hypostatic union is the first principle of all ontology..." (p. 266).

[35]DDI III, 3, 202 (ed., p. 24): "Haec autem est perfectissima operatio maximae dei potentiae infinitae et interminabilis, in qua deficere nequit; alioquin neque creator esset neque creatura."

is fulfilled in Jesus, the first-born of all creation, as described in Colossians 1. Everything that Scripture reveals about the Redeemer shows that in Jesus "we have every perfection and the redemption and remission of sins."[36] It is at this juncture, with the first mention of sin, that Cusanus, as he also does in his sermons, shows that the redemptive aspect of the Incarnation is fully consonant with the cosmological and anthropological primacy that has up to now been his focus.

It is important to reflect on the status of the argument that Cusanus has presented. The necessity of the God-man is not open to purely rational investigation (in this he clearly agrees with Aquinas). It is only through the *docta ignorantia* that goes beyond reason that we can hypothesize—not conceive —the maximum humanity of Jesus (*humanitas Iesu maxima*). Following his usual mode of argument, Cusanus provides an analogy to try to gain some understanding of how "all things exist in Jesus as in the Word, and every creature exists in this highest and most perfect humanity, which universally enfolds all creatable things."[37] In human knowing, sense knowledge is contracted to individuals, but since this contracted way of knowing exists, or is "supposited in," an intellectual creature, it can ascend to the level of the intellect, something which is not contracted to individuals, but which can grasp universal concepts. A further step—unknowable to us, but able to be hypothesized in *docta ignorantia* —is our faith as it exists in the intellect of Jesus, "in whom humanity is supposited in divinity." Faith holds that such a human intellect is *actually* and not just potentially all things—that is, it is the intelligible reality of the universe.[38]

The rest of book three of the *De docta ignorantia* is an exploration of how the mysteries of Christ's life—conception, birth, death, resurrection, ascension, and coming in judgment—realize the incarnational primacy laid out in the first four chapters. Cusanus concludes the book with a chapter devoted to ecclesiology, since the Church as the body, or extension, of Christ in this world and the world to come, is the necessary mediator of his universal primacy to our concrete historical existence.[39] All in all, the structure of book three cannot help but recall the second book of Anselm's *Cur Deus homo?*, which has a similar division into two parts with chapters 1-6 laying out the essential argument, and chapters 7-22 exploring the implications of this demonstration for the saving

---

[36]DDI III, 4, 203 (ed., p. 26): "...habemus perfectionem omnem, redemptionem et redemptionem peccatorum...."

[37]DDI III, 4, 204 (ed., p. 28): "...et omnis creatura in ipsa humanitate summa et perfectissima universaliter omnia creabilia complicanti, ut sit omnis plenitudo ipsum inhabitans."

[38]For another development of this argument, see DVD 22, 99-100.

[39]On this theme, see Reinhold Weier, "Christus als 'Haupt' und 'Fundament' der Kirche," in *Nikolaus von Kues, Kirche und Respublica Christiana: Konkordanz, Repräsentanz und Konsens,* ed. Klaus Kremer and Klaus Reinhardt (Trier, 1994), pp. 163-182.

events of Christ's life. Nevertheless, the difference in the answer each theologian gives to the fundamental question *Cur Deus homo?* is striking—purely soteriological for Anselm; essentially universal and primatial for Cusanus, though with a solid role for soteriology.

When we turn to cardinal Nicholas' sermons for further explorations of his thought on why God became man, we note that Cusanus, unlike Duns Scotus, never explicitly disagreed with the traditional view enshrined in the Augustinian axiom and favored by Thomas Aquinas. Christ *did* die to redeem humanity from Adam's sin—this is a necessary, though not exhaustive, motive for the Incarnation. Cusanus thought that the hypothetical question, "If Adam had not sinned, would God have become incarnate?," was the wrong kind of hypothesis. His conviction was that for the task of *fides quaerens intellectum* it was more important to explore as fully as possible all aspects of the Christological mystery revealed in Scripture than to pursue abstract and misleading *quaestiones*. A glance at four sermons that explicitly discuss the motive of the Incarnation helps make this evident in showing how the cardinal preached the Christology sketched out in the *De docta ignorantia*. They also indicate an evolution in Cusanus' thinking.

Cusanus' Sermon I, preached on Christmas 1430, took as its text the first verse of the Gospel of John. The third part of the homily, dealing with the motive of the Incarnation, is based on the satisfaction theology of Anselm and Bernard of Clairvaux. After a mini-drama employing Bernard's portrayal of the *pia discordia* in God as Truth and Justice argue the opposing sides of the case for sinful man's redemption,[40] the young Cusanus constructs an Anselmian-style argument for the necessity of the God-man that is close to *Cur Deus homo?* 1.5 and 2.6, but with a typically Cusan twist on the role of wisdom. He summarizes:

> Justice wills that the one who sinned make satisfaction and satisfy according to his sin. Man sinned; man makes satisfaction. Man wanted to be God; therefore, he sinned insofar as he wanted to be God. Therefore, the Man-God makes satisfaction. And because man wanted to be wise as God and the Son is the Father's Wisdom, it is fitting that not the Father, not the Holy Spirit, but the Father's Son-made-man make satisfaction.[41]

Although the motive of satisfaction for sin is given priority here, the sermon also contains two references to the other pole of Cusanus' theory of the

---

[40]Sermo I, 17-22 (h XVI/1, 14-17), using Bernard of Clairvaux, *In festo Annunciationis* 1.6-14. See *Sancti Bernardi Opera,* ed. Jean Leclercq et al., 10 vols. (Roma, 1957-1998); 5.16-29.

[41]Sermo I, 23 (h XVI/1, 18): "Vult autem iustitia ut, qui peccavit, satisfaciat et, secundum quod peccavit, satisfaciat. Homo peccavit, satisfaciat homo. Voluit homo esse Deus. Peccavit ergo tantum, quantum est Deus. Ideo Homo-Deus satisfaciat. Et quia homo voluit esse sapiens ut Deus, et Filius est Sapientia Patris, ideo congruit, ut non Pater, non Spiritus Sanctus, sed Filius Patris factus homo satisfaciat."

Incarnation. For example, in the debate between Justice and Mercy, the latter argues for the fittingness of sending the Redeemer on the basis of Paul's teaching in Romans 8:29 on the predestination of the elect "to be conformed to the image of the Son."[42]

A similar approach to the motive for the Incarnation emerges from another early sermon, number XVI, preached most likely in 1432. Again, Cusanus refers to the debate between Justice and Mercy over the fate of fallen humanity. Here Peace appeals to the Creator's *pietas,* detailing four reasons why "a Saving Doctor is needed for all, lest all the things that are written, especially what Paul explained so fully to the Ephesians, might be said to be empty and vain." The four reasons are a summary of the Pauline teaching on the predestination and primacy of Christ figured in the union of Adam and Eve as a type of the sacrament of the perpetual marriage of the Church and the Savior.[43] Again, although the satisfaction motif is the dominant argument, in appealing to prelapsarian type of Adam's marriage to Eve, Cusanus shows that he is continually mindful of the other, more universal, dimensions of *Cur Deus homo*?

When we consider later sermonic treatments of the motive of the Incarnation (*de causa et utilitate incarnationis*), postdating the *De docta ignorantia,* we find a shift in the homilist's emphasis. A good example can be found in Sermon XLV preached in 1444 at Mainz.[44] In this address Cusanus explicitly refers to the divergent views about the issue. "Some consider," he says, "as the angel said to the shepherds [Luke 2:10 and 14], that the cause is the salvation and perfection and repose of all creatures, and that the rational creature cannot share in the life of reason in fulfilling the peace of desire unless the Word were to assume the rational creature." Others—"most Catholics," he says—"consider the Incarnation as it looks to the restoration of humanity's fall through prevarication." Cusanus then gives his solution:

> We can resolve the two positions into one and say that the Incarnation took place so that all things might attain the end for which they were created in the Word, even man, who wandered away from the end through sin in the

---

42Sermo I, 19, lines 30-33 and 20, lines 6-7 (h XVI/1, 15-16).

43Sermo XVII, 2-3 (h XVI/3, 271): "Quare ut cunctis....opus esset salutifero medico, ne cuncta illa inaniter, nulliter scripta dicerentur, quae Paulus, Ad Ephesios praesertim, exuberantissime explicat...." The key Pauline texts on predestination and Christ's primacy cited in the four reasons of n. 2 include Eph 1:5, 4:15, 5:23, and 5:32; Rom 8:17, and 8:29; Col 1:15, 18-22, and 2:10; 1 Cor 11:3; Heb 1:1-4, and 6; and 1 Tm 6:15.

44There are many examples among the later sermons. Some of these have been utilized in Haubst's *Die Christologie des Nikolas von Kues.*

[first] parent and through himself. I say that the Incarnation is the fulfillment and the repose of creation.[45]

It is clear, then, that for Cusanus the "primatial" motive, namely that "all things attain the end for which they were created in the Word," includes the soteriological motive of redeeming erring humanity from sin. He underlines this by summarizing the Christological teaching found in the *De docta ignorantia* in the rest of the sermon. The nature of God's power makes it always possible for him to make a creature more perfect than any creature we know, "but when a creature is in that perfection in which it is supposited in God, the power of creating which is God is complete, because then there is no medium between creature and Creator and no closer union is possible."[46] Such a union can be realized only in man, because man, as possessed of intellect, is the *complicatio creaturarum*. Hence, Cusanus once again insists that Christ, that is the God-man and not just the *Verbum increatum,* has primacy as the "Firstborn of every creature" (Col 1:15). This primogeniture stands outside time, because in the mind of the Creator, as in that of any maker, "what is perfect is prior, that is, the house itself, even though it is last in execution." Cusanus insists that creation takes place in and for the God-man: "And 'because He is one, the world is one'; and because of Him all things in the world are what they are."[47]

Another text that explicitly discusses the motive of the Incarnation is sermon CCIII given at Brixen on September 8, 1455, the Feast of the Nativity of Mary.[48] Preaching on the text, "Who finds me will find life and will draw

---

[45]Sermo XLV, 3 (h XVII/3, 188): "Quidam ipsam considerant, prout angelus pastoribus locutus est, quod causa sit salvatio et perfectio et quies omnium creaturarum, ac quod creatura rationalis non potuit rationabilem vitam participare in complemento pacis desiderii, nisi Verbum assumeret rationalem creaturam. Alii considerant incarnationem, ut respicit restaurationem casus hominis per praevaricationem. Et haec est catholicorum plerumque. Possumus tamen resolvere ambas in unam et dicere, quod incarnatio facta est, ut omnia finem, ad quem creata sunt, in Verbo consequantur, sive sit homo, qui a fine per peccatum deviavit in parente vel per se. Dico incarnationem Verbi esse complementum et quietem creationis."

[46]Sermo XLV, 4 (h XVII/3, 188-189): "Sed quando creatura in ea est perfectione, quod in deo suppositatur, completa est potentia creandi, quae est Deus, quoniam tunc non est medium inter creaturam et Creatorem et est unio, qua nulla strictior esse potest."

[47]Sermo XLV, 5 (h XVII/3, 189): "...sicut in mente artificis prius est, quod perfectum, scilicet domus ipsa, quae tamen est ultima in exsecutione....Et 'quia ipse est unus, est unus mundus'. Et propter ipsum omnia, quae in mundo sunt, id sunt, quod sunt." Thomas Aquinas (e.g., *Summa theologiae* Ia, q. 47, a. 3) bases the unity of the world on the divine unity, not, as Cusanus does, on the unity of the God-man.

[48]I wish to thank Dr. Walter Andreas Euler of the Institut für Cusanus-Forschung at the University of Trier for making the text of this sermon, which has not yet

salvation from the Lord" (Prov 8:35), the cardinal begins his discussion from the necessity of salvation from sin, contrasting Mary, the vessel who bears Christ, with Eve, who brought death into the world. But in considering how God intended Mary to come into the world to show forth his glory, Cusanus draws out the wider implications of the economy of salvation. The world can only have one *principium,* the eternal Trinity which creates not through necessity (*via naturae*), but by its *ars,* that is, the Wisdom of God acting by means of will. Proverbs 8:31 says that the "Wisdom of God delights to be with the sons of men," because humanity is created by God with the capacity to receive divine Wisdom. Thus, the deepest motive for God becoming man is found in Wisdom's self-communication:

> Since Wisdom, [though] remaining in Himself, transfers Himself into the souls of the saints, then, willing to complete the most perfect work of all, He decides from all eternity to descend into human nature. And because that Eternal Art wished to unite Himself to man, from eternity He ordained a mother for Himself, in which He would put on human nature.[49]

The primacy of Christ, both in creation and in return, was a theme that Cusanus echoed again and again in other sermons and late treatises. Sermon 257 (Haubst enumeration), for example, says:

> God is the Creator, but Jesus is the creation itself, for only in Jesus does the power of the Creator appear. In Him the omnipotence of the one creating is revealed. By His creation God creates all, but the "creation" is Jesus "through which He made the ages" [Heb 1:2].[50]

In the *Cribratio Alcorani* we find a lapidary expression of Christ's creative primacy: "Hence, it is clear that Christ, of whose fullness all participate, is the absolute perfection of intellectual creatures. The perfection of every creature is in Christ the head...."[51] In the *De visione Dei,* although there is no explicit

---

appeared in the critical edition, available to me. This sermon is cited by Haubst in the older enumeration as No. 199.

[49]Sermo CCIII: "Et quoniam sapientia in se manens se transfert in animas sanctorum, tunc perfectissimum opus complere volens statuit ad aeterno in humanam naturam descendere. Et quia ars illa aeterna ordinavit sibi matrem, in qua indueret humanam naturam."

[50]Sermo 257, as quoted in Haubst, *Die Christologie,* p. 137 n. 47: "Deus est Creator, sed Iesus est ipsa creatio, nam solum in Iesu apparet vis Creatoris. In eo enim revelatur omnipotentia creantis: Deus enim creat creatione omnia. 'Creatio' autem est Iesus, 'per quem fecit et saecula'."

[51]*Cribatio Alcorani* III, 4, 175 (h VIII, 141): "Unde patet, quod Christus est perfectio absoluta intellectualium creaturarum, de cujus plenitudine omnes participant. In Christo igitur capite omnis creaturae est perfectio...."

discussion of the motive of the Incarnation,[52] Cusanus insists, as in the *De docta ignorantia,* that the union of God and humanity in Christ lies on the far side of the "wall of Paradise" (*intra murum*) as an absolute mystery.[53] This does not prevent him, however, from stressing Christ's primacy, especially in the final chapter.[54]

These treatments of the motive of the Incarnation indicate that the primacy of the God-man took on an increasingly larger role in Cusanus' thought after 1440. Along with the theme of filiation, to which the cardinal devoted a treatise in 1445, it emerges as a lynch-pin of his mature view of our relation to God. However, the connection between these two poles of his thought, i.e., Incarnation and filiation, remains a subject to be explored, especially because Cusanus' analysis of *filiatio* in the 1445 treatise is largely abstract, though it closes with the invocation that sonship can be realized only through the incarnate Jesus.[55] Filiation can be seen as an integral factor in the economy of a Christocentric universe, but, as is the case with some patristic authors, Cusanus seems to have treated becoming children of God through Christ as only implicitly and not explicitly part of motivation of the Incarnation.

Summarizing Nicholas of Cusa's view of the *Cur Deus homo?*, we can agree with Rudolf Haubst that the cardinal was not a follower of Duns Scotus. He never addresses the hypothetical question of whether the Word would have become incarnate if Adam had not sinned, and he always viewed atonement for sin as a motive for the *fact* of the Incarnation and not just for its mode of realization. (In this connection, it is worth noting that Cusanus did not follow the line of Ramon Llull either, although the Catalan thinker had considerable authority for him.) Nor was Cusanus a Thomist on this issue. For him it was not just the necessity of satisfaction for sin, but also—and indeed more centrally —the "fulfillment and repose of all creation" which unlocked the mystery of *Cur Deus homo?*. For the cardinal, the Pauline texts about Christ's primacy explain not only how all things *return* to God, they also reveal the manner in which the universe *came forth* from God's love in light of the God-man as the inner meaning of the entire creative process. Cosmology can only be understood in light of Christology.

---

[52]The closest Cusanus comes to giving a motivation for the Incarnation is DVD 23, 104 (Hopkins ed., p. 252): "Tu, deus, qui es ipsa bonitas, non potuisti satisfacere infinitae clementiae et largitati tuae, nisi te nobis donares. Nec hoc convenientius et nobis recipientibus possibilius fieri potuit, quam quod nostram assumeres naturam, qui tuam accedere non potuimus. Ita venisti ad nos, et nominaris Ihesus, salvator semper benedictus."

[53]DVD 20-21 (Hopkins ed., pp. 232-246).

[54]See DVD 25, 112 (Hopkins ed., p. 264).

[55]The *De filiatione Dei* can be found in h IV, 39-64. The treatise ends with the prayer: "...ut hinc translati filiationem dei adipiscamur in filio unigenito Iesu Christo semper benedicto" (IV, 64).

Nicholas of Cusa's analysis of the motive for the Incarnation, then, is neither that of Thomas Aquinas, nor that of Duns Scotus and other late medieval proponents of Christ's absolute predestination. In its positive aspect, it emphasizes the biblical presentation of Christ's universal primacy, without forgetting the scriptural passages that talk about Adam's sin and the necessity for atonement. In its negative aspect, it refuses to be trapped in the dichotomies set up by the wrong hypotheses, those that begin from "What if?," rather than being based upon sacred history. Nicholas of Cusa's position on *Cur Deus homo*? reflects a third option in the late medieval debate over the predestination of Christ.

The Third Option for the Motive of the Incarnation

Cusanus' position was not a new one, though he argued for it in his own way. With regard to this "third option" on the question of the motive of the Incarnation, the cardinal had many distinguished predecessdors in both east and west—some known to him; others not. Cusanus' line of argument, emphasizing the Christic reality of creation as the proper context within which to understand how and why the Word had become flesh to redeem humanity by His death and resurrection, can be seen as belonging to a tradition of spiritual reflection older and deeper than that of the opposed school traditions of Thomists versus Scotists. This third way may be broadly described as that of Christological ontology. In closing, I would like to take a brief look at some of its proponents.

In Eastern Orthodox thought, the seventh-century monk, Maximus the Confessor, is perhaps the most eloquent spokesman for the position that argues that creation cannot be understood apart from God's intention to become man. For Maximus, the deification of man is nothing more nor less than the hominization of God.[56] There is no evidence that Cusanus knew either Maximus' *Ambigua*, or his *Quaestiones ad Thalassium*, both of which had been translated by John Scottus Eriugena.[57] Nevertheless, although the way in which

---

[56]See, e.g., Maximus the Confessor, *Ambigua* 7 (PG 91.1084CD). Cusanus has a formula remarkably close to this in DVD 23, 100: "Verbum enim Dei es humanatum, et homo es deificatus" (Hopkins ed., p. 246).

[57]The absolute predestination of Christ is found in many of Maximus' speculative works, but especially in such texts as *Ambigua* 6-7 and 33, as well as the *Quaestiones ad Thalassium* 60. For the Latin text of the latter, see *Maximi Confessoris Quaestiones ad Thalassium II. Quaestiones LVI-LXV una cum latina interpretatione Ioannis Scotti Eriugenae*, ed. Carl Laga and Carlos Steel (CCSG 22; Turnhout, 1990), pp. 72-83. For Maximus' teaching, see Perl, "Metaphysics and Christology," pp. 253-270, who summarizes: "The cosmos, deified by perfect participation in God, is the created nature of the Word Himself, the creature which God has made to be Himself, in accordance with His will for self-incarnation which is the very basis of the creative act" (p. 261). See also Hans Urs von Balthasar, *Liturgie Cosmique* (Paris, 1947), pp. 203-208; and Paul M. Blowers, *Exegesis and Spiritual*

Maximus presented his argument is different from that found in Cusanus, there is a remarkable parallel between Maximus' doctrine of "enhypostazation" and what Cusanus has to say about human nature being "supposited" in the Word.[58] Maximus and Cusanus may be considered as independent spokesmen for what I have called the third option on the motivation of the Incarnation.

Could Cusanus have been influenced by John Scottus Eriugena in developing his middle ground for a universal understanding of *Cur Deus homo*? Although the cardinal had read some Eriugena, there are important differences in the ways that the two viewed Christ's cosmic primacy that lead me to doubt that the Irishman was a major influence on the cardinal. Briefly, for Eriugena the *Verbum* is essential for the procession of the first creation, the world of ideas or *causae primordiales* (i.e., the second species of genus *natura*), but it is only the fall from the second to the third species of our cosmos that makes the Word's Incarnation necessary as the unification of the *Sapientia creatrix* with concrete human nature, the *sapientia creata,* in order to initiate its return to God.[59] This does not seem to square with Cusanus' view.

The cardinal, as we have seen, certainly knew Anselm of Canterbury and he incorporated Anselm's satisfaction theory into his own Christology. Anselm's insistence on redemptive pay-back as the *ratio necessaria* for the God-man appears to have stimulated considerable discussion of the motive of the Incarnation in the 12th century. There were certainly those who disagreed with the archbishop. Among the earliest Latin authors to have explicitly challenged the Augustinian axiom that "Had not Adam sinned God would not have become incarnate" were two theologians of the period 1100-1150, Rupert of Deutz and Honorius Augustodunensis. A similar view, if one not so explicitly directed to

---

Pedagogy in Maximus the Confessor: An Investigation of the "Quaestiones ad Thalassium" (Notre Dame, Indiana, 1991), pp. 117-130.

[58]On enhypostazation, see Perl, "Metaphysics and Christology," pp. 257-261. Enhypostazation, as developed by the Neo-chalcedonians like Leontius of Jerusalem, meant that the humanity of Christ was not its own hypostasis, but was *enhyposatized* in the Person, or hypostasis, of the Word. Maximus extended this by showing how all creation is the body, or human nature, of Christ by personal not essential identity. As he put it in *Ambiguum* 7: "The things which are by nature far separated from each other return into one, converging with each other in the one nature of man, and God Himself becomes all things in all things, embracing and *enhypostasizing* all things in Himself" (PG 91.1092C; translation of Perl, "Metaphysics and Chrostology," p. 260).

[59]A text where Eriugena underlines this point can be found in *Periphyseon* 3.17 (PL 122.678CD). For an explicit discussion of the motive of the Word's descent to *save* the effects and return them to their causes, see *Periphyseon* 5.25 (PL 122.912AB). Consult Perl, "Metaphysics and Christology," pp. 262-267, on the differences between Maximus and Eriugena on this point. Of course, insofar as the "fall" from species two to species three may be considered to be a metaphysical necessity in Eriugena's system, the Incarnation of the Word could also be described as a crucial aspect of procession, but that is another story.

school debates, was expressed by their contemporary, the first great female
theologian, Hildegard of Bingen, between 1150 and 1175.

In the thirteenth book of his *De gloria et honore Filii hominis,* a commentary on Matthew written between 1125 and 1127, Rupert took up the
question of the motive of the Incarnation, advancing a different answer from
Anselm.[60] The feisty abbot does not agree that Christ's Incarnation was
primarily a remedy for sin, arguing that from all eternity God foreordained his
Son to take on flesh to reign as the King of creation (Rupert cites Prov 8:31,
Eph 3:8-11, and Heb 2:9-10 to good effect here).[61] Rupert, however, does not
emphasize the role of the God-man in the creative process itself, as Maximus had
before him, and Cusanus would do afterward. Rupert's contemporary, Honorius,
explicitly posed the question, *Utrum Christus incarnaretur, si homo in paradiso
perstitiesset,* in his *Libellus octo quaestionum,* written ca. 1145. Like Rupert,
Honorius will have none of the traditional Augustinian teaching, claiming that
since sin is not good but evil, it cannot be the cause of the Incarnation. "The
cause of Christ's Incarnation," says Honorius citing John 17:23, "is the predestination of human deification."[62] Honorius, like Cusanus, uses Paul's
reference to the marriage of Adam and Eve realized in paradise before the Fall as a
magnum sacramentum of the union of Christ and the Church (see Eph 5:31-32)
in order to argue that Christ's deifying action was predestined from all eternity.[63]
This appears to be the earliest use of this scriptural argument for the necessity of
an Incarnation intended apart from the Fall.

---

[60]On this work, see John Van Engen, *Rupert of Deutz* (Berkeley and Los
Angeles, 1983), pp. 352-360. The standard edition of the text is that of Raban
Haacke, *Rupertus Tuitiensis. De Gloria et Honore Filii Hominis super Mattheum*
(CCCM 29; Turnhout, 1979). Book 13 can be found on pp. 397-421. On Rupert's
Christology, see Mariano Magrassi, *Teologia e storia nel pensiero di Ruperto di
Deutz* (Roma, 1959), pp. 219-255.

[61]Rupert, *De gloria* 13 (ed., pp. 408-416). Rupert allows that Christ's sacrificial
atonement gave added glory to his Kingship.

[62]Honorius Augustodunensis, *Libellus octo quaestionum* 2 (PL 172.1187C):
"Causa autem Christi incarnationis fuit praedestinatio humanae deificationis."

[63]*Libellus* (PL 172.1187D): "Denique provida Scriptura ante peccatum hominis
promittit Christum, dicens: *Relinquet homo patrem et matrem, et adhaerebit uxori
suae et erunt duo in carne una.* Haec Apostolus exponit ita, dicens: *Sacramentum hoc
magnum est, ego dico in Christo et in Ecclesia.* Ecce adhuc nullum peccatum ab
homine committitur, et Christi et Ecclesiae conjunctio in una carne praedicatur. Unde
idem Apostolous: *Deus,* inquit, *ante mundi constitutionem elegit nos in Christo.*
Christus est Deus homo, in quo Deus ante mundi constitutionem praedestinatos ad
vitam elegit, quia in Christo nos deificari constituit."

Hildegard of Bingen was not only the first great woman theologian but also an original exegete.[64] Her position on what would later be called Christ's absolute predestination is evident throughout her works, but it is most effectively laid out in the two extended scriptural commentaries contained in her final major text, the *Liber divinorum operum* (ca. 1163-1173). Not surprisingly, these deal with the Prologue to John and the creation account in Genesis: two foundations of biblical exegesis.[65] The central theological concern of the two commentaries is not so much the cosmology of alternating principles whose interaction produces the "flourishing life force" (*viriditas*) of the cosmos, important as that is to her, but rather Hildegard's insistence on a pan-Christic ontology that holds that the Word creates precisely in order to become man. As she put it with exemplary conciseness in another treatise, "When God made the world, His plan from the beginning was to be made man."[66] In the comment on John, for example, the abbess shows little interest in the relation of the Word "back" to the Father, the traditional focus of commentary on the first verses. Her attention is directed forward on how the Word relates to the world as creator and redeemer. The Word that Hildegard is considering is not just the eternal *Verbum increatum*, but the *Verbum incarnatum* of our salvation, as she makes clear in her exegesis of the *Hexaemeron*. Here, like Cusanus, she identifies the Incarnate Son with the seventh day that expresses the goal and meaning of the whole creative process.[67]

The Christological link between creation and Incarnation also had an important effect on Hildegard's understanding of how *homo* is made to the image and likeness of God. In exegeting Genesis 1:25-26, she advances a novel interpretation of these famous verses by identifying the *imago* with "that tunic which will grow in the virgin's womb, which the Person of the Son will put on for the salvation of humanity."[68] The *similitudo* in this reading is the divine

---

[64]On Hildegard's exegesis, see Bernard McGinn, "Hildegard of Bingen as Visionary and Exegete," in *Hildegard von Bingen in ihrem historischen Umfeld*, ed. Alfred Haverkamp (Mainz, 2000), pp. 321-350.

[65]See *Hildegardis Bingensis Liber Divinorum Operum*, ed. Albert Derolez and Peter Dronke (CCCM 92; Turnhout, 1996). The commentary on John's Prologue can be found in 1.4.105 (pp. 248-264), and that on Gn 1:1-2:3 in 2.1.17-49 (pp. 285-344).

[66]This text is quoted from Hildegard's *Causae et Curae* in an improved, but not yet published, text of Peter Dronke, as cited in his *Women Writers of the Middle Ages* (Cambridge, 1983), p. 241: "Cum enim Deus mundum fecit, in antiquo consilio habuit quod homo fieri voluit...."

[67]*Liber divinorum operum* 2.1.48 (ed., p. 342.26-39).

[68]*Liber divinorum operum* 2.1.43 (ed., p. 328.25-29): "...faciamus hominem ad imaginem nostram, id est secundum tunicam illam, que in utero uirginis germinabit, quam persona filii pro salute hominis induens..." The entire passage on p. 328.19-40 is crucial for understanding Hildegard's anthropology.

rationalitas in which man also shares. Thus, humanity is created according to the image and likeness not just of the *Verbum increatum,* and not just internally (i.e., in the human mind, as most commentators held), but specifically to the entire human form of the *Verbum incarnatum,* body and soul.

Nicholas of Cusa probably did not read these twelfth century German proponents of the third option regarding the motive of the Incarnation. But there was a fourteenth century representative of this view with whom he was familiar. Meister Eckhart's *Expositio sancti evangelii secundum Iohannem* lays out the foundations of his Christology in its lengthy analysis of the Johannine Prologue.[69] The exegesis of John 1:1-10 deals with a familiar theme in Eckhart, the relation between the "just person" (*justus*) and Justice (*justitia*), but the analysis of verses 11-18 concentrates on the purpose of the Incarnation. The German Dominican emphasizes what we may call an anthropological motivation for the Incarnation centering on divinization. God's intention in sending his Son was that "man may become by the grace of adoption what the Son is by nature." Eckhart, however, understands this traditional motif of the distinction of son-ships in his own way, that is, as rooted in our transformation into the *very same image* that is the Son of God Himself (citing a favorite Christological text, 2 Cor 3:18). In interpreting verse 14a, Eckhart says, "It would be of little value for me that the Word was made flesh for man in Christ as a person distinct from me, unless He was also made flesh for me personally so that I too might become God's son."[70] Therefore, insofar as there is only one real Son, or *imago Dei,* if we are truly sons (as Scripture teaches), we are identically the same Son, *formally speaking.* This is the source for Eckhart's teaching, one which finds an echo in Cusanus,[71] that because the Word takes on common human nature and not a human person, all humans are one in Christ. This led the Dominican to conclusions he put more daringly than anything found in Cusanus, such as this passage from his German Sermon 5a: "He [i.e., Eckhart] also says that in everything whatever that God the Father gave to his Only-Begotten Son in human nature, He intended it more for me and loved me more than Him, and

---

[69]*Meister Eckhart: Die deutschen und lateinischen Werke,* 6 vols. (Stuttgart and Berlin, 1936-   ). The volumes containing the Latin works are customarily abbreviated as LW. The commentary on John (hereafter *In. Io.*) is found in LW 3, with the interpretation of the Prologue coming in nn. 4-198 (LW 3, 5-167). For an introduction to Eckhart's Christology, see Bernard McGinn, "Was Eckhart Christologically Challenged?," *The Eckhart Review* No. 8 (Spring 1999): 29-47.

[70]*In Io.* n. 117 (LW 3, 101-102): "Parum enim mihi esset *verbum caro factum* pro homine in Christo, supposito illo a me distincto, nisi et in me personaliter, ut et ego essem filius dei."

[71]See, e.g., the discussion of the union of all humans in Christ in DDI III, 6, 219; and III, 8, 227-228. This is to be distinguished from the higher and ultimate union of the saved in the Mystical Body of Christ in heaven as analyzed in DDI III, 12, 256, and 260-262.

gave it to me rather than Him;...I exclude nothing, neither oneness, nor the holiness of the Godhead, nor anything."[72]

When Eckhart reaches verse 14b of John's Prologue ("We saw his glory,....."), the universal aspects of His understanding of the Incarnation come to the fore. Here he claims that not only the procession of the Eternal Word from the Father, but also the glory of the Word Incarnate "...is contained in and taught by the properties of the things of nature, morality, and art. The Word universally and naturally becomes flesh in every work of nature and art and it dwells in things that are made or in which the Word becomes flesh."[73] The entire world of *creatio* and even human *factio,* then, has a Christological core. Eckhart provides an explanation for this in his comment on verse 17, contrasting the law given through Moses and the grace and truth available in Christ. The law is read ontologically as all forms of change and becoming, while Christ's grace and truth equals "existence, immutability, eternity, the one or unity" (n. 186). This is because the Incarnation is the necessary link between the eternal emanation of the Trinity and the whole of created reality. Eckhart concludes:

> It seems fittingly added that the Wisdom of God deigned to become flesh in such a way that the Incarnation itself, like a medium between the procession of the divine Persons and the production of creatures, tastes the nature of each. This happens in such a way that the Incarnation itself exemplifies the eternal emanation and is the exemplar of the entire lower nature.[74]

Thus, Eckhart has his own form of pan-Christic ontology in which the Incarnation as the hominification of God is the purpose and inner reality of creation.

My intention in noting these predecessors of Nicholas of Cusa's teaching that the motive of the Incarnation should not be restricted to satisfaction for sin,

---

[72]Pr. 5a, as found in the *Deutsche Werke* (DW 1.77.10-16): "Er spricht ouch, daz der vatter an allem dem, daz er sinem sun Jesum Chrm ye gegab in menschlicher natur, so hat er mich ee angesehen und mich mer liebgehebt dann in und gab mir es ee dann im:...ich nim nut usz weder eynung noch heilikeit der gottheit noch nutzend nit" (my translation).

[73]*In Io.* n. 124 (LW 3.108): "...supposita veritate semper historiae [i.e., Jn. 1:14], continere et docere rerum naturalium, moralium et artificialium proprietates. Notandum ergo quod universaliter et naturaliter in omni opere naturae et artis verbum caro fit et habitat in illis quae fiunt sive in quibus verbum caro fit."

[74]*In Io.* n. 185 (LW 3.154): "Rursus notandum est quod, quia 'verbum caro factum est', ut habitaret in nobis, ut supra expositum est,.....congrue subieciendum videtur quod Dei sapientia sic caro fieri dedignata est, ut ipsa incarnatio quasi media inter divinarum personarum processionem et creaturarum productionem utriusque naturam sapiat, ita ut incarnatio ipsa sit exemplata quidem ab aeterna emanatione et exemplar totius naturae inferioris." Eckhart goes on to draw as a conclusion from this that there can be no difference in *content* between philosophy and theology.

but also includes a universal cosmic aspect based on Christ's primacy, is not in any way meant to claim that the Christology of Maximus, Eriugena, or Meister Eckhart is all the same—or the same as that of Cusanus. Nor do I want to assert that Cusanus' view is that of his 20th century successors, such as Teilhard de Chardin and Karl Rahner, who also were convinced that the scholastic disputes over the absolute predestination of Christ were misplaced. My point is only that the third option, as I have called it, is not something new, but is deeply rooted in the history of Christian theology. Cusanus' attempt to go beyond the opposing positions of Thomists and Scotists was not a novelty, but a powerful restatement of tradition—*nova et vetera,* or if I may be permitted to adapt the cardinal's penchant for Latin neologisms, a position that might be described as *Christologia novetera.*

THE "ICON" AND THE "ICONIC TEXT"
IN NICHOLAS OF CUSA'S DE VISIONE DEI I-XVII

H. Lawrence Bond

*Domine deus, adiutor te quaerentium, video te in horto paradisi et nescio,
quid video, quia nihil visibilium video. Et hoc scio solum, quia scio me
nescire, quid video, et numquam scire posse. Et nescio te nominare, quia
nescio, quid sis.*

Nicholas of Cusa[1]

*Nicholas of Cusa: opening up. Magnificent discovery. I have been on to
him for a while, but not realizing how much was there!*

Thomas Merton[2]

Nicholas of Cusa's *De visione Dei* (1453) (*On the Vision of God*) is his most
eloquent writing, and it stands as a classic in the history of late medieval
Christian spirituality. It resonates with negative theology and takes the reader
down the path *in obscuro*, as Cusanus later will speak of it.[3] Employing both
admiratio and *contemplatio*, it nurtures equally an affective and a speculative
spirituality. He subtitles the work *Icona Dei*.[4]

Notwithstanding the contributions of Rudolf Haubst,[5] Erwin

---

[1]*De visione Dei*, xiii, #51.3-6 (h VI, 44). Hereafter referred to as DVD.

[2]November 14, 1963 entry from Merton's journal *Dancing in the Water of Life:
The Journals of Thomas Merton,* 5:1963-1965, ed. Robert E. Daggy (New York,
1997), p. 34.

[3]*De apice theoriae* #5.9-13 (h XII, 120). See also *De docta ignorantia* I, xxvi,
#86 and 89 (h I, 54-56). Hereafter referred to as DDI. See especially DDI I #89.13f.
(h I, 56) and the preface to DVD prol., #1 (h VI, 3-4).

[4]In *Trialogus de possest* #58 (h XI/2, 69.12), Cusanus refers to *conveniens
aenigma,* as set forth in his *libello Iconae.* See also his citation in his *De apice
theoriae* #16, where he employs the title *De icona sive visu Dei* (h XII, 130.6).

[5]See Rudolf Haubst's comment to Eric Meuthen, "Die Pfründen des Cusanus,"
MFCG 2 (1962): 25, n. 56a; his note in MFCG 18 (1989): 68; and his article "Die
erkenntnistheoretische und mystische Bedeutung der 'Mauer der Koinzidenz,'" MFCG
18 (1989): 167-195 and the accompanying reproduction of the Christ image in the
"cloth of Veronica" in the cloister of St. Nicholas' Hospital at Kues. Cusanus refers to
this and other similar omnivoyant in paintings in DVD Praefatio, #2.6-10 (h VI, 5):
"Harum etsi multae reperiantur optime pictae uti illa sagittarii in foro Norimbergensis
et Bruxellis Rogeri maximi pictoris in pretiosissima tabula, quae in praetorio
habetur, et Confluentiae in capella mea Veronicae et Brixinae in castro angeli arma
ecclesiae tenentis."

Panofsky,[6] Werner Beierwaltes,[7] Louis Dupré,[8] Alex Stock,[9] Michel de Certeau,[10] and others, two key questions remain unanswered regarding the mystical theology in Nicholas of Cusa's *De visione Dei*: (1) Cusanus' understanding of himself as a contemplative or mystical theologian, and (2) the nature and content of the icon that Cusa sent with the original text for use by the Benedictine monks at the abbey of St. Quirin in Tegernsee. Especially revealing are Cusanus' exchange of letters with their abbot, Kaspar Aindorffer, and with

---

[6]For the other examples of omnivoyant paintings cited by Cusanus include the painting of Roger van der Weyden (1400-1464), now lost, which is apparently now represented in a Flemish tapestry, see Gerd Heinz-Mohr and Willehad Eckert, *Das Werk des Nicolaus Cusanus* (Köln, 1963) pp. 30 and 72 and Erwin Panofsky, *"Facies illa Rogeri maximi pictoris,"* in *Late Classical and Mediaeval Studies in Honor of A.M. Friend, Jr.* (Princeton, 1955), pp. 392-400. *La vision de Dieu par le cardinal Nicolas de Cuse (1401-1464),* trans. Edmond Vansteenberghe (Paris, 1925) remarks that Cusanus had been well received in Brussels by Philip the Good at the end of 1452 and wonders if Cusanus had seen this remarkable painting at that time, p. 3, n. 1. Also see Panofsky's explanation of the *veronica* reference as *vera icona*, a portrait of Christ in Cusanus' chapel, *Facies* p. 395.

[7]See Werner Beierwaltes' rich analyses of Cusanus' notion of sight in *Visio absoluta: Reflexion als Grundzug des göttlichen Prinzips bei Nicolaus Cusanus,* (Sitzungsberichte der Heidelberger Akademie der Wissenschaften, Philosopisch-historische Klasse; Heidelberg, 1978): pp. 5-33 and "Visio facialis - Sehen ins Angesicht. Zur Coincidenz des endlichen und unendlichen Blicks bei Cusanus," MFCG 18 (1989): 91-124.

[8]Louis Dupré, "The Mystical Theology of Nicholas of Cusa's *De visione Dei,*" in *Nicholas of Cusa on Christ and the Church,* ed. Gerald Christianson and Thomas M. Izbicki (Leiden,1996), pp. 205-220.

[9]Stock's helpful theological-aesthetic analysis occurs in "Die Rolle der 'icona Dei' in der Spekulation 'De visione Dei,'" MFCG 18 (1989): 50-68. For further studies regarding the aesthetic qualties of the icon, see also Norbert Herold, "Bild der Wahrheit–Wahrheit des Bildes: Zur Deutung des Blicks aus dem Bild in der Cusanusischen Schrift *De visione dei,*" in *Wahreit und Begründung*, ed. Volker Gerhardt and Norbert Herold (Würzburg, 1985), pp. 71-98 and Alfred Neumeyer's analysis of illusion and image in *Das Blick aus dem Bild* (Berlin, 1964), especially pp. 9ff.

[10]The single most interesting analysis is surely that provided by Michel de Certeau, "The Gaze of Nicholas of Cusa," *Diacritics* 17 (1987): 2-38. For a fanciful dialogue between Cusanus and a Buddhist on "representation," see Roger J. Corless, "Non-referentiality in the Christian Icon and the Buddhist *Thangka,*" in *Nicholas of Cusa on Christ and the Church,* pp. 205-220.

their prior, Bernhard von Waging, from 1452 to 1458[11] as well as Cusanus' instructions in the treatise itself on the use of this particular icon.

The letters and the eventual treatise petitioned by the monks provide Cusanus with the specific opportunity to address then-current issues in *mystica theologia* including the relationship of *affectio* and *intellegere* to *synderesis*, theology as *experimentalis*, and knowing God by means of *translire* or *ascensus mentis*. In an earlier letter Aindorffer had raised the question of prevenient or concomitant knowledge in the soul's attaining to God,[12] a topic that Jean Gerson and Vincenz of Aggsbach had addressed and of vigorous interest to the Tegernsee Benedictines.[13]

On several occasions the monks at St. Quirin's had asked Cusanus to provide them with a further exposition of his notion of *coincidentia oppositorum* and also to include an explanation of mystical theology that would clarify his understanding of the respective roles of intellect and love in contemplative experience. Both in correspondence with the brothers and also in the treatise itself the word and concept *experimentalis* is very important.[14] The composition

---

[11]For Cusanus' correspondence with the monastery at Tegernsee and other documents of this time frame, see the first volume of of Wilhelm Baum and Raimund Senoner's two volume, bilingual edition, *Nikolaus von Kues Briefe und Dokumente zum Brixner Streit, 1: Kontroverse um de Mystic und Anfänge in Brixen (1450-1455)* (Wien, 1998). See especially Cusanus' letters of September 22, 1452 (pp. 92-95) and September 14, 1453 (pp. 96-103). Cf. Letter 5 of September 22, 1452 and Letter 6 of September 15, 1453 in the appendix to Edmond Vansteenberghe, *Autour de la Docte Ignorance: Une controverse sur la Théologie mystique au XVe siècle* (Münster, 1915), pp. 111ff. Ludwig Baur and Josef Koch emended the latter edition in *Cusanus- Texte, IV: Briefwechsel des Nikolaus von Cues, Erste Sammlung* (Sitzungsberichte der Heidelberger Akademie der Wissenschaften, Philosophisch-historische Klasse; Heidelberg, 1944), pp. 107-110. In addition to Vansteenberghe's summary and characterization of the letters in Chapters I-III, see also Margot Schmidt, "Nikolaus von Kues im Gespräch mit den Tegernseer Mönchen über Wesen und Sinn der Mystik," MFCG 18 (1989): 25-49 and Morimichi Watanabe, "Nicolaus Cusanus, Monastic Reform in the Tyrol and the *De visione Dei*," in *Concordia discors: Studi su Niccolò Cusano e l'umanesimo europeo offerti a Giovanni Santinello* (Padova, 1993), pp. 181-197.

[12]See Aindorffer's letter of September 22, 1452 in Baum and Senoner, *Briefe und Dokumente,* pp. 88-91. The letter appears as Letter 3 in Vansteenberghe, *Autour,* p.110.

[13]Cusanus was asked about the identification of mystical theology and contemplation in the writings of Jean Gerson, whom Aggsbach accused of confusing mystical theology and prayer. The treatise against Gerson and other writings of Aggsbach are contained in the appendix to *Autour,* pp. 189-218.

[14]Aindorffer also questioned Cusanus about the views of Jean Gerson, Hugh of Balma, and others regarding the roles of *affectus* and *synderesis* in the experience of God; see Baum and Senoner, *Briefe und Dokumente,* p. 90: "Est autem hec quaestio,

that Cusanus sent, *De visione Dei seu icona Dei*, "On the Vision or Icon of God," is intended to fulfill both requests.[15]

He accompanied the book with a copy of a face presenting an omnivoyant gaze.[16] He asks the brothers not merely to meditate on it but also to address it contemplatively. After a prefatory letter and a brief introduction, the author, like St. Augustine in the *Confessiones*, breaks into prayer so that the rest of the treatise is his own prayer, part *oratio*, part *meditatio* and part *contemplatio*.[17] His own prayerful experience of such an icon he later describes as rapturous.[18] He bids the monks to enter their own orative, meditative, and rapturous experience by gazing and marveling and allowing themselves to be transported experientially into a *sacratissimam obscuritatem*, a most holy darkness.[19]

At first Cusanus speaks of gazing at the icon and later of gazing at the gazer, at the person who would contemplate God. Cusanus opens his treatise with the following clarification:

> I will now explain dearest brothers, what I had earlier promised you about the facility of mystical theology.[20] For I know that you are led by a zeal for

---

utrum anima devota sine intellectus cognicione, vel etiam sine cogitacione previa vel concomitante, solo affectu seu per mentis apicem, quam vocant synderesim Deum attingere possit et in ipsum immediate moveri aut ferri." Regarding Gerson and the appeal to experience, see Vansteenberghe, *Autour*, pp. 110, 193.

[15]By early 1454, Aindorffer indicates that he has received Cusanus' treatise; see Baum and Senoner, *Briefe und Dokumente,* p. 107-111. Note Cusanus' reply of February 12, 1454, *Briefe und Dokumente,* pp. 110-113.

[16]The icon that Cusanus sent has not been found. Elisabeth Bohnenstädt, *Von Gotteschen: De visione Dei* (Schriften des Nikolaus von Cues: in deutscher Öbersetzung 4; Leipzig 1944), pp. 163-164, n.4) reports that in the Eisleben ms. 960 I (D19) an icon was attached to fol. 10v, but now only the caption can be seen. Also the München ms. Clm 18711 (Tegernsee 711), which includes letters to the abbot and brothers of Tegernsee, contains an image of the so-called "towel of Veronica" on the foreleaf.

[17]Cusanus' "prayer" begins at the start of Chapter Four: "Quod visio dei providentia, gratia et vita dicitur aeterna," following a list of three premises and his final instructions regarding the use of the icon: "Accede nunc tu, frater contemplator, ad dei eiconam, et primum te loces ad orientem, deinde ad meridiem ac ultimo ad occasum; et quia visus eiconae te aeque undique respicit et non deserit, quocumque pergas, in te excitabitur speculatio provocaberisque et dices: Domine, nunc in hac tua imagine providentiam tuam quadam sensibili experientia intueor," DVD iv, #9 (h VI, 13).

[18]DVD xvi, #70.1-3 (h VI, 57).

[19]DVD prol., #1.11-13 (h VI, 4): "Conabor autem simplicissimo atque communissimo modo vos experimentaliter in sacratissimam obscuritatem manuducere."

[20]For Cusanus' promise see his letter of September 14, 1453 in Baum and Senoner, *Briefe und Dokumente,* pp.100-103. Note also Cusanus' preceding

God, and I count you worthy for the uncovering of this most precious and bountiful treasure. But first I pray that there may be given to me the Word from on high and the all-powerful Discourse, which alone can disclose itself, to set forth, according to your grasp, the wonders that are revealed beyond all sensible, rational, and intellectual sight. But by means of a very simple and commonplace method I will attempt to lead you through experience into the most sacred darkness. While you abide there, feeling the presence of the inaccessible light, each of you, in the measure granted him by God, will of himself endeavor to draw continuously nearer and in this place to foretaste, by a most delicious sampling, that feast of eternal happiness to which we have been called in the Word of Life[21] through the Gospel of the ever blessed Christ. . . . So that you not be deficient in the exercise, which requires a sensible image of this kind, I am sending . . . a painting which I was able to acquire containing an all-seeing image, which I call an icon of God.

Hang this up some place, perhaps on a north wall. And you brothers stand around it, equally distant from it, and gaze at it. And each of you will experience that from whatever place one observes it the face will seem to regard him alone.[22]

The icon that Cusanus sent is no longer extant. We do not know its content nor even whether it was an icon of the face of Christ, i.e., whether or not it was a *vera icona*, a phrase sometimes collapsed into *veronica*.[23] The details of course may never be known without some later fortuitous discovery. I am wondering, however, about the aesthetic effect of the icon regardless of particulars.

Although omnivoyance is the dramatic effect, one should not make too much of the eyes, because it is not difficult to create the illusion of eyes following the viewer from whatever angle. In fact it is difficult to paint a portrait with eyes looking directly at you that does not seem omnivoyant.

I want to suggest a list of aesthetic characteristics inferred from Cusanus' brief description of his icon, from his contemplative directions, and from his theological applications in the text. Such an icon would present the viewer with:

---

statement: "Verum quomodo possimus ad misticam theologiam nos ipsos transferre, ut degustemus in impossibilitate necessitatem et in negacione affirmacionem, difficiliter tradi potest, nam degustacio illa, que sine summa dulcedine et caritate non potest esse, in hoc mundo perfecte non potest haberi. Et mihi visum fuit, quod tota ista mistica theologia sit intrare ipsam infinitatem absolutam, dicit enim infinitas contradictoriorum coincidenciam, scilicet finem sine fine; et nemo potest Deum mistice videre nisi in caligine coincidencie, que est infinitas. Sed de hoc lacius videbitis, Deo duce, que ipse dederit."

[21] 1 John 1:1.

[22] DVD prol., #1 (h VI, 3-4).

[23] Ewa Kuryluk, *Veronica and Her Cloth* (Oxford, 1991), p. 5, however, denies the derivation of the name "Veronica" ("the Latin form of Bernice") from *vera icon* as a false etymology.

-an omnivoyant face whose eyes rivet the attention
-an absolute presence and a generality of presence, outside any context, i.e. an absolute condition
-a timeless and unlocated face
-a direct but inexplicit glance, so direct that it would address each viewer and so inexplicit that it would look on all equally regardless of the angle of vision
-a face dominating its frame, either non-localized spatially or placed extremely forward so as to minimize context
-a general withdrawal of specific localizing information
-a non-episodic rendering, stripped of all the devices of narrative
-a primary and direct confrontation, i.e. an inescapable confrontation between image and viewer, not allowing the viewer to escape confrontation with it.

In overall effect the icon would present a relentlessly capturing gaze with nothing to release the viewer from a mysterious confrontation with it, and it would possess a vacancy or negation, with nothing included in the icon to let the viewer off.

This sounds very much like the icon known in the West as the Holy Visage. In the East it is called the icon "made without hands" (χειροποητος) or "the icon of the Lord on the cloth" (μανδλιον). According to Ouspensky and Lossky, this icon holds the principal position among icons of Christ. Such an image presumably made without hands is in keeping with the Mosaic repudiation of graven images (Ex 20:4):

> Instead of creating according to their own inclination, "with their hands," the image of the God-Man, iconographers must follow a tradition which attaches them to the original "acheiropoietos." This tradition acquired, at the start of the Fifth century, a legendary form in the story of Abgar, king of Edessa, who was said to have had a portrait of Christ painted. According to the Byzantine version, the Edessa image would be an impression of the face of the Saviour on a piece of linen, which Christ had pressed to His face and sent to the envoy of Abgar. Thus, the first images of Christ, the "mandilion" and its two miraculous reimpressions on bricks—the "keramidia"—would have been documents "made without hands," direct and so to speak, material testimonies of the Incarnation of the Word.[24]

"Documents" is a crucial word here, denoting icons as "texts." Cusanus' treatise seems to join a western and Benedictine spirituality of *lectio* to a Byzantine

---

[24]Leonid Ouspensky and Vladimir Lossky, *The Meaning of Icons*, tr. G.E.H. Palmer and E. Kadloubovsky (Crestwood, New York, 1989), p. 69. A copy of a so-called "true icon" or "veronica" of Christ's visage appears in the cloister of the St. Nikolaus Hospital that Cusa had constructed at Kues. See the photograph (Landesbildstelle Rheinland-Pfalz, Harald Goebel) in MFCG 18 (1989).

spirituality of gazing. Cusanus' icon becomes text; his text and the reader become icons. Not only does Cusanus supply a material icon for the monks to use, but he makes both text and also the contemplator iconic. The *De visione Dei* is intended to be read much in the way an icon is to be "read" but requires such a hermeneutical shift in the reader that the contemplative reader also becomes *figura*, icon, and text. The text is crafted to "picture" by its own rhetorical form and with a variety of linguistic devices so as not merely to "signify" but, in the manner of icons, to transpose the reader from the experiential state of a contemplator to that of one who is himself contemplated and to convey the reader from one contemplative state to another.

We may infer some principles from the series of comments that Cusanus makes on language throughout his treatment of mystical theology:

1. Symbols and images, such as Cusanus' icon, like terms with material accretion, require perception, but in "the mind's eye,"[25] of an invisible truth signified under the form of quantity and quality, yet a truth possessing neither.

2. A right consideration of icons, metaphors and images requires passing beyond and through the image, as if moving from the individuated nature to the exemplar.[26]

3. Theological language and symbols picture a *figura* of infinity, linguistically and in the mind, but do not picture infinity itself. By seeing through the figure the eye may penetrate the wall separating the human and God, and as a consequence the eye may experience "a kind of foretaste" of God's nature,[27] as Cusanus says he hopes to provide through this exercise.

4. The utility of an image is measurable by its effect on the intellect and the senses, by its ability, not to perfect the intellect, but to stir up an experiential inquiry after the exemplar's truth.[28] The Truth will do its own work when the mind is present and ready and moves from one stasis to another.

---

[25]DVD iv, #11.10; vi, #17.9 and #19.13; vii, #22.11; x, #38.5 (h VI 15, 20, 21, 24, 35). See also xviii, #80.3 and xxii, #94.3 ch VI, 63 and 74).

[26]Note especially Cusa's favorite hermeneutical metaphor *translire*: DVD vi, #20.4 and #21.6.12.15; vii, #23.3; and #48.2 (h VI, 22-23, 25, and xii, 41).

[27]DVD prol., #1.15 (h VI, 4). Cf. DVD xvii, #76.4; xvii #78.7; xxiv #107.7.13; xxiv #108.9; xxv #119.4 (h VI, 61-62, 82-83, 89).

[28]Cusa's letter of September 14, 1453 to Aindorffer in Baum and Sengner, *Briefe und Dokumente,* p. 100, speaks of a reference to such an image in his *Complementum theologicum*: ". . . et inserui capitulum, quomodo ex ymagine simul omnia et singula videntis, quam depictam habeo, quodam sensibili experimento ducamur ad misticam theologiam." Cf. *Complementum theologicum,* xiiif. (h X/2a, 70-75).

Image is a special case for Cusanus. By means of image, as a different kind of similitude than analogy or metaphor, the mind moves from a material to an immaterial reality, which is seen in the material as vestige or reflection. An image is a reflection disclosing another, which is partly contained or mirrored in the image, in some sense as its exemplar. Images may be devised by humans or given by God through nature, history, or direct experience. Depiction may be the function of other images, but icons—or words and images used iconically—are to rouse and transport the contemplative to the transcendent. Cusanus' most simple and commonplace method, a *via experimentalis*, is neither a philosophical nor a theological tool, nor any other pedagogical or cognitive device; rather, reaching beyond meditation, it is the pathway of the direct experience of spiritual perception.

When I speak of the text of Cusanus' *De visione Dei* as mystical theology I am making a distinction between the text as iconography and the text as iconic. As iconography, a text would, of course, describe, explain, and interpret the use and meaning of figures or icons but, as iconic, the text itself would serve as a kind of icon, ministering to the reader in the manner of an icon, picturing by its own form, with words or other symbols, so as to signify, convey, and transpose the reader from one state of awareness or experience to another.

In *De visione Dei* Cusanus takes the notion of coincidence to its limits, beyond itself and beyond his previous discussion in *De docta ignorantia* (1440) (*On Learned Ignorance*). However, to see coincidence is still not to see God. God as the apparent object of the human's effort to see, however, acts on our seeing as subject so that the searcher and observer discovers oneself searched out, observed, measured, defined. This is what I mean when I say that Cusanus posits the contemplative as text and icon. This is one of the more interesting features of Cusanus' treatise—the human being as *figura*, for example, the theologian discovering oneself as symbol; the searcher after the meaning behind symbols becomes oneself a symbol. The self becomes the text of a *lectio divina*.[29]

In *De visione Dei* one sees God through and, therefore, beyond image and icon—not merely by means of an icon but by passing through the image and moving from a meditation to a contemplation of the infinite, incomprehensible God beyond all concepts, figures and imaginings. Observing the icon is an exercise in *lectio divina* with Cusanus' all-seeing icon as the text; but for Cusanus, observing the observer is also an experience in *lectio divina* with the contemplator oneself becoming text.

For the human being in time and place there is no escaping image and icon. The very nature and condition of human seeing and knowing require images, comparisons, or similitudes. God, however, is beyond these, beyond everything a sentient being needs in order to know, and therefore cannot be reached or grasped by the human mind. How then, outside what Cusanus calls the wall of Paradise, can the mind see God? And what of God can one see in the present

---

29This is perhaps one of the reasons Martin Buber, *Between Man and Man*, tr. Ronald Gregor Smith (Boston, 1955), p. 131, attributed to Cusanus a praiseworthy new "earnestness" about human beings and the assertion that humans carry all things in themselves and thus can know all things.

life? Cusanus as theologian finds himself required to redefine seeing and knowing, really to redefine defining.

The *De visione Dei* might be more appropriately entitled "God's Sight," for the central focus is God's vision of us, not ours of God. The theme of seeing God seeing us affords Cusanus reflection on what it means to say God sees and on how God sees. For God, seeing is creating. God sees, and we become, all become. For us, seeing God means seeing God see all things, and therefore means seeing all things truly, seeing ourselves in the truest possible vision.

Cusanus offers a variety of ways in which we may see God but all are reducible to God's granting Godself to be seen. Therefore, there is one way in which we may see God—as God makes God accessible to sight, as God discloses God. There are many different ways we may speak of seeing God. In Cusanus' own list, we see God inwardly, contemplatively or mystically, incomprehensibly, metaphorically, transcendently, experientially, coincidentally, priorly, viz. before contradiction and distinction, and inclusively and exclusively, that is, seeing all things in God and seeing only God in all things. Yet these are at their core, the same way of seeing; iconic seeing that takes us beyond modes of seeing to Absolute Sight Itself.

The progression of Cusanus' talk about seeing God in Chapter Six, "*De faciali visione*," is interesting. When we behold God, even by means of the icon, we may say we look inwardly, seeing only with the eyes of the mind and understanding.[30] But the inward motion is also upward. If it can be said that we see God's face at all, we see transcendently, beyond all forms of faces and all figures, beyond concepts; above all these we see Absolute Face Itself. But this invisible truth of God's face is signified under a shadow and limitation in this life. So here God is seen immanently, in all faces, but veiled and in enigma. Whenever we see God, whether obliquely now or directly later, we see God as absolute, as absolutely all that God is, freed (*absolutum*) from every limitation. To see God's face, therefore, is to behold face that is true, unfettered, "absolved," the Absolute Face of faces, the exemplar and true type of all, containing all faces, while not contracted or restricted to any one face.[31]

If we truly see God here, we see in and through enigmata, and we see through and above all faces. In leaping beyond what the eye can of itself see, we see mystically, in a certain secret and mystic silence, Cusanus says, where there is no knowledge or concept:

> This cloud, mist, darkness, or ignorance, into which whoever seeks your face enters when one leaps beyond every knowledge and concept, is such that below it your face cannot be found except veiled. But this very cloud reveals your face to be there beyond all veils.[32]

---

[30]DVD vi, #17 (h VI, 20).

[31]DVD vi, #17-18 (h VI, 20-21).

[32]DVD vi, #21.4-8 (h VI, 23).

The cloud of ignorance is a sacred sign. The light in which we see God is a darkness, because it is a light beyond our seeing and must lack visible light. The denser the cloud or mist is known to be, the more truly we attain the invisible light in the darkness.[33] In such seeing, therefore, what can we say that we see? We see the Absolute, and not simply face itself, but all itself, the whole itself, truth itself, the adequate measure of all. Consequently, when God's face is seen, nothing is seen other than or different from each face which beholds God, "nothing which is other or different from itself, because it sees there its own truth."[34] We see all that we are and all that we can see. We see a face looking back in the same fashion as is the face of the one who looks on God, for the mind sees God according to the nature of its own contraction and passivity or responsiveness. We can only see humanly. We see a face attributed with the nature of the beholder; whether the observer is a human being or an eagle,[35] it will see its own face but as the absolute face, the "sole, truest and most adequate exemplar of all faces, the exemplar of all in such a way that it is the exemplar of each individually and is so most perfectly the exemplar of each as if it were the exemplar of no other."[36]

How then can I see God when all I can see is my own nature? If I see my own nature truly, if I see my own truest self, I see God, and I see God as enfolding all that I am and can be and as enfolding all else. It is not that God is only me, but that *for me* God is only me. All I can see of God is me, but in seeing me truly I see God and all else. When I do so, I must leap beyond the forms of all formable faces and all figures and see myself absolute in God. This is hermeneutics informed by *abstractio* and *ascensus mentis*.

In the next chapter, "*Quis fructus facialis visionis et quomodo habebitur,*" Cusa explains the mystery of this by analogy of power in relation to Absolute Power, specifically of seed to tree. In seeing God as Power, we leap across all knowable and conceivable powers and enter into an ignorance in which no vestige of contracted powers remain. Here alone are we able to see God as Absolute Power, really as the Absolute Itself, as power itself, unapproachable by any imaginable power, the principle giving being to all power, exalted above all, enfolding and containing absolutely whatever it gives to its effect. In the same way, then, God is seen absolutely as the face and exemplar of all faces and of each face, the truth and pattern, the absolute face and absolute power, the nature of all natures.[37]

33DVD vi, #21.20-21 (h VI, 24).

34DVD vi, #18.11-12 (h VI, 21). The English translations are my own; many are adapted from *Nicholas of Cusa: Selected Spiritual Writings,* tr. H. Lawrence Bond (New York, 1997).

35DVD vi, #19.19-22 (h VI, 21).

36DVD vi, #20.1-3 (h VI, 22).

37DVD vii, #24 (h VI, 25-26).

> O God, you have led me to that place in which I see your absolute face to be
> the natural face of all nature, the face which is the absolute entity of all
> being, the art and the knowledge of all that can be known.[38]

To see God's face, accordingly, is to see all things plainly. We see, however,
inasmuch as we are given to see. We see God as God disposes to reveal God to
us. Seeing God is a gift to which we are led. We see by means of unveiling.
Cusanus provides this formula: 1) I do not see God without having God; 2) I do
not attain God and possess God without God's self-revelation to me; and 3) God
does not give God to me without giving me heaven and earth and all that are in
them, without giving me my own self.[39]

He goes on to describe the seeing now at this stage as contemplative and free:

> And when I thus rest in the silence of contemplation, you, Lord, answer me
> within my heart, saying: "Be yours and I too will be yours!"

> O Lord, the Sweetness of every delight, you have placed (within me freedom
> to be my own if I am willing). Hence, unless I am my own, you are not
> mine, for you would constrain my freedom since you cannot be mine unless I
> also am mine. And since you have placed this in my freedom, you do not
> constrain me, but you wait for me to choose to be my own. This depends on
> me and not on you, O Lord, for you do not limit your maximum goodness
> but lavish it on all who are able to receive it.[40]

But how are we able to receive such a gift from God—except by receiving God's
enlightening, by listening to the divine Word speaking within oneself, outside
reason but illumining reason? Here seeing and hearing are one. The Word gives
us sight of God through its speech. For Cusanus epistemology at this level is
all contemplation or *theoria* now. Knowing is seeing and hearing and is
revelational and therapeutic. The Word unceasingly speaks within and would
continually enlighten reason. As we hearken to it, only then do we become our
own, free true selves and, beholding God's face, we become whole.[41]

In Chapter Nine, "*Quomodo est universalis pariter et particularis, et quae via
ad visionem dei,*" Cusanus also describes seeing God as coincidental. Seeing and
not-seeing coincide. It is necessary, Cusanus explains to the brothers, to enter
into the darkness and to admit the coincidence of opposites, beyond reason's
grasp, and to seek the truth where impossibility confronts us. This seeing, in
and through coincidence, occurs beyond even the highest ascent of intellect; it is
not post-ascent but an ascending beyond ascent, which for Cusanus is also

---

[38]DVD vii, #24 (h VI, 26.)

[39]DVD vii, #25 (h VI, 26-27).

[40]DVD vii, #25.15-19 (h VI, 27).

[41]DVD vii, #26 (h VI, 27).

descent. This is the darkest impossibility, the ascent "to that which is unknown to every intellect and which every intellect judges to be the most removed from truth."[42] Here is where God resides—beyond the wall of coincidence of contradictions—where the most remote impossibility coincides with the greatest necessity. Here God is unveiled, and nowhere else is God to be seen.[43]

In yet another refrain reminiscent of *De docta ignorantia*, Cusanus speaks of knowing or of seeing God where reason is vanquished.[44] God is seen incomprehensibly:

> Therefore, I thank you, my God, because you make clear to me that there is no other way of approaching you except that which to all humans, even to the most learned philosophers, seems wholly inaccessible and impossible.[45] For you have shown me that you cannot be seen elsewhere than where impossibility confronts and obstructs me.[46]

Chapter Eleven, "*Quomodo videtur in deo successio sine successione,*" continues the discussion by speaking of going in and out the door of coincidence, seeing by moving from creatures to God and back again, moving in and out simultaneously. This is a vision beyond disjunction and conjunction, for God is Power enfolding and unfolding simultaneously, without contradiction, absolute from all that can be spoken or thought.[47]

All these we can see as God gives us sight and concepts, beyond our own seeing and conceiving. God inspires images or similitudes for us that we may see beyond these what otherwise cannot be seen. The simple concept of a perfect clock, for example, is a mental icon by and through which we are led inward and upward to a higher order of sight. The frailty and corruption of our earthen vessel require that God feed and nourish us with what Cusanus calls the "milk of likenesses" until we are given more solid food.[48] Without God's tutelage and provision we see only darkness and not in and through it.[49]

It is necessary to look beyond similitudes, to proceed beyond one's own power, and to leap across the wall of coincidence, of invisible vision, beyond

---

42DVD ix, #36.5-6 (h VI, 34).

43DVD ix, #37.7-8 (h VI, 35).

44DVD ix, #37.8-10 (h VI, 35).

45Cf. Cusanus' letter of September 14, 1453 to Aindorffer in Baum and Sengner, *Briefe und Dokumente,* p. 98.

46DVD ix, #37.1-5 (h VI, 34).

47DVD ix, #46.6-11 (h VI, 40-41).

48Cf. Hebrews 5:12.

49DVD ix, #45.1-5 (h VI, 40).

which God is to be found.[50] Chapter Twelve, "*Quod ubi invisibilis videtur, increatus creatur*," makes the distinction, however, between God's invisibility in regard to God's own being and visibility in regard to the creature. God is "seen by everyone who sees . . . . both absolute from everything visible and infinitely exalted above all. . . [yet] seen in every visible thing and in every act of vision."[51] The notion of coincidence explains how, though God is infinite and therefore hidden beyond all sight, nevertheless God is to be seen of all and seen in all seeing. With God seeing is creating. God sees only Godself and is the object of God's own sight, for God sees, is to be seen, and is sight. With God, creating and being created are one, for God shares being among all. To share is to be created. So God is All in all but freed from all.[52]

Cusanus remarks that we exist only in the measure in which we behold God.[53] The measure occurs within a diversity of perspective—before, within, and beyond coincidence. What we see of God depends on where we stand. One might also add "if we stand." In the manner of a Benedictine spirituality Cusanus proposes a kind of necessary *stasis* interrupting motion if we are to contemplate truly. If we stand on this side of the wall, we imagine a creator creating; but, if, instead of entering we remain in the wall, we imagine a creatable creator. Once we cross the wall and enter the Garden, we reach a dynamic *stasis* in which we see God: as absolute infinity to whom is suited neither the name of creating creator nor that of creatable creator, then [we] begin to behold [God] unveiled.[54] When we see God as absolute and infinite, we see God as infinitely more than creator and as beyond the coincidence of creating and being created.[55]

But why is this so? Cusanus has been laying the groundwork for the answer throughout the first twelve chapters of the treatise. All are one in God. God does not have plural properties. To see one attribute is to see all. God is never merely power, or goodness, or beauty. Whatever God is, God is "that itself," for example, sight itself. Therefore, we may say God is absolute power itself or sight itself, for whatever God may be said to be, God is above all that may be given in comparison and above all modes of power, or of seeing, or of anything else. God is the Absolute and Infinite Itself of all. If we see God, this is what we see, however we may choose to speak. Since all coincide in God, who is the Absolute and Infinite, power, sight, and all else as enfolded in God are infinite and absolute and are one and the same. The accumulation of scattered but repeated references in the treatise point to a new look at coincidence. Not only

[50]DVD xii, #48.1-2 (h VI, 41).

[51]DVD xii, #47.10-13 (h VI, 41).

[52]DVD xii, #49 (h VI, 42-43).

[53]DVD xii, #47.9-10 (h VI, 41).

[54]DVD xii, #50 (h VI, 43).

[55]DVD xii, #49.14-16 (h VI, 43).

do all things coincide in God; but, in God, all is God and all exist not only prior to opposition but prior even to coincidence.

Cusanus writes as if he were presenting a series of reflections as they occur, as if each chapter were a separate meditation of its own, as if the author were himself in a process of discovering as he writes that each reconsideration of the gaze of God, first from one angle of his own inner vision and then from another, were leading him to the same contemplation: God as Absolute Infinity, not as philosophic hypothesis nor as concept, but as what I am calling "contemplative experience." This is a non-conceptual knowing, which is entirely a knowing, though it may be best described negatively as a not-knowing.

Chapter Thirteen, "*Quod deus omnia complicat sine alteritate,*" represents a kind of denouement in the book. As if a drama were being worked out, Cusanus' own soul or mind, seeking God in and through the meditation he is recommending to the brothers, reaches a critical moment of discovery:

> O Lord God, helper of those who seek you, I [behold] you in the garden of Paradise, and I do not know what I see, because I see nothing visible. I know this alone that I know that I do not know what I see and that I can never know. I do not know how to name you, because I do not know what you are.[56]

Not only is this the notion of learned ignorance; this is also the description of the experience of it. This is event, not concept. This is what I am calling the experience of God as beyond names:

> Should anyone tell me that you are named by this or that name, by the fact that one gives a name I know that it is not your name. For the wall beyond which I see you is the limit of every mode of signification by names. Should anyone express any concept by which you could be conceived, I know that this concept is not a concept of you, for every concept finds its boundary at the wall of Paradise. Should anyone express any likeness and say that you ought to be conceived according to it, I know in the same way that this is not a likeness of you. So too if anyone, wishing to furnish the means by which you might be understood, should set forth an understanding of you, one is still far removed from you. For a most towering wall separates you from all these and secludes you from everything that can be said or thought, because you are absolute from all the things that can fall within any concept. Accordingly, when I am lifted up to the highest, I see you as infinity. For this reason you cannot be approached, comprehended, named, multiplied, or seen.[57]

The intellect knows God via contemplative ascent, in and through the darkness of ignorance. The intellect must become ignorant, must become established in

---

[56]DVD xiii, #51.3-6 (h VI, 44).

[57]DVD xiii, #51.6-19 and #52.1-3 (h VI, 44).

darkness in order to see:[58] "O God, you are infinity, and no one can approach you except one whose intellect abides in ignorance, that is, one whose intellect knows that it is ignorant of you."[59] This is the kind of "learned ignorance" Cusanus speaks of, and this is the learned ignorance he knows presumably by his own experience as recapitulated in the treatise.

I am calling this a contemplative and sacred ignorance, as it is described here, because I see it presented in *De visione Dei* less as concept and more as *admiratio* and *adoratio*, as wonder and worship. The work is more than a manual of instruction; it is clearly also a confession of experiencing God. The details, the *affectio*, the cogency, the intellectual integrity of the work all strongly suggest that the treatise is a record of Cusanus' own practice of *theoria* or *contemplatio* as well as theological and philosophical analysis. Clearly this is the style and method of the writing: dialogue in contemplative experience of God. It is a journal of prayer and vision, however instructive Cusanus may also intend the work to be. Could anyone write such prayers without first having prayed them? This *manuductio* seems as much for Cusanus himself as for the reader.

How can the intellect be said to see or know God? The journey of the mind that Cusanus describes through Chapter Thirteen reaches into a dark cloud. But this is the beginning of seeing, though it occurs in an obscurity.[60]

Nicholas of Cusa entitles the chapter with the thesis: "*Quod deus videtur absoluta infinitas.*" For Cusa this is the moment of crisis in a meditation that urges an ascent of the mind: to move from textual meditation to contemplation beyond text, beyond mind, beyond seeing. What could be more impossible to see than *utter infinity* – unlimitedness beyond the powers of conception and abstraction? Cusa, therefore, opens the chapter with a plaintive confession of faith summarizing the core of his negative theology: "*hoc scio solum, quia scio me nescire, quid video, et numquam scire posse. . . . nescio, quid sis.*"[61]

Chapter Thirteen is a meditation on infinity, as set forth by the icon, the infinity of God seen contemplatively. This takes place above reason. One is tempted to say above mind, especially if by mind one means a grasping, percipient, comprehending organ. God can be said to be known only if the unknowable could be known, the invisible seen, the inaccessible attained, and the incomprehensible comprehended.[62] But the Infinite itself is not to be grasped at any level or by any means. We do not comprehend. Instead, we acknowledge the absurd: that the end is endless, that darkness is light, that ignorance is knowledge, that the impossible is necessary. This embraces some other kind of knowing. This is some other kind of coincidence. This coincidence of contra-

---

[58] DVD xiii, #52.8-9 (h VI, 45).

[59] DVD xiii, #52.11-12 (h VI, 45).

[60] DVD xiii, #52.6-8 (h VI, 45).

[61] DVD xiii, #51.4-6 (h VI, 44).

[62] DVD xiii, #52.13-18 (h VI, 45).

dictories is "contradiction without contradiction," "an opposition of opposites" and "an opposition without opposition." Why? Because God is infinity itself, and absolute infinity is simplicity itself. In infinity, which is simplicity, the opposition of opposites exists without opposition, just as in unity otherness exists without otherness because it is unity.63

Cusanus continues his meditation on infinity in Chapter Fifteen, "*Quomodo actualis infinitas est unitas, in qua figura est veritas,*" and reminds the contemplative reader of what one is expected to see. The gaze of the icon's painted face is not limited to an object or a place; it is not turned more to one beholding it than to another; yet it fixes its gaze on anyone looking at it as if it saw only this person and nothing else. The gaze is intended to represent an infinite gaze and therefore the infinite in itself. Consequently, one is able to see an image of infinity in it.64

Cusanus prays "Thus, O Lord, you appear to me as if absolute and infinite *posse esse*, formable and determinable by every form."65 Therefore, when we see in the icon an image of infinity, at first we appear to be seeing "formable prime matter" because the contemplated image seems to take on the form of whoever beholds it. But then meditation is transformed into contemplation by divine *elevatio* so that we may see that looking on God does not give God form; but rather we see ourselves in God for, in fact, we receive from God what we are. Cusanus goes on to address God as "the living mirror of eternity," in which one does not see an image but the exemplar itself, the truth of which the one who sees is the image.66

Who then are we who would see God? Cusanus takes special pains to delineate the divine and iconic seeing available to human beings. We are not the seers; we are the seen. Even when we contemplate, we contemplate ourselves. We are always the *imago,* never the subject of the highest seeing. We are "a living shadow," and God the original truth. Our seeing is a being seen. God is never the object of our sight; God is the eternal subject of seeing. The truth of our face is changeable; the absolute truth of God is not. Our face is truth insofar as it is image but image insofar as it is truth. Why then, in contemplating the icon, does God's face seem to change, while the truth of God's face always remains unchangeable? As we change, God does not abandon the truth of our face, which because it is the truth of an image and changeable could not exist without God's participation.67 Cusanus breaks into a doxology:

O profoundest Depth, my God, you who do not abandon your creatures and at the same time do not follow after them! O inexplicable Lovingkindness, you

---

63DVD xiii, #54.1-10 (h VI, 46).

64DVD xv, # 61.5-11 (h VI, 51).

65DVD xv, #61.11-12 (h VI, 51-52).

66DVD xv, #63 (h VI, 53).

67DVD xv, #65.1-10 (h VI, 54).

offer yourself to any of us looking on you, as though you receive being from us, and you conform yourself to us so that we will love you more the more you seem like us. For we cannot hate ourselves. Therefore, we love that which participates and accompanies our being. We embrace our likeness because we are shown ourselves in an image and we love ourselves in it.[68]

Cusanus insists that God presents God as if our creature in order to draw us to God: for the likeness that seems to be created by us is the Truth that creates us.[69] In Chapter Sixteen, "*Quod nisi deus esset infinitus, non foret finis desiderii*," Cusanus goes on to say that God appears to us in our very desire for God. God is said to "shine forth" in the desire that is insatiable by anything finite or comprehensible. Cusanus sets down this contemplative dictum: the more we comprehend God to be incomprehensible, the more we attain God because the more we attain the end of our desire.[70]

Cusanus completes his meditation of the icon in Chapter Seventeen, "*Quod deus non nisi unitrinus videri perfecte potest,*" with a summation of the icon's effect and special meaning. His words serve as a kind of caveat of humility and reverence to the reader and to himself as he acknowledges what he has and what he has not done:

I have set forth, Lord, by a likeness a kind of foretaste of your nature. But you who are merciful be sparing for I am attempting to depict the undepictable taste of your sweetness. For if the sweetness of an unknown fruit remains unable to be depicted by every picture and symbol or unable to be expressed by every word, who am I, a wretched sinner, to strive to show you who cannot be shown and to depict you who are invisible as visible and to presume to make savory your infinite and utterly inexpressible sweetness? I have never yet merited to taste it. And through that which I describe here I diminish rather than magnify it. But so great is your goodness, my God, that you even permit the blind to speak of the light and to herald the praises of him of whom they neither know anything nor can know unless it is revealed to them.[71]

Cusanus acknowledges that the "wall" of the coincidence of the hidden and revealed has shut out the power of the intellect. Yet the eye of the mind is permitted to look beyond into Paradise. But what the eye can see through the grace of contemplative experience it can neither say nor understand. Even after having been seen, divine truth remains hidden.[72]

---

[68]DVD xv, #65.11-17 (h VI, 54).

[69]DVD xv, #66.1-2 (h VI, 54).

[70]DVD xvi, #69.1-3 (h VI, 57).

[71]DVD xvii, #78.6-15-#79.1-3 (h VI, 62.)

[72]DVD xvii, #75.10-14 (h VI, 61).

In one final reconsideration Cusanus begins to speak of the experience of hope and the foretaste of joy in place of knowledge:

I have ventured to surrender myself to rapture in order to see you who are invisible and who are unrevealable vision revealed. You know how far I have reached, but I do not; yet your grace is sufficient . . . by it you both assure me that you are incomprehensible and also lift me up into the firm hope that through your guidance I may come to enjoy you forever.[73]

Neither revelation nor faith attains to the contemplative tasting of God, only to foretasting.[74] For Cusanus, in this life the consummation is foreseen and therefore foretasted not only through a divine gift in contemplative practice, but also by experiencing hope manifested in contemplative prayer:

O God, you have revealed to me that ear has not heard nor has there descended into the human heart the infinity of your sweetness, which has been prepared for those who love you.[75] This was revealed to us by Paul, your great apostle, who was caught up, beyond the wall of coincidence, into Paradise,[76] where alone you, who are the fountain of delights, can be seen without veil.[77]

This may be the book's denouement, but it is not its end. How does God provide for a knowing and seeing extended beyond our capacity for knowing and seeing? The rest of the *De visione Dei* comprises a series of meditations on Jesus, who reveals not only God but our truest human self.

This crucial point of resolution by the end of Chapter Seventeen, which is the treatise's last major appeal to the icon, leads quite naturally to the question of contemplative practice and the reading of *De visione Dei* as Cusanus might have us enter the text today. This poses special problems for the historian. In addition to the conventional historical questions about textual authenticity and interpretations appropriate to Cusanus' particular intentions, the topic also brings the historian closer *to* the work of the philosopher and of the theologian and, even more perilously, *into* the practice of the devout and the contemplative, into one's own practice of spirituality. Beyond questions of historicity, this topic asks of the text not only the philosophical theological questions—is it true and what kind of truth does it embrace, but also the spiritual and devotional

---

[73]DVD xvii, #79.9-14 (h VI, 63).

[74]Cf. *Idiota de sapientia* I,19 (h V2, 41-42) where Cusa stresses tasting wisdom experientially in oneself by an interior tasting.

[75]I Cor. 2:9.

[76]Is 64:4 and 2 Cor 12:4.

[77]DVD xvii, #4-9 (h VI, 62-63).

questions—how can it be true for me and how can I appropriate its truth within me.

I began this study by asking myself the larger question of the extent to which Cusanus' writings lend themselves to *contemplative* practice. It seemed obvious that many of his texts could be read *meditatively*. There is in fact already a book in English of paraphrased selections from Cusanus' writings entitled *Meditations with Nicholas of Cusa*.[78]

But I have posed the question of contemplation, and I see it as different from that of meditation and from the kind of philosophic contemplation that Aristotle and other classical writers had in mind. *Contemplatio,* as this essay comes to a close, is limited to a prayerful state, to a soulful reaching beyond articulation and cognition. I wondered to what extent Cusanus' writings could still accommodate the traditional Benedictine form of prayer—*lectio, oratio, meditatio,* and *contemplatio.*

I have emphasized several distinctions in the treatise's mystical theology —to the extent that one can differentiate between a meditation of the "icon" and a contemplation of it. I have also attempted to distinguish between a meditation on the icon and a meditation on both the text and contemplative reader and between meditation on all three and the contemplative practice issuing from it.

How then might meditative practice lead to contemplative prayer in a manner corresponding to the mystical theology of Cusanus' text? I want to end this essay by venturing to propose a model not only in conformity with Cusanus' iconic theologizing in the first sixteen chapters of *De visione Dei,* but also with his final reflections in the seventeenth chapter of what he himself has experienced in the course of his own meditation on the icon and what he hopes to accomplish for the reader.

---

[78]*Meditations with Nicholas of Cusa,* tr. James Francis Yockey (Santa Fe, New Mexico, 1987).

GUIDED MEDITATION ON "THE FACE"

BASED ON CHAPTER VI ¶17-21 FROM
NICHOLAS OF CUSA'S *DE VISIONE DEI SIVE DE ICONA*

I want to ask you to close your eyes
for a few moments and to image:

I want you to follow me
into a dark cloud,
a mist so dense
we are hidden from each other,
and although we can see,
there is nothing to be seen
except the darkness.

While there, in that dark place,
I want you to peer into the mist
and imagine the face of God,
like the face in the icon,
a face without narrative or locality,
a universal face,
that contains all faces,
all the faces of humanity
and all the faces of nature,
all the faces of being,
and of not-being,
of all creation
and of all not yet created,
an infinite face,
borderless, boundless,
itself uncontained
and yet containing all.

I want you to let this face observe you,
and, wherever you turn,
pursue you with its eyes,
and encompass you,
and penetrate you,
so that, when you dare to gaze back,
you see with God's eyes,
and now you see all things
embraced in the face of God,
and, among all the faces you might see,
you can see there too
your own face -- enfolded.
I want you now to imagine your own face,
as if you were the icon.

Examine carefully each line,
each mark
of time and experience.
Simply observe
the special characteristics
that comprise you.

Notice the wounds,
all the vestiges of pain,
every brokenness and defect.

And now find God's face in your face,
See how God has made
the broken places whole;
see how in God
your face is transformed.

Among all the features
you might see in your face,
observe the divine potentiality,
the latent power,
love, and all the other capacities
that are the traces of the divine,
just as you might discover
the parent's face in the child.
Contemplate carefully,
compassionately and
without judgment,
and see God unfolded in you.

THE CURSE OF CUSANUS: EXCOMMUNICATION
IN FIFTEENTH CENTURY GERMANY

Brian A. Pavlac

One of the few "weapons" canon law made available to clergy trying to discipline or punish people has been the infamous "curse" of excommunication. A notorious user of this punishment was the man who was the bishop of Brixen from 1450 to 1464, namely Cardinal Nicholas of Cusa, or Nicolaus Cusanus. He allegedly overused and misused this stricture while trying to reform ecclesiastical and political systems in his diocese. [1] But these excommunications (coupled with the imposition of interdicts) hardly achieved the obedience Bishop Nicholas sought. Instead, many observers have held that these excommunications contributed to his humiliating failure as bishop, a setback which has cursed his reputation ever since.[2] Nonetheless, the reason for his excommunications' failures needs to be clarified. Surveying some contemporary examples in the Holy Roman Empire of the 15th century and examining Nicolaus Cusanus' actual bans, it becomes clear that the problem was less with the person than with the sentence itself. Bishop Nicholas of Brixen's excommunications failed because contemporary secular and canon law, political practices, and the lack of a reforming spirituality undermined such sentences.

One could compare the overuse issue to a contemporary legal problem: drunk driving. Our contemporary society has decided drunk driving is a crime and has instituted various methods to combat it, especially arrest and imprisonment. Yet the complaints about sobriety checkpoints and abuse of police powers are frequent and loud. If dozens of persons are arrested for drunk driving, however,

---

[1] Pardon E. Tillinghast, "Nicholas of Cusa versus Sigmund of Habsburg: an Attempt at Post-conciliar Church Reform," CH 36 (1967): 390; Erich Meuthen, *Nikolaus von Kues 1401-1464: Skizze einer Biographie*, 5th ed. (Münster, 1982), p. 104; Andreas Posch, "Nikolaus von Cusa, Bischof von Brixen, im Kampf um Kirchenreform und Landeshoheit in seinem Bistum," in *Cusanus Gedächtnisschrift: Im Auftrag der Rechts- und Staatswissenschaftlichen Fakultät der Universität Innsbruck*, ed. Nikolaus Grass (Innsbruck-München, 1970), p. 250; in the same volume: Nikolaus Grass, "Cusanus als Rechtshistoriker, Quellenkritiker und Jurist: Skizzen und Fragmente," p. 136; Anselm Sparber, "Aus der Wirksamkeit des Kardinals Nikolaus von Kues als Fürstbischof von Brixen (1450-1464)," in *Niccolò Cusano agli inizi del mondo moderno: Atti del Congresso internazionale in occasione del V centenario della morte di Niccolò Cusano, Bressanone, 6-10 settembre 1964* (Firenze, 1970), pp. 530, 533. See also Albert Jäger, *Der Streit des Cardinals Nikolaus von Cusa mit dem Herzog Sigmund von Österreich als Grafen von Tirol: Ein Bruchstück aus den Kämpfen der weltlichen und kirchlichen Gewalt nach dem Concilium zu Basel*, 2 vols. (Innsbruck, 1861).

[2] For these and other reasons for his failure, see Brian A. Pavlac, "Nicolaus Cusanus as Prince-Bishop of Brixen (1450-64): Historians and a Conflict of Church and State," *Historical Reflections/Réflexions Historiques* 21 (1995): 131-154 and Morimichi Watanabe, "Nicholas of Cusa and the Tyrolese Monasteries: Reform and Resistance," *History of Political Thought* 9 (1986): 53-72. See also Hermann J. Hallauer, *Nikolaus von Kues als Bischof und Landesfürst in Brixen* (Trier, 2000).

the problem seems to be not the overuse of the arresting jurisdiction of the state but too many drunk drivers. Even one is too many in a state that has outlawed that behavior, except for the unfortunate reality that many people regularly violate drunk-driving laws. In addition, along many highways you can see posted the slogan: "Drunk drivers go to jail!" Still, it is quite obvious that many drunk drivers do not go to jail: those not caught, those not convicted, and even those let off with lighter sentences. To achieve these last two results, lawyers use all sorts of methods in the courtroom, from questioning police procedure and evidence to arguing mitigating circumstances, or appealing to the sympathies of the judge. The imposition of law has never been perfect or absolute, but the widespread scofflaw attitude about drunk driving clearly undermines respect for authority.

The sentence of excommunication or anathema in the late Middle Ages was facing still greater problems of enforcement than our own issue of drunk driving. As far as punishment went, it was supposed to be worse than jail. As Julius Goebel, Jr., puts it, excommunication would have been the ultimate punishment against the contumacious, since "it embodie[d] a curse that w[ould] either bring [a person] to grace or assure his eternal damnation."[3] In medieval society, where many believed in heaven and hell, excommunication was often seen as a real threat to salvation in the next world, as well as life in this one. In this life, it at least halted participation in the sacraments; and, in its greatest form, it prohibited all social, political and economic contact with other Christians. To be absolved from these strictures and reconciled to the Church, one had only to ask forgiveness from the proper authority, cease the bad behavior, and probably perform some sort of penance. The grounds for invoking excommunication covered a whole range of behaviors. Latent excommunication automatically inflicted anathema, without a formal sentencing, for acts such as violence against a cleric. Usually, a bishop, including the pope, needed to specifically pronounce and publish the excommunication, whether by announcing from the chancel or posting a notice on church doors.

In any case, the condemned may not have had a legal hearing to present their side of the matter. When the growing sophistication of lawyers and a legal mentality in the late Middle Ages did insist on a trial or hearing, often it took place after the official imposition. Whether a hearing had taken place or not, the accursed often lodged an appeal.[4] Thus a legal process frequently followed the punishment, even though, ironically, it was supposed to take away one's legal standing in court. And while on appeal, any restrictions could be considered

---

[3]Julius Goebel, Jr., *Felony and Misdemeanor: A Study in the History of Criminal Law* (Philadelphia, 1976): 263-264. For a brief description of excommunication and some examples of its successful use, see Brian A. Pavlac, "Excommunication and Territorial Politics in High Medieval Trier," CH 60 (1991): 20-36.

[4]Even Cusanus in his *Catholic Concordance,* CC II,31,227 (h XIV, 270-271), suggested that, if a bishop punished a cleric, that person should be able to appeal to the next higher authority; see also Paul E. Sigmund, *Nicholas of Cusa and Medieval Political Thought* (Cambridge, Massachusetts, 1963), p. 184.

suspended. Accordingly, the whole appeals process undermined the effectiveness of the sentence.[5] Anyone could simply ignore the provisions by saying they were under appeal. Adding to the success of appeals was the confusion of the excommunication law, which had enough loopholes to create all sorts of problems. The Council of Basel's minor attempt at reform only complicated the issue.[6] All of this supports the point made by Elizabeth Vodola in her major study of excommunication. She argues that the deathblow to excommunication came when it lost the shame factor based on a theology of penance and instead became associated with the sphere of law.[7] Without a spiritual sense of sin and reconciliation, excommunication became a mere rule, particularly vulnerable to innumerable scofflaws.

Nonetheless, church authorities applied this sanction frequently throughout the early fifteenth century. If we merely take the continuous flagrant disobedience of an ecclesiastical superior as justifiable grounds for excommunication, its use was certainly warranted many times (although just as ineffective). Consider two examples with which Nicolaus Cusanus would have been familiar.

First, the use of excommunication during the Hussite controversy by no means succeeded in bringing the Bohemians back to Catholicism. When John Hus himself was excommunicated in 1410, partly for refusing to obey a command to appear before the pope, the local populace ignored the sentence, running the archbishop out of town.[8] Key to resistance, of course, was the acquiescence of the local territorial prince, King Wenceslaus, whose vacillations allowed the Hussites to ignore excommunication. Additionally, Hus' lawyer, John von Jessenitz, filed an appeal in Rome, which held up implementation of Hus' excommunication for more than a year. Jessenitz then got himself cursed, condemned as a heretic and imprisoned, but escaped and quickly earned a legal degree at the University of Bologna despite his own excommunication![9] Only Hus' walking into the Council of Constance, where he was arrested and burned alive, allowed the Church to punish him.

His followers continued in their unorthodox ways, however. Despite two crusading military invasions which were soundly thrown back, the excommunicated heretics in Bohemia remained intransigent and defiant of the Church's denunciations. In the 1430's they tried to present their case to the Council of

---

[5]Donald Sullivan, "Nicholas of Cusa as Reformer: The Papal Legation to the Germanies, 1451-1452," *Mediaeval Studies* 35 (1974): 423.

[6]Elisabeth Vodola, *Excommunication in the Middle Ages* (Berkeley, 1986), pp. 142-145.

[7]Vodola, *Excommunication*, p. 193.

[8]Howard Kaminsky, *A History of the Hussite Revolution* (Berkeley and Los Angeles, 1967), pp. 73-74, 91.

[9]Albert Hauck, *Kirchengeschichte Deutschlands,* 5 vols. (Leipzig, 1911), 5/2.925, 939-949.

Basel. There Nicolaus Cusanus dealt with their grievances, which included the worldly power and wealth of bishops.[10] The nominally-excommunicated, heretical Bohemian delegates at the council seem to have been treated with respect, and Cusanus even tried to pressure them into joining the council (although they declared this a trick to tie them up in protocol). The council, in the name of the Church and the papacy, eventually accepted the Prague Compacts, which granted victory to these excommunicates without any real penance.

By the 1460's, however, the new Pope Pius II (1458-1464) hoped King George Podiebrand could mediate Bohemia's obedience to the Roman See.[11] In a conference with his representatives in March 1462, Cardinal Cusanus demanded that the Bohemians follow the orders of the pope and not "make a joke of the very word obedience."[12] They remained obdurate, notwithstanding. When Cusanus died in 1464, he was preparing for Pope Pius a final text of an excommunication bull against King George of Bohemia.[13] Postponed by Cusanus' and then Pius' passing, the Church pronounced King George's excommunication on December 23, 1466. Even then his people did not rebel against him. Both another crusade and the attacks by the kings of Hungary and Poland failed to break his position.[14] Neither excommunication nor military force substantially affected the course of the Bohemian schism.

A second example comes from Cusanus' homeland of Trier, where excommunication and interdict were the order of the day. A conflict had broken out between Ulrich von Manderscheid, who claimed to be the duly elected archbishop of Trier, and Hraban of Helmstädt, the bishop of Speyer, papally provided to that see[15] Hraban's connections with the pope led to excommunication and other

---

[10]Frantisek Smahel, "The Hussite Critique of the Clergy's Civil Dominion," in *Anticlericalism in Late Medieval and Early Modern Europe*, ed. Peter A. Dykema and Heiko A. Oberman (Leiden, 1991), p. 88. See also *Unity and Reform: Selected Writings of Nicholas of Cusa,* ed. John Patrick Dolan (South Bend, 1962), p. 27; Frederick G. Heymann, *George of Bohemia, King of Heretics* (Princeton, 1965), pp. 68-69.

[11]Wilhelm Baum, *Nikolaus Cusanus in Tirol: Das Wirken des Philosophen als Fürstbischof von Brixen* (Bozen/Bolzano, 1983), pp. 274-277.

[12]Heymann, *George*, pp. 267, 273.

[13]Edward Winter, "Das geistige Profil von Nikolaus von Kues im Widerstreit der Zeit," in *Nikolaus von Kues: Wissenschaftliche Konferenz des Plenums der Deutschen Akademie der Wissenschaften zu Berlin anläßlich der 500. Wiederkehr seines Todesjahres, Referate und Diskussionsbeiträge* (Berlin, 1965), p. 11.

[14]Manfred Schulze, *Fürsten und Reformation: Geistliche Reformpolitik weltlicher Fürsten vor der Reformation* (Tübingen, 1991), p. 44.

[15]Erich Meuthen, *Das Trierer Schisma von 1430 auf dem Basler Konzil: Zur Lebensgeschichte des Nikolaus von Kues* (Münster, 1964).

censures imposed on Ulrich and his supporters in 1431, which were not removed until December 26, 1435. In spite of these, Ulrich appealed over the head of the pope to the Council of Basel and chose Nicolaus Cusanus to argue his case there. Thus, during these years, Nicholas of Cusa himself consorted with the known excommunicate Ulrich in open defiance of ecclesiastical commands. Indeed, as representative of the interdicted and excommunicated Trier clergy and as Ulrich's advocate in the appeals to the council, Cusanus could himself have been considered excommunicated.[16] While Nicholas issued legal rationales for his patron's candidacy and against recognizing the efficacy of spiritual weapons, Ulrich launched the Manderscheidsche Fehde. Ulrich, his relatives, and noble allies began military campaigns to control the castles and cities of the Trier see. He besieged Trier itself through the Easter season and again in late summer 1433 (although in the latter siege, a chronicler claimed that no man or animal had been injured, through the grace of God, except one dog).[17] After many delays, in May 1434 the Council of Basel finally decided the election controversy in favor of Hraban. Yet the fighting continued until February 1436, when a compromise was negotiated that basically bought off Ulrich and left Hraban heavily in debt.[18] Excommunication had not really influenced the events at all: lawyers, soldiers and cash seem to have been what counted.

A few years after these fights, Hraban was succeeded by Archbishop Jacob I von Sierck (1439-1456), who also ran into excommunication.[19] While a Trier cleric denigrated Jacob as "greedy," the renowned humanist Aeneas Sylvius Piccolomini praised him for being "as virtuous as he was noble."[20] Jacob ran afoul of excommunication when he and Archbishop Dietrich von Mörs of

---

[16]Meuthen, *Das Trierer Schisma*, pp. 121, 127, 136, 139, 258; see also Joachim W. Stieber, "The 'Hercules of the Eugenians' at the Crossroads: Nicholas of Cusa's Decision for the Pope and against the Council in 1436/1437—Theological, Political and Social Aspects," in *Nicholas of Cusa in Search of God and Wisdom: Essays in Honor of Morimichi Watanabe*, ed. Gerald Christianson and Thomas M. Izbicki (Leiden, 1991), pp. 232-233.

[17]Johann Leonardy, *Geschichte des Trierischen Landes und Volkes*, second ed. (Trier, 1877; reprint Trier, 1982): 560; see also Meuthen, *Das Trierer Schisma*, p. 176.

[18]Meuthen, *Das Trierer Schisma*, pp. 219, 250; Peter L. McDermott, "Nicholas of Cusa: Continuity and Conciliation at the Council of Basel," CH 67 (1998): 266; Sigmund, *Nicholas of Cusa*, pp. 219-220.

[19]Coincidentally, Jacob was almost Hraban's predecessor, since his quarrel with Ulrich von Manderscheid had sparked the original electoral controversy. As his coadjutor, Jacob was practically running the see in Hraban's last years. Ulrich died in 1438 on his way to visit the pope.

[20]*Memoirs of a Reniassance Pope: The Commentaries of Pius II*, trans. Florence A. Gragg (New York, 1959), p. 40. On Aeneas and Cusanus, see Wilhelm Baum, "Enea Silvio Piccolomini (Pius II.), Cusanus und Tirol," *Der Schlern* 56 (1982): 174-195.

Cologne worked together to maintain good relations with the now anti-papal Council of Basel and the anti-pope Felix, while they avoided proper obeisance to Pope Eugene IV (1431-1447). A minor dispute between the archbishop of Trier and his cathedral chapter, though, gave Eugene the chance to excommunicate and declare the deposition of both Jacob and Dietrich in 1446.[21] Yet most German princes ignored these castigations and both prince-archbishops maintained their leadership positions.[22] For example, at the meeting at Frankfurt in September 1446 to settle issues of Empire and Church, the archbishops of Cologne and Trier, although excommunicated and deposed, met with other electors, bishops, princes as well as representatives for the pope: Aeneas Sylvius, Cardinal Juan Carvajal and Nicolaus Cusanus. For the archbishops it seems that deposition was a more serious issue than excommunication. Had their subjects recognized that punishment, they might actually have lost power.[23] By early 1447, both had come to some terms with the papacy, although full relations were only restored with Eugene's successor, Pope Nicholas V (1447-1455) and neither really petitioned for forgiveness.[24] Other examples from the empire would make clear that although excommunication was a constant threat and some people may have feared it, politics were more important.[25]

How did Cusanus fare with his own use of excommunication? Bishop Nicholas first used it outside of his own see. As legate for the pope, Cardinal Cusanus often threatened and sometimes used excommunication during his great legation journey through Germany during 1451 and 1452. Yet he seems to have had little success with it, as the cases of Cloister Wülzburg or of the bleeding hosts of Wilsnack illustrate.[26] Despite Germany's notable resistance to reform,

---

[21]Joachim W. Stieber, *Pope Eugenius IV, the Council of Basel, and the Secular and Ecclesiastical Authorities in the Empire: The Conflict over Supreme Authority and Power in the Church* (Leiden, 1978), p. 276; Rudolf Holbach, *Stiftsgeistlichkeit in Trier: Studien zur Geschichte des Trierer Domkapitels und Domklerus im Spätmittelalter* (Trier, 1982), p. 240.

[22]Stieber, *Eugenius*, p. 277. Holbach, *Stiftsgeistlichkeit*, p. 240, notes how Jacob at the same time tried to use excommunication against regional rivals like Count Henry of Nassau-Beilstein.

[23]Stieber, *Eugenius*, pp. 288, 290.

[24]Stieber, *Eugenius*, p. 308. Ironically, Holbach, *Stiftsgeistlichkeit*, pp. 240-241, notes how Pope Nicholas then had to excommunicate and interdict the Trier clergy in order to help Jacob restore his authority.

[25]Stieber, *Eugenius*, pp. 321-322.

[26]Many of the documents concerning this legation are now published in *Acta Cusana: Quellen zur Lebensgeschichte des Nikolaus von Kues*, ed. Erich Meuthen, 2 vols., 1/3A (Hamburg, 1996-2000); see especially Nr. 1694, 1829, 1211. See also Stieber, *Eugenius*, pp. 340-341; Sullivan, "Nicholas of Cusa," p. 404; Erich Meuthen, "Die deutsche Legationsreise des Nikolaus von Kues 1451-1452," in

Cusanus determined to carry on with his mission upon entering his own see of Brixen. He maintained high standards, held reforming synods, preached regularly, and called on other clerics to assist him in the reformation of religious foundations. His reforms for the laity also carried the sharp stick of the threat of anathema.[27] In trying to change laypeople's behavior, he made significant use of its latent form. Modern historians criticize Cusanus' excommunications and interdicts as unfairly hurting the poor mountain farmers, expecially when he forbade the use of milk products during Lent[28] or when he unfairly threatened vassals with excommunication for not paying their tax bills on time.[29] Further, he unreasonably applied excommunication for carrying weapons on church holidays or for dancing then.[30] According to Cusanus, rowdy dancing and weapons could lead to scandals displeasing to God. Concerning any actual unhappiness among the people, however, little reliable evidence exists about how many were actually affected or how deeply they felt about it.

One exception pertains to dancing, which, strangely enough, actually led to an explicit excommunication—or perhaps not so strangely, because the target was Casper von Gufidaun, a powerful noble whose family was implicated in a plot to kidnap or murder the bishop in 1457. Back in 1455, however, the family had benefited from monies collected for providing security surrounding the dancing at festivals. When they protested Cusanus' new ordinance against dancing, Casper found himself excommunicated. Finally, after three years, Casper von Gufidaun, with all humility, acknowledged Nicolaus Cusanus' authority and petitioned for the removal of the censures. Once again he could enjoy entering churches, partaking in the sacraments and visiting cemeteries.[31] Although his words of repentance sound sincere, how much did this rough noble really believe them?

The crux of Cusanus' reform program was the status of the clergy, who, as agents of the Church, stood as examples and guides for the laypeople. Thus

---

Lebenslehren und Weltentwürfe im Übergang vom Mittelalter zur Neuzeit: Politik-Bildung-Naturkunde-Theologie (Bericht über Kolloquien der Kommission zur Erforschung der Kultur des Spätmittelalters 1983 bis 1987.), ed. Hartmut Boockmann, Bernd Moeller and Karl Stackmann (Göttingen, 1989), pp. 421-499; and Josef Koch, *Der deutsche Kardinal in deutschen Landen: Die Legationsreise des Nikolaus von Kues (1451/2)* (Trier, 1964).

[27]Sullivan, "Nicholas of Cusa," p. 402, Meuthen, "Die deutsche Legationsreise," p. 470.

[28]Nikolaus Grass, *Cusanus und das Volkstum der Berge* (Innsbruck, 1972), pp. 40-49.

[29]Winter, "Das geistige Profil," p. 10.

[30]Grass, *Cusanus und das Volkstum*, p. 63; Tillinghast, "Nicholas of Cusa," p. 385; Watanabe, "Tyrolese Monasteries," p. 57. Wilhelm Baum and Raimund Senoner, *Nikolas von Kues: Briefe und Dokumente der Brixiner Zent,* 2 vols. (Wien, 1998), 2.106-109.

[31]Baum, *Cusanus in Tirol*, pp. 355-356.

Bishop Nicholas needed to improve the lives of his see's priests and monks, backed up by latent ecclesiastical censure. Priests who had not abandoned concubines, who deviated from the standard missal, or used a host made of mixed grains faced excommunication.[32] Resisting correct observance of a monastic rule might bring down the malediction. Concern about this led some monks to complain that the threat of excommunication by Nicolaus Cusanus made them fear that any little infraction might lead to damnation. He tried to reassure them that the curse was meant for the truly rebellious who resisted reform.[33] Again it is unclear how many explicitly suffered this punishment.

More infamously, however, Cusanus dealt out several serious ecclesiastical censures to specific members of his Tyrolean clergy. One example was the curse of the contrary canons. Bishop Nicholas wanted to grant the benefices that had belonged to the canon Leonhard Wiesmair to his own nephew Simon von Wehlen. This transfer had become complicated because Wiesmair was the bishop-elect whom Cusanus had himself replaced as a papal provision.[34] Further, Wiesmair had subsequently become the bishop-elect of the neighboring diocese of Chur and was likewise temporarily caught up in an electoral conflict over that see, earning him papal excommunication. In this dispute about the benefices, Cusanus had excommunicated four canons who openly disapproved of the reassignment of the prebends.[35]

While some historians criticize Cusanus for peremptory behavior, these four canons had formed a legal contract, bearing together any financial costs, in their open defiance of the bishop. They even nailed a huge complaint to the door of the cathedral while Cusanus was celebrating mass, and one denounced the bishop loudly in church as he left the choir.[36] How could any authority figure tolerate such planned insubordination? One can imagine that Cusanus had finally had enough of this group of malcontents. Yet when one, Christian von Freiberg, later disturbed the mass in another church, he wrote that he did not consider himself excommunicated: first, because he did not feel that he had done anything

---

[32]Tillinghast, "Nicholas of Cusa," p. 381. Baum and Senoner, *Nikolaus von Kues: Briefe*, 2.70-71, also indicate that he dismissed the penalty for incorrect missals, showing forbearance.

[33]Baum and Senoner, *Nikolaus von Kues: Briefe*, 1.280-287.

[34]Stieber, "Hercules of the Eugenians," pp. 249-53; Wilhelm Baum, "Nikolaus Cusanus wird Bischof von Brixen (mit Edition unveröffentlichten Cusanus- und Kaiserurkunden)," *Der Schlern* 60 (1986): 379-388.

[35]Wilhelm Baum, "Nikolaus Cusanus und Leonhard Wiesmair: Der Kardinal und sein Gegenspeiler, Kanzler von Tirol und Bischof von Chur—mit Edition von unveröffentlichten Cusanus-Texten," *Der Schlern* 57 (1983): 437; Sparber, "Aus der Wirksamkeit," p. 525; Meuthen, *Nikolaus von Kues*, pp. 101-102.

[36]Baum, *Cusanus in Tirol*, p. 230; Tillinghast, "Nicholas of Cusa," p. 384; Baum and Senoner, *Nikolaus von Kues: Briefe*, 2.58-71.

wrong and, second, because the pope and/or the archbishop of Salzburg had not yet considered his appeal. There lay the problem. The resolution of the conflict was unclear, but the contumacious canons clearly found support both within the chapter and from Duke Sigismund.[37] It seems that excommunication hardly affected these clerics' lives.

The next three cases dealt with leaders of religious foundations, which Cusanus had explicit papal authorization to reform (a fact often ignored by his opponents).[38] Of these, the first and worst was the curse of the rebellious abbess. If anyone deserved excommunication, it was Abbess Verena of Sonnenburg.[39] Although some have admired Verena's forthright defense of her perceived rights, from Cusanus' first moments in the diocese, the abbess and her eight nuns resisted reform. They defied not just the strict claustration Cusanus sought to impose, but also any serious conformity to the Benedictine Rule, while constantly entreating the abbey's technical advocate, Duke Sigismund, to interfere.[40] After enduring years of prevaricating visitation and the flouting of his authority, in April 1455 Cusanus first excommunicated her in secret, giving the nuns one last chance to obey the Rule and even allowing Verena the opportunity to be obedient to the papal will. Her continued waffling led him, at the end of June, to publish Verena's excommunication, to have it broadcast from every pulpit, and to have it posted all over the diocese.

It took another three years and a battle between the bishop's troops and the nun's mercenaries before this "Jezebel," as Nicolaus Cusanus called her, was

---

37Baum, *Cusanus in Tirol*, pp. 231-232.

38Watanabe, "Tyrolese Monasteries," p. 60.

39Hermann Hallauer, "Eine Visitation des Nikolaus von Kues in Benediktinerinnenkloster Sonnenburg," MCFG 4 (1961): 116-118; Tillinghast, "Nicholas of Cusa," p. 382. See also Anselm Sparber, *Die Brixener Fürstbischöfe im Mittelalter: Ihr Leben und Wirken* (Bozen/Bolzano, 1968), pp. 156-157; Morimichi Watanabe, "Nicolaus Cusanus, Monastic Reform in the Tyrol and the *De visione Dei*," in *Concordia discors: Studi su Niccolò Cusano e l'umanesimo Europeo offerti a Giovanni Santinello* (Padova, 1993), pp. 184-185, 192. See also Karl Wolfsgruber, "Das Benediktinerinnenstift Sonnenberg," *Der Schlern* 54 (1980): 416-420; Paul Schreckenthal, "Die Abdankung der Abtissen Verena von Sonnenburg." *Der Schlern* 14 (1933): 391-394.

40Hans Liermann, "Nikolaus von Cues und das deutsche Recht," in *Cusanus Gedächtnisschrift,* p. 219; support is echoed in the same volume by Kolumban Spahr, "Nikolaus von Cues, das adelige Frauenstift Sonnenburg OSB und die mittelalterliche Nonnenklausur," p. 313. See also Jäger, *Streit,* 1.55-57, 73, 95; Robert Gismann, *Die Beziehung zwischen Tirol und Bayern im Ausgang des Mittelalters: Herzog Sigmund der Münzreiche und die Wittelsbacher in Landshut und München von 1439 bis 1479*, Ph.D. Dissertation, University of Innsbruck, 1976, pp. 97, 608 n. 95; Baum, *Cusanus in Tirol*, pp. 171-216. Note Bernhard von Waiging's concerns, Baum and Senoner, *Nikolaus von Kues: Briefe*, 1.112-119, 140-141.

forced from power, as arranged with Duke Sigismund.[41] Even then Verena long refused to ask to be absolved in person, since it would have been an act of dishonor. Meanwhile, Cusanus insisted on a grand public ceremony which would attest to her errors.[42] After yet another year of negotiation, Verena received absolution in private. During all these political machinations, the duke seems to have been more important than the spiritual terrors of anathema in bringing about resolution.[43]

Another of Cusanus' significant excommunications, the curse of the prevaricating prior, seems less justifiable. The case involved Prior Caspar Aigner of Neustift near Brixen, who up until his excommunication seemed one of Nicolaus Cusanus' supporters and even a friend.[44] Prior Casper was caught between his spiritual and temporal superiors as Cusanus wanted a second visitation and reform of Neustift. When the prior asked for advice from the priory's advocate, Duke Sigismund, Cusanus peremptorily excommunicated him. Despite having recorded the cardinal's displeasure, the prior did not even comprehend his position and tried to celebrate mass the next day. The services were interrupted by a messenger with a letter from the cardinal's own hand, reminding the prior of the punishment of excommunication. Prior Casper soon got Duke Sigismund to mediate and a successful reform visit was achieved.

It might seem harsh that Cusanus would excommunicate one of his own supporters. Perhaps Cusanus excommunicated in this case because he thought that sentence would be obeyed for once. Although many people disregarded the ramifications of the sentences, surely a reforming prior would take it seriously. But Cusanus got that wrong, too. That the prior ignored his own excommunication again illustrates how little excommunication intimidated. Besides, this bickering did not even ruin their relationship. In subsequent conflicts in the diocese it seems Cusanus could rely somewhat on Prior Casper. The prior

---

41See Hermann Hallauer, "Die 'Schlacht' von Enneberg 1458: Neue Quellen zur Biographie des Nikolaus von Kues," in *Niccolò Cusano agli inizi del mondo oderno,* mpp. 447-469; Franz Klein-Bruckschwaiger, "Um die rechtliche Bewertung der Enneberger Schlacht im Jahre 1458," *Der Schlern* 47 (1933): 300-309. Cusanus calls her Jezebel in, e.g., Baum and Senoner, *Nikolaus von Kues: Briefe,* 1.162-167, 180-185.

42William Kurtz Gotwald, *Ecclesiastical Censure at the End of the Fifteenth Century* (Baltimore, 1927), p. 13.

43Edmond Vansteenberghe, *Le Cardinal Nicolas de Cues (1401-1464): L'action — La pensée* (Paris, 1920; reprint Frankfurt, 1963), p. 147.

44Watanabe, "Tyrolese Monasteries," pp. 58, 61-63; Baum, *Cusanus in Tirol,* pp. 102, 104, 443; Hermann Hallauer, "Cusanus und Neustift," in *Festschrift Nikolaus Grass zum 60. Geburtstag dargebracht von Fachgenossen, Freunden und Schülern,* ed. Louis Carlen and Fritz Steinegger, 2 vols. (Innsbruck-München, 1974), 1.309-324; Peter Hofer, *Nicolaus Cusanus in seinem Verhältnisse zum Kloster Neustift,* Ph.D. Dissertation, University of Pavia, 1978.

probably deserved excommunication least of all of Cusanus' targets, considering his usual obedience.

His last major excommunication, the curse of the absent abbot, once more entailed resistance to Cusanus' leadership. Abbot George Ried of the Cistercian monastery at Stams had been lukewarm to Cusanus' reforms and had avoided helping in the reform of Sonnenburg in May 1457.[45] The final straw was the abbot's missing a synod later that year, claiming exemption because of the privileges of his Cistercian order. The synod (not just Cusanus alone) declared him and other absentee prelates excommunicated, although, out of generosity, the cardinal did delay its implementation for a month so that the abbot could justify his absence. At that time two representatives from the abbot arrived, but without proper credentials. They produced some documents, which Cusanus found unsatisfactory. So he demanded once more that the abbot arrive in person, although he granted George an additional three months so he could look after the well-being of his monastery. In addition, Cusanus suspended the abbot's representatives from celebrating mass and threatened them with excommunication because of their frivolous appeal. While these last censures seem vindictive to some historians, as legate, cardinal and episcopal ordinary, Cusanus was surely frustrated that so many made excuses not to carry out the necessities of reform. Moreover, he recognized petty legal machinations and delays. Regardless, Abbot George did not appear before the cardinal but rather solicited the good offices of Duke Sigismund, Emperor Frederick III, and the new pope Calixtus III (1455-1458), who was no friend of Cusanus. Consequently, the pope upheld the exemption of the Cistercian order from episcopal synods and voided the excommunication.

The last significant excommunications associated with Cusanus are certainly blamed on him, but were not pronounced by him. These included the curse of the dangerous duke. Soon after the excommunication of Abbot George, the mysterious Wilten Affair allegedly endangered Cusanus' life. As a result, even Pope Calixtus, cool to Cusanus, imposed on the Tyrol an interdict in November 1457 and threatened excommunication of Sigismund.[46] Sigismund appealed the interdict, which was hardly upheld by most clergy anyhow. Through the sympathy and mediation of the next pope, Aeneas Sylvius Piccolomini, namely Pope Pius II, Cusanus and Sigismund were briefly reconciled. Yet the truce between Cusanus and Sigismund ended at Easter 1460 when the duke besieged the bishop in his castle in Bruneck and coerced capitulations out of the captive

---

[45]Watanabe, "Tyrolese Monasteries," pp. 58, 65-68; Baum, *Cusanus in Tirol*, pp. 150-162; Baum and Senoner, *Nikolaus von Kues: Briefe*, 2.76-87.

[46]Gotwald, *Ecclesiastical Censure*, pp. 13-14; Morimichi Watanabe, "Duke Sigmund und Gregor Heimburg," in *Festschrift Nikolaus Grass,* 1.563. See also Karl Franz Zani, "Mordplan gegen Kardinal Nikolaus Cusanus (1457)," *Der Schlern* 56 (1952): 224-225; Hans (Hermann) Lentze, "Nikolaus von Cues und die Reform des Stiftes Wilten," *Veröffentlichungen des Museum Ferdinandeum in Innsbruck* 31 (1951): 501-527; Baum and Senoner, *Nikolaus von Kues: Briefe*, 2.312-321.

cardinal.[47] As a result of this attack on a cleric, on August 8, Pius excommunicated Sigismund, his officials and his allies, also encouraging that his properties and goods be confiscated and that foreign princes make war on the Tyrol.[48] Only the Swiss responded to these exhortations, largely for their own reasons and to conquer one small province.[49] In the subsequent years Pius reinforced these excommunications several times, clearly explaining his grounds. Just as frequently Sigismund's appeals claimed that the pope and Cusanus spread falsehoods, since he himself had done nothing wrong.[50]

Many of these appeals were written by the lawyer Gregor Heimburg, Cusanus' intellectual nemesis in the Tyrolean Affair, who had also argued against him at the Council of Basel concerning Ulrich of Trier.[51] Heimburg appealed to a better-instructed future pope and council, in direct contravention to Pius' bull *Execrabilis* issued at the Council of Mantua in 1460.[52] The pope soon excommunicated Heimburg and declared him a heretic. Suspicion of heresy always followed dangerously close on the heals of stubborn excommunicates.

---

[47]Hermann Josef Hallauer, "Bruneck 1460: Nikolaus von Kues—der Bischof scheitert an der weltlichen Macht," in *Studien zum 15. Jahrhundert: Festschrift für Erich Meuthen*, ed. Johannes Helmrath und Heribert Müller, 2 vols. (München, 1994), pp. 381-412; Anselm Sparber, "Wie kam es zur Gefangennahme des Fürstbischofs und Kardinals Nikolaus von Cues in Bruneck?," in *Brunecker Buch: Festschrift zur 700-Jahr-Feier der Stadterhebung* (Innsbruck, 1956), pp. 97-107; Hans Hörtnagl, "Der Brunecker Überfall des Herzogs Sigmund und sein Ritt an die Etsch zu Ostern 1460," *Der Schlern* 7 (1926): 467-470.

[48]Baum, *Cusanus in Tirol*, pp. 398-399.

[49]Erich Meuthen, "Pius II und die Besetzung des Thurgaus," in *Festschrift Nikolaus Grass,* 1.67-90. Wilhelm Baum, "Nikolaus von Kues und der Konflikt Herzog Sigmunds von Österreich mit den Schweizer Eidgenossen," *Zeitschrift für Schweizerische Kirchengeschichte* 82 (1988): 5-32.

[50]Gotwald, *Ecclesiastical Censure*, p. 17

[51]Paul Joachimsohn, *Gregor Heimburg* (Bamberg, 1891); Watanabe, "Duke Sigmund und Gregor Heimburg," p. 564; Hartmut Boockmann, *Laurentius Blumenau: Fürstlicher Rat—Jurist—Humanist (ca. 1415-1484)* (Göttingen, 1965), pp. 174-175; Harald Zimmermann, "Der Cancer Cusa und sein Gegner Gregor-Errorius: Der Streit des Nikolaus Cusanus mit Gregor Heimburg bei Thomas Ebendorfer," in *Harald Zimmermann: Im Bann des Mittelalters, Ausgewählte Beiträge zur Kirchen- und Rechtsgeschichte, Festgabe zu seinem 60 Geburtstag,* ed. Immo Eberle and Hans-Henning Kortüm (Sigmaringen, 1986), pp. 133-151.

[52]Arnold Esch, "Enea Silvio Piccolomini als Papst Pius II.: Herrschaftspraxis und Selbstdarstellung," in *Lebenslehren und Weltentwürfe im Übergang vom Mittelalter zur Neuzeit: Politik-Bildung-Naturkunde-Theologie (Bericht über Kolloquien der Kommission zur Erforschung der Kultur des Spätmittelalters 1983 bis 1987),* ed. Hartmut Boockmann, Bernd Moeller und Karl Stackmann (Göttingen, 1989), pp 121-123; Joachimsohn, *Gregor Heimburg,* p. 188.

The pope sent special bulls to Heimburg's home towns of Nuremburg and Würzburg, demanding that the cities' authorities, and all German princes, confiscate his property and arrest him. Many princes, such as the archbishops of Mainz, Trier, and Cologne, however, read Heimburg's manifestos and pamphlets, supported Sigismund's appeals, and ignored the papacy.[53] Meanwhile, Heimburg lived on unmolested for some time, publishing his propaganda pamphlets which denounced and insulted the papacy and Cusanus. Heimburg blithely began working for Archbishop Dieter von Isenburg of Mainz (embroiled in his own excommunication troubles), corresponded with the hard-liner Cardinal Carvajal, and even represented Venice in negotiations with the pope, with papal permission despite his excommunication. Heimburg then went on to advise the "heretic" King George Podiebrand of Bohemia. As far as we know, Heimburg remained under excommunication's curse, nominally, for the rest of his life.[54]

In the end, the papal fulminations on behalf of Cusanus came to nothing.[55] Special priests entered the Tyrol to support Cusanus' position, and Cusanus himself pleaded with the people in Brixen not to risk becoming heretics by receiving the eucharist from banned priests. Most Tyroleans, nonetheless, ignored the excommunications and interdicts. After the deaths of Cusanus and Pius II, Duke Sigismund's excommunication was nullified through the mediation of Emperor Frederick III, with the duke escaping all blame or punishment. In this matter Nicolaus Cusanus had earlier emphasized that, if the pope did not end up with honor in this matter, in the future it was goodbye to excommunication and interdict in Germany.[56] Let us all wave farewell.

Still, we also have to ask, what were Cusanus' alternatives? He was "a middle-aged man in a hurry," whose religious goals would be adopted by other humanists and leaders of the Reformation.[57] He led an unblemished personal life; he regularly preached the good news; he tried to get people to work together. How much patience should he have had? Giving an order and expecting it to be

---

[53]Heymann, *George*, p. 222; Gotwald, *Ecclesiastical Censure*, pp. 17, 20; Winter, "Das geistige Profil," p. 10.

[54]Heymann, *George*, p. 416; Gotwald, *Ecclesiastical Censure*, pp. 18-20; Watanabe, "Duke Sigmund und Gregor Heimburg," pp. 569-570; Pardon E. Tillinghast, "An Aborted Reformation: Germans and the Papacy in the Mid-fifteeenth Century," *Journal of Medieval History* 2 (1976): 74.

[55]Baum, *Cusanus in Tirol*, pp. 411-412, 417; Erich Meuthen, *Die letzten Jahre des Nikolaus von Kues: Biographische Untersuchungen nach neuen Quellen* (Cologne, 1958), p. 59; Sparber, "Wie kam es," p. 107.

[56]Baum, *Cusanus in Tirol*, p. 418; Jäger, *Streit*, 2.361.

[57]Tillinghast, "Nicholas of Cusa," pp. 377-378; on personality issues see also Pavlac, "Nicolaus Cusanus," pp. 139-142.

obeyed is in the nature of most authorities.[58] Some historians instead suggest he should have been less choleric, prideful and authoritarian.[59] Or even more, should he have used sweet persuasion, "warmth and patience?"[60] Or rather, should he have practiced more "love, tolerance and understanding?"[61] Do these methods sound as if they would have worked for the spiritual princes of his times? Not in fifteenth century Germany, where saints did not get very far in politics.

Certainly, the complex interaction of prince-bishops' temporal and spiritual rule complicated matters.[62] Not just as bishop of the diocese of Brixen, but also as the ruler of the territorial principality of Brixen, Cusanus was trying to get people to heaven. He wrote in his *Catholic Concordance* that every prince "holds public office for the public benefit. But the public benefit consists in peace. The foundation of peace is to direct one's subject to their eternal end."[63] Unfortunately, peace was bound to be in short supply unless Cusanus surrendered what he saw as the liberty of the Church. The complicated history of Brixen and the weakness of the bishop's temporal power there, unlike in Trier, undermined Cusanus' authority. Therefore, the main route to success in clerical reform needed to go through Duke Sigismund. But that road was closed because of the many disagreements between duke and bishop, beginning with Cusanus' papal provision. Like many lay princes, the duke was uninterested in supporting a clerical agenda where it did not specifically enhance his own authority.[64] And the growing

---

[58]See his own sermon on obedience in Baum and Senoner, *Nikolaus von Kues: Briefe*, 2.174-183; *Cusanus-Texte, 1/7: Untersuchungen über Datierung, Form, Sprache und Quellen: Kritisches Verzeichnis sämtlicher Predigten*, ed. Josef Koch (Heidelberg, 1942), p. 147, no. 189.

[59]Sullivan, "Nicholas of Cusa," pp. 414, 425; Baum, *Cusanus in Tirol*, p. 162; Leo Stern, "Nikolaus von Kues als Kirchenpolitiker und Diplomat," in *Nikolaus von Kues: Wissenschaftliche Konferenz des Plenums der Deutschen Akademie der Wissenschaften zu Berlin anläßlich der 500. Wiederkehr seines Todesjahres, Referate und Diskussionsbeiträge* (Berlin, 1965), p. 47; Heymann, *George*, p. 414. See also Hallauer, "Bruneck," p. 405; and Cusanus did write that church leaders should be more ready to absolve than to condemn, except, however, where they had an express written precept of the Church; Baum and Senoner, *Nikolaus von Kues: Briefe*, 1.106-107.

[60]Watanabe, "Tyrolese Monasteries," p. 71.

[61]Suggested by Baum, *Cusanus in Tirol*, p. 236.

[62]Pavlac, "Nicolaus Cusanus," pp. 134-136. For Cusanus' own early criticism of mixing secular and spiritual, see DCC II, 29, 223 (h XIV,265).

[63]Sigmund, *Nicholas of Cusa*, p. 202 quoting DCC III, 7, 348 (h XIV,359-360), translation from Nicholas of Cusa, *The Catholic Concordance*, ed. Paul E. Sigmund (Cambridge, 1991), p. 237.

[64]Stieber, *Eugenius*, p. 335.

power of secular, national, and territorial states was changing everything. The overlapping confusion of jurisdictions, the compromised papacy, the impotent emperor, and the entrenched nobility all did not bode well for gradual reform.[65]

In conclusion, Nicholas of Cusa's use of excommunication was doomed to fail in his conflict with Duke Sigismund of the Tyrol, even though it was so often justified. Likewise, excommunication failed to gain the pope much leverage in his dealings with German princes.[66] If you were powerful, had powerful friends or good lawyers, then excommunication was meaningless, regardless of whether it was justified or not. To achieve moral change, the Church had the carrot of the sacraments and the stick of excommunication. But excommunication was not even a big stick, since many kept getting the carrots while being little intimidated by the stick. Lacking a true spiritual depth, by the fifteenth century excommunication often had an impact only if political consequences followed. And Nicolaus Cusanus lacked the "secular arm" to enforce the sentence, to coerce anyone take the punishments seriously.[67] As Nicolaus Cusanus wrote in the *Catholic Concordance*: "Law without coercion has no sanction and loses its effectiveness. It no more merits to be called a law than a corpse should be called a man."[68] It was Cusanus' misfortune, if not curse, that the law of excommunication was ready for embalming in the fifteenth century.

---

[65]Baum, *Cusanus in Tirol*, pp. 90-91, admits how reform found little resonance in society; see also Vansteenberghe, *Cardinal Nicolas*, p. 133.

[66]Schulze, *Fürsten und Reformation*, p. 45.

[67]Pavlac, "Nicolaus Cusanus," pp. 152-153; Sigmund, *Nicholas of Cusa*, pp. 288-289 points out how Cusanus often threatened to invoke the "secular arm" but as two hierarchies working together, not one subordinate to the other. See also Meuthen, *Das Trierer Schisma*, p. 109. Excommunication had not been taken seriously in the Tyrol by one of Sigismund's predecessors, either; see Brian A. Pavlac, "Die Verhängung des Kirchenbannes über Graf Meinhard II. von Tirol (1259-95)," *Veröffentlichungen des Tiroler Landesmuseums Ferdinandeum* 75/76 (1995/6): 219-232.

[68]DCC III, 26, 486 (h XIV,427-428), translation from Sigmund, *The Catholic Concordance*, p. 287. See also Sigmund, *Nicholas of Cusa*, p. 211.

PART THREE

CUSANUS' LEGACY

ST. NICHOLAS HOSPITAL AT KUES
AS A SPIRITUAL LEGACY OF NICHOLAS OF CUSA

Morimichi Watanabe

When we regard Nicholas of Cusa as one of the most original thinkers of the fifteenth century and remember the year 2001 as the 6th centennial year of his birth, our attention is naturally turned to two monuments that still stand at his place of birth in Kues, Germany: the impressive stone house of his birth (Nikolausufer 49) at the corner of Nikolausufer and Kardinalstrasse, and St. Nicholas Hospital on the left bank of the Moselle river. Cusanus' birth house undoubtedly represents his physical beginning. St. Nicholas Hospital eloquently symbolizes his spiritual and intellectual development and growth. It is the second monument which we wish to examine in this paper as a spiritual legacy of Nicholas of Cusa.

There is a host of questions about the hospital that can be raised and examined. What prompted him to build it? What was its main purpose? How was it organized and managed? What did it contain? When did its construction begin and end? Who paid for the cost? How has it been able to survive momentous and often destructive events for over 500 years? Even though we shall not attempt or be able to answer each of these questions fully, we shall try to show below how and why the hospital is an important institution as a spiritual legacy of Cusanus the man and the thinker.

I

The idea of founding the hospital in Kues seems to have arisen in the minds of Cusanus, his older sister Margareta († before1447), his younger brother Johann (†1456), and his youngest sister Klara (†1473) even before the death of their father, Johan or Henne Cryfftz,[1] in 1450 or 1451. Johan Cryfftz, a boat owner or operator (*nauta*), was a man of considerable economic power and social standing, serving as a juror (*Schöffe*) in the village. He is said to have made a monopoly of boat traffic on the Moselle, fishing rights, and landed property. At his death he left houses, vineyards, fields and other property, which were worth 3,000 Rhenish gold florins.[2] Although known for his unpretentiousness and lack of

---

[1]About Cusanus' family, see Edmond Vansteenberghe, *Le Cardinal Nicolas de Cues (1401-1463): L'action—la pensée* (Paris, 1920; reprint Frankfurt am Main, 1963), pp. 3-6; Erich Meuthen, *Nikolaus von Kues 1401-1464: Skizze einer Biographie,* 7th ed. (Münster, 1992), pp. 7-12.

[2]Meuthen, *Nikolaus von Kues,* pp. 8-11; Morimichi Watanabe, "Following Cusanus' Footsteps (26), Cues (Kues): Part 2: Hospital of St. Nicholas," *American Cusanus Society Newsletter,* 17/1 (2000): 14-17. Sometimes Cusanus is described as the son of a poor fisherman (*filium cuiusdam pauperis piscatoris*). About his father and his social and economic position, see further Erich Meuthen, "Neue Schlaglichter auf das Leben des Nikolaus von Cues," MFCG 4 (1964): 37-53; Anton Lübke, *Nikolaus von Kues: Kirchenfürst zwischen Mittelalter und Neuzeit* (München, 1968),

interest in material possessions, Cusanus himself was a man of considerable economic acumen and accumulated a number of benefices over the years, for which he was sometimes criticized.[3] His elevation to the cardinalate in 1449 certainly strengthened his financial status and dossier.

Cusanus' sister Margareta married a magistrate of Trier, Matthias, but died young without a child. Her house in Trier was later donated to the hospital from her estate. His brother Johann was, by 1453, priest of the parish church of St. Michael at Bernkastel on the opposite bank of Kues. There was an agreement by which Johann and his sister Klara consented to forgo their share of the father's property.[4] In his testament, signed on the day of his death, May 7, 1456, Johann donated his entire estate to the hospital.[5] After the death of her first husband, Johann Plynisch, who was a citizen and magistrate of Trier, the childless Klara married on 21 June, 1441, Paul von Brystge, who was a magistrate and later mayor of Trier from 1458 to 1468. As a result, she could live an affluent life. In her will, executed shortly before her death in 1473, Klara left almost all of her possessions to the hospital, which amounted almost to 30,000 Rhenish golden florins.[6] Her beautiful sarcophagus, which was built in the hospital according to her will, still attracts the attention of visitors to the hospital. It is, therefore, certainly possible to say that all four members of Cusanus' family, at least the three younger ones Nicholas, Johann, and Klara, were the founders of the hospital.

What was the purpose of the hospital? Who was to be admitted? In Rome on December 3, 1458, Cusanus, *doctor decretorum,* executed a foundation deed (*Stiftungsurkunde*) which in 15 articles prescribed how the hospital was to be

---

pp. 13-14.

[3]One of the best characterizations of Cusanus as a simple, modest and unpretentious person was given by Vespasiano da Bisticci (1421-1498). See Vespasiano da Bisticci, *Renaissance Princes, Popes and Prelates: The Vespasiano Memoirs, Lives of Illustrious Men of the XVth Century,* trans. William George and Emily Waters (New York, 1963), p. 156: "Messer Nicolo di Cusa, of German nationality, was a man of worship, a great philosopher, theologian and platonist. He was of holy life, well lettered, especially in Greek. . .He cared nothing for state or for possessions, and was one of the most needy of the cardinals, thus giving an excellent example in all his doings." See also Meuthen, "Neue Schlaglichter," p. 47. About Cusanus' acquisition of numerous benefices, see Erich Meuthen, "Die Pfründen des Cusanus," MFCG 2 (1962): 15-66.

[4]The agreement is printed in Jakob Marx, *Geschichte des Armen-Hospitals zum h. Nikolaus zu Cues* (Trier, 1907), pp. 245-246, "Kritisches Verzeichnis der Londoner Handschriften aus dem Besitz des Nikolaus von Kues (KVLHBNK)," MFCG 3 (1963): 16-100.

[5]Marx, *Geschichte,* pp. 46, 245-246.

[6]Marx, *Geschichte,* pp. 253-260.

organized and administered.[7] Cusanus later showed a great concern about the strict observance of these articles. According to the deed, the hospital was to shelter 33 poor, worn-out (*elaborati*) males who were above 50 years of age and who were men of good reputation.[8] The hospital was essentially a place of refuge and a *hospitale pauperum*.[9] Cusanus added, however, that, if it is easy to have them, 6 priests and 6 noblemen should be included, making the number of laymen 21.[10] It is interesting to note that, to express his gratitude to the family of Manderscheid, he designated a room of the hospital for the use of Count Dietrich von Manderscheid and his heirs.[11] Needless to say, the total number of residents represents the life span of Jesus Christ.

Without any class distinction, all residents were to wear a grey habit and to live according to the customary ways of the region. They were also to live like the canons of the Augustinian Congregation at Windesheim in the Netherlands.[12] It is clear that on visiting the Windesheim Congregation during his famous legation journey in 1452, Cusanus was impressed by the way in which the congregation was run.[13] Cusanus wanted his own hospital at Kues to be administered as a really religious institution in its purpose and character.

---

[7]The deed is printed in Marx, *Geschichte,* pp. 53-63 in Latin and German. See also J. Thomas, "Der Wille des Cusanus in seiner Stiftungsurkunde vom 3. December 1458," *Trierer Theologische Zeitschrift* 67 (1968): 363-368.

[8]Marx, *Geschichte,* p. 54: "...in terris Trigintatres pauperes, elaborati senes quinquagenarii et ultra, homines masculini sexus tantum, bonarum fame, conditionis...."

[9]Marx, *Geschichte,* p. 54.

[10]Marx, *Geschichte,* pp. 56, 70.

[11]Marx, *Geschichte,* p. 59: "Item domino Theoderico de manderscheit et heredibus suis unam cellam nobilium." On the legend about Cusanus' debt to the Manderscheid family, see Erich Meuthen, "Cusanus in Deventer," in *Concordia discors: Studi su Niccolò Cusano e l'umanesimo europeo offerti a Giovanni Santinello,* ed. Gregorio Piaia (Padova, 1993), pp. 39-54 at pp. 44-45.

[12]Marx, *Geschichte,* p. 59: "...quod modus vivendi in dicto hospitali sit communis illius terre; et quantum poterunt se conformabunt fratribus Canonicorum regularum de Capitulo de Windeshem, Similiter de hora comedendi, surgendi, dormiendi et orandi...."

[13]Cusanus made a detour to go to Windesheim on his legation journey and stayed in Windesheim on August 21-22, 1451. See Meuthen, "Cusanus in Deventer," pp. 53-54; *Acta Cusana: Quellen zur Lebensgeschichte des Nikolaus von Kues* [=*AC*], ed. Erich Meuthen and Hermann J. Hallauer, 2 vols., 1976-*Lieferung 3a* (Hamburg, 1976-2000), 1/3A, pp. 1079-1084 (Nr. 1632-1640).

The foundation deed also stipulated that the hospital be directed and managed by a rector (*Rector hospitalis*).[14] After Cusanus' death in 1464, Johann Römer von Briedel, a relative of Cusanus' mother, nee Katherina Römer von Briedel, served as first rector briefly from 1464 to 1466. Jakob Marx published a list of rectors from 1464 to 1898 in his important work, *Geschichte des Armen-Hospitals zum h. Nikolaus zu Kues* (Trier, 1907).[15] In the very early period of the hospital, three rectors, Simon Kolb von Cues (1466-1467), Dietrich von Xanten (1467-1488), and Peter Wymar von Erkelenz (1488-1498), made especially important contributions to the stability and development of the hospital.

Simon Kolb von Cues, a canon of the church of St. Simeon at Trier, was an uncle of Simon von Wehlen, Cusanus' relative and an assistant (*Koadjutor*) to Rector Johann Römer.[16] Serving as rector for 21 years, from 1467 to 1488, Rector Dietrich von Xanten, a canon of Aachen, was also instrumental in founding the Bursa Cusana at Deventer in the Netherlands on June 28, 1469 to help 20 poor clerical students.[17] A canon of Aachen, Peter von Erkelenz, who also served as Cusanus' secretary for many years and was at Cusanus' deathbed at Todi in 1464, was an influential rector of the hospital from 1488 to 1494 and was buried in the inner court of the hospital.[18]

The foundation deed further provided that the hospital should be visited by inspectors (*visitatores*) yearly and that they should be the prior of the Carthusian monastery on the Beatusberg near Koblenz, which is nowadays in Koblenz, and the prior of the Windesheim Congregation on the island of Niederwerth near Koblenz. It is indicated in the deed that they were chosen because of singular devotion (*devotionem singularem*).[19] Here again, we see the influence of the Augustinian canons of Windesheim on Nicholas of Cusa. It is known that, when he was dean of the cathedral chapter of the *Florinskirche* in Koblenz in 1429, he was in close touch with the Windesheim Congregation of Niederwerth and, in all

---

[14]Marx, *Geschichte,* p. 56: ". . .sit unus Rector hospitalis, qui continue in loco resideat." See also p. 64.

[15]Marx, *Geschichte,* pp. 1-2.

[16]Marx, *Geschichte,* pp. 64, 107.

[17]Marx, *Geschichte,* pp. 82-84,108. The Statutes of the Bursa Cusana at Deventer are printed in Marx, *Geschichte,* pp. 260-265. See also Meuthen, "Cusanus in Deventer," pp. 39-54.

[18]Marx, *Geschichte,* pp. 38-39, 43, 108, 117. See also Erich Meuthen, "Peter von Erkelenz (ca. 1430-1494)," *Zeitschrift des Aachener Geschichtsvereins* 84/85 (1977/78): 701-744.

[19]Marx, *Geschichte,* pp. 57, 59.

likelihood, he contacted the congregation when he was in Koblenz in March 1452 on his legation journey.[20]

The actual construction of the hospital began in 1451 or, at the latest, in 1452, after the death of the father.[21] Probably because of Cusanus' promotion to cardinal in 1448, his appointment as bishop of Brixen in April 1450, and his legation journey to Germany and the Low Countries in 1451 and 1452, the beginning of the construction was delayed. The overall architect of the hospital is not known, although Dietrich von Xanten was designated as architect (*Baumeister*) and manager (*Verweser*) of the hospital.[22] When Cusanus came to Bernkastel on November 9, 1451 on his legation journey and, no doubt, also visited Kues, the hospital was not yet completed. On May 1, 1453, the hospital, with the exception of its chapel, was finished. It was on May 5, 1456 that the entire building was constructed, but not yet consecrated.[23]

The hospital remained unused for many years. The cardinal himself wanted to receive the first residents after the consecretion of the chapel; but he could not come to the hospital for that purpose because of his busy schedule. Only after the consecration ceremony held on July 22, 1465, one year after his death, were the first residents admitted to the hospital.[24]

Cusanus himself stated that the construction of the hospital cost more than 10,000 Rhenish gold florins.[25] On March 30, 1457, he sent a letter from Brixen to the jurors of Bernkastel and Kues, in which he proudly spoke of the completion of the hospital: "We have constructed a costly building (*Wir haben darnach einen kostlichen baw getan. . . .*)."[26] In another letter of 1458, which Cusanus sent to the jurors of Bernkastel, he wrote in praise of God:

> Since our Savior says, "Therefore stay awake, for you do not know the hour," prompted by this divine warning, we have earnestly weighed what a rich reward the Giver of all good things gives for the deeds of hospitable mercy which we render to the poor and the suffering. Therefore, we have, with a fortune which God bestowed on us, erected in a costly building a new chapel with the cloisters, a dining room, houses and cells and other rooms which are necessary for the reception and lodging of the poor and the needy,

---

[20]Marx, *Geschichte,* pp. 59, 61-62, 78-80; Meuthen, "Cusanus in Deventer," p. 41; Meuthen, "Die Pründen," p. 65; *AC,* 1/3B, pp. 1513-1517 (Nr. 2361-2371).

[21]Marx, *Geschichte,* pp. 41-42.

[22]Marx, *Geschichte,* pp. 42-43.

[23]Marx, *Geschichte,* p. 42. About Cusanus' stay in Bernkastel, see *AC,* 1/3B, p. 1274 (Nr. 1983).

[24]Marx, *Geschichte,* p. 46.

[25]Marx, *Geschichte,* p. 42.

[26]Marx, *Geschichte,* pp. 42, 247-248.

that is, the worn-out persons, in accordance with the number of years which Christ, our Redeemer, spent on earth.[27]

In a third letter, which Cusanus had sent to Archbishop Jakob I of Trier (1439-1456) on December 14, 1453, he wrote:

> I have placed my entire property before the Eternal Father and withheld nothing, but shall place everything - whether it be the income from my benefices or that from my father's property - at the disposal of the hospital in Kues. . . . For this is my firm intention. *What God sends me should belong to the poor.* [28]

These three letters, together with the picture of the kneeling cardinal and his brother Johann[29] under the cross in the altar painting of the chapel, eloquently express his pious and sympathetic desire to serve and contribute to the poor and the needy whom he saw and encountered in his busy life. In this connection, it is important to remember that towards the end of his life, Cusanus founded St. Andreas Hospice in Rome for the sick German officials of the papal curia. Sympathizing with those Germans abroad, he revised his second will of August 6, 1464 in order to establish the hospice as a part of the well-established German Brotherhood in Rome, *B. Maria de Anima Teutonicorum de Urbe.*[30] The hospice no longer stands in Rome, thus enhancing the importance of St. Nicholas Hospital in Kues as a true monument to Cusanus' piety, charity, and spirituality.

---

[27]*Das Werk des Nicolaus Cusanus: Eine bibliophile Einleitung,* ed. Gerd Heinz-Mohr and Willehad Paul Eckert (Köln, 1963), p. 109.

[28]Josef Koch, *Nikolaus Cusanus und seine Umwelt: Untersuchungen zu Cusanus-Texte: IV Briefe,* Erste Sammlung (Heidelberg, 1948), p. 80; Koch, "Nikolaus von Cues als Mensch nach dem Briefwechsel und persoenlichen Aufzeichnungen," in *Humanismus, Mystik und Kunst in der Welt des Mittelalters,* ed. Josef Koch, 2nd ed. (Leiden-Köln, 1959), pp. 57-63 at p. 62; Koch, "Die Stiftung des Kardinals Nikolaus von Kues," *Archiv für Kultur und Geschichte des Landkreises Bernkastel* 2 (1964/65): 37-39 at p. 38.

[29]Marx, *Geschichte,* p. 44. Recent studies state that the younger man keeling behind the cardinal is not Johann Krebs, but Peter von Erkelenz. See, for example, Heinz-Mohr and Eckert, *Das Werk,* p. 109.

[30]About Cusanus' hospice at Santa Maria dell'Anima in Rome, see Erich Meuthen, *Die letzten Jahre des Nikolaus von Kues: Biographische Untersuchungen nach neuen Quellen* (Köln and Opladen, 1958), p. 105; Hermann J. Hallauer, "Das St. Andreas-Hospiz der Anima in Rom Ein Beitrag zur Biographie des Nikolaus von Kues," MFCG 19 (1991): 25-52. See also Clifford W. Maas, *The German Community in Renaissance Rome 1378-1523* (Freiburg, 1981).

II

The physical facilities of St. Nicholas Hospital, which were jointly founded by Cusanus and his brother and sisters, are indeed impressive and beautiful. Especially noteworthy are its chapel and the inner court with its surrounding cross-aisles. The chapel, where, in accordance with his wishes, Cusanus' heart was buried, is indeed a religious center of the hospital. But another important part of the hospital which must draw our close attention as we consider the spiritual significance of the hospital is, no doubt, its library.

Why did Cusanus add a library to his *hospitale pauperum*? There are at least a few reasons which we should consider. First, Cusanus undoubtedly thought it convenient to keep many or most of his collected manuscripts in one place. For this purpose, no place was better suited than the hospital to be established at his birthplace. It is conceivable that, in his later years, Cusanus wanted to live in the hospital himself in contemplation of God. Although, as is well known, he thought of obtaining a room for retirement at the Benedictine monastery in Tegernsee,[31] St. Nicholas Hospital at Kues was a good candidate for his later life.

Secondly, along with the chapel of the hospital, which was the spiritual and religious center for all the residents of the hospital, the library symbolized Cusanus' intellectual and cultural pursuit of the truth. The chapel was the heart of the hospital; the library represented its head. It was natural that the two areas were interconnected through a small window, expressing the unity and interdependence of Cusanus' religious and philosophical yearnings.[32]

Thirdly, as Jakob Marx suggested, Cusanus probably thought that not only the residents of the hospital, especially the rector, the clergymen, and the nobles, but also some scholars and specialists from the outside might, in the future, wish to use or consult some manuscripts in the collection.[33]

Finally, it is conceivable that Cusanus was influenced by the idea of the *studiolo* (private study) which affected the design of many Italian palaces and

---

[31]In his letter of February 12, 1454 from Brixen to Abbot Kaspar Ayndorffer (1402-1461), Cusanus expressed his desire to obtain a cell in the monastery: "propterea fratribus dixi michi cellam parari. Utinam concederetur michi sacro ocio frui inter fratres, qui vacant et vident, quoniam est suavis dominus!"; see *Nikolaus von Kues: Briefe und Dokumente zum Brixner Streit, Kontroverse um die Mystik und Anfänge in Brixen (1450-1455),* ed. Wilhelm Baum and Raimund Senoner (Wien, 1998), p. 112. See also Nicolas de Cues, *Lettres aux moines de Tegernsee sur la docte ignorance (1452-1456): Du jeu de la boule (1463),* trans. Maurice de Gandillac (Paris, 1985), p. 32; Morimichi Watanabe, "Nicolaus Cusanus, Monastic Reform in the Tyrol and the *De visione Dei*," in *Concordia discors,* pp. 181-197.

[32]Marx, *Geschichte,* p. 41. It is interesting to note that both the choir of the chapel and the library have a single pillar in the center that no doubt expresses a unitive principle.

[33]Marx, *Geschichte,* p. 50.

residences of the fifteenth century. The *scrittoio* or *studiolo*, whose most famous early example is in Petrarch's house in Arquà, can be found, for example, in the Palazzo Davanzati in Florence, Lionello d'Este's Palazzo Belfiore near Ferrara, the Palazzo Medici in Florence, Pope Pius II's Palazzo Piccolomini at Pienza, and Duke Federico da Montefeltro's Ducal Palaces at Urbino and Gubbio.[34] The *studiolo* of Pius II's Palazzo Piccolomini is naturally of special importance because of his close relations with Cusanus. We note that the *studiolo,* in many cases, was located near a chapel and a spiral staircase like in the hospital at Kues. Although a *studiolo* is not exactly a *libraeria,* Cusanus may have been influenced by its usefulness.

How were Cusanus' manuscripts brought to Kues? According to a notarized inventory of Cusanus' manuscripts, silver, clothing and other personal belongings that Giovanni Mantese found in 1960 in the Archivio di Stato in Vincenza, there were 167 manuscripts which belonged to Cusanus.[35] They were probably in Rome.[36] Pietro Barbo, cardinal of the titular Church of St. Mark in Rome and bishop of Vincenza (1451-1464), was one of the three executors designated by Cusanus in his second, last will of August 6, 1464. Although Pietro Barbo was elected pope on August 30, 1464, only 19 days after Cusanus' death in the episcopal palace at Todi, Umbria, and was crowned as Paul II on September 16, 1464, the busy new pope did not neglect to carry out his duties as

---

[34]Il Kim, "Quattrocento Studioli: The Historical Background of Fifteenth-century Humanism in Italy and the Changing Reception of *De vita solitaria, Literary Eloquence, Moral Philosophy, and the Planning of Studioli," Annual Report of the Collegium Mediterranistarum Mediterraneus* 21 (1998): 91-119+[3] at pp. 103-113. On the *studiolo* of the 15th century, see Wolfgang Liebenwein, *Studiolo: Die Entstehung eines Raumtyps und seine Entwicklung bis um 1600* (Berlin, 1977); Wolfgang Liebenwein, *Studiolo: Storia e tipologia di uno spazio culturale* (Modena, 1988); Olga Raggio, *The Liberal Arts Studiolo from the Ducal Palace at Gubbio* (New York, 1996).

[35]Giovanni Mantese, "Ein notarielles Inventar von Büchern und Wertgegenständen aus dem Nachlass des Nikolaus von Kues," MFCG 2 (1962): 85-116.

[36]Where were the manuscripts housed? In Rome? How many of Cusanus' manuscripts were there? Were they in his house? Where was his house in Rome? Was it near St. Peter in Chains (*apud sanctum Petrum in domibus nostre solite residentie ibidem*) in the 1450's? Or was it in St. Peter's that is the Vatican (*apud sanctum Petrum*), after Cusanus was recalled to Rome from Brixen in 1458 by his friend Pope Pius II? About Cusanus' house in Rome, see Josef Koch, *Cusanus-Texte: IV, Briefwechsel des Nikolaus von Kues,* Erste Sammlung (Sitzungsberichte der Heidelberger Akademie der Wissenschaften [hereafter HSB], Jahrg. 1942/43. 2. Abh; Heidelberg, 1944), p. 95; Meuthen, *Die letzten Jahre,* pp. 90, 218-229; Concetta Bianca, "La biblioteca Romana di Niccolò Cusano," in *Scrittura biblioteche e stampa a Roma nel quattrocento,* ed. Massimo Miglio (Città del Vaticano, 1983), pp. 669-708. Although Bianca speaks of Cusanus' "Roman years" and "Roman library," she does not indicate clearly where in Rome his manuscripts were located.

Cusanus' executor.[37] With the help of his friends, Francesco Mauroceno or Morosini, Marco Marini de Spalatro and Heinrich Valpot or Walpod, Pope Paul II made sure that point 8 of Cusanus' first will of June 15, 1461, which stipulated that his manuscripts be given to St. Nicholas Hospital at Kues,[38] be carried out. It was in all likelihood Heinrich Valpot who brought the manuscripts to Kues.[39] It is not clear what the number was.[40]

When we consider the impact of many events since the establishment of St. Nicholas Hospital, such as the Protestant and Catholic Reformations, the French Revolution, the secularization of the monasteries in 1802, World Wars I and II, it is really remarkable that Cusanus' collection of manuscripts in the library survived them all without much damage and loss.

It is known, however, that some of Cusanus' manuscripts in the hospital library were sold to outsiders or somehow lost and can now be found in London, Brussels, and other places. How did this come about? We shall pay attention here to the so-called Harley Collection of the British Museum in which Jakob Marx thought there were 17 Cusanus manuscripts in 1907,[41] Paul Lehmann discovered 26 Cusanus manuscripts in 1930,[42] and B.L. Ullman found 33 Cusanus manuscripts in 1938.[43] Sending Alois Krchnák to the British Museum in 1964,[44] the Cusanus-Gesellschaft in Bernkastel-Kues began intensive studies of Cusanus manuscripts in the Harley Collection. According to the results of recent research,

---

[37]Marx, *Geschichte,* p. 25; Mantese, "Ein notarielles Inventar," p. 88.

[38]Marx, *Geschichte,* p. 250: "(8) Item voluit, quod libri apud eum existentes et qui sui non sunt restituantur illis, quorum sunt, suos autem libros omnes dedit et legavit dicto eius hospitali volens illos ibidem adduci et reponi." See also Marx, *Geschichte,* p. 50; Mantese, "Ein notarielles Inventar," p. 86.

[39]Mantese, "Ein notarielles Inventar," p. 93. See also Bianca, "La biblioteca," p. 697. There are still questions about how Cusanus' manuscripts, if they were in Rome, were transferred to Kues. Mantese suggests (p. 92) as one of the three possibilities that before leaving Rome in 1464 for his trip to Ancona to meet Pope Pius II there, Cusanus asked Morosini to take charge of his house in Rome. Peter von Erkelenz has also been mentioned as one who brought the manuscripts to Kues.

[40]Mantese estimated that the number was 167. Bianca, "La biblioteca," p. 67.

[41]Marx, *Geschichte,* p. 142 and n. 1. See also mention at p. 167.

[42]Paul Lehmann, "Mitteilungen aus Handschriften II," *Sitzungsberichte der Bayerischen Akademie der Wissenschaften, Philosophisch-historische Abteilung,* Jahrg. 1930, Heft 2 (1930): 18-27.

[43]Berthold L. Ullman, "Manuscripts of Nicholas of Cues," *Speculum* 13 (1938): 194-197 at p. 194.

[44]Alois Krchnák, "Neue Handschriften in London und Oxford - Reisebericht," MFCG 3 (1963): 101-108.

there are at least 48 Cusanus manuscripts in the collection.[45] All of them have been described and analyzed in detail by specialists in the *Mitteilungen und Forschungsbeiträge der Cusanus-Gesellschaft* from 1963 to 1982 under the heading: *Kritischer Verzeichnis der Londoner Handschriften aus dem Besitz des Nikolaus von Kues.*[46]

It has become clear that a good many Cusanus manuscripts were sold and dispersed from the hospital library during the rectorship of Johann Hugo Shaanen (1717-1721) and Heinrich Brechels (1721-1726; 1737-1747).[47] Especially notable are the purchases made by George Suttie, who as a foreign agent of the book dealer Nathaniel Noel (*fl.* 1681-*c.* 1753) bought many Cusanus manuscripts for Edward Harley, 2nd Earl of Oxford and a fabulous collector of manuscripts and books.[48] The famous *Diary* or *Journal* of Humfrey Wanley (1672-1726), who as Library-Keeper of Lord Harley negotiated with many book dealers, including Nathaniel Noel, was edited and published by C.E. and Ruth C. Wright in 1966.[49] The editors wrote:

---

[45]Rudolf Haubst said, in his report, "Aus dem Institut für Cusanus-Forschung," MFCG 2 (1962): 14, that there were at least 38 manuscripts in the collection. The first report of the search, among several, was published as Institut für Cusanusforschung.

[46]For the complete "Kritische Verzelchnis der londoner Handschriften," "Kritische Verzelchnis," see MFCG 3 (1963): 16-100; MFCG 7 (1969): 129-145; MFCG 8 (1970): 199-237; MFCG 10 (1973): 58-103; MFCG 12 (1977): 18-71; MFCG 15 (1982): 43-56. See also Alois Krchnák, "Neue Handschriften in London and Oxford," MFCG 3 (1963): 101-108; Robert Danzer, "Nikolaus von Kues in der Überlieferungsgeschichte der lateinischen Literatur nach Ausweis der Londoner Handschriften aus seinem Besitz," MFCG 4 (1964): 384-394; Rolf Winau, "Medizinische Handschriften aus dem Besitz des Nikolaus von Kues im Britisch Museum," MFCG 5 (1965): 137-161; Hermann J. Hallauer, "Neue Handschriften in London," MFCG 7 (1969): 146-157; Hermann J. Hallauer, "'Habent sind fata libelli' Von der Mosel zur Themse: Handschriften des St. Nikolaus-Hospitals in der Bibliotheca Harleiana, Vorläufiger Abschluss des Kritischen Verzeichnisses der Londoner Handschriften aus dem Besitz des Nikolaus von Kues," MFCG 17 (1986): 21-56.

[47]C.E. Wright and Ruth C. Wright, *The Diary of Humfrey Wanley, 1715-1726,* 2 vols. (London, 1966), 1.xl and n. 2. Marx spelled the 25th rector's name as "Schaanen," not like some others who spelled the name "Schannen."

[48]Wright and Wright, *The Diary,* 1, passim. C.E. Wright discussed "Nathaniel Noel and George Suttie" in his article, "Manuscripts of Italian Provenance in the Harleian Collection in the British Museum: Their Sources, Associations and Channels of Acquisition," in *Cultural Aspects of the Italian Renaissance: Essays in Honour of Paul Oskar Kristeller,* ed. Cecil H. Clough (Manchester and New York, 1976), pp. 462-484 at pp. 473-475.

[49]Wright and Wright, *The Diary,* 1. See note 48 for bibliographical information.

Probably the most important event of 1717 or perhaps early 1718, however, was the acquisition of a large group of MSS. from the Continent through Noel (presumably from Noel's agent Suttie) which included a considerable number of MSS. from Cues on the Mosel. The only reference to this in Harley's letters is in one of the 17th November in which he says: "Are the Books come from Holland? Among which you make mention will come Cardinal Cusanus's MSS. Fusts Bible in 1462 and other Books of Antient Dates and all extream valuable, what is become of this mighty Cargo? I am afraid the 500 Galons of rhenish wine has drunk them all up."[50]

In his detailed study of the purchases made by Suttie at Kues, Hermann J. Hallauer showed that Suttie was in Kues at least four times, July 3, 1717; August 8, 1717; after November 17, 1718; and perhaps March-April, 1722, to purchase Cusanus' manuscripts from St. Nicholas Hospital.[51] During his first visit to Kues on July 3, 1717, Suttie made a purchase of some manuscripts from Rector Shaanen at very low prices. Returning soon to Kues on August 8, 1717, the enthusiastic buyer Suttie acquired additional manuscripts from the same rector, who in two summer months sold at least 13 precious manuscipts to Suttie not so much for financial reasons as for his lack of appreciation of their value. Although we have little information about Suttie's third stay at Kues in 1718, it is estimated that he obtained 7 manuscripts.[52]

After the death of Rector Shaanen on December 4, 1721, Suttie was able to make the most fruitful purchase during his fourth stay in Kues. He bought at least 21 manuscripts from the new rector, Brechels. Since Rector Brechels was not installed officially until the end of 1723 or the beginning of 1724, no financial or other records about 1722 are extant. We note that the controversial rector was later accused of having sold a large number of manuscripts cheaply to an Englishman and that he fled to Luxemburg, where he died on May 22, 1742.[53] The Harley Collection's gain was a big loss to St. Nicholas Hospital.

III

It can be said that a collection of manuscripts or books reveals the interest, character and personality of the collector. Seen from this point of view, how does Cusanus' collection as a whole look? As Van de Vyver pointed out, we must remember that some of his manuscripts were not in the library of St. Nicholas Hospital; that some of his manuscripts in the library were, as seen

---

[50]Wright and Wright, *The Diary*, 1.xxxix. See also Hallauer, "Habent sind fata libelli," MFCG 17 (1986): 28, where the quote is cited.

[51]Hallauer, "'Habent sind fata libelli'," pp. 26-27.

[52]Hallauer, "'Habent sind fata libelli'," pp. 27-29.

[53]Hallauer, "'Habent sind fata libelli'," p. 33.

above, later dispersed; and that there are manuscripts now in the library that did not belong to Cusanus.[54] As a result, it would not be easy to gain an exact evaluation of his total collection. But we shall attempt to understand the general characteristics of his entire collection by briefly examining the nature of the larger collections of his manuscripts in Kues, London, and Brussels.

In his important list of Cusanus' manuscripts in Kues, which will be referred to as Cod. Cus., Jakob Marx described and discussed the manuscripts under the following headings in his famous book, *Verzeichnis der Handschriften in der Armen-Hospital zum h. Nikolaus* (Trier, 1905):[55]

1. Bible and Commentaries	Cod. Cus. 1-27
2. Church Father	28-57
3. Scholastic Theology	58-117
4. Sermons	118-130
5. Liturgy	131-155
6. Geography and History	156-170
7. Liberal Arts and Philosophy	171-206
8. Astronomy	207-216
9. Works of Nicholas of Cusa	217-222
10. Canon Law	223-278
11. Roman Law	279-292
12. Medicine	293-310
13. Others	311-314

Marx believed that of the 314 manuscripts and incunabula in the library, about 270 were Cusanus' own.[56]

Giovanni Andrea Bussi (1417-1475), Cusanus' secretary and the first librarian of the Vatican Library, testified that Cusanus was very well versed in the ancient and medieval works of history and poetry;[57] but literary writers are not very strongly represented in the library at Kues. We find, however, the works of some

---

[54]Emil Van de Vyver, "Annotations de Nicolas de Cues dans plusieurs manuscrits de la bibliothèque royale de Bruxelles," in *Nicolò da Cusa: Relazioni tenute al Convegno interuniversitario di Bressanone nel 1960* (Firenze, 1962), p. 47.

[55]Jakob Marx, *Verzeichnis der Handschriften in der Armen-Hospital zum h. Nikolaus* (Trier, 1905; reprint Frankfurt a.M., 1966), passim. According to Marx and others, there are 132 incunabules in the library but only two were printed before Cusanus' death. See Albert Kapr, "Gab es Beziehungen zwischen Gutenberg und Nikolaus von Kues?," *Gutenberg Jahrbuch* (1972): 32-40; Bianca, "La biblioteca," p. 692.

[56]Marx, *Geschichte,* p. 50. About the incunabules in the library, see also Hallauer, "'Habent sind fata libelli'," pp. 36-37.

[57]Martin Honecker, *Cusanus-Studien: II, Nikolaus von Cues und die griechische Sprache: Nebst einem Anhang, Die Lobrede des Giovanni Andrea dei Bussi* (HSB, Jahrg. 1937/38, 2. Abh.; Heidelberg, 1938), pp. 70-73 at pp. 71-72. See also Heinz-Mohr and Eckert, *Das Werk,* p. 124.

medieval or late medieval writers like Ioannes de Garlandia, Leonardo Aretino, Petrarch, and Leonardo Bruni, but not Dante.[58] Ancient philosophers were in a better position. Certainly, Plato (Cod. Cus. 177,178) and Aristotle (Cod. Cus. 179-184; 187-189), as well as Proclus (Cod. Cus. 185, 186, 195) and Boethius (Cod. Cus. 190, 191) were well known to him.[59]

In addition to the various kinds of the Bible and the commentaries, including Nicholas de Lyra's *Lectura in psalmos* (Cod. Cus. 22), many works of the Church Fathers are found. The Greek Fathers include Origen (Cod. Cus. 50), Cyprian (Cod. Cus. 28, 29), Eusebius (Cod. Cus. 41), Optatus Milevis (Cod. Cus. 50), Gregory of Nazianzus (Cod. Cus. 48), Chrysostom (Cod. Cus. 29, 46, 47, 52, 53, 56, 58), and others. The Latin Fathers are represented in the library by Augustine (Cod. Cus. 31-35, 52, 53, 55, 57, 64), Gregory the Great (Cod. Cus. 49, 130), Ambrose (Cod. Cus. 38, 52, 53), Isidore of Seville (Cod. Cus. 29, 42, 116), and others.[60] Pseudo-Dionysius the Areopagite, who influenced Cusanus deeply, is naturally found there (Cod. Cus. 43-45).[61] There is no doubt that Cusanus preferred the Church Fathers to scholastic theologians. It is interesting to note, however, that under the heading "Scholastic Theology" (Cod. Cus. 58-117), Marx listed the works of many medieval writers: St. Anselm of Canterbury, St. Bernard of Clairvaux, St. Thomas Aquinas, Hildegard of Bingen,

---

[58] Heinz-Mohr and Eckert, *Das Werk,* p. 124.

[59] Marx, *Verzeichnis,* pp. 164-179. Cusanus' view of Plato is discussed in Martin Honecker, "Des Cusanus Verhältnis zu Platons Schriften," in *Nikolaus von Kues und die griechische Sprache* (HSB, Jhrg. 1939/40, 2. Abh.; Heidelberg, 1940), pp. 61-65; Johannes Hirschberger, "Das Platon-Bild bei Nikolaus von Kues," in *Nicolò Cusano agli inizi del mondo moderno:* Attidel Congreso internazionale in occasione del V centenario della morte di Niccolò Cusano. Bressanine, 6-10 Setteme ???? (Firenze, 1970), pp. 113-140. On Cusanus and Aristotle, see Peter Volkelt, "Die Philosophenbildnisse in den Commentarii ad Opera Aristotelis des Cod. Cus. 187," MFCG 3 (1963): 181-213. On Cusanus and Proclus, see Raymond Klibansky, *Ein Proklus-Fund und seine Bedeutung* (HSB, Jahrg. 1928/29, 5. Abh.; Heidelberg, 1929), pp. 25-29; ed. Hans Gerhard Senger, *Cusanus-Texte: III. Marginalien, 2. Proclus Latinus. Die Exzerpte und Randnoten des Nikolaus von Kues zu den lateinischen Übersetzungen der Proclus-Schriften, 2.1. Theologia Platonis - Elementatio theologica,* (Abhandlungen der Heidelberger Akademie der Wissenschaften, Philosophisch-historische Klasse, Jahrg. 1986, 2. Abh., Heidelberg, 1986); Bianca,*"*La biblioteca," pp. 697 and n. 97, 698-699.

[60] Marx, *Geschichte,* pp. 21-63 (Cod. Cus. 28-57); Bianca, "La biblioteca," p. 681. See also Hans Gerhard Senger, "Griechisches und biblisch-patristisches: Erbe im cusanischen Weisheitsbegriff," MFCG 20 (1992): 147-181.

[61] For a recent study of the influence of Pseudo-Dionysius on Cusanus, see Hans Gerhard Senger, "Die Präferenz für Ps.-Dionysius bei Nicolaus Cusanus und seinem italienischen Umfeld," in *Die Dionysius-Rezeption im Mittelalter: Internationales Kolloquium in Sofia vom 8. bis 11. April 1999 unter der Schirmherrschaft der Société Internationale pour l'Étude de la Philosophie Médiévale,* ed. Tzotcho Boiadjieve, Georgi Kapriev and Andreas Speer (Turnhout, 2000), pp. 505-539.

St. Bonaventure, Peter Lombard, Joannes Duns Scotus, Meister Eckhart, Ludolf von Saxony, Ramon Llull, St. Albertus Magnus, Aegidius Romanus, Heimericus de Campo, Johannes de Turrecremata, and others.[62] The manuscripts of Lull (Cod. Cus. 81, 82, 83, 85, 88, 118) are especially notable and constitute the largest collection of works by any writer.[63] Many collections of sermons are also found in the library (Cod. Cus. 118-130).

Cusanus' inclination towards Neo-Platonic philosophy is manifested in his interest in mathematics, but no important mathematical works by others are found in the library. In the field of geography, the library, in addition to Strabo's *Geographia* (Cod. Cus. 156) translated by Gregorius Tiphernes, contains the *Roma instaurata* and *Italia illustrata* of Flavio Biondo (c.1388-c.1463), secretary of Popes Eugenius IV and Pius II (Cod. Cus. 157).[64] Cusanus' passion for astronomical and astrological manuscripts is manifested in the 18 manuscripts, which include Ptolemy (Cod. Cus. 209), Joannes de Ligneris (Cod. Cus. 210), Gerhard of Cremona (Cod. Cus. 212, 213), and Al-Kindi (Cod. Cus. 208, 212). The astronomical instruments which he bought in Nürnberg in September 1444 (Cf. Cod. Cus. 211) are still on display in a glass case in the library.[65] Medicine is another subject in which he was interested as far as it was related to many of his philosophical problems. The 19 medical manuscripts (Cod. Cus. 222, 293-310), which together show his great interest in medicine, include the works of Hippocrates (Cod. Cus. 293, 294, 298, 307), Galen (Cod. Cus. 293, 296, 297, 298), Johannitius (Cod. Cus. 293, 295, 306, 310), Theophilius (Cod. Cus. 293, 295), Philaret (Cod. Cus. 222, 293), Rhasis (Cod. Cus. 302), Avicenna (Cod. Cus. 298, 299, 300), Bernard de Gordon (Cod. Cus. 304, 308, 309), and others.[66]

---

[62]Marx, *Verzeichnis,* pp. 64-114 (Cod. Cus. 58-117).

[63]Marx, *Verzeichnis,* pp. 81-93, 115-116. See Martin Honecker, "Lullus-Handschriften aus dem Besitz des Kardinals Nikolaus von Cues," *Spanische Forschungen der Görresgesellschaft* 6 (1937): 252-369; Eusebius Colomer, *Nikolaus von Kues und Raimund Lull aus Handschriften der Kueser Bibliothek* (Berlin, 1961); Charles Lohr, "Ramón Lull und Nikolaus von Kues: Zu einem Strukturvergleich ihres Denkens," *Theologie und Philosophie* 56 (1981): 218-231; Theodor Pindl-Büchel, "Nicholas of Cusa and the Lullian Tradition in Padua," *American Cusanus Society Newsletter* 5/2 (1988): 35-37.

[64]Marx, *Verzeichnis,* pp. 143-144; Bianca, "La biblioteca," pp. 681, 691, 694.

[65]See Johannes Hartmann, *Die astronomischen Instrumente des Kardinals Nikolaus Cusanus* (Abhandlungen der königlichen Gesellschaft der Wissenschaften zu Göttingen, Mathematisch-physikalische Klasse, N.F., Bd. x, Nr. 6; Berlin, 1919); Alois Krchnák, "Die Herkunft der astronomischen Handschriften und Instrumente des Nikolaus von Kues," MFCG 3 (1960): 109-180.

[66]Marx, *Verzeichnis,* pp. 219-220, 281-303 (Cod. Cus. 222, 293-310). See Rudolf Creutz, *Cusanus-Studien: IV, Medizinisch-physikalisches Denken bei Nikolaus von Cues und die ihm als "Glossae Cardinalis" irrig zugeschriebenen*

Cusanus' collection of canon law and Roman law manuscripts in the library is especially prominent and outstanding. A *doctor decretorum* from the University of Padua and an active participant in the Council of Basel from 1434 to 1437, he managed to collect 70 legal manuscripts (Canon law: Cod. Cus. 223-278; Roman law: Cod. Cus. 279-292), with numerous marginal notes of his own.[67] In addition to Gratian's *Decretum* with the gloss (Cod. Cus. 223), there are many canon law manuscripts by such notable canon lawyers as Bartholomeus Brixiensis, Henricus de Bohic, Hostiensis, Huguccio, Joannes Andreae, Joannes de Lignano, Joannes Teutonicus, Raymundus de Pennaforte, and William Durant (Cod. Cus. 168) that deal with the organization of the Church. Justinian's *Digest* and *Institutes* with the *Glossa ordinaria* are there (Cod. Cus. 279-285), together with the works of such distinguished civilians as Azo, Hugolinus and Bartolus of Sassoferrato, and a manuscript of *Schwabenspiegel* (Cod. Cus. 292).[68] It is only natural that as a participant in the Council of Basel, he had manuscripts on the Councils of Pisa, Constance, and Basel (Cod. Cus. 164-168) that include the speeches of Henry of Langenstein and Pierre d'Ailly. In addition to the collections of his own works (Cod. Cus. 217-222), a manuscript on numismatic and three Hebrew manuscripts complete the 314-manuscript collection of St. Nicholas Hospital.[69]

In its richness and variety, the library reflects the mind of a universal man interested in a broad range of human knowledge. As stated above, about 270 of 314 manuscripts in St. Nicholas Hospital are his own. Although some serious studies have been made, further work is necessary to identify exactly which manuscrupts are his own.[70] Besides, there are some other manuscripts, as stated above, which he collected but which are found at present in other places. It is clear that in order to appreciate and understand the characteristics of Cusanus' manuscripts as a whole, we must at least briefly examine two other important collections of his own manuscripts outside of Kues, that is, in London and Brussels.

---

medizinischen Handschriften, (HSB, Jahrg. 1938/39, 3. Abh.; Heidelberg, 1939). See also Franz Josef Kuntz, "Medizinisches bei Nikolaus Cusanus," MFCG 12 (1977): 127-136.

[67]Marx, *Verzeichnis,* pp. 220-268; 269-281. See also Alois Krchnák, "Die kanonistischen Aufzeichnungen des Nikolaus von Kues in Cod. Cus. 220 als Mitschrift einer Vorlesungen seiner Paduaner Lehrers Prosdocimus de Comitibus," MFCG 2 (1962): 67-84.

[68]Marx, *Verzeichnis,* p. 280.

[69]Marx, *Verzeichnis,* pp. 149-157.

[70]In addition to the studies mentioned in note 47, see, for example, Emil Van de Vyver, "Die Brüsseler Handschriften aus dem Besitz des Nikolaus von Kues," MFCG 4 (Mainz, 1964), pp. 323-324.

In analyzing the 48 Cusanus manuscripts that are at present in the Harley and other collections of the British Museum, Hermann J. Hallauer grouped them, somewhat like Jakob Marx, under the following headings:[71]

1. Ancient poets, historiographers, grammarians, rhetoricians
2. Philosophy and history of philosophy
3. Theology and canon law
4. Astronomy and astrology
5. Medicine and pharmacy
6. Chemistry and alchemy
7. Manuscripts in Greek language
8 Manuscripts in Hebrew language
9. Others: manuscripts in French language and geography

A quick examination of Cusanus manuscripts in the Harley and other collections in the British Museum shows that a considerable number of the works of ancient poets, such as Virgil, Horace, Lucan, and Aurelius Prudentius are included, and that ancient philosophers, historians and writers like Plato, Aristotle, Cicero, Laertius Diogenes, Sallust, Livy, Polybius, Cassiodorus, Suetonius, and Plutarch are rather well represented in them, too. George Suttie had a good professional eye as he examined the manuscripts at Kues. He knew well that these were the works which Lord Harley, because of the influence of Humfrey Wanley, would find particularly interesting.[72] These works of ancient writers also show that Andrea Bussi was right about Cusanus' interest in them. In addition to the ancients, medieval writers like Peter Lombard, Walter Burley, and Thomas Bradwardine (Cod. Harl. 3243) are included. Cusanus' strong interest in scientific subjects, especially medicine, is clearly seen in the works of Hippocrates, Galen, Constantinus Africanus, Avicenna, Bernard de Gordon, and others (Cod. Harl. 3698, 3745, 3748, 3757, 5098, 5792), with many marginal notes in his own hand. Other manuscripts in Greek and Hebrew languages demonstrate Cusanus' strong interest in them.[73]

---

[71]Hallauer, "'Habent sind fata libelli'," p. 41. The Harley Collection manuscripts will be cited below as "Cod. Harl."

[72]Wright and Wright, *The Diary,* 1.xi-lxxxiii.

[73]On medical manuscripts, see Winau, "Medizinische Handschriften." Kuntz points out that when the Faculty of Medicine of the University of Paris had 12 medical manuscripts in the 15th century, Cusanus owned 26 medical manuscripts altogether, of which 19 can now be found in Kues and 7 in the British Museum. Kunz, "Medizinisches," p. 128. When Honecker discussed in 1939/40 Cusanus' knowledge of the Greek language in his article, "Nikolaus von Kues und die griechische Sprace," he was not impressed; but recent studies take a more positive view. See, for example, "Kritische Verzeichnis," MFCG 3 (1963): 105-106; MFCG 8 (1970): 226; MFCG 10 (1973): 84-85; MFCG 12 (1977): 41; *AC* 1/1.202-204 (Nr. 297); 221 Anm. 13; 223-224 (Nr. 333); 227 (Nr. 344). On Hebrew language manuscripts (Cod. Harl. Orient

What then does the Brussels collection of Cusanus manuscripts, which is the third in size, look like? Remigo Sabbadini counted 11 Cusanus manuscripts in the Royal Library in Brussels in 1914.[74] Emil Van de Vyver spoke of 7 Cusanus manuscripts there in 1956[75] and Concetta Bianca mentioned 14 of them in 1983.[76] But recent research indicates that two of the manuscripts mentioned by them (Cod. Brux. 8873-8878 and Cod. Brux. 5092-5094) did not belong to the Cusanus library in Kues.[77]

Many of these manuscripts once belonged to the Bollandist Museum in Antwerp. It is known that two Bollandist hagiographers, Father Godefridus Henschenius (Godfried Henschen) (1601-1681) and Daniel Papebrochius (Daniel van Papenbroeck) (1628-1714), went on a journey in July 1660 which lasted 29 months and visited Germany and Italy to collect materials for the *Acta Sanctorum*.[78] Although they went from Cologne to Koblenz, thence to Mainz, Worms, Speyer, Frankfurt, Aschanffenburg, Würzburg, Bamberg, Nürnberg, Eichstätt, Ingolstadt, Augsburg, München, Innsbruck, and Trent in Germany before entering Italy, they apparently did not go to Kues. Undertaking a second journey in 1668 after the publication of the three March volumes of the *Acta Sanctorum*, the fathers visited the banks of the Meuse and the Moselle. Only a portion of the account of this journey has been found.[79] Whether they were able to borrow or buy some of the manuscripts in the hospital library in Kues remains unclear.[80] It would be helpful to find more information about how these manuscripts went to Antwerp.

Many of the manuscripts now in the Royal Library in Brussels have Cusanus' glosses or marginal notes. In addition to one manuscript (Cod. Brux. 11.479-84) which contains two of Cusanus' own works, *De mathematicis*

5655, 5705, 5708), see Lothar Tetzner, "Die hebräischen Handschriften aus dem Besitz des Kueser Hospitals im British Museum," MFCG 8 (1970): 227-237.

[74]Remigo Sabbadini, *Le scoperti dei codici latini e greci ne' secoli XIV a XV* (Firenze,1914), 2.26 and n. 131.

[75]Van de Vyver, "Annotations," p. 47.

[76]Bianca, "La biblioteca," p. 677. On Cod. Brux. 3819-20, 10615-729, 11196-97, as well as Cod. Cus. 52, see Karl Manitius, "Eine Gruppe von Handschriften des 12. Jahrhunderts aus dem Trierer Kloster St. Eucharius-Matthias," *Forschungen und Fortschritte,* Jahrg. 29, Heft 10 (1955): 317-319.

[77]Van de Vyver, "Die Brüsseler Handschriften," pp. 323-324.

[78]Hippolyte Delehaye, *The Work of the Bollandists through Three Centuries, 1615-1915* (Princeton, 1922), p. 65.

[79]"Voyage littéraire des pères Godefroid Henschenius et Daniel Papebrochuis, an l'année 1668," *Analectes pour servir à l'histoire ecclésiastique de la Belgique* 4 (1867): 337-348 [cited by Delehaye]; Delehaye, *The Work,* p. 78.

[80]Delehaye, *The Work,* p. 78.

complementis,[81] written by Peter von Erkelenz, and *De theologicis complementis,* the Royal Library has those of Plato, Priscian, Lucius Apuleius, Burchard of Worms, Heymericus de Campo, Guido Pisanus and Henricus Bate.[82] Emil Van de Vyver has studied the marginal notes in the *Speculum Divinorum et quorundam Naturalium* of Henricus Bate (Cod. Brux. 271) closely.[83]

IV

In conclusion, it can be said that because of the complex conditions under which the manuscripts once owned by Cusanus are now placed, it would be very difficult to gain a total, exact view of his entire collection.[84] But a careful investigator who examines the lists and contents of manuscripts in Kues, London, Brussels, and other places would be very much impressed by the wide range of interests Cusanus had. As pointed out by Hallauer, the further advancement of careful and comprehensive studies of the marginal notes in Cusanus' manuscripts is an important area of investigation for future Cusanus research.[85]

---

[81]On the *De theologicis complementis,* see Carolus Bormann and Adelaida Dorothea Riemann, "Nicolai Cusani *De theologicis complementis:* Nonnula in proemio editionis criticae notanda," in *Concordia discors,* pp. 217-235.

[82]Van de Vyver, "Annotations," pp. 47-61; Van de Vyver, "Die Brüsseler Handschriften," pp. 323-335. On Cod. Brux. Albert 1er 10054-56, which contains the *Opuscula* of Apuleius and the *Asclepius* of Hermes Trismegistus, see a recent study, Pasquale Arfé, "The Annotations of Nicolaus Cusanus and Giovanni Andrea Bussi on the *Asclepius,*" *Journal of the Warburg and Courtauld Institutes* 62 (1999): 29-59.

[83]Emil Van de Vyver, "Marginala van Nicolaus van Cusa in Bate-Codex 271 en andere Codices van de Koninklijke Biblioteek te Brussel," *Tijdschrift voor Philosophie* 18 (1956): 439-456.

[84]In addition to about 270 Cusanus manuscripts at Kues, 48 in the British Museum and 14 at Brussels, Bianca mentions 3 at Oxford and the Vatican and 1 each at Paris, Strasbourg, Brixen and Volterra; see Bianca, "La biblioteca," pp. 677-678. See also Josef Koch, "Über eine aus den nächsten Umgebung des Nikolaus von Kues stammende Handschrift der Trierer Stadtbibliothek (1927/1426)," in *Aus Mittelalter und Neuzeit. Gerhard Kallen zum 70. Geburtstag dargebracht von Kollegen, Freunden und Schülern,* ed. Josef Engel und Hans Martin Klinkenberg (Bonn, 1957), pp. 117-135; Wladyslaw Sénko, "Les manuscripts des oeuvres de Nicolas de Cues conservés en Pologne," *Mediaevalia Philosophica Polonorum* 13 (1968): 82-99.

[85]Hermann Josef Hallauer, "Cusana in der Bibliothek des Priesterseminars zu Brixen," MFCG 19 (1991): 53-54. See also Hans Gerhard Senger, *Cusanus-Texte:* III, *Marginalien, 2, Proclus Latinus, Die Exzerpte und Randnoten des Nikolaus von Kues zu den lateinischen Übersetzungen der Proclus-Schriften, 2/1: Theologia Platonis - Elementatio theologica* (Abhandlungen der Heidelberger Akademie der Wissenschaften, Philosophisch-historische Klasse, Jahrg. 1986, 2. Abh.; Heidelberg, 1986); *Cusanus-Texte:* III, *Marginalien, 3. Raimundus Lullus, Die*

The collections of Cusanus manuscripts, not only in Kues, but also in other places, demonstrate as a whole that the collector was a person who was keenly interested in the religious, philosophical, historical, legal, and scientific ideas and writings of ancient and medieval times. Aeneas Sylvius Piccolomini described Cusanus as *homo in omni genere literarum tritus.*[86] In this regard, it is clear that although the number of manuscripts has been somewhat reduced, the library of St. Nicholas Hospital has the most important collection of Cusanus' own manuscripts.

St. Nicholas Hospital is an important spiritual legacy with a precious library which Nicholas of Cusa left in Kues for the glory of God and for the benefit of the poor and the needy. St. Andreas Hospice in Rome and the Bursa Cusana in Deventer no longer exist, but St. Nicholas Hospital still stands on the left bank of the Moselle river in this sixth centennial year of his birth as an irreplaceable monument to his spirituality and learning.

Exzerpte und Randnoten des Nikolaus von Kues zu den Schriften des Raimundus Lullus, Extractum ex libris meditacionum Raymundi, ed. Theodor Pindl-Büchel (Abhandlungen der Heidelberger Akademie der Wissenschaften, Philosophisch-historische Klasse, Jahrg. 1990, 1. Abh.; Heidelberg 1990); Ulli Roth, *Cusanus-Texte:* III, *Marginalien* 4, *Raimundus Lullus, Die Exzerptensammlung aus Schriften des Raimundus Lullus im Codex Cusanus 83,* ed. Ulli (Schriften der Philosophisch-historische Klasse der Heidelberger Akademie der Wissenschaften, 23; Heidelberg, 1999).

[86]See Bianca, "La biblioteca," p. 676 and n. 21. Aeneas also described Cusanus as "homo et priscarum literarum eruditissimus et multarum rerum usu perdoctus." See Aeneas Sylvivs Piccolominvs (Pius II), *De Gestis Concilii Basiliensis Commentariorum, Libri II,* ed. Denys Hay and W.K. Smith (Oxford, 1967), p. 14. See also Meuthen, *Die letzten Jahre,* pp. 218-219.

JEAN GERSON (1363-1429), NICHOLAS OF CUSA (1401-1464), JACQUES LEFÈVRE D'ETAPLES (1450-1537): THE CONTINUITY OF IDEAS

Yelena Matusevich

Gerson and Cusanus
"As the Fifteenth Century drew to a close, the
star of Gerson's fame was mounting to its zenith."[1]

It is completely infeasible here to present, however superficially, all aspects of the continuity of ideas between Jean Gerson and Nicholas of Cusa and the subsequent relevance of the ideas of Gerson and Cusanus to those of Jacques Lefèvre d'Etaples. It is impossible because of the very large amount of materials and because the detailed analysis of these ideas has yet to be done. More immediately necessary for this volume are a short resumé of the major links among these three thinkers and a brief recapitulation of the beginnings and development of the late medieval mystical tradition.

Jean Gerson (1363-1429) does not need an introduction. The great late medieval theologian, religious leader, chancellor of the University of Paris and passionate supporter of Joan of Arc was extremely influential; and his ideas were omnipresent in the spiritual and philosophical climate of the fifteenth century Europe.[2] The cult of the spirit of the chancellor was observed in many monasteries, and his teachings were put on a par with that of the great men in the congregation of the Canons of Windesheim.[3] Due to the art of printing and the sympathy of ideals that bound all religious orders together, the tracts of Gerson soon became common property.[4] Vincent von Aggsbach, the contemporary of Nicholas of Cusa, expressed the reputation that Gerson's name enjoyed: *"Gerson habet nomen juxta nomen magnorum in terra."*[5]

Even if Nicholas of Cusa's personal library possessed, according to Vansteenberghe, only one work of Gerson, *Concilium publicum in causa communionis laicalis*, this fact does not prevent us from thinking that Cusanus

---

[1]James L. Connolly, *John Gerson, Reformer and Mystic.* (Louvain, 1928), p. 355.

[2]The expression is of Jean-Pierre Massaut, *Josse Clichtove, L'humanisme et la réforme du clergé* (Paris: 1968), p. 127. James Connolly, *John Gerson,* p. 272. "One of the striking indications of the power of the ideas of Gerson was that they immediately became general property. The art of printing had much to do with this dissemination of his works, but the printers simply responded to a great demand. When Nider ... was lauding the teaching of Gerson, and when Nicholas of Cusa was carrying with him ... a determination to make more known the theories of the Chancellor what wonder if men sought after his writings."

[3]James Connolly, *John Gerson,* p. 375.

[4]James Connolly, *John Gerson,* p. 356.

[5]Edmond Vansteenberghe, *Autour de la Docte Ignorance* (Beiträge zur Geschichte der Philosophie des Mittelalters; München, 1915), p. 195: "The name of Gerson is found next to the names of the biggest names on earth." Unless stated otherwise the translation is mine.

was familiar with Gerson's ideas.[6] The readiness with which Cusanus defended Gerson's ideas during the Vincent von Aggsbach controversy proves his respect for and appreciation of the chancellor's teachings. Also, even if he was familiar with Gerson's ideas on mystical theology only through his critic, Vincent von Aggsbach, and the explanations of Kaspar Aindorffer,[7] his argument itself proves his full understanding of Gerson's position. Finally, in the era when the popularity of an author was measured by, on one hand, the anonymous circulation of his ideas and, on the other hand, by the attribution of his ideas to other authors, the influence of such an omnipresent thinker as Gerson cannot be measured only by direct citations and references.[8] Gerson's spirituality was the "air du temps" of the fifteenth century and especially present to and revered by the contemplatives of the *devotio moderna,* whose longtime protector was Nicholas of Cusa.[9] However, the emphasis will be placed on the continuity of themes and on the cohesion of opinions rather than on Cusanus' extension of received notions.[10]

It seems very probable that Cusanus was influenced by certain of Gerson's political and religious ideas. First of all, there are political sympathies. In 1434 Cusanus finished his *De concordantia catholica,* where he exposed his ideas about the superiority of the council over the papal authority and on the necessity of the

---

[6]John Major expressly put the names of Gerson and Cusanus side by side (John Major, 1518, in *Oeuvres Complètes de Gerson,* 1.148): "Hoc tenuerunt varii cardinales, ut Joannes Patriarcha Antiochenus, Petrus de Alliaco, Nicolaus de Cusa cardinaliis; doctor vocatis christianissimus Joannes Gerson, cancellarius Parisensis, profecto munquam satis laudatus". "Several cardinals such as John the Patriarch of Antioch, Peter of Ailly, Nicholas of Cusa, as well as Jean Gerson, called the most Christian doctor, who was very greatly praised, maintained the following...."

[7]Cusa refers to Aggsbach in the following passage (Edmond Vansteenberghe, *Le cardinal Nicholas de Cues, action et pensée,* Paris, 1920, p. 115): "Et quamvis religiosus ille cartusiensis exquisite scripta cancellarii Gerson legerit, et iudicet eundem non recte sensisse, maxime quia misticam theologiam dicat contemplationem." "...Whatever says this Carthusian monk who, after having carefully read works of the chancellor Gerson, judged them as wrong, and particularly the identification of mystical theology with contemplation...."

[8]It is very true for Gerson. Gerson's texts have been manipulated many times. Also several texts of other authors were attributed to him, which certainly testifies to his enormous popularity in the fifteenth century. For example *Alphabeto divini amoris* of John Nider (died in 1438) was for a long time attributed to Gerson in spite of the affirmation of John Mombaer: "Johannes Nider docet in suo *Alphabeto Amoris.*" *Imitatio Christi, Means of Uniting and Reforming the Church in the General Council* by Dietrich von Nieheim, published in 1410, and *La danse macabre* have also been attributed to Gerson. The newest *Anthologie de la poésie française,* ed. Michel Cazenave (Paris, 1994) still presents *La danse macabre* as Gerson's poem.

[9]Nicholas of Cusa charged the priest John Busch with imposing the rule of Windesheim in the dioceses of Sax. See Willem Moll, *Die vorreformatorische Kirchengeschichte des Niderlääande,* ed. P. Zuppke (Leipzig, 1985), 2.287-295.

[10]As has been noted by H. Lawrence Bond, recently emphasis was "placed less on Cusa's originality and more on his extension of received notions"; see Introduction to *Nicholas of Cusa, Selected Spiritual Writings* (New York, 1997), p. 15.

Church as a republic based on elections, instead of the Church as a monarchy. In this domain the continuity with Gerson's thesis is obvious, since the chancellor was widely known for his ideas on the superiority of the council over papal authority. These are precisely the ideas that the chancellor expressed during the Council of Constance. Indeed, Cusanus expressly refers to the Council of Constance in his letter to Pope Pius.[11]

Like Gerson and his friend Pierre d'Ailly, Nicholas of Cusa was first of all concerned with the unity and the welfare of the Church.[12] In the same letter to Pope Pius, Cusanus expressed his indignation about the corruption of the Church. His exasperated tone reminds one of Gerson's famous speech *For the Reform of the Kingdom.*[13] Like Gerson, he did not know how to flatter: "If you can bear to hear the truth, I like nothing which goes on in this Curia."[14]

---

[11]Nicholas of Cusa, "Letter to Pope Pius," cited by Bond in the Introduction to *Selected Spiritual Writings,* p. 11: "[...]you have no regard for the oath you swore to the Sacred College. . . that you would on no account create Cardinals unless with the consent of the majority of the College and according to the decrees of the Council of Constance." On this subject see Morimichi Watanabe, "Nicholas of Cusa and the Reform of the Roman Curia," in *Humanity and Divinity in Renaissance and Reformation: Essays in Honor of Charles Trinkaus,* ed. John W. O'Malley, Thomas M. Izbicki, and Gerald Christianson (Leiden, 1993), pp. 185-203.

[12]Pierre Ailly, *De corrupto statu seu de ruina Ecclesiae.*

[13]Gerson, *Oeuvre française,* in *Oeuvres complètes de Gerson,* ed. Palémon Glorieux, (Paris, 1961), 7.1153: "Ce n'est doncques riens d'aide ou faveur de commun; folz est qui s'y fie. C'est le conseil du prophete Amos (5:13): in illo tempore vir prudens tacebit quia tempus malum est. Et n'est pas le temps mauvais, mais tres mauvais? Certes si est. Si se fault taire. Qui de tout se tait, de tout a paix. Laisse aler; laisse chascun bien se conviegne; sauve soy qui peust. Ne faiz pas des grans seigneurs, desquelz tu as receu et peus encorez recevoir grant faveur, tez ennemis' Les subiectz qui sont eulz pour corriger leur seigneur, et disciplez leur maistres? A eulz est d'obeir, tant soient seigneurs desordonnes [...] Mais aussi par lequel bout, dy moy, se doit commencier ceste reformation, et a la quelle fin on en venroit?" "Helping or favoring public interests brings nothing good; the one who does it is foolish. It is the advice of the prophet Amos [5, 13]: 'prudent man will remain silent in those times because those times are bad. Aren't our times not bad but rather very bad? They are indeed. It is better not to say anything. Who always remains silent, always has peace. Let it be; let everybody do what one likes; save yourself who can. Do not make great lords, from whom you received everything and from whom you can still receive, your enemies. But if the subjects who are here to correct their masters... would only obey the disordered lords... where, from which place, tell me, will start the reform and to which end would we come?."

[14]Nicholas of Cusa, "Letter to Pope Pius," cited above, p. 11. Cusanus' position is reminiscent of the one taken toward the corruption of the Church by Gerson: "Even if the clergy knows or notices that errors against good morals and heresies against the faith are spread everywhere to the perdition of the kingdom or Christendom, the clergy should not allow that because of some peace treaty those errors or heresies remain without correction or suitable repentance." *Oeuvres complètes,* 7.1029: "Si le clergie sent ou apperçoit que erreurs contre bonnes moeurs et heresies contre la foy aient esté publiees au prejudice de tout le royaume ou de chrestienté, clergie ne doit point ce faire, pour traittie quelconque de la paix fait ou faire, que les dites erreurs ou heresies demeurent sans correction ou convenable reparation."

Then there is similarity of methods. Like Gerson, Cusanus saw the remedy against the decay of the Church in the careful instruction of priests and the simple faithful. In his pastoral activity he followed Gerson's pedagogical and psychological approach to preaching. For example, he used Gerson's method when he ordered to inscribe *Pater Noster*, *Ave*, *Credo* and the *Ten Commandments* on the big wooden surface that was suspended in the Church of St. Lambert of Hildesheim for public education.[15]

Cusanus' evolution as a humanist parallels in many aspects the development of Gerson rather than that of the Italian humanists. Like him, Cusanus subjugated his erudition to theology and viewed the study of classical letters as the way to enrich it. He still belongs to the type of theologian-humanist that first appeared in the generation of Jean Gerson and Nicholas de Clamanges.[16] Contrary to Valla and the Petrarchists, Cusanus did not break with the medieval tradition. He certainly was a philosopher rather than philologist, and his humanistic activity was entirely devoted to the service of the Church. Unlike Italian humanists, his genius is all theological and religious.

However, even tightly connected to the previous period, Cusanus definitely pertains to another generation, the next after the generation of Gerson and intermediate between the first humanists and the complete victory of the Renaissance in the sixttenth century. Late medieval concepts were adjusted and forged by the cardinal into his own spirituality and *Weltanschauung*. It is in his cosmology that the evolution of mentality can be observed the best, since his ideas about the universe appear to be as different from those of the Italian thinkers as from those of Gerson.

Gerson's cosmology has not yet been the object of serious study.[17] However, his work contains many elements that could enrich our knowledge of medieval

---

15Edmond Vansteenberghe, *Le cardinal Nicholas de Cues l'action et la pensée*, p. 102: "the idea was simple . . . but it is not absolutely new. The honor belongs to the admirable pedagogue who was our great Gerson." Gerson spoke of this practical method in the following passage: "Agant igitur praenomini quod doctrina hujus Libri inscribatur, tabellis assignatur tota vel per partes in locis communibus, utpote in Parochialibus Ecclesiis, in Scholis, in Hospitalibus, in locis religiosis," *Opera*, in ed. L. Ellies du Pin (Antwerp, 1706), 1.427. According to Vansteenberghe (p. 102) this painting is still in the museum of Hildesheim. It measures one meter and a half and has 43 lines.

16The question whether Gerson can be called a humanist appears to be finally resolved to his favor. The titanic work accomplished by the French scholar Gilbert Ouy was entirely devoted to this task. To those familiar with Ouy's work there is no further doubt—Gerson is one of the first French humanists in the full sense of this term. However, it may take a much longer time for popular and even academic opinion to acknowledge this fact.

17I am in a process of preparing a book that includes the study of Gerson's cosmology.

mentality and chronotope if we use the terms of Mikhail Bakhtin.[18] His work represents the summit and resume of all late-medieval beliefs and conceptions about the universe and man in the same manner as Dante's *Divine Comedy* represents the encyclopedia of the "classical" medieval mentality.[19]

According to Gerson one presence fills the universe above all realities —the Holy Spirit. This presence is radically necessary because without it no ontological subsistence is possible. This presence is not only proper to the Trinity but the whole universe:

> *Hinc Job ait: Spiritus Domini ornavit coelos (Job. XXVI.13) concorditer ad ordinans nomina Dei per respectum ad creaturas posuit bonum, quod appropriatur Spiritu Sancto, esse primum nomen Dei.*[20]

This *bonum* is very significant. Contrary to the majority of the Rhine mystics, Gerson chose among all the names of God Good rather than Being. This association of the Holy Spirit with the Good rather than with Being allows him to build the universe on the priority of the moral law and find an agreement, on this level of generality, between Christian theologians and certain pagan philosophers and poets: "*ideo bene definiendo inquit Aristoteles: Bonum est quod omnia appetunt.*"[21]

In his desire to find agreement between his beloved pagan thinkers and Christian dogma Gerson was certainly following the classical pattern of the Christian humanists.[22] However, the similarity stops there. First of all, Gerson spoke as a mystic, not as a philosopher. Second, the universe where the Holy Spirit dwells is much less the metaphysical one than the universe of grace. Third, Gerson indicated precisely that he did not mean the spirit of the universe, but the life-giving Spirit of which Jesus spoke:

------

[18]Mikhail Mikhailovich Bakhtin, *The Dialogical Imagination* (Cambridge, MA, 1984), pp. 278 and 252: "Since authors model whole worlds, they are ineluctably forced to employ the organizing categories of the worlds that they themselves inhabit, [thus] emerge the reflected and created chronotopes of the world represented in the work."

[19]As "classical" medieval period we understand the twelfth and thirteenth centuries.

[20]Jean Gerson, *Spiritus Domini,* in *Oeuvres Complètes,* 5.522: "Job said this: The Holy Spirit adorns the skies (Job 26:13) according to the psalmist. That is, what the divine Dyonisius saw who, while ordering the names of God relative to creatures, decided that the Good, which corresponds to the Holy Spirit, was the first name of God."

[21]"Therefore Aristotle, defining it well, said: The good is what all seek."

[22]Jean Gerson, *Spiritus Domini*, p. 522: "Hoc et Plato, et multi poetarum inter suos theologi sub quodam involucro somniasse videntur dum dixerunt cumVirgilio si bene memini: Principio coelum etc...." "Plato and many theologians among the [pagan] poets seem to have been meditating about it under the veiled form when they said with Virgil (if I recall rightly): In the beginning were skies etc...."

Et bene Spiritus Domini, non spiritus mundi, non spiritus carnis, non spiritus daemonii quos in Apocalypsi Joannes vidit egredientes de ore Bestiae. Spiritus insuper ... quia Spiritus est qui Vivificat Joan. VI. 64.[23]

His perspective is purely scriptural and anthropocentric. According to Aaron Gurevitch, this constant return to the topic of the anthropomorphic nature and cosmic man is neither a traditional pose nor a conventionality.[24] In Gerson's universe man is *orbis terrarum*. Although man has an earthly body, he can still advance toward God thanks to two divine forces that God provided for him. One is interior: it is God's permanent presence in man's soul—synderesis.[25] Synderesis is a central concept for Gerson, for it is a "power of the soul that takes on a certain natural inclination to the good."[26] Another is God's presence in the universe—the breath of the Holy Spirit.

Gerson developed his theory of microcosm and macrocosm: "*Denique sicut homo omnis creatura, dicitur cultura mundi, dicitur microcosmus, sic eum nominare orbem terrarum fas putamus.*"[27] Once more, Gerson spoke not as a philosopher but as a theologian and mystic. What he meant by microcosm and macrocosm does not belong to the physical matter. Everything here is biblical and moral since "spatial concepts are indissolubly bound up with religious and

---

[23]*Spiritus Domini*, p. 524: "Therefore the Holy Spirit, not the spirit of the world, not the spirit of the flesh, not the spirit of the demon whom Saint John saw coming out of the mouth of the beast in Apocalypses... It is the Spirit above because the Spirit is the one who gives life."

[24]Aaron Jakovlevitch Gurevitch, *Categories of Medieval Culture*, trans. G.L. Cambell (London, 1985), p. 60.

[25]The function of the synderesis is generally recognized by the Catholic tradition. One can cite the *Summa theologiae* of Saint Thomas Aquinas: "Synderesis dicitur instigare ad bonum, et murmurare de male" (I, q. 79, a. 12). St. Jerome found the basis of this concept in these two passages of St. Paul: 1 Thess 5:23 and Rom 8:26. The word comes from Greek. One can find this term in Gregory of Nazianzus, Albert the Great, St. Thomas and St. Bonaventure. The doctrine of St. Bonaventure that probably influenced Gerson considers synderesis according to the Franciscan tradition as the power that inclines the man to the good. On this subject see Heinrich Appel, *Die Lehre der Scholastiker von der Synteresis* (Rostock, 1891).

[26]Jean Gerson, *Sermon sur St. Bernard,* in *Oeuvres Complètes,* 7/1.336, trans. Brian Patrick McGuire, in *Gerson, Early Works* (New York, 1998), pp. 279-280: "[...] synderesis is simply present with respect to the final good, without any admission of evil... It can also be called a virginal part of the soul, or a natural stimulus to the good, or the apex of the mind....."

[27]Jean Gerson, *Spiritus Domini,* p. 523: "Since man is called the global creature, the consciousness of the world and microcosm, therefore, we can rightfully call him the universe."

moral concepts."[28] For Gerson, the philosophical language serves traditional orthodoxy. What man and the universe have in common is their origin and the Holy Spirit that dwells in both. The plenty of the Spirit that fills up the universe is one and the same Spirit that the Apostles received on the day of Pentecost. The world and the human soul tend toward good thanks to the Holy Spirit and the memory that the Holy Spirit left in the soul—synderesis.

However, the common law uniting the universe and man is not the law of nature or any kind of cosmic solidarity. Gerson is certainly a forerunner of Pomponazzi:

> *Spiritus Domini replet hominem incolam orbis terrarum facit hoc non quadam Naturali ne necessitate sedgratuito spontaneoque voluntatis atque libertatis arbitrio. Defecit ad hujus considerationis imperscrutabilem abyssem omnis pene philosophorum, astrologorum, Epicureorum, Stoicorum ... perscrutatio dicentium vel Deum non esse vel non curare res extra se vel agere necessitate naturae, sicut solem et ignem.*[29]

Freedom of God and man's moral responsibility is particularly emphasized by Gerson. The relationship between macrocosm and microcosm is neither direct nor natural nor reciprocal. This relation is essentially supernatural and indirect since it is transcendent. It is not really reciprocal since, because of its highly moral character, it concerns mostly the microcosm. It is not the result of the structure of the cosmos but represents its moral life. This relation proceeds neither from Neoplatonic sympathy, nor from the determinism of the natural causality; the relation between microcosm and macrocosm derives from the sovereign action of God.[30] It can be formulated as following: the notable moral mutation in the microcosm provokes notable mutations in the macrocosm: "*Colligimus ex praemissis, quod ad morum mutationem notabilem in microcosmo, scilicet in hominibus, consequens est mutationes in macrocosmo, hoc est in majori mundo.*"[31] For Gerson there is no doubt that the tribulations that France suffered in his time were nothing but punishments sent by God for

---

[28]Gurevitch, *Categories,* p. 72.

[29]*Spiritus Domini,* p. 526: "The Spirit of the Lord, when it fills up the man as it fills up the universe, does so not according to necessity but according to the free and spontaneous volition and free will. The idea of almost all philosophers, astrologists, Epicureans and Stoics contradicts this concept, thus creating an unfathomable abyss by saying that either there is no God or he is not concerned with what is external to him, or he acts out of the natural necessity like sun or fire."

[30]Jean Gerson, *De consolatione theologiae,* p. 204.

[31]*Spiritus Domini,* p. 536.

the correction of sinners and that the Great Schism was the result of too many guilty mutations of numerous microcosms.[32]

However, the universe is equally responsive to acts of virtue and to spiritual progress. Since the interior structure corresponds to the exterior structure and the intimate world of the soul is part of the mystical universe, personal spiritual progress participates in the evolution of the whole macrocosm.[33] Gerson always insists on the moral aspect, but it has nothing to do with virtue, with the virtue of Pomponazzi and even with the virtue of obedience in the Old Testament. Moral progress, the purification of the soul, participates in the purification of the universe, since virtue is the guardian as well as the keystone of the existence of the macrocosm. Therefore, every spiritual victory brings joy and relief to the universe, and the saintly life of one man or woman can improve the global situation:

> En apries, ils [les contemplatifs] pourfitent en oraisons devotes pour tous les aultres; et advient souvent que pour leur merite Dieu fera par le moïien d'aulcuns mondains voire qui seront bien mauevais un tres grand bien, comme une paix des royaumes.[34]

Accordingly, human responsibility before the macrocosm is joined to responsibility before the community of Christians. Therefore, by his individual life man participates in the historico-biblical destiny of humanity's temporal aspect. By his moral and spiritual state man-microcosm influences the entire macrocosm of the universe, its spatial aspect. Thus categories of time (the chronotope) and of space (microcosm-macrocosm) meet in Gerson's vision of the entirely spiritualized world where nothing is ethically neutral. One can say that in this world man apprehended reality on four different levels situated in two parallel perspectives: 1) on the level of his local life and on the level of the universal history (temporal dimension); 2) on the level of his own personal

---

[32]Jean Gerson, *Discours pour la Réforme du Royaume*, in *Oeuvres Complètes*, 7.1155: "Les maulz qui regnent et les peches ne sont ilz pas assez grans, si detestables, si horribles et abhominables ... que terre ne les deveuroyt soustenir, mais engloutir?" "The evils and sins that reign, aren't they so great, so detestable, so horrible and abominable ... that the earth should not endure them but swallow them?."

[33]Gurevitch, *Categories*, p. 126: "The Christian philosophy of history endorsed a belief in progress, in contradistinction to the radical pessimism with which antiquity viewed history. But 'progress' in this medieval context ... referred only to the spiritual life: in the course of history men draw near to a knowledge of God, as his truth penetrates them."

[34]Jean Gerson, *The Mountain of Contemplation*, trans. McGuire, in *Gerson, Early Works*, p. 100: "Second, contemplatives benefit all others because of their prayers. It often happens that because of their merit God will act through the agency of worldly persons, even evil ones, and provide a great good, such as piece between kingdoms."

being, soul and body, and as a part of the universe (spatial dimension). For example, Gerson's choice to speak to the Council of Constance about the microcosm and macrocosm is not a simple *topos*. By using this theme, he simultaneously appealed to the collective consciousness of his audience and to the spiritual mission granted to every Christian.

This vision reinforces the belief in God's justice and nourishes the joy so universal that even Hell is compelled to take part in the mystical harmony of the world: "*Quia pleni sunt coeli et terra majestatis gloriae Spiritus Sancti, hinc coelum laudadibus intonat, mundus exultans jubilat, gemens infernus ululat.*"[35] The optimism and joy that animate the chancellor come from the central position of love in the Christian universe. By love—the Holy Spirit—man is guided toward Good—God: "*Hic est cunctis communis amor.*"[36]

Contrary to Gerson's conception, the cosmos occupies such a big place in *De docta ignorantia* that one wonders, according to the expression of Gandillac, whether it is not precisely the cosmos that serves as a mediator between infinite and finite, between creator and the creature.[37] However, it is not exactly so and Cusanus' mysticism is neither "cosmocentric" nor pantheistic nor ecstatic. The thought of Cusanus remained deeply theistic and oriented toward the inside, the interior world of the human soul. For Cusanus there is no question of the world once created and then abandoned by its creator. Cusanus' world is not exterior to its creator. It does not have an independent existence from God. Contrary to the spirit of the Renaissance that placed the individual in front of the universe in an arrogant independence,[38] for Cusanus the position of the human being is not yet exteriorized.

His world, like the world of Gerson, is not static either; it is in the perpetual movement in and with the creator. Creation is a voluntary and simultaneous action of God and not a natural and necessary emanation. Born from the living thought of God, from the act of divine will, and created through and by love, the universe also tends toward love. Therefore, the similarity with the Gersonian universe consists not only in the rejection of all necessity of creation and in the conception of the creation as a voluntary and free act; Cusanus' universe also tends toward Good, and universal love constitutes the essential connection between the elements: "And this spirit is the motion of the loving bond of all

---

[35]*Spiritus Domini*, p. 521: "Hence skies and earth are full of the shiny glory of the Holy Spirit, skies attune praises for him, the universe is exceedingly glad and the hell scrims groaning." Musical analogies are characteristic of Gerson.

[36]*Spiritus Domini*, p. 523. Gerson cites Boethus, *De consolatione philosophiae*, IV, metr. 6, v. 40-48, PL 63.823A : "Love is common to all."

[37]Maurice de Gandillac, Introduction to *Oeuvres choisies de Nicholas de Cues* (Paris, 1942), p. 34.

[38]See Maurice de Gandillac, "Nicholas de Cues," in *Dictionnaire de Spiritualité* (Paris: 1964), 11.262-268.

things and toward unity."[39] Thus his universe remains deeply spiritualized and has nothing of the physical and objective cosmos of modern science.

It has been said above that the cosmos of both Gerson and Cusanus is in perpetual movement (we mean by this a moral and spiritual movement rather than a geological one). Nevertheless, the movement of Cusanus' universe is quite different from the movement of the Gersonian cosmos. For Cusanus' universe, though spiritualized, is much more conceptual and less anthropomorphic:

> In the creation of the world God made use of arithmetic, geometry, music, and astronomy. Therefore, the machine of the world cannot perish.[40]

This citation shows that, contrary to Gerson, Cusanus insisted on "the technical side" of God's plan, its physical and mathematical dimensions for which Gerson had little interest. In Cusanus the universal movement appears less dependent on man and the spiritual relation between the cosmos and the individual.

Gerson especially insisted on the beneficial or noxious influence of the microcosm on macrocosm, what represents, in the vertical medieval world, the ascending movement. Cusanus expressly asserted a rather opposite direction—the descending movement from the universal to the particular.[41] Compared to Gerson, it is a remarkable change in direction. Even if Cusanus believed, like Gerson, that the human microcosm is called, in spite of original sin, to make the world more worthy of its creator, for Cusanus the cosmic movement no longer represents the ongoing moral exchange between the microcosm and the macrocosm.

Cusanus' universe is much more Neoplatonic than the universe of Gerson. This difference is striking. It appears particularly clear when one considers the abstruse question of the notion of Spirit in Cusanus' work. Gerson's vision does not leave any ambiguity. The chancellor energetically refused the assimilation of *Spiritus Domini* with the Neoplatonic vision. As was shown above, Gerson carefully avoided all possible confusion with the Neoplatonic concepts when he spoke of the "Spirit that gives life"—*Spiritus qui vivificat.*[42]

In Cusanus this distinction is not so clear anymore. At least it is not clear always and everywhere. The *Spiritus vitae* of which Cusa speaks in *On Seeking*

---

[39]Nicholas of Cusa, *On Learned Ignorance,* in *Selected Spiritual Writings*, p. 157.

[40]Nicholas of Cusa, *On Learned Ignorance*, p. 166.

[41]Nicholas of Cusa, *On Learned Ignorance,* p. 156: "In the same way, motion descends by degrees from the universal to particular...."

[42]See the fragment cited above: "Et bene Spiritus Domini, non spiritus mundi ...."

God[43] cannot be really amalgamated with Gerson's *Spiritus qui vivificat.* For Gerson, *Spiritus qui vivificat* is the breath of life or the life itself that replenishes the universe and man: "*Spiritus Domini replet hominem incolam orbis.*" Cusanus speaks of several different spirits and sub-spirits.

If for Gerson the material sense of the breath of life and the spiritual sense of the divine origin completely coincide, being one universal *Spiritus Domini,* Cusanus explicitly distinguishes *spiritus vitae* as the interior law proper to creatures but not to elements.[44] The *spiritus vitae* appears different from another spirit that Cusanus defines as "spirit of connection," "contracting agent," or "esprit synthétique" according to Gadillac's French translation: "But this movement or spirit descends from the divine Spirit, who moves all things by this motion."[45] Therefore, the divine Spirit does not move the universe directly but through the spirit of connection. This spirit of connection is a "created spirit"[46] emanating "from God who is Spirit from whom all motion descends."[47] However, this created spirit also proceeds from the potentiality of matter that "ascends toward actual being" and from the soul of the world that "descends in order to have a contracted existence in possibility."[48] The spirit that connects matter and form, otherwise called the soul of the world, is called synthetic or the spirit of connection precisely because it combines in itself two motions: "ascending and descending."[49] According to Cusanus, "this spirit, which is called nature, is diffused throughout and contracted by the entire universe and by each of its parts."[50] However, while speaking about the descending movement of the universe in *De docta ignorantia,* Cusanus clearly evokes *Spiritus Domini* as the third person of the Trinity: "But it is evident that this connection [of matter and form] descends

---

[43]Nicholas of Cusa, *On Seeking God,* in *Selected Spiritual Writings,* p. 225: "And in the same way, the creature possessing the spirit of life is more perfect, the more it participates in the light of life."

[44]Nicholas of Cusa, *On Seeking God,* p. 225.

[45]Nicholas of Cusa, *On Learned Ignorance,* p. 156.

[46]Nicholas of Cusa, *On Learned Ignorance,* p. 157: "This created spirit, therefore, is a spirit without which nothing is one or able to exist but through this spirit ... the entire world and all that are in it are, naturally and connectively."

[47]Nicholas of Cusa, *On Learned Ignorance,* p. 156.

[48]Nicholas of Cusa, *On Learned Ignorance,* p. 156.

[49]Nicholas of Cusa, *On Learned Ignorance,* p. 156.

[50]Nicholas of Cusa, *On Learned Ignorance,* p. 156. Nature should be understood as the result born of the motion of the synthetic movement.

from the Holy Spirit, who is the infinite connection."[51] In order not to give a picture of the universe totally detached from the biblical origin, Cusanus introduced *Spiritus Domini* which, however, takes a much more abstract aspect, closer rather to the Neoplatonic One than to the Holy Spirit of the Scriptures. Gerson's unmediated, euphonious and poetic presence of the Holy Spirit is replaced, but with the not-less-transcendent, yet still complex and sophisticated system of "connecting agents." Consequently, if *Spiritus Domini* replenishes Cusanus' universe, it does so in a quite different manner than in the macrocosm of Gerson.

There are also theological and spiritual affinities. Nicholas of Cusa shares with Gerson the same sources of inspiration: Richard and Hugh of St. Victor, St. Bernard and St. Bonaventure. Like Gerson, he especially retained from St. Bernard his theory of affective contemplation. In St. Bonaventure Cusanus particularly admired the balance between the intellectual illumination and the priority of love. Like his predecessors, the cardinal also defined contemplation by its affective and gratuitous character: "And what, Lord, is my life, except that embrace in which the sweetness of your love so lovingly holds me!"[52]

Another important influence comes from the German mystics. Cusa possessed *Horlogium* of Heinrich Suso and a great number of Eckhart's works. In spite of the substantial influence that Eckhart had on Cusanus, the latter held a rather reserved position toward the father of German theology. Cusanus did not consider the reading of Eckhart suitable for the unprepared public, fearing that "too rough nourishment would hurt stomachs that are too young."[53] In his reservations Cusanus echoed the similar attitude of Jean Gerson.

First of all there is the question of the mystical union with God. Eckhart saw this union as a complete self-abnegation of the human soul in the "perfect identity" with God in which the soul will be totally absorbed in God and consequently lose its personality. Eckhart and Marguerite Porete both used the image of water.[54] This conception of the mystical union always met with vigorous opposition from Gerson:

---

[51]Nicholas of Cusa, *On Learned Ignorance,* p. 146.

[52]Nicholas of Cusa, *On the Vision of God,* p. 240.

[53]Maurice de Gandillac, Introduction to *Oeuvres choisies de Nicholas de Cues,* p. 24.

[54]Marguerite Porete used this image in the chapter 82 of *The Mirror of Simple Souls,* trans. Ellen Babinsky (New York, 1993), p. 45: "And therefore, she loses her name in the One in whom she is melted and dissolved through Himself and in Himself. Thus she would be like a body of water which flows from the sea, it loses its course and its name with which it flowed in many countries in accomplishing its task." In his book *Master Eckhart and the Beguine Mystics: Hadjewich of Brabant, Mechtild of Magdeburg and Marguerite Porete,* ed. Bernard McGinn (New York, 1994), McGinn recently proved that Eckhart was familiar with Porete's writings.

This unity is not essential, nor does it exist through a precise likeness, but only assimilation and participation are there meant. [...] For assimilation does not take away our nature; it perfects it. Nor does it remove the being that a creature has in its own genus, since a rational soul cannot lose this except through annihilation.[55]

Cusanus shared the same opinion: "For human nature cannot cross over into essential union with the divine, just as the finite cannot be infinitely united to the infinite, because the finite would cross over into an identity with the infinite, and thus, when infinite would be proved true of it, the finite would cease to be finite."[56]

Cusanus also had some other theological disagreements with Eckhart. In the *Sermon on Eternal Death* Eckhart supposed that the Divinity comes with perfect passivity and self-abandonment.[57] To this position Gerson opposed the active seeking of God under the specifically Gersonian form of spiritual mendicancy. Cusanus' opinion appears to be closer to Gerson's position than to Eckhart's quietism. Contrary to Eckhart, for Cusanus the mystical union does not take place by the total abandonment of self but by the active seeking of God and a perpetual self-overcoming: "And God wills to be sought and wills to give to seekers the light without which they are unable to seek God."[58] Cusanus even spoke about a "spiritual hunt."[59]

Eckhart considered that not only an absolute "No" to the world but also the complete abnegation of all desires, even the desire of God, is the only way of mystical deification. For Cusanus the negation does not exclude affirmation from the beginning. In the beginning these two methods are complementary in order to be overcome by the synthesis that unites them by transcendence "*in copulacionem et coincidenciam, seu unionem simplicissimam que est non lateralis sed directe supra omnem ablacionem et posicionem, ubi ablacio*

---

[55]Jean, Gerson, *First and Second Letters to Barthélemy Chantier*, in *Early Works*, pp. 207 and 251.

[56]Nicholas of Cusa, *On the Vision of God*, pp. 274-275.

[57] Meister Eckhart, "Sermon on the eternal death", translated by R.B. Blakney in *Late Medieval Mysticism*, ed. by Ray C. Petry, p. 180: "He [God] removes the active intellect and puts himself in its place and takes over its complete function." See also further in the same text, p. 182: "The rays are really emitted by the sun and come from it, not from the air. They are only received by the air and passed on to anything that can be lighted up. It is like this with the soul."

[58]Nicholas of Cusa, *On Seeking God*, p. 226.

[59]Nicholas of Cusa, *On the Hunt for Wisdom*, completed in 1462.

coincidit cum positione."[60] For Cusanus, as for Gerson, only ecstatic love and beatific intuition can put an end to learned ignorance, because the renouncement of the discursive reason on the summit of contemplation must necessarily be crowned by love: "[...] after long meditations and ascensions one would see most sweet Jesus as alone to be loved and, forsaking all else, would joyously embrace him as one's own true life and everlasting joy."[61]

However, Gerson's spirituality is less intellectual than the spirituality of Nicholas of Cusa. The good example of it is the representation of the God-soul relationship. In Gerson there are many beautiful lyrical passages devoted to the dialogues between God and the human soul. The most striking feature of these dialogues is the intimacy and familiarity of tone in which the soul conveys its worries, complaints or prayers to God:

> O Dieu tout bon, tout doulx, tout misericors, o Pere! Se la personne se sent faible, elle se doibt demander doucelement pardon à Dieu et son ayde, ainsi comme l'enfant qui est cheu tend la main a mère.[62]

Gerson insisted on the parental nature of this relationship and mostly expressed it in such terms. This relationship is so parental that Gerson frequently used the metaphor of maternal love to express it. We find the same topic of parental filiation in Cusanus:

> Thus, because you are lovable love, the created will which loves can obtain in you, its lovable God, union and happiness. For whoever receives you, O God, who are rational receivable Light, will be able to come to such a union with you that one will be united to you as a child to a parent.[63]

In spite of the fact that Cusanus shows the union with God as possible only by filiation when knowledge of God means "experiencing God as loved and loving

---

60Nicholas of Cusa, "Ad dominum abbatum et fratres in Tegernsee," in Vansteenberghe, *Autour de la Docte Ignorance*, p. 8: "Synthesis and coincidence, the most simple form of union which is not oblique but which overcomes all ablation and position because ablation coincides with position in it and negation coincides with affirmation."

61Nicholas of Cusa, *On Learned Ignorance*, p. 206.

62Jean Gerson, *Contre conscience trop scrupuleuse,* in *Oeuvres complètes*, 7/1.140: "O God the kindest, the sweetest, the most merciful, o father... If the person feels weak she should ... gently ask God for forgiveness and help like a child who is fell down giving his hand to his mother."

63*On the Vision of God*, p. 271.

children of the lovable Parent,"[64] the return of the soul to its creator is expressed in subtle Neoplatonic language. It is very different from the not-only-parental, but also familiar, sympathetic and affectionate relationship with God to Whom the human soul returns like a lost child home, to whom it complains and with whom it dialogues in a simple manner. While the chancellor languished for peace after a life filled with pain and the typical Gersonian anguish, the cardinal longs for "imparticipable and the infinite light."[65] It is important to understand that it is not so much the theology which is different here but rather its expression and representation: more earthly, emotional, literary and confidential in Gerson and more ideational, metaphysical and sophisticated in Cusanus.

The famous controversy of 1453 revealed the common ground between Cusanus and Gerson. The Carthusian monk Vincent von Aggsbach, first very much in favor of Gerson, as we could see from the earlier citation, turned against him later and accused him, in very violent terms, of fundamental infidelity to the meaning of the *Mystica theologia* of Dionysius the Areopagite. Vincent detected this "infidelity" in Gerson's work with the same title *De mystica theologia practica: "insanis Gerson, multe te littere as insaniam perducunt."*[66] Vincent especially attacked certain passages of Gerson's work:

Habet hanc proprietatem mystica theologia quod in affectu reponitur, aliis omnibus scientiis repositis in intellectu. Et quoniam omnis affectio vel amor est vel ab amore consurgit secundum philosophicam deductionem, nonne ideo rationabiliter ipsa theologia mystica nominari debeat ars amoris vel amandi scientia?[67]

For Vincent understood contemplation as *exclusively* based on affection without any participation of reason. On this matter he did not want to accept any compromise and Gerson's discourse appeared to him too mild. Indeed Vincent was an ardent partisan of a certain interpretation of the Areopagite's theology, the one traditionally associated with Dionysian mysticism. He was particularly fond of the Dionysian commentator Hugh of Balma (Vincent erroneously called

---

[64]Bond, in *Selected Spiritual Writings,* p. 50.

[65]*On Seeking God,* p. 226.

[66]Cited by Vansteenberghe in *Autour,* p. 199: "insane Gerson, much reading led you to perdition."

[67]Jean Gerson, *De mystica theologia practica,* in *Oeuvres complètes*, 8.32, trans. McGuire, in *Gerson, Early Works,* p. 310: "Mystical theology has the property of being located in affectivity, while all other forms of knowledge are found in intellect. All affection either is love or arises from love. Therefore, according to philosophical deduction, is it not then in accord with reason that this mystical theology should be named the art of love or the science of loving?"

him Hugh of Palma) and his clearly anti-intellectual theology. When Vincent reread Gerson's *De mystica theologia practica* and compared it to the writings of Dionysian mystics like Thomas Gallus and Hugh of Balma, he found Gerson guilty of usurping and corrupting the Areopagite's mystical theology.

In spite of his respectful age, Vincent von Aggsbach put so much zeal in his criticism that the affair became quickly known and ended up seriously confusing minds. Since Cusanus was considered to be the greatest authority on Pseudo-Dionysius, his longtime friends, Benedictine monks, asked him to pronounce his judgment in this dispute. The cardinal immediately took upon himself the defense of Gerson and declared that the latter did no violence to the Dionysian doctrine. In his letter of September 14, 1453, addressed to Kaspar Aindorffer, Cusa rejected Vincent's position in favor of Gerson's. To the question of whether the mystical ascent could be effectuated only by love without any know-ledge, Cusanus gave a clear, "No": "*[...] michi videtur nequaquam Dyonisium voluisse Thymoteum ignote debere consurgere, nisi modo quo predixi, et non modo quo vult cartusiensis, per affectum linquindo intellectum.*"[68] In the same letter Cusanus argued that in order to love an object one should possess some knowledge of it.[69] Therefore, for Cusanus, as for Gerson, affective mysticism is not opposed to speculative theology but is rather complimentary to it.

Cusanus' position concerning mystical theology is indeed closest to Gerson's. They each reacted to the theological challenge of their age: Gerson to excessive intellectualism, Cusanus to the opposite extreme. The chancellor wanted to make mystical theology more accessible and less intellectual by bringing to it the concept of ecstatic love that crowns the mystical ascension. However, he never abandoned the intellect and his main concern was precisely the balance between intellect and love. We should remember, however, that Gerson learned the Areopagite's mysticism indirectly, from Albert the Great and especially through the same Hugh of Balma. Therefore, he dealt with the Dionysian tradition that rendered the Areopagite's thought much more affective than it was originally. In spite of his debt to Balma, from whom Gerson borrowed the notion of the mystical theology as affective positivity, the chancellor did not share Balma's strictly anti-intellectual position. In *De elucidatione scholastica mystica theologiae,* where Gerson analyzed Balma's

---

[68]"Correspondance de Nicholas de Cusa avec Aindorffer et de Waging ", in *Le cardinal Nicholas de Cues*, p. 115: "[...] it seems to me that Dionysius did not pretend that Timothy had to ascend by pure ignorance unless in the way that I described and not at all according to the interpretation of this Carthusian, namely by affection abandoning all intellection."

[69]"Correspondance de Nicholas de Cusa avec Aindorffer et de Waging ", in *Le cardinal Nicholas de Cues*, p. 115: "Necesse est enim omnem amantem ad unionem amati ignote consurgentem premittere cognicionem qualemcumque...."

response to the question of "whether affectivity can bring to God without any prior and concomitant knowledge," he mentions his disagreements with Balma:[70]

3. It cannot be affirmed that love, even natural, appears and remains without any joined or separate knowledge;

11. It cannot be said that the mystical theology exists in man without some kind of knowledge of God.[71]

His arguments are reminiscent of the arguments of Cusa. In fact in the *De mystica theologia speculativa* the similarity of arguments is even greater.

Gerson: At that point we understand that many have devotion "but not according to knowledge" (Rom 10:2). Such persons are clearly susceptible to errors, even more so than those lacking devotion. The angel of Satan brought this piece in them . . in transfiguring himself into an angel of light.[72]

Cusanus: Therefore this method that consists in elevating in pure ignorance is not sure and it should not be taught in writing. For the Angel of Satan would easily misguide the novice by transfiguring himself into an angel of light.[73]

---

[70]Precisely these disagreements will provoke *post mortem* the anger of Vincent von Aggsbach. St. Thomas Aquinas was also aware of the Dionysian theory of "negative knowledge," and in the introduction to *Summa Theologiae*, I, 1.3, he has his famous statement about knowing "what God is, or rather is not."

[71]Jean Gerson, *De elucidatione scholastica mystica theologiae*, in *Oeuvres complètes*, 8.156: "Stare non potest quod amor etiam naturalis fiat aut maneat absque omni cognitione conjuncta vel separata"; ibid., p. 159: "11. Stare nequit ut theologia mystica sit in hominis mente sine qualicumque Dei cognitione."

[72]Jean Gerson, *On Mystical Theology*, trans. McGuire, in *Gerson, Early Works*, p. 272. Gerson's phrasing differs slightly from the Vulgate, which does not mention the angel of Satan (*angelus satane*), but rather Satan himself: "et non ipse enim Satanas transfigurat se in angelum lucis." Interestingly enough, Cusa's wording is the same as in Gerson's.

[73]"Correspondance de Nicholas de Cues avec Aindorffer ", in *Le cardinal Nicholas de Cues*, p. 115: "Ideo via illa ubi quis niteretur consurgere ignote non est secura, nec in scriptis tradenda. Et angelus satane in angelum lucis se transferens, abduceret confidentem facilime...."

Although they started from opposite ends, Gerson from the need to "democratize" the Areopagite's sophisticated theory[74] and Cusanus by defending the place of the intellect against excessive sentimentalism, the result was similar in both cases: the conception of a theology where intellect is balanced by affection. This concern about the balance between love and intellect brings about a more general question of the divorce between rationality and affectivity. This question has lost nothing of its actuality. Gerson foresaw the catastrophic consequences of such a divorce and did his best to prevent it. Cusanus, by his quick support of this balanced position, seems to share the same worries. Now, when the divorce between intellectual knowledge and affectivity has already taken place, the solidarity of two great thinkers on this question appears prophetic.

Finally, both thinkers have two other interesting common features. Gerson and Cusanus created their mystical works rather as a spiritual remedy or *cura animarum* than as *speculativa*.[75] Their writings do not fit the category of dogmatic and systematic theology of *summa theologiae* but represent a more open conception of theology, inclusive rather than exclusive.

Lefèvre d'Etaples and Nicholas of Cusa

The greatest among the French humanists at the end of the fifteenth and the beginning of the sixteenth centuries, Jacques Lefèvre d'Etaples (1450-1537), belongs to the next generation of humanist theologians, who will profit from the efforts of their predecessors as well as from now victorious Renaissance culture.[76] Lefèvre d'Etaples never became a doctor of theology and started his humanistic career as a scholar of ancient philosophy, first of Aristotle, then of Plato.[77] These studies led him to Italy where he met the most celebrated Italian

---

[74]Mark Stephen Burrows, *Jean Gerson and De consolatione theologiae* (Tübingen, 1991).

[75]The theme of theology as a remedy is very present in Gerson's writings, for example, the sermons *La medecine de l'âme* and *De remediis contra tentationes*.

[76]On Jacques Lefèvre d'Etaples see Massaut, *Josse Clichtove* and *Critique et tradition à la veille de la Réforme en France: étude suivie de textes traduits et annotés* (Paris, 1974); Charles-Henri Graf, *Essai sur la vie et les écrits de Jacques Lefèvre d'Etaples* (Genève, 1970), reprint of the edition of 1872; Eugene Rice, "Jacques Lefèvre d'Etaples and the Medieval Christian Mystics," in *Florilegium Historiale: Essays Presented to Wallace K. Ferguson*, ed. I.G. Rowe and "The Humanist Idea of Christian Antiquity: Lefèvre d'Etaples and his Circle," in *Studies in the Renaissance* 9 (1962): 126-160.

[77]Jacques Lefèvre d'Etaples, *In Aristotelis octo physicos libros paraphrasis*: J. Higman, 1492, in-4, Bibl. De Besançon, Inc. 432; *Ars moralis in Magna Moralia Aristotelis introductoria*, 13 juin 1494, in-4 (Hain 6637); *Introductio in libros*

philosophers and spiritual thinkers Marsiglio Ficino and Pico de la Mirandola. Their influence awoke his interest in Neoplatonic ideas and Hermetic studies. [78] Back in Paris Lefèvre experienced, together with his fellow humanists Gaguin and Fichet, a deep spiritual crisis. Following his longtime admiration of the monastic way of life, he tried to enter the orders. However, serious health problems, caused by exhausting scholarly activity, prevented him from executing his project. [79] From then on he considered his editorial work a spiritual mission and turned his attention to the ancient treasure of Christian literature. [80] Later he would gradually become interested first in patristic and then in medieval thinkers, including the Greek fathers, St. Bernard, Richard and Hugh of St. Victor, St. Bonaventure, Ruysbroeck and Gerson. Lefèvre was familiarized with the latter under the influence of the spiritual author John Mombaer, author of *Rosetum exircitiorum spiritualium et sacrarum meditationum*. [81] Mombaer faithfully patterned his thought on Gerson's theology; and, at the end of the fifteenth century, his book represented the surest path to following the counsels of the

---

Ethicorum Aristotelis; 1496, W. Hopyl, in-4; *Athenagoras de Resurrectione; Xenocrates Platonis auditor de Morte; Cebelis Thebani Aristotelis auditoris Tabula miro artificio vite instituta continens*, Guy Marchand, 18 août 1498, in-4; in 1491 he published in Italy the second edition of Plato's works followed by *Théologia Platonica de immortalitate animorum*.

[78]Mercurii Trismegistii *Liber de potestate et sapientia Dei per Marsiliam Ficinum traductus*; W. Hopyl, 30 août 1494, in-4; *Theologia vivificans. Cibus solidus. Dionysii coelestis Hierarchia, divina Nomina, mystica Theologia...*, J. Higman and W. Hopyl, 6 février 1498, in f; *Contenta in hoc volumine: Pimander. Mercurii Trismegistii liber de sapientia et potestate Dei. Asclepius. Ejusdem Mercurii liber de voluntate divina. Item Crater Hermetis a Lazarelo Septempedano...*: H. Estienne, 1 avril 1505, in-4. See Jean Dagens, "Hermétisme et cabale en France de Lefèvre d'Etaples à Bossuet," *Revue de Littérature Comparée* (janvier-mars, 1961): 5-16.

[79]Letter of Lefèvre of 1505, cited by Guy Bedouelle, *Lefèvre d'Etaples et l'Intélligence des Ecritures* (Genève, 1976), pp. 18-19. "Dum igitur differo, dum fugam protelo, desiderio tamen saepe aestuans, propositum fovebam visitando sanctos opinione hominum viros. Colebam insuper mirifice eos, qui zelo Dei mindum calcantes et verbis et operibus accedentium mentes ad Deum elevabant. Momburnum, inquam, sancte memorie Liveriacensem abbatem, Burgonium, Rolinum ..., Joannem Standucium austeritate vitae (dum viveret)...."

[80]Lefèvre and his closest friend and cooperator Josse Clichtove published numerous works of medieval mystics: *Hugonis de S. Victore* (Paris 1516); *Guillelmi Parisiensis* (Paris 1507); *Opus insigne B. Patris Cyrilli* (Paris 1509); *Epistolae Pauli* (Paris 1509); *Theologia Damasceni IV libris*, (Paris 1513); *Bernardi Opera* (Paris 1508, Lyon 1515, Paris 1535).

[81]Paris, Josse Bade, 13 août 1510.

chancellor.[82] Lefèvre was deeply impressed by Mombaer's book, which he truly admired.[83] Following Mombaer's advice the French humanist spent some time in Cologne with the Brothers of the Common Life studying Ruysbroeck,[84] Thomas of Kempen, Gérard Groote and Gerson; their library owned the most complete edition of Gerson's works at that time.[85] At the beginning of the sixteenth century he formulated his sources of inspiration in the following passage:

> *In rationali valuit Aristoteles, in intellectuali forte Parmenides, Anaxagoros, Heraclites et Pythagoros. Ergo si ita est, Aristoteles studiorum vita est, Pythagorus autem mors, vita superior; Hinc rite docuit hic tacendo, ille vero loquendo, sed silentium actus est et vox privatio ... in Paulo et Dionysio multum silentium, deinde in Cusa et Victorini ... in Aristotele autem vocum multum, nam silentium dicit et tacet voces, sequindem voces diceret, simpliciter taceret.[86]*

Three of these sources are traditional: ancient philosophy, patristic literature and medieval theology. The fourth is new: the spirituality of Nicholas of Cusa. It is absolutely impossible to present here the full analysis of Cusanus' influence on Lefèvre's writings. Here this influence interests us only as far as the transition between Gerson and Lefèvre, in other words between late medieval and Renaissance humanism as parts of one spiritual tradition.

Even if one cannot really speak about Cusanus' school of theology, it is exclusively thanks to the efforts of Lefèvre d'Etaples that Cusanus became

---

[82]Connolly, *John Gerson*, p. 377.

[83]See note 74. Lefèvre asked his friend Josse Bade to give the first edition of *Rosetum* in France.

[84]The direct proof that Lefèvre read Gerson is found in his commentaries on Ruysbroeck, *Devoti et venerabilis patris Joannis Rusberi ... de Ornatu Spiritualium Nuptiarum libre...* 3 août 1512, BN, Rés. D 5826 bis. Eugene Rice speaks about it in his article "Jacques Lefèvre d'Etaples and the Medieval Christian Mystics," p. 91: "Jean Gerson whom Lefèvre respected as a man of piety and weighty authority, with the mind of a monk under the garb of a secular priest."

[85]The complete work of Gerson in four volumes appeared in Cologne in 1483.

[86]Jacques Lefèvre d'Etaples, Paris, Letter of 1501, BN. Sig. a I-a, ii: "Aristotle is the most worthy in the rational, Parmenides, Anaxagoras, Heraclitus and Pythagoras in the intellectual ... Consequently, if it is the case, Aristotle is life and Pythagoras is death which is superior to life. Therefore one taught usually by the silence and the other by the word but the silence is action and the voice is deprived of it ... [...I]n saint Paul and saint Denys there is a lot of silence as well as in Cusanus and the Victorines [...]. In Aristotle there is a lot of voice; it is because the silence speaks and the voice is silent, the subaltern voice saying what was better to keep in silence."

known in France in order to grow to be one of the spiritual guides of French humanists. Lefèvre discovered Cusanus' *Dialogus de annunciatione* in the papal library in Rome, brought Cusanus' manuscripts to Paris and published two volumes of his work in 1514-1515. In Cusanus Lefèvre especially appreciated beatitude, an open mind and the balance between the intellect and love. By appreciating the openness of Cusanus' doctrine, Lefèvre, consciously or not, appreciated the same quality that the cardinal himself appreciated in Gerson.

Through Cusanus Lefèvre d'Etaples procured the theme of Christ the mediator: "God, therefore, is all things in all things, and all are in God through this Mediator."[87] This theme has already been developed in Gerson's writings, for example in *De consolatione theologiae:*[88] "*Hanc autem gratiam nulli dedit neque datarus est, nisi per medium Mediatoris Dei et hominum.*"[89] As a mediator Jesus represents the beginning and the end of the contemplative development.[90]

Contrary to the *devotio moderna,* which mostly exalted the physical and human side of Jesus' sufferings, Gerson and Cusanus privileged the mystical side of Christ, the Word and the Son of God.[91] In his vision of Christ's double nature Lefèvre followed this mystical interpretation, and it provoked his famous quarrel with Erasmus of Rotterdam.

The controversy started in 1512 when Lefèvre published his translation of the New Testament. In his translation he corrected the Vulgate by translating Hebr. 2:7: "*Minuisti eum paulominus a Deo*" instead of "*Minuisti eum paulominis ab angelis*" of the Vulgate. Erasmus did not accept this philologically unjustifiable modification and explained Lefèvre's error, first quite courteously, in his *Annotations on the New Testament,* published in 1516. However, he did not convince Lefèvre, who saw in Erasmus' philological criticism the will to "diminish" Christ, His transcendence and divinity, since Erasmus' translation

---

[87]*On Learned Ignorance*, p. 192. Also see the same text p. 190: "Unless I am not mistaken, you see that there is no perfect religion, leading to the final and most desired end of peace, that does not embrace Christ as mediator and savior, God and human, the way, the truth, and the life."

[88]Jean Gerson, *De consolatione theologiae*, in *Oeuvres complètes*, 9.208.

[89]*De consolatione theologiae,* p. 196: "Therefore this grace was not given and will not be given to anybody except by the agency of the mediator between God and man...."

[90]*The Mountain of Contemplation,* trans. McGuire, in *Gerson, Early Works,* p. 115: "By this I conclude that Saint Bernard began his contemplative life and found his way of ascent by thinking about the life of our Lord Jesus Christ."

[91]Nicholas of Cusa, *On Learned Ignorance*, p. 179: "Since, therefore, God is in all things in such a way that all are in God, it is clear that, without any change to God and in equality of being all things, God exists in unity with the maximum humanity of Jesus, for the maximum human can exist only maximally on God."

implied that God placed Jesus below the angels. According to Lefèvre, Erasmus insisted too much on the humanity of Christ. The French humanist reacted vigorously, claiming that the divine majesty of Christ never deserted Him, even during His time among humans.

This debate may appear technical and absurd to the modern reader, but it is, nevertheless, very revealing. For example, Bernard Roussel finds a real paradox in the fact that Lefèvre's Christ is, on the one hand, "a condescending God who reveals Himself and comes toward people" and, on the other hand, "the Christ that always keeps His elevated aspect," which Roussel says qualifies Christ as "almost abstract."[92] Roussel sees in this paradox "Lefèvre's difficulty." It is as if the consolation were incompatible with transcendence. In other words, Roussel considers difficult the presumed contradiction between the affective and the personal character of Lefèvre's Christology and the accent put on the transcendent and mysterious aspect of Christ. This difficulty is not new and already exists in Gerson's writings. However, when looked upon more closely, there appears to be no difficulty, neither in Gerson nor in Lefèvre. In the transcendent medieval universe, where the frontiers between natural and supernatural, real and imaginary, tangible and spiritual were not impenetrable yet, one did not feel any need to identify precisely the moment when Christ became or ceased to be "human." For a miracle does not need any rational justification; and earthly time is not in opposition to eternity, as long as it is spiritualized and participates in the salvation of the mankind. For Gerson, Cusanus and Lefèvre d'Etaples there is no contradiction between the transcendence and the humanity of Christ, between the incomprehensible mystery of the Incarnation and the intimacy of every believer with the Lord. The Christ of Gerson and Lefèvre is still vertical and transcendent. It is precisely Jesus' double nature that assures the connection between humanity and its creator: "*Nam non duo Christi corpora, sed unum, non duo spiritus sed unus spiritus,*" insists Lefèvre d'Etaples.[93] Lefèvre's words echo Cusanus' statement: "And here, in highest union, the true human Christ Jesus is united with the Son of God in so great a union that the humanity exists only in the divinity, and it exists in the divinity through an ineffable hypostatic union in such a way that it cannot be more highly and more simply united, while the truth of the nature of the humanity remains intact."[94] The mystery of the Incarnation does not prevent the believer from feeling Christ closely and affectionately already in this life on earth: "*Nam quicumque mortui sumus*

92*Actes du Colloque d'Etaples, les 7 et 8 novembre 1992* (Paris, 1995), pp. 206-207.

93Jacques Lefèvre d'Etaples, *Sancti Pauli Epistolae*, Eph. 5, 6, cited by Renaudet in *Préréforme et humanisme* (Paris, 1916; reprinted Genève, 1981), p. 626.

94Nicholas of Cusa, *On Learned Ignorance*, p. 204.

peccatis, [...] jam in mysterio sedentes cum eo in dextera patris."[95] On the contrary, the mystery preserves and assures the transcendent connection that unites the faithful to God. Therefore, if Erasmus' Christ appears more comprehensible to the modern reader, it is precisely because such a conception is closer to the horizontal mentality of today.

In Erasmus' reasoning Lefèvre foresaw, behind the separation of philological and theological arguments, the pending separation of Jesus' divine and human natures. Divine and human natures gradually become distant and placed on separate existential levels. For Lefèvre, although he naturally acknowledges the difference of essence of the divine and human natures of Christ, there is neither separation nor division of essences. Even if Lefèvre was certainly wrong on the material level of the text, he was right in his diagnosis. The pious French humanist discerned the new perception of the Incarnation that announces the radical change in the chronotype of European culture: the introduction of the earthly limits of time and space into the spiritual sphere. This change reveals the historization and rationalization of the Scriptures and, therefore, the desacralization of the universe. The reconstitution of events and earthly life of the Savior is evidently not deprived of interest, but the historical knowledge that does not lead the reader toward moral improvement and illumination by faith remains sterile. Lefèvre followed Gerson and Cusanus on the notion of Christ the mediator and Minimum-Maximum. Lefèvre remained faithful to the transcendent God of Gerson and Cusanus; his position is more vertical than the position of Erasmus and, consequently, more removed from the mentality of modern times.

The continuity of ideas is also found concerning another Christological aspect of Lefèvre's theology: the theme of *imitatio Christi*. Gerson devoted many pages to this theme and, for a long time, was considered the author of the famous book with the same title. "*Nos itaque Jesum debemus imitari,*"[96] he says in *De consolatione theologiae*. This topic is equally present in the *Mountain of Contemplation:*

Bernard made, so to speak, a bunch of myrrh, which he constantly placed on his breast in holy memory and in compassion with Christ. By this I conclude that St. Bernard began his contemplative life and found his way of ascent by thinking about the life of our Lord Jesus Christ.[97]

---

[95]*Sancti Pauli Epistolae*, Eph., II, 5, 6, cited by Augustin Renaudet, *Préreforme,* p. 626: "All of us who are dead to sin ... already we sit with him [Jesus] on the right of the Father."

[96]*De consolatione theologiae*, p. 208.

[97]*The Mountain of Contemplation*, trans. McGuire, in *Gerson, Early Works,* p. 115.

Nicholas of Cusa found a new expression for this theme—*Christiformitas*.
Cusanus explained what he understood under *Christiformitas* in the end of *On
Learned Ignorance*: "Great, indeed, is the power of faith that makes a person
Christlike so that one forsakes sensible things, strips off the contaminations of
the flesh, walks reverently in the ways of God, follows joyously in the footsteps
of Christ."[98] For Lefèvre, as he states in his commentary of chapter 3 of St.
Paul's epistle to the Colossians, the sense of the Christian life consists precisely
in *Christiformitas*: "*interiorem adjuvabis (quae spiritum respecit)
Christiformitatem non sequens doctrinas hominum sed exemplar quod in caelis
est et coelestem habebis imitationem.*"[99]

Lefèvre was interested in Cusanus' ideas because they certainly echoed his
own and also because he perceived in them the unbroken line of the mystical and
medieval tradition to which Lefèvre remained faithful. Although he belongs to
the third generation of French humanists he still represents the same type of
humanist theologian as Gerson and Cusanus: "*Nam si qua est sapientia,
theologia sapientia est.*"[100] He saw in *De docta ignorantia*, first of all, the pious
humility of reason and the best preparation for the perfect contemplation. Indeed
he expresses his ideas in purely Cusan language: "*[...] ad intellectualem aspirare
debemus, in qua ad invisibilis et incomprehensibilis lucis spectacula raptamur,
ubi se videre credentes cecutiunt, et se non videre scientes aspiciunt, ubi potior
ignorantia quam scientia judicatur.*"[101]

These words come from Lefèvre's preface to his edition of *De superdivina
Trinitate* of Richard of St. Victor, whom Gerson considered "the first theologian
after Denys."[102] Lefèvre saw in the theology of Richard of St. Victor the link
between Dionysius the Areopagite and Nicholas of Cusa, whom he considered
the best interpreter of the Areopagite's mystical thought:

---

[98]Nicholas of Cusa, *On Learned Ignorance*, p. 200.

[99]*Sancti Pauli Epistolae*, ed. 1515, BN, fol 178r: "you will help the internal
Christlikehood (the one that concerns the spirit) not by following the doctrine of
men but the example that is in heaven, and you will have the celestial imitation."

[100]Jacques Lefèvre d'Etaples, *Egregii Patris et clari theologi Ricardi...*, H.
Estienne, nineteenth of July 1510, cited by Renaudet, *Préreforme,* p. 600: "Therefore
if there is a wisdom, theology is this wisdom."

[101]Jacques Lefèvre d'Etaples, H. Estienne, nineteenth of July 1510, cited by
Renaudet, *Préreforme,* p. 599: "we should aspire to the intellectual knowledge which
elevates us to the contemplation of the invisible and incomprehensible light, so
those who think that they see are blind and those who think that they don't, do see;
therefore the ignorance appears to be superior to the knowledge."

[102]However, Gerson often confused Richard with Hugh of St. Victor.

[...] Ut intellegas ... theologiam Cusae ad primam illam intellectualem theologiam totam pertinere, et qua nulla magis juvamur ad sacra Dionysii Areopagitae adyta et eorum qui generosius et sublimius de Deo philosophati sunt iacta conquirenda.[103]

In Cusanus' theology Lefèvre saw a brilliant illustration of the triumph of his favorite mystic, Pseudo-Dionysius. "I have never encountered anything, after Scriptures, that seemed to me so great and so divine than books of Denys," affirms Lefèvre in *Theologia vivificans.*[104] Like Gerson and Cusanus before him, Lefèvre sees in the ecstatic love the crowning of the *docta ignorantia* and the purely negative theology of the Areopagite. Nevertheless, in spite of the very affective tendency in Lefèvre's writings, full of lyrical passages that remind one of the literary style of Gerson in many of his mystical texts, the French theologian never denies intelligence its place. Instead of the anti-intellectual position of leaders of the Reformation, he rather calls for the parity of the intellectual and affective quests.[105] It is precisely this parity that was questioned by Vincent von Aggsbach and brilliantly defended by Nicholas of Cusa. For Lefèvre it is the question of two "*cognoscendi modos,*" intellectual and mystical, that can be united by faith:

---

[103]Jacques Lefèvre d'Etaples, *Haec accurata recognitio trium voluminum operum clarissimi Patris Nicolae Cusae Cardinalis ex officina ascensiana recenter emissa est* ... Paris: J. Bade, 1514, a ii v, cited by Renaudet, *Préreforme,* p. 664: " [there is only] the theology of Cusa, this first intellectual theology ... in order to understand how to grasp the secret and mysterious part of the writings of Dionysius the Areopagite and of those who knew to meditate about God with the most of nobility, grandeur and sublimity."

[104]Jacques Lefèvre, *Theologia vivificans*, aiii r, cited by Renaudet, *Préreforme,* p. 375: " [...] michi nunquam post sancta eloquia ... quicquam his magni et divini Dionysii operibus occurrisse sacratius."

[105]The relationship between, on the one hand, Lefèvre and Erasmus and, on the other hand, Lefèvre and Luther, were the objects of several studies. On Erasmus see Augustin Renaudet, *Préréforme;* Massaut, *Critique et Tradition;* more in detail Andre Stegmann, "Erasme et la France (1495-1520)," in *Colloquium erasmianum* (Mons, 1968) and M.-M. de La Garanderie, "Les relations d'Erasme avec Paris au temps de son séjour aux Pays-Bas méridionaux (1516-1521)," in *Scrinium erasmianum: Mélanges Historiques...,* ed. Joseph Coppens, 2 vols. (Leiden, 1969) 1.29-53 n. 104. On Luther see Bedouelle, *Lefèvre d'Etaples et l'intelligence de l'Ecriture* and Renaudet, the two cited works; more in detail see Jean Boisset, "Erasme de Rotterdam et la réforme," *Bulletin de la Societé de L'Histoire du Protestantisme Français* 116 (Paris: 1970): 23-40.

Et fides maxime divina lumen est animorum et primae veritatis infulgentia.
Quo fit ut nullus sit fode superior cognoscendi modus.[106]

Finally, there is a clear continuity of thought concerning the question of divine grace. This theological issue is complex and very important for the understanding of pre-Reformation mysticism. Here, however, we will be limited to three particular aspects of this issue, concerning the human part in the receiving of the grace: the capacity of human nature for grace; voluntary preparation for grace; and cooperation with grace.

The theology of grace received a full and original development in Gerson's writings. Since it is clearly impossible to present his conception of grace in detail in this study, we will articulate only the main ideas. Without in any way diminishing God's initiative, Gerson developed the theory of *via media*, the "reciprocal" or "cooperative" theology where man not only seeks God but welcomes His grace. In other words man is able to prepare himself spiritually in order to be receptive to grace. Gerson spoke of the necessity of human "consent" to receive grace so that "we help ourselves as He [God] wants us to...."[107] Cusanus definitely shares this position:

> O Lord, you have given me being of such kind that it can make itself even more capable to receive your grace and goodness. [...] By it I can increase or restrict my capacity for your grace.[108]

The same motif is found in Lefèvre d'Etaples. For him, as for Gerson and for Cusanus, human free will consists precisely in the receptivity of the soul to grace. Lefèvre spoke about human freedom to "resist" God's grace, lose it or augment it, according to the effort.[109] Lefèvre does not hesitate to speak about the cooperation of man with God's design: "coopérons à la lumière évangélique,"

106Jacques Lefèvre d'Etaples, *De superdivina Trinitate Egregii Patris et elari theologi Ricardi...*: "The faith is the biggest divine light of the spirit and the brilliance of the first truth. Therefore, no means of knowledge is superior to faith...."

107Jean Gerson, *Pour le mercredi des Cendres,* in *Oeuvres complètes,* 7/2.577: "Pourtant se nous ne donnons nostre consentement a sa grace et misericorde que ainsy nous promet, et se nous ne l'ensuyons, se nous ne nous aidons nous mesmes se nous ne metons la main a nous aidier comme il soit ainsy que il veut ...."

108Nicholas of Cusa, *On the Vision of God,* p. 240.

109Jacques Lefèvre d'Etaples, *Epistolae divini Pauli apostoli cum Commentariis* 1513, Ad 2 Cor. 5:14, cited by Charles-Henri Graf, *Essai sur la vie et les ecrits de Jacques Lefèvre d'Etaples* (Genève, 1970), p. 64.

he exhorted his readers and listeners in his sermon *For the Feast of the Ascension.*[110]

Through the theology of Nicholas of Cusa Lefèvre returned to the sources of the mystical tradition of the *moderni*. This mystical tradition, according to Augustin Renaudet, "protested for three quarters of the century against the dryness and the sterility of dialecticians and sought, like Jean Gerson, the interior religion uniting the negative theology of Pseudo-Dionysius, the affectivity of St. Bernard, the psychological insight of St. Augustine, the theological balance of St. Bonaventure and the erudition of Italian humanism." It is at the crossroad of these theological, spiritual and humanistic currents that the name of Nicholas of Cusa is found. The continuity of ideas, or rather the solidarity of ideals that links these three famous late medieval-Renaissance thinkers, consists in the ideal of theology as *theologia media*, non-dogmatic, dynamic, moderate, open and balanced theology. Although this type of theology was not destined to win the battle of history, which always seems to prefer revolutionaries to "evolutionaries," it did not lose its attraction to the modern reader concerned with eternal questions of human destiny, relationship to God and the universe. It is also possible that the peaceful voices of our three theologians will be more carefully heard in the future, because history did not stop and what won yesterday may be discredited tomorrow. Maybe it is not their ideas and ideals that became dated for the modern humanity, but it is humanity that is not yet ready for them.

---

[110]Jacques Lefèvre d'Etaples, "Fête de l'Ascension" Marc XVI, *Epîtres et Evangiles pour les 52 dimanches de l'an*, ed. Guy Bedouelle et Giacone Franco (Leiden, 1976), p. 200.

APPENDICES

NICHOLAS OF CUSA: THE LITERATURE IN ENGLISH, 1994-2001

Thomas M. Izbicki

This list supplements those already published in *Nicholas of Cusa in Search of God and Wisdom: Essays in Honor of Morimichi Watanabe by the American Cusanus Society*, ed. Gerald Christianson and Thomas M. Izbicki (Leiden: E.J. Brill, 1991) and *Nicholas of Cusa on Christ and the Church: Essays in Memory of Chandler McCuskey Brooks for the American Cusanus Society*, ed. Gerald Christianson and Thomas M. Izbicki (Leiden: E.J. Brill, 1996). Many articles and books have appeared in this period, and more are forthcoming. Most notable, however, are the several translations, especially those by H. Lawrence Bond and Jasper Hopkins. Few major works by Cusanus remain untranslated, but more attention to the sermons and mathematical works would be most welcome.

I. General Studies of Life and Works

Christianson, Gerald, "Nicholas of Cusa and the Presidency Debate at the Council of Basel, 1434," in *Nicholas of Cusa on Christ and the Church: Essays in Memory of Chandler McCuskey Brooks for the American Cusanus Society*, ed. Gerald Christianson and Thomas M. Izbicki (Leiden: E.J. Brill, 1996), pp. 87-103.

Izbicki, Thomas M., "Nicholas of Cusa," in *Encyclopedia of the Renaissance*, ed. Paul Grendler, 6 vols. (New York: Charles Scribner' Sons, 1999), 4.317-320.

McDermott, Peter L., "Nicholas of Cusa: Continuity and Conciliation at the Council of Basel," *Church History* 67 (1998): 254-273.

Pavlac, Brian, "Nicolaus Cusanus as Prince-Bishop of Brixen (1450-64): Historians and a Conflict of Church and State," *Historical Reflections* 21 (1995): 131-153.

Röll, Johannes, "A Crayfish in Subiaco: A Hint of Nicholas of Cusa's Involvement in Early Printing," *Library* 16 (1994): 135-140.

II. Individual Works

General:

Cranz, F. Edward, "The Late Works of Nicholas of Cusa," reprinted in F. Edward Cranz, *Nicholas of Cusa and the Renaissance*, ed. Thomas M. Izbicki and Gerald Christianson (Aldershot: Variorum, 2000), pp. 43-60.

Compendium:

Hopkins, Jasper, *Nicholas of Cusa on Wisdom and Knowledge* (Minneapolis: A.J. Banning Press, 1996), pp. 373-441.

De aequalitate:

Cranz, F. Edward, "The *De aequalitate* and the *De principio* of Nicholas of Cusa," in *Nicholas of Cusa on Christ and the Church*, pp. 272-280. [Reprinted in Cranz, *Nicholas of Cusa and the Renaissance*, pp. 61-70.]

Hopkins, Jasper, *Nicholas of Cusa: Metaphysical Speculations, [Volume 1]* (Minneapolis: A.J. Banning Press, 1998), pp. 74-125.

De apice theoriae:

Hopkins, Jasper, *Nicholas of Cusa: Metaphysical Speculations, [Volume 1]*, pp. 239-251.

De beryllo:

Hopkins, Jasper, *Nicholas of Cusa: Metaphysical Speculations, [Volume 1]*, pp. 35-72.

De coniecturis:

Hopkins, Jasper, *Nicholas of Cusa: Metaphysical Speculations, Volume 2* (Minneapolis: A.J. Banning Press, 2000), pp. 149-247.

De docta ignorantia:

Bond, H. Lawrence, "Nicholas of Cusa from Constantinople to 'Learned Ignorance': The Historical Matrix for the Formation of the *De docta ignorantia*," in *Nicholas of Cusa on Christ and the Church*, pp. 135-163.

Casarella, Peter J., "*His Name Is Jesus*: Negative Theology in Two Writings of Nicholas of Cusa from 1440," in *Nicholas of Cusa on Christ and the Church*, pp. 281-307.

Fubini, Riccardo, "Humanism and Truth: Valla Writes against the Donation of Constantine," *Journal of the History of Ideas* 57 (1996): 79-86.

De ludo globi:

Hopkins, Jasper, *Nicholas of Cusa: Metaphysical Speculations, Volume 2*, pp. 251-319.

De principio:

Cranz, F. Edward, "The *De aequalitate* and the *De principio* of Nicholas of Cusa," in *Nicholas of Cusa on Christ and the Church*, pp. 272-280. [Reprinted in: Cranz, *Nicholas of Cusa and the Renaissance*, pp. 61-70.]

Hopkins, Jasper, *Nicholas of Cusa: Metaphysical Speculations, [Volume 1]*, pp. 129-149.

De quadratura circuli:

Reprinted in *Toward a New Council of Florence: "On the Peace of Faith" and Other Works*, trans. William F. Wertz Jr., rev. ed. (Washington, DC: Schiller Institute, 1995), pp. 595-610.[1]

De theologicis complementis:

Hopkins, Jasper, *Nicholas of Cusa: Metaphysical Speculations, [Volume 1]*, pp. 5-32.

De venatione sapientiae:

Hopkins, Jasper, *Nicholas of Cusa: Metaphysical Speculations, [Volume 1]*, pp. 152-235.

De visione Dei:

Corless, Roger J., "Non-Referentiality in the Christian Icon and the Buddhist *Thangka*," in *Nicholas of Cusa on Christ and the Church*, pp. 265-269.

Dupré, Louis, "The Mystical Theology of Nicholas of Cusa's *De visione Dei*," in *Nicholas of Cusa on Christ and the Church*, pp. 205-220.

Führer, M., "The Consolation of Contemplation in Nicholas of Cusa's *De visione Dei*," in *Nicholas of Cusa on Christ and the Church*, pp. 221-240.

---

[1]All works reprinted from the first edition appear on the same pages as in that earlier release.

Olds, Clifton, "Aspect and Perspective in Renaissance Thought: Nicholas of Cusa and Jan van Eyck," in *Nicholas of Cusa on Christ and the Church*, pp. 251-264.

Idiota:

Hopkins, Jasper, *Nicholas of Cusa on Wisdom and Knowledge*, pp. 86-371.

Pater noster:

"The 'Our Father' Commentary," trans. William F. Wertz, Jr., reprinted in: *Toward a New Council of Florence*, rev. ed., pp. 575-594.

Reformatio generalis:

Watanabe, Morimichi, and Thomas M. Izbicki, "Nicholas of Cusa, *A General Reform of the Church*," in *Nicholas of Cusa on Christ and the Church*, pp. 175-202.

Sermones:

Casarella, Peter J., "*His Name Is Jesus*: Negative Theology in Two Writings of Nicholas of Cusa from 1440," in *Nicholas of Cusa on Christ and the Church*, pp. 281-307. [Translation of Sermo XX, pp. 298-307.]

Izbicki, Thomas M., "An Ambivalent Papalism: Peter in the Sermons of Nicholas of Cusa," in *Perspectives on Early Modern and Modern Intellectual History: Essays in Honor of Nancy S. Struever*, ed. Joseph Marino and Melinda W. Schlitt (Rochester, NY: University of Rochester Press, 2001), pp. 49-65.

III. Doctrines

A. Speculative Thought

Arfé, Pasuale, "The Annotations of Nicolaus Cusanus and Giovanni Andrea Bussi on the *Asclepius*," *Journal of the Warburg and Courtauld Institutes* 62 (1999): 29-59.

Brient, Elizabeth, "Transitions to a Modern Cosmology: Meister Eckhart and Nicholas of Cusa on the Intensive Infinite," *Journal of the History of Philosophy* 37 (1999): 575-600.

Cranz, F. Edward, "The (Concept of the) Beyond in Proclus, Pseudo-Dionysius and Nicholas of Cusa," in *Nicholas of Cusa and the Renaissance*, pp. 95-108.

Cranz, F. Edward, "Cusanus' Use of Pseudo-Dionysius," in *Nicholas of Cusa and the Renaissance*, pp. 137-148.

Cranz, F. Edward, "Development in Cusanus?," in *Nicholas of Cusa and the Renaissance*, pp. 1-18.

Cranz, F. Edward, "Nicolaus Cusanus and Dionysius Areopagita," in *Nicholas of Cusa and the Renaissance*, pp. 109-136.

Cranz, F. Edward, "Reason and Beyond Reason in Nicholas of Cusa," in *Nicholas of Cusa and the Renaissance*, pp. 19-30.

Cranz, F. Edward, "Reason, Intellect and the Absolute in Nicholas of Cusa," in *Nicholas of Cusa and the Renaissance*, pp. 73-94.

Cranz, F. Edward, "Saint Augustine and Nicholas of Cusa in the Tradition of Western Thought," reprinted in *Nicholas of Cusa and the Renaissance*, pp. 31-40.

Decorte, Jos, "Medieval Philosophy as a 'Second Voyage': The Case of Anselm of Canterbury and of Nicholas of Cusa," *Quodlibetaria: Mediaevalia*, Texts e Estudos, 7-8 (1995): 127-151.

Dupré, Wilhelm, "Absolute Truth and Conjectural Insights," in *Nicholas of Cusa on Christ and the Church*, pp. 323-338.

Dupré, Wilhelm, "Nicholas of Cusa and the Experience of Immortality," *Mitteilungen für Anthropologie und Religionsgeschichte* 9 (1994): 55-76.

Euler, Walter Andreas, "Does Nicholas of Cusa Have a Theology of the Cross?," *Journal of Religion* 80 (2000): 405-420.

Heimsoeth, Heinz, *The Six Great Themes of Western Metaphysics and the End of the Middle Ages*, tr. Ramon J. Betanzos (Detroit: Wayne State University Press, 1994).

Helander, Birgit H., "Nicholas of Cusa as Theoretician of Unity," in *Nicholas of Cusa on Christ and the Church*, pp. 309-321.

Hoenen, Maarten J.F.M., "Tradition and Renewal: The Philosophical Setting of Fifteenth-Century Christology, Heymericus de Campo, Nicolaus Cusanus and the Cologne *Quaestiones vacantiales* [1465]," in *Christ Among the Medieval Dominicans: Representations of Christ in the Texts and Images of the Order of Preachers*, ed. Kent Emery, Jr. and Joseph Wawrykow (Notre Dame: University of Notre Dame Press, 1998), pp. 462-492.

Hösle, Vittorio, "Platonism and Anti-Platonism in Nicholas of Cusa's Philosophy of Mathematics," in *Aristotelica et Lulliana: Magistro doctissimo Charles Lohr septuagesimum annum feliciter agenti dedicata*, ed. Fernando Domínguez, Ruedi Imbach, Theodor Pindl and Peter Walter (The Hague: Martinus Nijhoff International, 1995), pp. 517-543.

McTighe, Thomas P., "A Neglected Feature of Neoplatonic Metaphysics," in *Christian Spirituality and the Culture of Modernity: The Thought of Louis Dupré*, ed. Peter J. Casarella and George P. Schner (Grand Rapids: Eerdmans, 1998), pp. 27-49.

Mojsisch, Burkhard, "The Epistemology of Humanism," *Bochumer Philosophische Jahrbuch* 1 (1996): 127-152.

Mojsisch, Burkhard, "The Otherness of God as Coincidence, Negation and Not-Otherness in Nicholas of Cusa: An Explication and Critique," in *The Otherness of God*, ed. Orrin F. Summerell (Charlottesville: University of Virginia Press, 1998), pp. 60-77.

Philippoussis, John, "Cusanus' Novel Interpretation of Plato," *Skepsis* 7 (1996): 71-94.

Wertz, William F., Jr., "The Method of Learned Ignorance," *Fidelio* 4/1 (1995): 38-52.

B. Ecumenism

Nederman, Cary J., "*Natio* and the 'Variety of Rites': Foundations of Religious Toleration in Nicholas of Cusa," in *Religious Toleration: "The Variety of Rites" from Cyrus to Defoe*, ed. John C. Laursen (New York: St. Martin's Press, 1999), pp. 59-74.

Nederman, Cary J., *Worlds of Difference: European Discourses of Toleration, c. 1100c. 1550* (University Park: Pennsylvania State University Press, 2000), pp. 85-97, c. 6: Nationality and the "variety of rites " in Nicholas of Cusa.

C. Reform

Sullivan, Donald, "Cusanus and Pastoral Renewal: The Reform of Popular Religion," in *Nicholas of Cusa on Christ and the Church*, pp. 165-173.

Watanabe, Morimichi, "The German Church Shortly Before the Reformation: Nicolaus Cusanus and the Veneration of the Bleeding Hosts at Wilsnack," in *Reform and Renewal in the Middle Ages and the Renaissance: Studies in Honor of Louis Pascoe, SJ*, ed. Thomas M. Izbicki and Christopher M. Bellitto (Leiden: E.J. Brill, 2000), pp. 210-223.

D. Political and Ecclesiological Thought

Biechler, James E., "The Conciliar Constitution of the Church: Nicholas of Cusa's 'Catholic Concordance'," in *Open Catholicism, The Tradition at Its Best: Essays in Honor of Gerard S. Sloyan*, ed. David Efrogmson and John Raines (Collegeville, MN: The Liturgical Press, 1996), pp. 87-110.
Black, Antony, "Christianity and Republicanism: A Response to Nederman," *American Political Science Review* 92 (1998): 919-921.

Hendrix, Scott H., "Nicholas of Cusa's Ecclesiology between Reform and Reformation," in *Nicholas of Cusa on Christ and the Church*, pp. 107-126.

Nederman, Cary J., "The Puzzling Case of Christianity and Republicanism: A Comment on Black," *American Political Science Review* 92 (1998): 913-918.

Sigmund, Paul E., "Nicholas of Cusa on the Constitution of the Church," in *Nicholas of Cusa on Christ and the Church*, pp. 127-134.

Wertz, William F., Jr., "'Man Measures His Intellect Through the Power of His Words': How Nicholas of Cusa's Revolution in the Platonic Christian Concept of Natural Law Laid the Basis for the Renaissance Invention of the Modern Nation-State," *Fidelio* 3/4 (1994): 69-85.

E. Cusanus and Later Thinkers

Bruno, Giordano, *Cause, Principle and Unity and Essays on Magic*, ed. Richard J. Blackwell and Robert de Lucca (Cambridge: Cambridge University Press, 1998), pp. xi-xii, xiv-xvii, xix, 97.

Cranz, F. Edward, "A Common Pattern in Petrarch, Nicholas of Cusa and Martin Luther," reprinted in *Nicholas of Cusa and the Renaissance*, pp. 151-167.

Cranz, F. Edward, "The Transmutation of Platonism in the Development of Nicolaus Cusanus and of Martin Luther," reprinted in *Nicholas of Cusa and the Renaissance*, pp. 169-193.

Cranz, F. Edward, "Cusanus and Luther and the Mystical Tradition," reprinted in *Nicholas of Cusa and the Renaissance*, pp. 195-203.

Hedley, Douglas, "Coleridge's Intellectual Intuition, the Vision of God and the Walled Garden of Kubla Khan," *Journal of the History of Ideas* 59 (1998): 115-134.

Reynolds, Bryan, "The Transversality of Michel de Certeau: Foucault's Panoptic Discourse and the Cartographic Impulse," *Diacritics* 29 (1999): 63-80.

Tracy, David, "Fragments of Synthesis?: The Hopeful Paradox of Dupré's Modernity," in *Christian Spirituality and the Culture of Modernity*, pp. 9-24.

IV. Manuscripts, Editions and Library

Cranz, F. Edward, "Bibliographic Background to *De visione Dei* of Cusanus," in *Nicholas of Cusa and the Renaissance*, pp. 207-216.

V. Bibliographic Sources

Izbicki, Thomas M., "Nicholas of Cusa: The Literature in English, 1989-1994," in *Nicholas of Cusa on Christ and the Church*, pp. 341-353.

Addendum to Previous Bibliographies

Gay, John H., "Four Medieval Views of Creation," *Harvard Theological Review* 56 (1963): 243-273.

Spruit, Leen, *Species intelligibilis: From Perception to Knowledge* (Leiden: Brill, 1994-1995), vol. 2, Part 1, VI. 1.1, pp. 20-28: Nicholas of Cusa.

WORKS BY NICHOLAS OF CUSA CITED

INDEX

Persons

INDEX

Places

Aachen: 220
Antwerp: 233-234
Avignon: 63, 65

Basel: 73-74
Bernkastel-Kues: 218, 221, 225
Bologna: 63, 66-67, 72
Brixen/Bressanone: ix, 89-93, 96, 98-100, 137, 166, 205, 211, 221
Bruneck: 89-90, 210-211
Brussels: 225, 228, 231-234
Buchenstein: 89-90

Cloister Wülzburg: 204
Cologne: 56, 59, 211, 233
Constance: 73
Constantinople: 80

Deventer: 220, 235
Düsseldorf: 56

Egypt: 42, 44

Ferrara: 67, 224
Florence: 65-66, 73, 224
Frankfurt: 204, 233

Hildesheim: 240

Jerusalem: 41, 43, 81

Koblenz: 79, 86, 220-221, 233
Kraków: 56

Leipzig: 65
London: 225, 228, 231-234
Luxemburg: 227

Mainz: 56, 165, 211, 233
Melk: 58
Milan: 65
Montoliveto: 89

Namur: 59
Nazareth: 42-43, 49
Neustift: 208
Nuremburg: 211, 233

Padua: 65-67, 70-72
Paris: 63, 255
Pienza: 224
Pisa: 66
Prague: 56, 64-65

Rome: 218, 222, 224, 235, 257

Sierck: 56
Sonnenburg: 207, 209
Stams: 209

Tegernsee: 34, 58, 90, 178, 223
Todi: 220, 224
Trier: 30, 53-56, 58-59, 80, 202-203, 210-213, 218, 220

Urbino: 224

Venice: 65-67, 71, 211
Vincenza: 224

Wilsnack: 30, 204
Wilten: 209
Windesheim: 219-220

INDEX

Subjects

Studies in the History
of Christian Thought

FOUNDED BY HEIKO A. OBERMAN †

EDITED BY ROBERT J. BAST

51. O'MALLEY, J. W., IZBICKI, T. M. and CHRISTIANSON, G. (eds.). *Humanity and Divinity in Renaissance and Reformation.* Essays in Honor of Charles Trinkaus. 1993
52. REEVE, A. (ed.) and SCREECH, M. A. (introd.). *Erasmus' Annotations on the New Testament.* Galatians to the Apocalypse. 1993
53. STUMP, Ph. H. *The Reforms of the Council of Constance (1414-1418).* 1994
54. GIAKALIS, A. *Images of the Divine.* The Theology of Icons at the Seventh Ecumenical Council. With a Foreword by Henry Chadwick. 1994
55. NELLEN, H. J. M. and RABBIE, E. (eds.). *Hugo Grotius – Theologian.* Essays in Honour of G. H. M. Posthumus Meyjes. 1994
56. TRIGG, J. D. *Baptism in the Theology of Martin Luther.* 1994
57. JANSE, W. *Albert Hardenberg als Theologe.* Profil eines Bucer-Schülers. 1994
59. SCHOOR, R.J.M. VAN DE. *The Irenical Theology of Théophile Brachet de La Milletière (1588-1665).* 1995
60. STREHLE, S. *The Catholic Roots of the Protestant Gospel.* Encounter between the Middle Ages and the Reformation. 1995
61. BROWN, M.L. *Donne and the Politics of Conscience in Early Modern England.* 1995
62. SCREECH, M.A. (ed.). *Richard Mocket, Warden of All Souls College, Oxford, Doctrina et Politia Ecclesiae Anglicanae.* An Anglican Summa. Facsimile with Variants of the Text of 1617. Edited with an Introduction. 1995
63. SNOEK, G.J.C. *Medieval Piety from Relics to the Eucharist.* A Process of Mutual Inter-action. 1995
64. PIXTON, P.B. *The German Episcopacy and the Implementation of the Decrees of the Fourth Lateran Council, 1216-1245.* Watchmen on the Tower. 1995
65. DOLNIKOWSKI, E.W. *Thomas Bradwardine: A View of Time and a Vision of Eternity in Fourteenth-Century Thought.* 1995
66. RABBIE, E. (ed.). *Hugo Grotius, Ordinum Hollandiae ac Westfrisiae Pietas (1613).* Critical Edition with Translation and Commentary. 1995
67. HIRSH, J.C. *The Boundaries of Faith.* The Development and Transmission of Medieval Spirituality. 1996
68. BURNETT, S.G. *From Christian Hebraism to Jewish Studies.* Johannes Buxtorf (1564-1629) and Hebrew Learning in the Seventeenth Century. 1996
69. BOLAND O.P., V. *Ideas in God according to Saint Thomas Aquinas.* Sources and Synthesis. 1996
70. LANGE, M.E. *Telling Tears in the English Renaissance.* 1996
71. CHRISTIANSON, G. and T.M. IZBICKI (eds.). *Nicholas of Cusa on Christ and the Church.* Essays in Memory of Chandler McCuskey Brooks for the American Cusanus Society. 1996
72. MALI, A. *Mystic in the New World.* Marie de l'Incarnation (1599-1672). 1996
73. VISSER, D. *Apocalypse as Utopian Expectation (800-1500).* The Apocalypse Commentary of Berengaudus of Ferrières and the Relationship between Exegesis, Liturgy and Iconography. 1996
74. O'ROURKE BOYLE, M. *Divine Domesticity.* Augustine of Thagaste to Teresa of Avila. 1997
75. PFIZENMAIER, T.C. *The Trinitarian Theology of Dr. Samuel Clarke (1675-1729).* Context, Sources, and Controversy. 1997
76. BERKVENS-STEVELINCK, C., J. ISRAEL and G.H.M. POSTHUMUS MEYJES (eds.). *The Emergence of Tolerance in the Dutch Republic.* 1997
77. HAYKIN, M.A.G. (ed.). *The Life and Thought of John Gill (1697-1771).* A Tercentennial Appreciation. 1997
78. KAISER, C.B. *Creational Theology and the History of Physical Science.* The Creationist Tradition from Basil to Bohr. 1997
79. LEES, J.T. *Anselm of Havelberg.* Deeds into Words in the Twelfth Century. 1997
80. WINTER, J.M. VAN. *Sources Concerning the Hospitallers of St John in the Netherlands, 14th-18th Centuries.* 1998
81. TIERNEY, B. *Foundations of the Conciliar Theory.* The Contribution of the Medieval Canonists from Gratian to the Great Schism. Enlarged New Edition. 1998
82. MIERNOWSKI, J. *Le Dieu Néant.* Théologies négatives à l'aube des temps modernes. 1998
83. HALVERSON, J.L. *Peter Aureole on Predestination.* A Challenge to Late Medieval Thought. 1998.
84. HOULISTON, V. (ed.). *Robert Persons, S.J.: The Christian Directory (1582).* The First Booke of the Christian Exercise, appertayning to Resolution. 1998
85. GRELL, O.P. (ed.). *Paracelsus.* The Man and His Reputation, His Ideas and Their Transformation. 1998
86. MAZZOLA, E. *The Pathology of the English Renaissance.* Sacred Remains and Holy Ghosts. 1998.
87. 88. MARSILIUS VON INGHEN. *Quaestiones super quattuor libros sententiarum.* Super Primum. Bearbeitet von M. Santos Noya. 2 Bände. I. Quaestiones 1-7. II. Quaestiones 8-21. 2000
89. FAUPEL-DREVS, K. *Vom rechten Gebrauch der Bilder im liturgischen Raum.* Mittelalterliche Funktionsbestimmungen bildender Kunst im *Rationale divinorum officiorum* des Durandus von Mende (1230/1-1296). 1999

90. KREY, P.D.W. and SMITH, L. (eds.). *Nicholas of Lyra. the Senses of Scripture.* 2000
92. OAKLEY, F. *Politics and Eternity.* Studies in the History of Medieval and Early-Modern Political Thought. 1999
93. PRYDS, D. *The Politics of Preaching.* Robert of Naples (1309-1343) and his Sermons. 2000
94. POSTHUMUS MEYJES, G.H.M. *Jean Gerson – Apostle of Unity.* His Church Politics and Ecclesiology. Translated by J.C. Grayson. 1999
95. BERG, J. VAN DEN. *Religious Currents and Cross-Currents.* Essays on Early Modern Protestantism and the Protestant Enlightenment. Edited by J. de Bruijn, P. Holtrop, and E. van der Wall. 1999
96. IZBICKI, T.M. and BELLITTO, C.M. (eds.). *Reform and Renewal in the Middle Ages and the Renaissance.* Studies in Honor of Louis Pascoe, S. J. 2000
97. KELLY, D. *The Conspiracy of Allusion.* Description, Rewriting, and Authorship from Macrobius to Medieval Romance. 1999
98. MARRONE, S.P. *The Light of Thy Countenance.* Science and Knowledge of God in the Thirteenth Century. 2 volumes. 1. A Doctrine of Divine Illumination. 2. God at the Core of Cognition. 2001
99. HOWSON B.H. *Erroneous and Schismatical Opinions.* The Question of Orthodoxy regarding the Theology of Hanserd Knollys (c. 1599-1691). 2001
100. ASSELT, W.J. VAN. *The Federal Theology of Johannes Cocceius (1603-1669).* 2001
101. CELENZA, C.S. *Piety and Pythagoras in Renaissance Florence the* Symbolum Nesianum. 2001
102. DAM, H.-J. VAN (ed.). *Hugo Grotius, De imperio summarum potestatum circa sacra.* Critical Edition with Introduction, English Translation and Commentary. 2 volumes. 2001
103. BAGGE, S. *Kings, Politics, and the Right Order of the World in German Historiography c. 950-1150.* 2002
104. STEIGER, J.A. *Fünf Zentralthemen der Theologie Luthers und seiner Erben.* Communicatio – Figura – Imago – Maria – Exempla. Mit Edition zweier christologischer Frühschriften Johann Gerhards. 2002
105. IZBICKI T.M. and BELLITTO C.M. (eds.). *Nicholas of Cusa and his Age: Intellect and Spirituality.* Essays Dedicated to the Memory of F. Edward Cranz, Thomas P. McTighe and Charles Trinkaus. 2002

Prospectus available on request

BRILL — P.O.B. 9000 — 2300 PA LEIDEN — THE NETHERLANDS